Outdoor Life's

COMPLETE
FISH & GAME
COOKBOOK

A.D. Livingston

Drawings by Dolores R. Santoloquido

SEDGEWOOD® PRESS, New York

Published by
  Popular Science Books
  Sedgewood® Press
  750 Third Avenue
  New York, New York 10017

Distributed by Meredith Corporation, Des Moines, Iowa

Designed by Jeff Fitschen

Library of Congress Cataloging-in-Publication Data

Livingston, A. D., 1932–
    Outdoor life's complete fish and game cookbook / by A.D.
  Livingston ; drawings by Dolores Santoloquido.
        p.   cm.
      Includes index.
      ISBN 0-696-11026-1
      1. Cookery (Game)   2. Cookery (Fish)   I. Outdoor life.
    II. Title.   III. Title: Complete fish and game cookbook.
    TX751.L58   1989
    641.6′9--dc20   89-31879
                                                                              CIP
10 9 8 7 6 5 4 3
Manufactured in the United States of America

CONTENTS

PART 2: **GAME BIRDS**

PART 3: **GAME ANIMALS**

INTRODUCTION

While headed West as a fairly young man, some years ago, I learned by radio of a cafe in Winters, Texas, that served up buffalo steaks. After pulling off the road, I circled Winters on the map and decided to take a quick dog-leg detour from my route.

Several hours later, I enjoyed a big T-bone, cooked medium rare. Licking my lips, I quickly paid up, in cash money, and hurried on toward El Paso. Speeding on for the next several hundred miles, however, didn't rid my mind of the rich red meat. A little sweeter than prime beef. Finally, I parked at Indian Mountain Lodge, a quaint adobe place, and wrote an article about the buffalo T-bone.

After the article came out in a magazine some months later, the owner of the cafe wrote me a letter. He thanked me nicely—but requested rather firmly that I write nothing else about his cafe. "Folks have come in here from 27 states," he explained, "and they have et every buffalo in this part of the country!"

Following the same line of thought, I at first had reservations about writing this book. Many of our game animals, birds, and fish are just too good (with proper handling) as compared to supermarket foods! Moreover, wild game animals and birds are typically very low in fat as compared to pen-raised chickens and feed-lot cattle. Also, the nutritional advantages of fish are well known and daily touted. In short, I feared that the regular hunters and fishermen would be joined by zealous gourmets, plump dieters, and the gaunt, half-starved health food nuts, so that folks from 47 states and Greenwich Village would be chasing swamp rabbits in Louisiana, stalking elk in Wyoming, or angling for eelpout in the north of Minnesota.

But I proceeded with the book, and made it fatter, when I considered that there are no doubt more wild turkeys in this country now than there were 30 years ago. Whitetail deer and a number of other animals have also enjoyed population booms in many parts of the country. The reason is that modern game management programs, from state to state, as well as nationally and internationally for such migratory birds as the sandhill crane, have given us good hunting and fishing. It's true that some fish and game species are in trouble in some areas. There are, of course, some sad stories in game management. But for the most part hunting and fishing in North America are better now than before World War II.

Why? Because hunters and fishermen paid for it. The bill is not being footed by bird watchers in sneakers or water skiers in swim suits. We the hunters buy the hunting licenses. We the anglers buy the fishing licenses. We the waterfowlers buy the duck stamps. More importantly, we pay the excise tax. *Excise tax*? Yes. Excise tax. It's not a sales tax, which we also pay. It's not an income tax, which we also pay. It's not a duty on imports, which we also pay. It's an excise tax. Ten percent of fishing tackle at the manufacturer's end. Guns and ammo are taxed even

more. This tax pulls in millions and millions of dollars per year, and it is earmarked for the preservation and improvement of hunting and fishing. Yes, we pay the bills for our sport—and good eating is our bonus.

ACKNOWLEDGMENTS

I would like to thank the following individuals, publishing houses, magazines, or agencies for their permission to use material from their letters or publications.

Henrietta Goplen of Saskatoon, Canada, for quotes from her book *The Sportsman's Gourmet Guide*; Freda Gibbons for permission to use quotes from Euell Gibbon's book *Stalking the Wild Asparagus*; the Maine Department of Inland Fisheries and Wildlife for recipes and quotations from *The Maine Way*; the South Carolina Wildlife and Marine Resources Department for permission to use material from *The South Carolina Wildlife Cookbook*; Northwest Territories Renewable Resources for a brief quote from *A Way of Life*; Outdoor Life Books for permission to quote from their *Complete Book of Outdoor Cookery* by Mel Marshall, *Game Cookery* by E.N. and Edith Sturdivent, and *Venison from Field to Table* by John Weiss; the Oklahoma Wildlife Federation for two recipes from their book *Wildlife Chef*; New Century Publishers for material reprinted from *Complete Fish and Game Cookery of North America* copyright 1983 by Frances MacIlquham by permission of Winchester Press, Piscataway, N.J.

The Arkansas Game and Fish Commission

for material from *Arkansas Game and Fish Magazine*; the Texas Parks & Wildlife Department for material provided by news releases; Art Boebinger and the Kentucky Department of Fish and Wildlife Resources for material from the *Happy Hunting Ground* magazine; The National Wild Turkey Federation for a turkey recipe; *Sports Afield*, a division of the Hearst Corporation, for permission to quote from articles; Henry Holt and Company for permission to use a short quote from *McClane's New Standard Fishing Encyclopedia*, edited by A.J. McClane; Van Nostrand Reinhold for two short quotes from *Butchering, Processing and Preservation of Meat* by Frank G. Ashbrook; the North Carolina Wildlife Resources Commission for quotes from a collection of wildlife recipes; Tanny Ryan of the Montana Department of Fish, Wildlife and Parks; the Illinois Department of Conservation for material from their *Outdoor Highlights* publication; the Nova Scotia Department of Fisheries.

Ducks Unlimited, Inc., for a short quote from an article in their magazine; The Commonwealth of Virginia's Department of Game and Inland Fisheries for material from *Virginia Wildlife*; Times Mirror Magazines for material from articles originally published in *Outdoor Life* and *Field & Stream*; Chandler S. Cheek for quotes from his book *Answering the Call to Duck Cookery*; Missouri Department of Conservation for short recipes and quotes from *Wild Edibles of Missouri* by Jan Phillips, from *Cy Littlebee's Guide to Cooking Fish & Game* by W.O. Nagel, and from *Frogs and Toads of Missouri*; Eva Babcock for material quoted from the book *Cooking in Wyoming*; the South Dakota Department of Game, Fish, and Parks for reci-

pes from *Cooking the Sportsman's Harvest*; the Mississippi Department of Conservation for material from their magazine *Mississippi Outdoors*; Surfside Publishing for material from *Seminole Indian Recipes* by Marina Polvay; B.A.S.S., Inc. for material from an editorial by Larry Teague published in *Southern Outdoors* magazine; the Alaska Department of Fish and Game for material from their *Wildlife Cookbook*.

Nancy Davis and UNC Sea Grant for material from booklets; the University of Minnesota Sea Grant Extension Program; the Oklahoma Outdoor Wildlife News Service; the New Hampshire Fish and Game Department for material published in booklet form; Stackpole Books for material reprinted from *Microwave Game & Fish Cookbook* by J. Del Guidice; George Nelson for material and recipes sent by letter from Manitoba; the Florida Game and Fresh Water Fish Commission for material from news releases and *Florida Wildlife*; Southern Progress Corporation for short quotes from the *Progressive Farmer Southern Cookbook*; Bradford Angier for material from his interesting book *Gourmet Cooking for Free*; Crown Publishers, Inc., for a recipe from *The Manhattan Chile Company Southwest American Cookbook* by Michael McLaughlin, copyright 1986 by The Manhattan Chile Company.

Macmillan Publishing Company for material from *Jack Ubaldi's Meat Book* by Jack Ubaldi and Elizabeth Crossman, copyright 1987 by Jack Ubaldi and Elizabeth Crossman; Pelican Publishing Company for material from *The Forgotten Art of Flower Cookery* by Leona Woodring Smith, copyright 1973 by Leona Woodring Smith; Charles Scribner's Sons, an imprint of Macmillan Publishing Company, for material from *Cross Creek Cookery* by Marjorie Kinnan Rawlings, copyright 1942 by Marjorie Kinnan Rawlings, copyright renewed 1970 by Norton Baskin; Atheneum Publishers, an imprint of Macmillan Publishing Company, for material from *Joe's Book of Mushroom Cookery* by Jack Czarnecki, copyright 1986 by Jack Czarnecki. Crown Publishers Inc. for material quoted from *Larousse Gastronomique*; Doubleday, a division of Bantam, Doubleday, Dell Publishing Group, Inc., for material from *The Varmint and Crow Hunter's Bible* by Bert Popowski, copyright 1962 by Bert Popowski; The University of North Carolina Press for material from *Coastal Carolina Cooking*, edited by Nancy Davis and Kathy Hart, copyright 1986 by the University of North Carolina Press.

In addition to the above, more specific acknowledgments have been made in the text, as appropriate. I would also like to acknowledge two quotations from *Book of the Eskimo* by the late Peter Freuchen. Several attempts to locate the current copyright holder have not been successful. If more recent information is obtained, updated credits will be given in any revised editions of this work.

Finally, I would like to thank Henry Gross, my editor at Outdoor Life Books, for his many helpful comments and suggestions.

ABOUT INGREDIENTS

Most of the recipes in this book list ingredients that are commonly available in supermarkets nationwide. In a few cases, however, I broke my own ground rules, either by conviction that my choice of ingredient would be significantly better than a substitute or by ignorance of what is or is not available in Midway, Missouri; Seattle, Washington; or Long Island, New York. The short list includes Creole mustard, Rotel tomatoes, water-ground white cornmeal, and a few others.

Including a list of suppliers would, I believe, be more frustrating than rewarding. While writing this book, I wrote seven firms that were listed in other books as mail-order sources for ingredients. Three of the letters were returned because the firms in question had moved or no longer exist, three were never answered, and one replied that they had gone into the resort business.

In view of this potential problem, I have arranged to obtain these ingredients from a local source and will ship them to readers upon written request. For a current price list and an information sheet send a stamped, self-addressed envelope to A.D. Livingston, P.O. Box 326, Headland AL 36345.

—A.D. Livingston

PART ONE

GAME FISH

1

FRIED FISH,
PLAIN and FANCY

Frying is America's favorite way of cooking fish. The reason is simply that fried fish are good. The trouble is that all cooks have their own preferred methods, batters, and so on. Once, for example, I had to stand between two guys, one from Connecticut and the other from California, who disagreed on whether to shake fish in white flour or yellow cornmeal before frying them.

Back then, I myself championed good causes, such as the culinary superiority of the Tennessee horneyhead over ordinary fare like the New England brookie or the Northern California Dolly Varden. For flavor and crunch, nothing beats fresh, properly fried hornyheads, provided that fine-ground *white* cornmeal and *peanut* oil are used.

But I look for no argument in these pages, and want to get on with a variety of recipes wide enough to suit everyone, North, South, East, and West. My personal favorite for fried fish is set forth next, along with my reasons for liking it. But catch lots of fish—and try everything.

Ninety Miles from Opp

Dick Wood, a talented advertising professional who is responsible for a lot of those pretty ads in the slick magazines, once told me that the late Lew Childre, the founder of the tackle firm, didn't trust or abide by any fisherman who wasn't born within a 90-mile radius of Opp, Alabama. As the crow flies, I'm certainly within that radius. Thus, I consider myself not only qualified but also trustworthy to say that you require only a short list of ingredients in order to fry the world's best fish:

good fresh fish
peanut oil
fine-ground white cornmeal
salt and pepper

Fillet or pan dress the fish. Heat an inch of peanut oil in a large skillet and put on high heat. Salt and pepper a few fish at a time, as you need them. Shake the fish in a bag of cornmeal, then fry in very hot peanut oil. Drain the fish on brown paper grocery bags. Serve hot. If you have lots of folks to feed, start them eating before all the fish are cooked. You'll have to add more cooking oil if you have lots of fish to fry.

Serve the fish with corn bread and lots of good salad, cole slaw, or (my favorite) sliced fresh tomatoes.

The corn bread is made as follows: mix cornmeal, salt, and pepper with hot water until it gets to a good "spooning" consistency. Let it sit for about 15 minutes or more, during which time it will firm up a bit. Then add a little peanut oil and mix. Heat oil to medium heat (not nearly as hot as for the fish). Spoon meal mixture into frying pan and cook until browned. Turn and brown the other side. Drain on brown paper bag.

Because the corn bread cooks slower than the fish, it is a good idea to cook it first. Or use two frying pans.

The success of this recipe—and most of the other recipes for fried fish—depends not so much on ingredients as on careful attention to detail. Thus, the following points are important:

1. The oil should be very hot while the fish are frying. I constantly adjust the heat while cooking, turning it up to high when new fish are put into the oil and turning it down a bit

Too Hot?

I usually recommend that fish be fried in very hot oil, just short of the smoking point. But there are exceptions. Skate and ray, for example, contain lots of moisture and tend to pop violently if dropped into very hot oil. So, proceed with caution.

Also, a pan full of hot oil can be very dangerous if it catches on fire. The best bet is to extinguish the fire with baking soda or a suitable fire extinguisher. Don't use water. Many people will take a burning frying pan by the handle and run for the door before it "smokes up the house." But note that it's better to smoke up the house than to burn yourself. Fall down with a pan full of burning oil and it could kill you—or burn up the house. Open a door and wind could blow the flames back on you, burning your arm and face.

So . . . be careful with hot grease. Minor burns can be treated by holding your hand or arm under cold running water as soon as possible. Most serious burns should also be cooled quickly, and, if possible, should be kept cold en route to a doctor or hospital.

as the fish heat up. We use peanut oil because it has a high smoke point, and has no unpleasant flavor. And no cholesterol.

2. The fish should not be cooked too long. If your oil is at the right temperature, this point pretty much takes care of itself simply because the fish will burn on the outside before they overcook on the inside. But if the oil isn't hot, the fish will dry out while you are trying to brown the outside. In fact, some of the worst fish I've ever eaten were cooked by this recipe. The only problem was that they were fried in a large iron pot on a small camp stove. The stove simply would not get the oil hot enough.

3. The fish should be drained and left on absorbent paper. They'll be soggy if you take them out of the frying pan and pile them high on a platter. In fact, we serve fried fish on brown grocery bags.

4. The cornmeal should be very fine, like flour.

5. Serve the fish hot.

Trout Amandine

If you're looking for an elegant but easy fish dish to prepare, get some very good white wine and cook trout amandine, a classic dish that was popular in early American restaurants. A number of variations of the basic recipe are good and can be found in many cookbooks and magazines. My favorite was influenced heavily by the *Heritage Cookbook* from the Better Homes and Gardens folks:

The Fish
4 to 6 small trout
salt and pepper
2 tablespoons cooking oil
2 tablespoons butter
1 egg
¼ cup half and half or light cream
¼ cup flour
The Topping
¼ cup slivered almonds
¼ cup melted butter
2 tablespoons lemon juice

Bone the trout, removing the fins and leaving the heads on. Whisk the egg and stir in the cream. Heat oil and 2 tablespoons of butter in a frying pan. Roll the trout in flour, then dip in the egg mixture. Fry in hot oil until the fish is golden in color and flakes easily. Place trout on a warm serving platter.

Quickly, melt ¼ cup of butter in a pan and brown the almonds. Remove from heat and stir in lemon juice. Pour mixture over fish and eat at once. *Serves 2 or 3.*

Smallfry

This particular recipe, or method, is based on *Bull Cook and Authentic Historical Recipes and Practices* by George Leonard Herter and Berthe E. Herter. They called it "Indian Method of Cooking Small Fish," saying that (1) fish in some areas run small and (2) you must eat them to supplement your diet in some cases in order to survive!

Anyhow—poach, boil, or steam the fish

for a few minutes, then flake the meat with a fork. Salt and pepper to taste. Heat up a little oil or butter in an Indian frying pan. Add fish and sizzle until browned. Drain. Eat. Survive. Catch more fish.

Also try the next recipe for frying very small fish.

Italian Fried Spanish Mackerel

Here's a recipe that I enjoy using on Spanish mackerel, mullet, and other fatty fish from salt water. To cook it, however, I use a lower frying temperature than with most similar recipes simply because the batter tends to burn, on all-out high heat, before the fish gets done. Also, I prefer this recipe cooked in a deep fryer instead of a frying pan.

> **2 pounds fillets**
> **cooking oil for deep frying**
> **1 cup Italian bread crumbs**

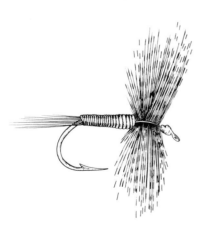

1 cup Parmesan cheese
salt and pepper
egg
lemon

Heat oil in deep fryer. Mix bread crumbs and cheese. Salt and pepper fillets, then dip in egg and roll in crumb mixture. Fry the fish until it flakes easily and is golden brown. Slice a lemon or two for garnish and juice for those who want it. *Serves 4.*

Flaked Fish Fry

A number of recipes for fritters, fish balls, patties, and so on are set forth in Chapter 4, on fish flakes. But a little duplication of topic is certainly justified in this case simply because fish patties are so very good—and easy to cook.

> **2 cups fish flakes**
> **oil**
> **2 large eggs**
> **salt and pepper**

Boil or poach your fish for a few minutes, until it flakes easily. Drain and flake. Salt and pepper to taste. Whisk the egg, then mix with fish. Spoon mixture into pan. (The mixture will be runny, but it will firm up as it cooks.) Fry in very hot oil for a couple of minutes, or until fish is brown. Remember, the fish has already been cooked before flaking, so don't fry any longer than necessary to brown. *Serves 3 or 4.*

With a simple fish flake recipe like this, I prefer to pan fry the flakes, using two spatulas to turn them gently. However, they can be cooked by any frying process, from griddle to deep fryer. The shape of the final product, from round to flat, will be influenced by the frying process and the depth of the oil used.

Note: In this recipe, the primary purpose of the egg is as a bonding agent to hold the fish together while cooking it. I have purposely kept this recipe simple, but remember that you can use everything from buttermilk to elderberry blossoms in fish patties and fritters. See Chapter 4 for more ideas.

Beer Batter Fish Fingers

If you like a very crispy batter, here's one to try. I modified the idea from a more basic batter recipe that was published by the Oklahoma Wildlife Federation in their *Wildlife Chef*:

    2 or 3 pounds fish fingers or small
        whole fish
    cooking oil for deep frying
    ½ cup melted butter
    ½ cup beer
    2 large eggs, separated
    1 cup flour
    ½ cup cornstarch

Beat egg yolks and mix with beer and melted butter. Then stir in flour and cornstarch. Whisk or beat egg whites until they stiffen, then add to flour mixture. Heat oil on medium-high in deep fryer. Salt and pepper fish to taste, then dip each piece into batter.

(Or you can add seasoning to the batter if you prefer.) Deep fry until golden brown. Drain on absorbent paper or brown grocery bags before serving. *Serves 4 to 6.*

Note: A medium high heat works best for this recipe. If the oil is too hot, the batter tends to pop away from the fish.

Shallow Fried Pigfish

Here's an interesting fried fish recipe from a booklet called *Pigfish*, published by the UNC Sea Grant:

The Fish
    6 pigfish (also called grunt) about ¾
        pound each, dressed
    6 tablespoons cornstarch
    10 tablespoons oil
    3 tablespoons coarsely minced, peeled
        ginger
    12 small whole scallions, coarsely
        chopped
The Sauce
    6 tablespoons light soy sauce
    6 tablespoons dry sherry
    6 tablespoons red wine vinegar
    6 teaspons sugar
    4 tablespoons sesame oil

"Score fish on a slant 3 times on each side. Dust well with cornstarch. Combine sauce seasonings in a small bowl. Heat large, heavy skillet over high heat until very hot; add oil and heat. Scatter in ginger and scallions; stir briskly until scallions are bright green and aromatic. Push to side of pan. Brown fish in pan 1 minute on each side. Turn heat to low and shallow-fry each side about 4 minutes, until crisp and brown. With heat on high, splash sauce directly onto fish, basting and turning them once as sauce sizzles. Remove with spatula to hot serving dish, spooning ginger and scallions on top. *Serves 6.*

Zesty Griddle Fish

Here's a tasty recipe that I use from time to time when I'm in a hurry to feed one or two people:

> fish fillets
> Zesty Italian dressing
> salt
> bread slices

Salt fish to taste. Heat griddle and pour a little Zesty Italian dressing onto the surface.

Thick or Thin?

Many of the thick and fancy batters for frying fish are of course nice and crunchy. But I recommend that all such recipes be tested before you cook fish for guests. Sometimes, if you are a little off in mixing or cooking a recipe, the batter comes off the fish or burns—or both. Also, thick batters, no matter how tasty and crunchy they may be, tend to hold more grease than a light coating of meal or flour.

Put fillets in the middle of griddle. With wide spatula, move most of the salad dressing to the center. Tear bread slices in half and arrange them around fish. Cook for 4 minutes and turn fish. Turn bread. Cook fish another 3 minutes and remove them to a plate. Check bread for toastiness.

Variations: Try other clear salad dressings that contain about ½ oil. Experiment. But remember that many of the dressings contain a lot of vinegar and won't behave like pure oil when heated. Creamy dressings may not work at frying and grilling temperatures.

Rockfish Wingo

If you like a golden, crunchy batter and sweet-tasting fish, try this one from my friend Carl Wingo of Woodbridge, Virginia. (That's Chesapeake Bay country, where "rockfish" is a popular name for the striped bass.)

> rockfish fillets
> salt
> 2 eggs
> frosted flakes
> cooking oil

If you have large fillets, cut them into fingers. Beat two eggs with 1 tablespoon water added. (The water, Wingo says, breaks down the egg so that it isn't so globby.) Crunch up the frosted flakes. Heat cooking oil. Salt fillets, dip in egg, roll in frosted flake crumbs, and fry on high heat. But be careful; the frosted flake batter will burn quickly. Cook

Frying for 1 or 100

When planning this book, I thought I would get into a long-winded discourse on the merits of frying fish by different methods, such as pan frying or deep frying. There is a good deal of difference, of course, but I now think that the choice should be a practical one. For example, most people wouldn't want to heat up a deep fryer full of expensive oil to cook fish for one person. Thus, my advice is to choose a method that is suited to the number of people that you have to feed.

Fish for one or two people can be sautéed in a pad of butter without making up batters or heating lots of oil.

Fish for three or four people can easily be fried in a frying pan, with oil from ⅛ to 1 inch deep, depending on how you like it and on how many people you have to feed. Of course,

more people can be fed from a frying pan simply by cooking more batches and adding more oil as needed.

Fish for five to ten or more are best fried in a deep fryer simply because it is quicker. It is also easier in that you don't have to worry about when the fish is done. If a particualr piece of fish floats, it's ready to eat.

Fish for a hundred or so people can be fried (usually outside) with special equipment. A large cast iron pot, as was used for washing clothes, works nicely if you can heat it properly. But be very careful. This much hot oil can be dangerous. Even larger pots can be used. For example, a local group of farmers fry fish for several hundred people in a large cast iron vat that was at one time used for scalding hogs.

---

fillets until they are golden brown.

Wingo says that his daughters love the sweetness in frosted flake batter, but he himself prefers to mix half frosted flakes with half cornflakes. In any case, try frosted flake batter; the sugar caramalizes, thereby producing more crunch than ordinary batters.

Flatfish Parmesan

Here's a tasty dish that works well with thin fillets, such as those from flounder or other flatfish. (Fillets from rounder fish can be put between wax paper and flattened a bit with a smooth mallet.)

**2 pounds thin fillets
cooking oil
1 tablespoon onion juice
salt
pepper
1 egg
¾ cup fine cracker crumbs
¾ cup Parmesan cheese, grated**

Stir onion juice into 1 cup of cooking oil. Marinate fish fillets for about two hours. Heat marinade oil in skillet. Salt and pepper fillets to taste. Mix cracker crumbs and

cheese. Whisk egg. Dip fillets in egg, roll in cracker crumb mixture, and quickly brown in the hot marinade oil. (Add more oil if needed.) Eat the fish while they are hot. *Serves 4 or 5.*

Potato Fried Fish

This is a very tasty recipe, but it requires onion soup mix that has been reduced almost to a powder. This is easily accomplished with a food processor. If you don't have a food processor, try a mortar and pestle—and lots of elbow grease.

>   2 pounds fish fillets
>   salt and pepper
>   cooking oil
>   1 egg, beaten
>   1 cup instant mashed potato flakes
>   1 pack (2 envelopes) onion soup mix
>   (2.6 ounces)

Put onion soup mix into a food processor and zap it several times, or grind it with a mortar and pestle. (I've also put it in a cloth

bag and pounded it with a mallet.) Add instant potatoes and mix. Heat oil in a frying pan or deep fryer. Salt and pepper fillets to taste. Roll fillets in potato mix. Dip in beaten egg, then roll again in potato mix. Fry in oil, at medium high heat, until fillets are golden brown. *Serves 4 or 5.*

Note: This batter burns quickly on high heat, so watch the fish closely.

Pan-Fried Jamaican Fish Steaks

Here's a good recipe for frying fish that are large enough to cut into steaks instead of filleting. Steaks can be cut with a knife, but an electric slicer works best. If you've got a 20-pound grouper, redfish, or something similar, see if your butcher will steak it for you.

The Fish
>   2 pounds fish steaks, 1-inch thick
>   salt and pepper
>   flour
>   2 tablespoons oil or butter
The Topping
>   1 clove garlic, minced
>   ⅛ teaspoon cayenne pepper
>   1 small onion, sliced in rings
>   ½ medium green pepper, sliced in
>   rings
>   ½ medium red pepper, sliced in rings

Heat 2 tablespoons oil or butter in a large frying pan. Salt and pepper fish steaks. Shake the steaks in flour, then brown them in the frying pan. Cook the steaks for about 6 minutes on each side. Add oil as necessary. Carefully put fish steaks on a serving platter.

Put a little oil into the frying pan if needed and fry the minced garlic. Add onion, green pepper, and red pepper. Sprinkle with cayenne. Stirfry on high heat for 3 minutes. (Use a wok if you have one; if not, the frying pan will do.) Spoon the vegetables onto the fish. *Serves 4 or 5.*

Catfish Buddy Platt

Here's a good one, from a friend of mine, for cooking catfish with a little more pep:

> **catfish fillets**
> **Louisiana hot sauce (or Tabasco sauce)**
> **fine white corn meal**
> **peanut oil**
> **salt**
> **water**

Put catfish fillets in a dish or bowl and shake the hot sauce on them. Let sit for six to eight hours, turning several times.

Heat oil in deep fryer. Salt the fillets, then shake in fine-ground corn meal. (Note that the fish is not dipped in egg or milk before mealing.) Fry in very hot oil until brown. Do not overcook. Drain. Serve hot with corn bread and lots of salad.

Buddy says that shaking the fish in a mixture of half flour and half meal will make it look pretty, but he usually uses pure meal. He is of more firm opinion about using only fine ground meal, saying that medium or

Chain Pickerel

Often called jacks, this fish of medium-low oil content is considered by many people to be very good. It has a series of small bones that runs down each fillet and these are difficult to deal with. Most people "gash" them with a sharp knife in one way or another, often with crosshatches. Then they fry them crisply and eat bones and all.

coarse meal tends to come off the fish and collect in the bottom of the pan.

Apalachicola Fry

In many parts of the rural South, using flour instead of fine-ground white cornmeal for frying fish would be simply out of the question. Unthinkable. Flour is for frying chicken. Period. But I have a booklet titled *How to Fish for Snook* which sets forth a recipe called "Spicy Apalachicola." Astoundingly, it calls for flour.

First, let me say that snook don't often roam as far north as Apalachicola, which is a fishing village in the Big Bend area of Florida's Gulf of Mexico's coastline—but I wouldn't argue that point. Second, I don't know as fact that anyone in Apalachicola actually uses flour instead of meal. But I do know that if anyone in this area, and as far North as Wewahitchka, chooses to use flour when frying fish, then they will damn well do so! And if they want to fish for snook in Dead Lakes, they'll do so.

In any case, the following recipe is unusual not only because of the flour but also because mustard is administered in an offbeat manner. I tried it and hereby confess that it's good:

fish
1 egg
salt
mustard
flour
cooking oil for deep frying

Whisk an egg. Stir in 1 tablespoon of prepared mustard sauce. Salt fillets, then dip in egg and mustard mixture. Roll in flour and fry in deep fat.

Pickerel Fillets Doria

Here's a recipe out of Winnipeg, Manitoba, which was sent to me from Saskatoon, Saskatchewan, by a fisheries ecologist. Besides being good, it makes interesting use of

---

Too Big to Eat?

Once I had the pleasure of fishing for several days with the late Lew Childre, a genius of the international fishing tackle trade, at his camp on the lower Apalachicola River in Florida. We were expecting Lew's advertising executive, a manufacturing representative from Japan, a lure maker, and other VIPs of the angling world. We were to have fish to eat that night before getting down to business.

Of course, Lew and I were expected to catch the bass, and we set out before sunup. On the third cast, just as the sun was peeping through the Spanish moss in the cypress trees, Lew caught a nice largemouth. About 5 pounds. Looked like another great day. "He's too big to eat, Lew," I said. "Throw him back and let's keep some smaller fish."

Holding the fish by the lower lip, Lew lowered it gently back into the Apalachicola.

Well, we plugged the banks. We pulled spin-nerbaits across the flats. We jigged the depths. We flipped into log jams. We pushed back into the sloughs. All morning we fished without a strike. Lew held silent during our lunch. After eating, he said he would take me to a secret hole or two if I would promise not to show them to Shag Shahid. I promised and we headed up the Appalachicola at full throttle. At Lew's honey holes, we fished worms, crankbaits, spoons, and spinnerbaits. We fished them deep. We fished them shallow. We fished them far and wide, fast and slow. At 3 p.m., we still hadn't had another strike. We hadn't even seen a fish. At about 4:30, however, I threw a deep running crankbait across a point where a creek entered the Apalachicola. Wham. I connected with an 8-pounder.

After we had the fish safely in the net, Lew said, "I don't care how big he is. We ain't going to throw him back!"

garlic clove and cucumber. And I have ulterior motives for including this recipe, which may become clear at the end of the directions.

This recipe doesn't deal with tiny bones in pickerel and other pikes. You may therefore want to substitute boneless fillets. Or debone the pickerel.

6 pickerel fillets
salt
pepper
flour
1 large egg
2 tablespoons milk
3 ounces fine bread crumbs
2 tablespoons cooking oil
½ ounce butter
1 clove garlic
3 cucumbers
1 ounce butter
2 tablespoons chopped parsley

Beat a large egg and whisk in 2 tablespoons of milk. Salt the fillets to taste and shake them in flour. Dip each fillet into the beaten egg mixture, then roll it in bread crumbs.

Heat the oil and ½ ounce of butter. Sauté the garlic in the oil mixture until it browns. Discard the garlic and sauté the pickerel fillets until they are browned on each side. Drain the fillets on absorbent paper.

While the fish are cooking, peel the cucumber and cut it into 2-inch segments. Then cut each piece lengthwise into 4. Melt 1 ounce of butter in frying pan and sauté the cucumber until the pieces are tender. Season the cucumber with salt and pepper, then serve on a platter with the fried fish fillets. Sprinkle fish and cucumber with chopped parsley. *Serves 6.*

Note: I confess that I haven't gone full course on this recipe. I'll eat most anything, at least once, but I have four good reasons for not eating cucumber, even for testing purposes.

First, the stuff simply doesn't agree with me. If I eat cucumber even in a salad I taste it on lettuce, tomatoes, mushrooms, and such.

Second, my wife once served up some cucumber soup for my dinner, even though *I* was on no diet. Cucumber soup. That was fifteen years ago, come July, and I have to use every opportunity to remind her of the fact. Within six months of the cucumber soup event, she made ham sandwiches for lunch—but she "forgot" to put the meat in mine, and was none too generous with the mayonnaise. Maybe she was trying to tell me something, and I still puzzle on it from time to time. And I remember to eat no cucumber, raw or cooked, in soup, salad, or fish, whatsoever.

Third, too many people call cucumbers "cukes," which, for some reason, grates on my nerves.

Fourth? I don't want to seem fussy, but . . . well, a good, well-seasoned, deeply blackened cast iron skillet is the only thing that I like to fry fish in. A man's frying pan is a personal thing, and, frankly, I don't want any cucumbers in mine.

2

BAKING FISH

I'll be honest about it. Some of the worst fish I have ever eaten was baked. Usually, such sorry fare was the result of a weekend angler catching a lunker fish and wanting to show it off, whole, at the dining table. This is entirely understandable, and of course a whole baked fish, even with the head on, can be delicious. But proceed with caution—and don't count on your lunker for Sunday dinner unless you or your chef has experience in baking whole stuffed fish. The bigger the fish, the greater the hazard. Unless you are quite experienced in baking whole fish, your best bet is to skin the larger fish and fillet or otherwise cut it down to size. If you want stuffing, it's best to put it between the fillets.

On the other hand, some of the best fish I have ever eaten was baked, and the text below includes recipes for whole stuffed fish as well as baked fillets, steaks, and other pieces. Also, see the fish roll recipes in the next chapter.

Fillets and Mushrooms

The following dish is quite good, and can be cooked with almost any fish. I prefer rather lean fillets, skinned and boneless.

2 pounds fish fillets
12 ounces mushrooms, sliced
¼ cup butter
2 tablespoons flour
2 tablespoons sherry
1 cup heavy cream
1 teaspoon prepared mustard

salt
pepper
½ **cup grated cheese**

Preheat oven to 400 degrees. Melt butter in a frying pan and sauté mushrooms. Add sherry and mustard. Stir in flour until smooth. Bring to heat, then turn to simmer. Slowly stir in cream. Salt and pepper to taste. Stir in cheese.

Arrange fish fillets into a well-greased baking dish. Pour sauce over the fish and bake for 20 minutes, or until fish flakes easily when tested with a fork. This dish goes nicely with hot, buttered French bread and French-cut green beans. *Serves 4.*

Chipper Drum

Here's an easy-to-fix and easy-to-remember recipe that I adapted from information provided by the Gulf and South Atlantic Fisheries Development Foundation. It calls for drum, but any suitable white-fleshed fillets can be used.

2 **pounds drum fillets, skinless**
½ **cup creamy Caesar salad dressing**
1 **cup potato chips, crushed**
½ **cup sharp cheddar cheese, shredded**
salt
pepper

Preheat oven to 500 degrees. Place individual fillets between wax paper and pound them flat, to about ¼ inch thickness. Salt and pepper fillets to taste, then dip them in salad dressing. Place fillets, skin side down, into a wide, shallow, well-greased baking dish or pan. (If you're cooking larger measures, don't overlap fillets; if your baking pan isn't wide enough to accommodate the batch of fillets that you are cooking, try the broiling pan without rack.) Sprinkle potato chips on each fillet. Sprinkle cheese evenly over chips and each fillet. Bake for 10 minutes, until fish flakes easily. If cheese hasn't begun to melt and brown, leave in oven a little longer—but watch closely. Using a spatula, carefully lift each fillet and place, cheese side up, onto individual serving plates. *Serves 4 to 6.*

Easy and Inexpensive Fish and Shrimp

This dish is not only easy to prepare and cheap. It is also very, very tasty. Most any sort of fresh or frozen fish will work, but I prefer mild, white-meat fillets. Flounder works nicely. So does channel and blue catfish.

2 **pounds boneless fillets**
1 **can cream of shrimp soup (10¾ ounce size)**
4 **ounces fresh or canned mushrooms, sliced**
4 **ounces cheddar cheese, shredded**
salt
pepper
paprika
butter or margarine

Baking Tip

Fish baked whole with the skin on them tend to curl up. The longer the fish, the more likely it is to curl badly. Gashing, or scoring, the skin will help prevent curling; this should be done crossways, or diagonally to the backbone. Scoring can also help in basting the fish, but note that it will also permit more of the natural juices to escape. In any case, I don't recommend that the fish be gashed all the way to the backbone (unless you're trying to cook it quickly); cutting the skin itself is what helps to prevent curling.

Preheat oven to 375 degrees. Place fish fillets into a flat casserole dish that has been heavily greased with butter. Salt and pepper to taste (but go easy on the salt). Pour soup into dish and spread it out smoothly. Distribute cheese atop soup, then sprinkle with paprika. Bake for 20 minutes, or until fish flakes easily with a fork. *Serves 4 or 5.*

Butterflied Trout with Dill Cream

This excellent recipe, from *Sunset*, requires both baking and broiling. But it is cooked primarily by baking, then browned under a broiler. Hence, I put it in this chapter.

6 trout (6- to 8-inch size) boned

2 teaspoons minced fresh dill (or 1 teaspoon dried dill weed)
butter
salt
white pepper
¼ cup dry white wine (or regular strength chicken broth)
2 tablespoons lemon juice
½ cup whipping cream
fresh dill or parsley
lemon wedges

Preheat oven to 350 degrees. Open boned trout and arrange, skin side down, in a 12-by-18-inch baking pan, well greased with butter. Sprinkle fish with dill. Salt and pepper to taste. Drizzle wine and lemon juice over fish. Put a sheet of aluminum foil loosely over pan and bake for about 15 minutes.

While fish is baking, beat whipping cream until it holds a peak. Take fish out of oven, then set the oven to broil. Spoon cream equally on each fish. Put back in oven and broil 2 inches from heat for about 3 minutes, or until the cream browns lightly.

Carefully transfer the fish to a warm platter. Garnish with lemon wedges and parsley or fresh dill. *Serves 6.*

Creole Fish Fillets

In this recipe, mild-tasting fillets from such fish as flounder or smallmouth bass are recommended.

The Fish
2 pounds boneless fillets
1 medium onion, thinly sliced

salt
pepper
¼ **stick margarine**
several sprigs fresh parsley
Sauce
½ **cup mayonnaise**
¼ **cup Creole mustard (or Dijon)**
½ **teaspoon Tabasco sauce**
¼ **cup sautérne**

Preheat oven to 300 degrees. Put fish in an oven-proof shallow Pyrex serving dish, well greased. Salt and pepper to taste. Cover with onion slices. Melt margarine and pour over onions and fillets. Bake for 20 minutes.

While fish is baking, make a sauce by mixing mayonnaise, mustard, Tabasco sauce, and sautérne. After fish has cooked for 20 minutes, remove dish from oven and turn on broiler. Cover with fish sauce, then put the dish under the broiler for a few minutes—just long enough to brown the top. Garnish with parsley. *Serves 4 to 6.*

Baked Minted Trout

Here's one that I adapted from material sent to me by the New Hampshire Fish and Game Department:

4 **to 6 trout**
½ **cup milk**
½ **cup flour**
½ **cup fine bread crumbs**
¼ **cup melted butter**
¼ **teaspoon dried mint**
salt
pepper

Preheat oven to 450 degrees. Melt butter, stir in dried mint, and let steep. Salt and pepper fish to taste. Dip in milk and roll in flour. Dip again in milk and roll in bread crumbs. Put trout carefully into a well-greased baking dish. Baste trout with butter and mint sauce. Bake for 10 to 12 minutes. *Serves 4 to 6.*

Oven Frying?

There is much confusion of cooking terms and even a simple concept like frying is not without misunderstanding, as for example the difference between a frying pan and a skillet. "Oven frying" has not been covered in the chapter about fried fish simply because I believe that anything cooked by this method is baked, not fried. But the term is widely used, and the results can be quite tasty.

The trick is to work with good fillets. Dip them in milk, salt and pepper to taste, and coat heavily with dry bread crumbs, cracker crumbs, crushed cornflakes, or some such dry ingredient. Then baste the fish with melted butter and put it into a very hot oven (500 degrees) for 10 minutes or so, or until the fish flakes easily when tested with a fork. If everything works right, the butter-basted batter will also take up the juices from the fish, and will be a golden brown color when it is done.

Try the method—but don't try to tell me that fish cooked in an oven are fried!

Barbecued Fish Steaks

2 pounds fish steaks (or fillets)
⅓ cup cooking oil
½ cup catsup
½ cup chile sauce
2 tablespoons red wine vinegar
½ cup finely chopped onion
1 clove garlic, minced
2 tablespoons brown sugar
1 tablespoon Worcestershire sauce
1 teaspoon salt
¼ teaspoon black pepper

Preheat oven to 350 degrees. Heat oil in frying pan. Sauté onion and garlic. Add other ingredients, except fish, and simmer for 20 minutes. Grease a baking pan and place fish steaks into it. Pour sauce over fish and bake for 20 to 30 minutes, or until fish flakes easily when tested with a fork. *Serves 4.*

Fish with Horseradish and Sour Cream

If you want something different for your fish fillets and have access to fresh horseradish, try the following dish. Basically, it's a Russian recipe, which I adapted from Elizabeth Schneider's book *Uncommon Fruits & Vegetables: A Common Sense Guide.*

2 firm fish fillets, about ½ pound each
salt and pepper
1 tablespoon lemon juice
1 teaspoon softened butter
2 ½ tablespoons finely grated fresh horseradish
3 tablespoons sour cream

Adjust the rack in the oven so that the dish will be baked in the upper one-third section, then preheat the oven to 425 degrees. Select a baking dish that will hold the fish fillets rather tightly without lapping. (The dish should also be suitable for serving.) Butter the baking dish and put the fillets into it. Sprinkle the fillets with lemon juice, then rub with softened butter. Salt and pepper the fillets to taste, then sprinkle evenly with the grated horseradish. Divide the sour cream equally for each fillet, then spread it to coat fillets. Bake for 15 minutes, or until fish flakes easily when tested with a fork. Do not overcook. Eat with vegetables, salad, and vegetables of your choice. *Serves 2.*

Fish Jekyll Island

Once I was a sort of editor at *Southern Living* magazine, which published lots of articles about foods. One of the best things that I got from that outfit was a recipe called Shrimp Dejonghe, which apparently came from Jekyll Island. After leaving the magazine and taking a fling at freelancing and quickly had a family. Seldom did I have money to spare for shrimp, but during this good time I caught and ate more fish than I care to admit and therefore modified the recipe somewhat. Here goes:

2 pounds skinless fish fillets
½ cup of butter
1 cup soft bread crumbs
1 tablespoon chopped parsley
2 cloves garlic, minced
salt
⅛ teaspoon cayenne pepper
¼ cup sherry

Preheat oven to 375 degrees. Cut fillets into chunks, about the size of shrimp, and put into a well-greased casserole dish. Melt the butter. Mix butter, bread crumbs, sherry, cayenne pepper, salt to taste, garlic, and parsley. Spread mixture over fish. Bake for 25 minutes. When done, the topping should be a little brown, and fish should flake easily. *Serves 4 or 5.*

Warning: This dish is strong in garlic. If you object to the smell or flavor, reduce measure to 1 clove.

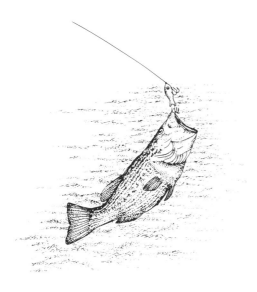

Stuffed Fish with Almond Butter Sauce

Here's a recipe for stuffed fish that's hard to beat. Try it with either smallmouth or largemouth bass. Also try it with mild saltwater fish, such as red snapper, which is especially good when baked whole.

The Fish
  4 or 5 pound bass or other good fish
  salt
  1 tablespoon butter
The Stuffing
  8 ounces fresh mushrooms, sliced
  1 medium onion, minced
  ½ cup of butter
  1 tablespoon freshly squeezed lemon juice
  3 cups of soft bread crumbs
  ¼ cup slivered almonds, toasted
  ¼ teaspoon celery seed
  ½ teaspoon salt
  ⅛ teaspoon pepper
The Sauce
  ½ cup butter
  2 tablespoons freshly squeezed lemon juice
  ¼ cup slivered almonds, toasted

Clean the fish, leaving it whole (head on or off) for stuffing. Preheat oven to 425 degrees.

To make the stuffing, melt ½ cup of butter in a frying pan. Sauté the mushrooms and onions. Add ¼ cup toasted slivered almonds, bread crumbs, ½ teaspoon salt, ⅛ teaspoon pepper, celery seed, and 1 tablespoon of lemon juice. Stir.

Spoon about a cup of stuffing mixture into fish cavity. Put the stuffed fish into a well-greased baking pan of suitable size. Dot fish with 1 tablespoon of butter. Place a baking pan into the oven. Put the rest of the stuffing in a separate casserole dish and put it into the oven with the fish. Bake for about 25 minutes.

To make the sauce, melt ½ cup of butter in a small pan. Stir in the slivered almonds and the lemon juice. Heat but do not boil. Pour the sauce over the fish just before eating. *Serves 6.*

Huachinango Acapulco Style

One of my favorite fish dishes comes from south of the border. It's a fine dish for red snapper, black bass, or blue catfish:

**red snapper or other fish, about 5
   pounds, head on**
½ cup of butter
2 red chili peppers
2 green chili peppers
2 small white onions, sliced
1 lemon or lime
2 medium tomatoes, fresh
1 cup white wine
½ cup red wine
a little more butter

Clean the fish. Preheat oven to 400 degrees. Peel the tomatoes and quarter. Slice the chili peppers lengthwise. Grease a Pyrex

or similar baking pan with part of the butter. Put the rest of the butter into the pan. Cover the bottom of the pan with pepper slices, then put a layer of sliced onions over the pepper. Place the fish on onions. Squeeze the juice of a lemon or lime over the fish. Place tomatoes over the fish. Add both kinds of wine. Tear off a sheet of aluminum foil and grease the dull side of it with butter. Place it, butter side down, over the fish.

Bake for 15 minutes. Remove the aluminum foil and bake for another 15 minutes. Carefully transfer the fish to a serving platter, then top with onions, peppers, and pan drippings. *Serves 6.*

Fiskgratin with Crawdad Sauce

This dish was developed by the Scandinavians over the years, probably using cod or some other cold-water ocean fish. I've tried it with warm-water bass fillets and a sauce made from freshwater crawfish; but the main dish can be made with any good fish fillets, and the sauce can be made with a few shrimp—frozen, fresh, or canned.

The Fish
   **2 pounds of fresh fish fillets (dressed
      weight)**
   1 teaspoon salt
   ½ teaspoon dill weed
   **3 cups mashed potatoes (seasoned to
      taste and rather stiff)**
   2 tablespoons melted butter

½ cup shredded Swiss cheese
paprika
The Sauce
1 cup crawfish tails, minced (or use
   shrimp)
¼ cup of onion, minced
2 tablespoons melted butter
2 tablespoons flour
milk as needed to thicken sauce
2 beaten egg yolks
1 tablespoon lemon juice
½ teaspoon dill weed

Preheat oven to 425 degrees. Arrange the fish in a large, shallow baking dish on a heat-proof platter. Sprinkle the fish with 1 teaspoon salt and ½ teaspoon dill weed. Cover the fillets with aluminum foil and bake for 10 minutes. Take the dish out of the oven. Remove aluminum foil, tilt dish a little toward one corner, and spoon out any liquid that might have collected. Spoon 6 large dollops of mashed potatoes into either end of the dish. Drizzle 2 tablespoons of melted butter over the fish and potatoes. Return the dish, uncovered, to the oven for 10 minutes, or until fish flakes easily when tested with a fork. Sprinkle cheese and paprika over the potatoes and return to the oven long enough for the cheese to melt.

To make the sauce, sauté the minced crawfish for 4 or 5 minutes in 2 tablespoons of butter. Add the onion and cook until it is tender. Stir in the flour and ½ teaspoon of salt. Add milk a little at a time and stir constantly until the sauce thickens. Beat the egg yolks in a bowl. Add a small amount of the hot sauce to the egg yolks, stir, then add the yolks to the rest of the sauce, beating constantly. Add the crawfish, onions, lemon

juice, and ½ teaspoon of dill weed. Stir. Pour part of the sauce over the fish fillets, and put the rest into a serving dish. *Serves 4 to 6.*

Fish Jambalaya Casserole

2 cups of cubed fish (skinless and
   boneless)
1 cup of cubed cured ham (precooked,
   preferably baked)
2 strips of thin-sliced bacon
2 ½ cups of diced tomatoes (peeled)
½ cup chopped green pepper
½ cup chopped onion
½ clove garlic, finely chopped
¼ cup Italian bread crumbs
2 tablespoons flour
¼ cup Parmesan cheese, grated
2 tablespoons melted butter
5 ounces extra thin spaghetti

Break spaghetti in half and cook in salted water. Drain and rinse in cold water. Preheat oven to 300 degrees. Cook bacon in a large

Bluefish

Here's a fish with a dual reputation. Many folks in the northeast rate it as purely excellent, whereas many folks in the southeast treat it as a trash fish. The fish is high in oil content and has a rather darkish meat. It is usually baked, broiled, or grilled.

frying pan and set aside. In bacon drippings, cook onion, garlic, and green pepper until the onions start to brown. Add tomatoes and stir in flour. Cook and stir until mixture thickens. (Stir in more flour if necessary.) In a casserole dish, mix ham, crumbled bacon, fish, and cooked spaghetti. Mix bread crumbs, cheese, and butter; top casserole with this mixture. Bake for 35 minutes. *Serves 5 or 6.*

Microwave Fillets with Orange Sauce

2 pounds of fish fillets
2 tablespoons of frozen orange juice concentrate, thawed
2 tablespoons of soy sauce
juice of 1 lemon
1 tablespoon of catsup
2 cloves of garlic, mashed (or 2 teaspoons garlic juice)
salt and pepper to taste

Salt and pepper the fish fillets and let stand for a few minutes. In a garlic press, mash two cloves (or use 2 teaspoons of bottled garlic juice). Mix a sauce with orange juice concentrate, soy sauce, lemon, catsup, and mashed garlic or garlic juice. Arrange fish in a 7- by 12-inch glass baking dish, platter, or some such container suitable for serving and for cooking in microwave ovens. Pour the sauce over the fish, then roll fish around, making sure that both sides are covered with sauce. Cover dish with plastic wrap. Turn the micro-

wave on high for 6 minutes. Test fillets with a fork. If fish doesn't flake easily, microwave it on high for another 2 minutes. Let the fish stand for a few minutes (leaving plastic wrap over the dish) before serving. *Serves 4.*

Easy Microwave Fillets

2 pounds fish fillets, boneless
2 tablespoons yogurt
1 tablespoon prepared mustard
¼ teaspoon black pepper

Grease a wide, shallow pan that is suitable for cooking in a microwave. Arrange the fish in it, preferably in a single layer. Make a sauce of the yogurt, mustard, and pepper. Spread over the fish and cover with a plastic wrap. Microwave on high heat for 8 minutes, then let it stand covered with the wrap for 5 minutes. *Serves 4.*

Fillets en Papillote

I've eaten a number of fish cooked in a paper sack and called some fancy name. But the best dish of this sort that I've ever eaten wasn't in a New Orleans restaurant. It was cooked in my own oven, and the fish was put into a plastic baking bag. I agree that the brown paper or "parchment" might add a touch of quaintness, or something, for the sophisticate, but I've always been afraid that the things would catch on fire in the oven. In any case, the plastic baking bags available at any good supermarket suit me just fine, and here's one of my favorite recipes:

> 3 pounds good fish fillets, boneless and skinned
> ¼ cup melted butter
> 2 small bell peppers, cored and sliced into rings
> 2 medium onions, sliced into rings
> juice from 1 lemon
> 2 teaspoons salt
> ¼ teaspoon black pepper
> paprika (optional)
> lemon wedges

Preheat oven to 375 degrees. Baste the fillets with about half the melted butter mixed with about half the lemon juice, then sprinkle them with salt and black pepper.

Put a plastic baking bag into an oven-proof dish or pan. Put onion rings, pepper rings, and lemon slices into the baking pan. Pour remaining lemon juice and remaining melted butter into the bag. Carefully place the fish fillets on top of the vegetables. Close the bag and punch a few holes into it (follow the directions on the package). Bake for 30 minutes.

The easiest way to serve this dish is to leave the bag in the baking dish. Slit the bag, and serve directly onto plates, sprinkling each helping of fish fillets with paprika. Or, carefully remove the fillets, arrange them on a platter, sprinkle with paprika, and put the vegetables around them. Garnish with lemon wedges. *Serves 5 or 6.*

Dillpout (microwave or regular)

I found this one in a booklet called *Eelpout (Burbot): the Fish Minnesotans Love to Hate*. It is good, and my wife is especially fond of the sauce. It calls for eelpout, but most any good fish can be used.

> 1 to 2 pounds eelpout fillets
> ¼ cup sour cream
> ¼ cup butter or margarine
> 1 teaspoon dill weed

Melt the butter in a small sauce pan, then mix in sour cream and dill weed. Place the fillets in a baking dish suitable for microwave. Place the thicker edges and the larger pieces toward the outside of the dish, and overlap thinner portions of the fillets so that the thickness will be more uniform. Pour sour cream mixture over the fillets. Cover the dish with plastic wrap and pierce it to let steam out. Bake the fish in a mircowave oven on high for 7 or 8 minutes.

If you prefer a regular oven (as I do), wrap the dish with aluminum foil and bake it for 25 to 30 minutes at 350 degrees. *Serves 2 to 4.*

3

---◆---

ROLL YOUR OWN

Once my wife and I lived in a little red-roofed house beside a blue-water lake in Florida. It was in a rural area, a true fried-fish, grits, and watermelon place, on the outskirts of the Big Scrub. Our neighbor happened to come in one day while I was beating bass fillets on the kitchen counter. She dropped whatever she was chattering about and watched me, as though she had now seen everything.

"We roll them and bake them," my wife said, as though an explanation were necessary. "When they are flattened, they are easier to stuff."

"It also changes the texture," I said. "Makes the meat firmer."

"You really ought to try it," my wife said, knowing full well that she wouldn't.

But she *should*. The first step is to place a skinned fillet on a piece of wax paper. (A large chopping block is desirable, but any large chopping block is desirable, but any smooth, solid surface will do. In Florida, I used our kitchen countertop.) Next, place another piece of wax paper over the fillet. With a large wooden mallet, start pounding in the middle of the fillet and work toward either end. Proceed easily at first, and lift the wax paper after a few strokes to see how you are doing. After you've beaten half a dozen or so, you'll get the hang of it.

"What do you stuff them *with*?" the woman asked.

"With whatever you think will be good," my wife said. "We try all sorts of things."

"I'll bet you do," the woman said, no doubt recalling some of my experiments with fish liver, rattlesnake, pickled golden shiner, smoked spotted gar, and so on. "All sorts of things, huh?"

It's true. We used whatever sounded good and happened to be on hand. Often, we had four or five kinds of stuffing at one meal, so that everybody got to try different ones. It was fun, and the kids loved it. I still feel that it is best to use your own imagaination for fish rolls, simply because you'll enjoy it more that way.

In Florida, we normally used small bass about 12 inches long, but any mild flavored fish will do. Skin the fillets. Some fillets, such as those from small flounder, won't require as much beating as the bass simply because they are flatter to start with.

If you want to try it, here are a few recipes and ideas to get you started:

Bass Roll Italian

   6 fillets from small bass
   1 cup ground beef, venison, or turtle
   6 tablespoons spaghetti sauce
   6 teaspoons finely chopped
      mushrooms
   Parmesan cheese
   salt and pepper to taste

Beat the fillets as described above until they are about ¼ to ½ inch thick. If you don't have a wooden mallet, use a 2-by 4-foot board and a hammer. Cover the fillet with a sheet of wax paper. Place the board firmly over the fillet, then pound the board with the hammer. After you've beaten all the fillets, set them aside.

Preheat oven to 350 degrees. Brown the ground meat in a frying pan. Salt and pepper the fillets and cover them with the ground meat, spreading evenly. Put 1 tablespoon of spaghetti sauce and 1 teaspoon of finely

chopped mushrooms over each fillet. Sprinkle with Parmesan cheese. Roll the fillets carefully and pin with tooth picks. Put the rolls into a greased baking dish and bake for about 30 minutes. *Serves 6*.

Note: In all the recipes in this chapter, any remaining stuffing can be put on top of the fillet rolls. If the rolls are stood on end, a cup can be formed in the top, and this cavity can be used to hold additional stuffing, or it can be filled, after cooking, with such toppings as sour cream. If you want a cup, it's best to start with the small end of the fillet and roll toward the big end. Don't hesitate to try whatever topping sounds good with a particular stuffing. Also, don't hesitate to use the juices and drippings left in the baking dish either as a basting sauce or thickened into a gravy. As a rule, allow at least ¼ pound of fish fillets per person when the stuffing calls for other meat; allow from ⅓ to ½ pound of fish fillets per person when the stuffing contains no other meat.

In the following recipes, the procedure for beating, stuffing, and cooking the fillets will not be repeated, and the names refer only to the stuffing:

Grouper

There are a number of fish in the grouper family, and most of them are purely excellent eating. They are medium-low in oil content, and have firm, white, mild flesh. However, some of the groupers have a bitter skin. So, skin them. The groupers can be cooked in any style.

Crab Stuffing

½ pound crab meat
1 cup dry bread crumbs
¼ cup butter
2 tablespoons minced onion
1 tablespoooon minced bell pepper
1 tablespoon minced celery
1 clove of garlic, minced
1 teaspoooon chopped parsley
2 beaten eggs
1 lemon
salt and pepper to taste

Sauté the onion, celery, and pepper in butter until tender. Stir in the parsley, bread crumbs, eggs, salt, and pepper. The stuffing is now ready to spread over the fillets for rolling. (Follow instructions in the first recipe.)

The recipe makes enough stuffing for 8 to 10 small fillets. Serve these fillet rolls with individual lemon wedges or lemon slices as a garnish, so that a drop or two of lemon juice can be used as desired.

Vegetable Stuffing

6 tablespoons chopped tomato
6 tablespoons chopped onion
6 tablespoons chopped mushrooms
6 teaspoons minced bell pepper
salt and pepper to taste

This recipe makes enough stuffing for 6 small fillets. Put 1 tablespoon each of tomato,

---

Snappers

The red snapper has a very good reputation as table fare, owing in part to its pretty red-orange skin. But the other snappers, such as the smaller mutton snapper and the larger black snapper, are also quite good. All of the snappers have a medium low oil content and can be cooked by most any reasonable method. They have rather meaty throats and heads, which can be used in soups and chowders.

onion, and mushroom on each fillet, then add 1 teaspoon of grated bell pepper. Or you can mix all the vegetables together and spread evenly.

Cream Cheese and Onion Soup Mix

3 ounces cream cheese
1 envelope of onion soup mix (1.4 ounce)
1 tablespoon finely chopped parsley
salt and pepper to taste

Mix all ingredients and spread evenly over fillets for rolling. Makes enough stuffing for four small fillets.

Variation: Try dipping the fillet rolls, after stuffing, into beaten eggs. Then roll in bread crumbs or crushed cereal, drizzle with melted butter, and bake as usual. But watch closely so that the crumbs don't get too brown.

Tomato Paste

> **tomato paste**
> **Italian bread crumbs**
> **salt and pepper to taste**

Salt and pepper fillets to taste, then cover them on one side with tomato paste and sprinkle with Italian bread crumbs. Roll as usual.

Also try this recipe with a strip of thin bacon wrapped around each fillet roll and pinned with a toothpick. Bake as usual, or until the bacon is brown and crisp.

Green Tomato Stuffing

I'm fond of fried green tomatoes, and fillets rolled with them and baked is one of my favorite dishes.

White Perch

This fish is often confused with the white crappie, but it is in fact a separate fish. It has good white flesh, rather firm, and low in oil content. It is rated very highly as table fare.

> **green tomatoes (not yet ripe)**
> **cooking oil**
> **salt and pepper to taste**

Slice the green tomatoes thinly (about ¼ inch) and fry in hot oil until brown. Place fried tomatoes on fillets, salt and pepper to taste, and roll as usual. This recipe is also good with a slice of thin bacon wrapped around each fillet roll.

Ham and Cheese Stuffing

> **thinly sliced pieces of boiled ham**
> **grated cheddar cheese**
> **salt and pepper to taste**

Cover each fillet with a thin slice of ham and sprinkle with grated cheese. One teaspoon of cheese for each fillet will be about right.

Mushroom Stuffing

> **1 cup cooked bass flakes (or other fish flakes, see Chapter 4)**
> **1 cup chopped mushrooms**
> **⅓ cup milk**
> **1 tablespoon flour**
> **1 tablespoon parsley flakes**
> **½ teaspoon dry mustard**
> **½ teaspoon Worcestershire sauce**
> **1 egg, beaten**
> **butter**

Sauté mushrooms and parsley in butter for about 10 minutes. Mix in fish flakes. Add milk and egg, then stir in all other ingredients. Spread evenly over beaten fillets as usual. This recipe makes enough stuffing for 8 to 10 fillets. Be sure to try this recipe, and, if you want something a little more impressive for company, try crab meat or chopped shrimp instead of bass flakes.

Asparagus Bundle

1 16-ounce can asparagus tops
1 can cream of celery soup
1 lemon
1 tablespoon Worcestershire sauce
1 medium onion, minced
Parmesan cheese
salt and papper to taste

The ingredients in this recipe are about right for 5 or 6 fillets, but the stuffing procedure is a little different from that used in the preceding recipes. First, preheat the oven to 350 degrees. Divide asparagus heads into equal amounts, making a bundle for each

---

American Grayling

This fine fish has firm white flesh of medium oil content. It can be cooked by any method.

---

fillet. Roll a beaten fillet around each bundle and place in an 8- by 10-inch baking dish. Mix all other ingredients and pour over the fillet and asparagus rolls. Sprinkle liberally with Parmesan cheese. As in the other recipes, bake for 30 minutes.

Variations: Try this recipe with cream of mushroom soup or clam chowder. You can also use tender French-cut beans instead of asparagus.

Eggplant and Cream Cheese Stuffing

My wife has cooked some delicious batches of bass rolls with eggplant stuffing, but unfortunately the recipes were not written down and have escaped me. You might experiment with any good eggplant puree stuffing, or with thin slices of fried eggplant. Or maybe with bundles of fried eggplant sticks. One reason that I forgot the recipes is that we quit experimenting when we came upon the following:

1 large eggplant
½ pound cream cheese (room
   temperature)

Snook

There are several types of snook, and all of them are very good fish of medium oil content. They can be cooked by any method. Some of the snooks, however, should be skinned instead of scaled.

White Suckers and the Redhorse

I was brought up eating a little white sucker from small streams, and, when fried by ordinary methods, they were very tasty—once you got past the bones. I still rate them as very, very good as table fare. Yet, I read in other books that they are mushy and have no flavor! We also ate the larger redhorse sucker, and it too was good.

At the same time, local people used to almost spit out the words "pond sucker" as if it had a bad taste. I don't think I ever ate a pond sucker, and I'm not sure what they are. I bring the matter up in order to suggest that the sucker's habitat might well have a bearing on its flavor. The ones I eat come from cool streams in the fall of the year, winter, or early spring. In fall or winter, the suckers are baited in holes and caught with hook and line. It's hard to tell when you're getting a bite, but you sure as hell know it when you hang one. In spring, the suckers are taken at night with net, seine, traps, or gig in shoal areas of small streams, where they spawn. In some sections of the country, a lot of people consider the spring sucker run just as much a part of the sportsman's calendar as the early fall dove season. A town in Missouri even has a spring festival in honor of the sucker run!

Many people call the sucker, especially the redhorse, buffalo fish. There are dozens of species of such fish, and all of them are in the sucker family. The bigmouth buffalo has a rather good reputation in the midwest as table fare, but, unfortunately, it is seldom taken on hook and line.

2 tablespoons parsley, finely chopped
bread crumbs, dry and fine
cooking oil
salt and pepper to taste

Preheat oven to 350 degrees. Peel the eggplant and slice it to the thickness of your beaten fillets. Sprinkle the slices with salt and drain on absorbent paper for 20 or 30 minutes. Rinse and pat dry with absorbent paper. Heat a little oil in a skillet and fry the eggplant slices until they are tender. Drain on absorbent paper. Mash cream cheese with a fork and mix in parsley. Spread cream cheese over fillets evenly, then top each fillet with a slice of fried eggplant. Roll fillets, put them into a suitable pan, and bake for 30 minutes.

This might well be my favorite fish dish!

4

COOKING with FISH
FLAKES

Filleting has always been my favorite method of preparing most fish for the table, regardless of whether they are to be fried, baked, or broiled. But I always feel downright guilty when I throw away all that good meat around the backbone and rib cage. If I take a sport fish from a lake or stream, I feel that I ought to make full use of it. (In view of the world's food shortage, a similar statement could easily be made against wasting protein by filleting commercial fish bought in the market.)

In short, I use all the meat more often than not. Although some filletists maintain that the actual waste is less than meets the eye, I have found that saving all the meat is very much worthwhile. It's easy, too, either by

flaking the fish or using the Livingston Family Cut as described in Chapter 19. Here's how the flaking works:

After setting the fillets aside for baking or frying or whatever, poach the backbone, rib cage, throat, and possibly the head for a few minutes, until the meat can be separated easily from the bone. Then remove the fish from the water and flake the meat off with the aid of a fork. The entire operation, including the filleting, goes smoother if the dorsal and anal fins are removed first. This is easily accomplished by making a deep incision around the fine bones with a sharp knife, then pulling out the fins and associated bones. (If a whole fish is to be flaked, as will often be the case after you get into fish flake

COOKING WITH FISH FLAKES

cookery, it is usually easier to skin the fish first. Then remove the fins, tail, and insides. Small fish will flake nicely when poached whole, but big ones should be cut up first.)

Once the meat has been flaked off the bones, it can be used in a variety of tasty dishes. If properly seasoned, it is good as is, or it can be "scrambled" in butter until brown. It can be used in all manner of chowders and soups and gumbos. (It can be used, with excellent results, in many recipes that call for crab meat or shrimp; the next time you are in a grocery store, price shrimp and crab meat, then remember the $ signs when you start to throw away a 5-pound bass after it has been filleted.) Flaked fish can also be used in salads, or pickled and used in relishes. Because finely flaked poached or boiled fish will congeal when refrigerated (owing to a natural pectin content), the meat can be formed into a loaf and sliced like cold cuts with a sharp fillet knife.

Clearly, the possibilities for fish flakes are almost endless. So, experiment! Or try the following:

Fish n' Potatoes

1 cup fish flakes
¼ pound bacon
1 medium potato
1 large tomato
½ cup leek (or mild onion) chopped
salt
pepper
½ cup cream or half and half
Parmesan cheese, grated

Slice potato thinly (from ⅛- to ¼-inch thick) and boil for about 10 minutes. Fry bacon crisp, crumble, and set aside. Poach fish and flake. Preheat oven to 400 degrees. Chop leek. Grease a shallow casserole dish or

Fish Flakes Save Freezer Space

If you've made a big catch and don't know quite what to do with all the fish, consider flaking and freezing. This will quickly reduce a very large stringer into a few small packages. If you have a large batch, it's best to skin the fish, then boil or steam them until the flesh flakes easily. Cool the fish and, with a fork, flake off the meat.

I normally freeze fish flakes in units of 2 cups, because that amount seems to work in lots of recipes. But units of 1 cup, or more, can

be used, depending on your requirements. Just be sure to label the contents carefully. I like to use a Zip Lock or similar zipper-close bag, simply because it's easy to use and freezes flat and very compactly.

The key, of course, is to put the bag on a flat surface and smooth it out. Zip the bag closed, then open one corner and squeeze down on the bag, forcing out the air. I use a 7-by 4-inch bag that opens the long way.

baking pan. Place potato slices in bottom; ideally, the potato slices should cover the bottom of the pan but should not overlap. Pour cream over potatoes. Sprinkle fish flakes evenly. Sprinkle leeks evenly. Slice tomato and cover the top of dish with a layer. Sprinkly with Parmesan cheese. Bake for 10 to 15 minutes, or until cheese starts to melt. *Serves 2.*

Fish Flake Breakfast

Some time ago, the Texas Parks and Wildlife Department recommended a healthy seafood breakfast that was based on shrimp and eggs. I have adapted the recipe for fish flakes as follows:

2 cups fish flakes
6 eggs, whisked
4 slices of bacon
½ cup chopped onion
½ cup chopped green pepper
¼ cup cream or half-and-half
½ teaspoon Worcestershire sauce
¼ teaspoon cayenne pepper
salt to taste

Fry bacon until crisp. Remove bacon and drain. Sauté onion and green pepper in the bacon drippings until tender. Add the fish flakes and seasonings. In a separate container, combine eggs, Worcestershire sauce, and crumbled bacon. Add this mixture to the fish flake mixture in the frying pan and cook over low heat, stirring occasionally, until the eggs are firm. *Serves 4.*

Fish n' Bacon for Two

If you enjoyed the above recipe for breakfast and have some fish flakes left over, try this recipe for lunch:

1 ½ cups fish flakes
¾ cup dry bread crumbs
1 large egg
2 tablespoons chopped onion
1 tablespoon Worcestershire sauce
sour cream
4 slices of bacon
salt and pepper to taste

Fry two of the four pieces of bacon until very crisp. Drain and crumble. Preheat oven to 400 degrees. Mix fish flakes, bread crumbs, eggs, onions, and seasonings. Form two patties on a well-greased baking pan. Patties should be about 3 ½ inches in diameter and of uniform thickness. Wrap each pattie with a strip of bacon and pin with toothpicks. Bake for 20 minutes, or until the bacon begins to crispen. Carefully remove the patties from the pan and place them on individual serving plates. Put about 1 tablespoon of sour cream atop each pattie and then sprinkle with crumbled bacon. The patties should be served quite hot—but with cold sour cream. *Serves 2 to 4.*

Easy Fish Loaf

3 cups fish flakes
2 cups crumbled cornflakes

½ teaspoon baking powder
1 cup chopped celery
1 cup chopped onion
¼ cup chopped green pepper
¼ cup minced pimento
¼ cup lemon juice
1 ¼ cups milk
salt and pepper to taste

Preheat oven to 350 degrees. Mix baking powder into crumbled cornflakes. Then mix all ingredients and place in a greased loaf pan, or in any suitable oven-proof serving dish. Bake for 35 to 40 minutes. *Serves 5 or 6.*

Livingston's Favorite

This dish is very rich, but we like it as a main course together with a green salad and sourdough bread. It can also be served as a side dish, or with crackers as an appetizer. No matter how you serve it, you aren't likely to have any left over. If you do, freeze it for a rainy day. On one such rainy day, we served up a seafood dinner for some rather sophisticated international guests. Fearing that we wouldn't have enough, I thawed and warmed up some leftovers of this dish. It took the menu honors away from such competition as expensive stone crab claws! If you want to try it, here's what you need:

2 cups fish flakes
1 large eggplant
2 medium onions, minced
2 medium tomatoes, peeled and diced
1 clove garlic, minced

1 lemon
1 cup Italian bread crumbs
Parmesan cheese
salad oil
salt and pepper

Peel the eggplant, wrap tightly in aluminum foil, and bake in preheated 400-degree oven for about an hour. Remove from oven and set aside. While eggplant is cooling, pour a little salad oil in a skillet, heat, and sauté the pepper, onion, and garlic for about 10 minutes. Add diced tomato and simmer for about 5 minutes. Transfer to a casserole dish of suitable size. Dice the eggplant and add to the other vegetables. Add ½ cup of the bread crumbs and the juice from the lemon. Stir carefully until the ingredients are mixed pretty well, adding salt and pepper to taste. Mix in the fish flakes. Baste with oil or melted butter and sprinkle the remaining bread crumbs onto mixture. Then sprinkle liberally with grated Parmesan cheese. Bake in 350-degree oven until the cheese begins to brown. *Serves 6 or 7.*

Note: As already stated, the leftovers from this dish are very good. And freeze even a small amount of leftovers to try as stuffing for a fillet roll, as discussed in Chapter 3.

Fish Patties with Sauce

The Patties
    2 cups of fish flakes
    2 eggs
    flour
    fine-ground white cornmeal

1 teaspoon Worcestershire sauce
peanut oil
salt and pepper to taste
The Sauce
1 can tomato paste (6-ounce size)
1 small onion, finely chopped
¼ cup vinegar
½ teaspoon Worcestershire sauce
¼ teaspoon Tabasco sauce
salt and pepper to taste
water

Whisk the eggs and mix with fish flakes. Add Worcestershire sauce. Stir in ⅓ cup of flour and ⅓ cup of cornmeal. Salt to taste. Mix thoroughly. Now mix together ½ cup of flour with ½ cup of cornmeal and roll patties in it. Heat about ½ inch of peanut oil in a large frying pan. Fry patties in hot oil on both sides until they are browned. Set aside on absorbent paper.

To make the sauce, mix the can of tomato paste with 1 can of water in a small pan. Stir in onion, vinegar, Worcestershire sauce, and Tabasco sauce. Bring to a quick boil, reduce heat, salt and pepper to taste, and simmer for a few minutes. Pour sauce over the fish patties and serve as soon as possible. *Makes 4 hefty servings.*

Tasty Fish Cakes

1 cup fish flakes
¼ cup cracker crumbs
¼ cup seasoned Italian bread crumbs
1 small onion, diced finely
1 egg
salt
pepper
butter or margerine

Combine fish, crumbs, onion, and egg. Salt and pepper to taste. Shape mixture into patties about ¾ inch thick. Heat oil in skillet and fry patties. Brown on both sides. Serves two for light lunch. Double if you're hungry. Measures can be increased to serve more people.

Cod

Several kinds of cod and closely related fish are quite good, having lean white, meat. The term "cod liver oil" gives the wrong impression of these fine fish. Although the liver itself might indeed be oily, the flesh is quite low in oil content. Members of this family include Atlantic cod, Pacific cod, haddock, hakes, and freshwater burbot (also called ling).

Fish Flake Pie Littlejohn

Here's a good recipe that I adapted from *Coastal Carolina Cooking*. It was submitted to that publication by Frances Drane Inglis of Edenton, North Carolina, who says that she got it from one of her ancestors, Mary M. C. Littlejohn.

1 whole fish, about 2 ½ pounds
water
3 cups mashed potatoes (cooked)

Mako Shark

Low in oil content, the mako is highly regarded as table fare in some circles. It's flesh has a pleasant flavor and good texture. The fish can be cooked by most any method.

1 can anchovies (see note below)
4 tablespoons butter
6 tablespoons flour
1 large egg
salt
pepper
juice from ½ lemon

Dress fish, cut up, and poach in a saucepan with about 3 cups of water. Remove the fish (retaining the liquid) and flake it with a fork. Put bones back onto sauce pan and simmer in the liquid.

Melt butter, add flour, and mix. Strain ¼ cup of fish stock from pan and add to flour and butter. Stir until well mixed. Add lemon juice, egg, anchovy, and fish. Salt and pepper to taste.

In a deep 9-inch pie pan, spread half of the mashed potatoes (1 ½ cups). Spread fish mixture onto potatoes, then top with the rest of the mashed potatoes. Bake in 350 degree oven for 20 minutes. I like to sprinkle mine with paprika, just for color, but the Outer Bank folk might not truck with this idea! *Serves 4 to 6*.

Note: The original recipe, as printed in *Coastal Carolina Cooking*, called for 1 heaping teaspoon of anchovy paste. I changed this to 1 can (2 ounces) of anchovies, finely chopped. Anyone who wants a milder flavor can decrease the anchovy measure—or omit it entirely.

Fish and Avocado Vinaigrette

In another book on fish and game cookery, the authors set forth a recipe that mixes venison and chocolate. Well, I'm not knocking it. I'm not trying it, either. I mention it here only to render speechless any critic who might be tempted to label the tangy combination below as strange.

2 large avocados
1 cup fish flakes
6 slices thick bacon
bacon fat
¾ cup chopped onion
juice from ½ lemon
¼ cup apple cider vinegar
1 teaspoon salt
¼ teaspoon pepper
mayonnaise (optional)

Prepare fish flakes by any method set forth at the beginning of this chapter. Fresh poached fish is preferred. Cook bacon until well browned. Remove bacon and crumble. To 2 tablespoons bacon fat, add onions, vinegar, crumbled bacon, lemon juice, salt, and pepper. Cover and cook for a few minutes, until onions are tender. Mix in fish flakes.

Cut avocados in half and scoop out meat in small chunks. (Or peel and cube.) Put equal amounts of avocado in bowls, then spoon on fish . If desired, top with a tad of mayonnaise. Also, avocado halves may be stuffed with fish mixture, then topped with mayonnaise and sprinkled with paprika. By the way, my wife says this might be her favorite fish dish. But I might add that she's nuts about avocado anyhow. *Serves 4.*

Flounder Flake au Gratin

I'm not too fussy, usually, about what sort of fish is used in most of the recipes in this chapter, but for this one I prefer a mild, white-fleshed fish, such as flounder and similar flatfish, or small Pea River bass.

    4 cups flounder flakes
    2 cups milk
    1 cup grated cheese
    1 can mushroom soup
    ½ cup sautérne
    ½ cup flour
    ½ cup butter (or ½ stick of margarine)
    ¼ cup chopped parsley
    1 medium onion, finely chopped
    1 green pepper, finely chopped
    ½ teaspon turmeric
    bread crumbs, buttered
    salt and pepper to taste

Preheat oven to 350 degrees. Sauté onion and pepper in butter until onion starts to brown. Mix flour into milk. Then mix all ingredients except crumbs and cheese. Put

into a well-greased, oven-proof serving dish about 15 inches long and 10 inches wide. Top with buttered crumbs, then sprinkle on grated cheese. Bake until cheese begins to brown. *Serves 7 or 8.*

Note: Consider serving this dish with the fish rolls below.

Flaked Bluefish Casserole

    1 pound dressed bluefish
    1 can cream of celery soup (10 ¾ ounce)
    2 hard boiled eggs, sliced
    ¼ cup milk
    1 cup crushed potato chips
    1 teaspoon salt
    ½ teaspoon pepper
    1 can Le Sueur early (small) green peas (8 ½-ounce size)

Preheat oven to 350 degrees. Poach fish for about 10 minutes, until it flakes when tested with a fork. Drain and flake. Turn oven to 350 degrees. Put soup and milk into a casserole dish and stir. Add eggs, fish, salt, pepper, and drained peas. Bake for 25 minutes. Sprinkle top with crushed potato chips and bake for another five minutes. *Serves 4.*

Fish Rolls

    2 cups flaked fish
    1 medium onion, grated

½ **green pepper, grated**
biscuit mix
milk
salt and pepper to taste

Mix biscuit dough according to directions on the package and roll into ¼-inch thickness, forming an oval shape. Set aside. Preheat oven to 350 degrees. Mix fish flakes, green pepper, and onion with a little milk. Salt and pepper to taste. Spread mixture evenly on dough sheet. Roll together, forming a loaf. Cut loaf every inch or so, but do not completely sever pieces. Bake loaf on a well-greased pan for 15 to 20 minutes, or until the loaf is biscuit-brown. *Serves 4.*

Note: I sometimes serve fish rolls instead of bread when we have Flaked Flounder au Gratin and similar dishes. The loaf can also be served with a mild cheese sauce.

Fish & Rice

3 **cups fish flakes**
½ **cup grated cheese**
1 **onion, chopped**
2 **stalks celery, chopped**
1 **green pepper, chopped**
1 **can tomatoes (16-ounce size)**
rice
butter
paprika
salt and pepper

Preheat oven to 350 degrees. Sauté green pepper, onion, and celery in butter. Mix with fish flakes, cheese, and tomatoes. Put into a well-greased casserole dish. Bake for about 20 mintues; be sure that the cheese has melted before removing from oven. Serve hot over separately cooked rice. Sprinkle lightly with paprika. *Serves 5 or 6.*

Quick Fish Cakes

2 **cups fish flakes**
1 **cup of Italian bread crumbs**
½ **cup finely chopped onion**
⅓ **cup mayonnaise**
1 **large egg**
1 **teaspoon Worcestershire sauce**
1 **teaspoon dry mustard**
salt and pepper to taste

Mix all ingredients in a large bowl. Shape into patties about ¾ inch thick. Heat the frying pan, using just enough oil to prevent sticking. Cook the patties on each side for 3 or 4 minutes, or until browned. *Serves 4.*

Fish Flake Fritters

2 **cups of flaked fish**
1 **egg, lightly beaten**
½ **cup biscuit or pancake mix**
1 **onion, finely chopped**
1 **teaspoon Worcestershire sauce**
1 **tablespoon milk**
cooking oil
salt and pepper to taste

Mix milk, egg, diced onion, salt, and pepper with fish flakes. Thicken the mixture slowly with approximately ½ cup of biscuit mix or pancake mix until the mixture can be formed into patties. Fry in ½ inch of hot oil. *Serves 4.*

Fish n' Eggs

This dish always brings back a lot of memories for me. I first cooked it about 13 years ago. At the time, my wife and I had three children to feed and not a whole lot of money to do it with. But we did have plenty of fish, and I fed them to my family in a variety of ways. Thinking I was doing something special for the recipe below, I splurged with some real butter (as compared to margarine). I didn't realize it, but our family, and most others, I suspect, always called margarine "butter" at the table. My wife and I enjoyed the real thing on toast, but the kids wouldn't eat it! "What's this stuff?" they yelled, almost spitting it out. Times do change, and I admit that I don't always keep up. If real butter is back in vogue, then use it in the recipe below. If not, use margarine.

2 cups fish flakes
6 eggs
4 tablespoons butter
1 tablespoon chopped parsley
1 tablespoon chopped chives
salt and pepper to taste

Measures

A friend of mine once asked me for a recipe for a fish flake and radish salad that I used to make. He commented later that it took too many fish to make a cup! I laughed, but his comments didn't quite sink in. At the time, most of my fish flakes were made from fish left from filleting. I didn't really realize how much it takes to fill a cup until I went out on the lake to catch enough fish to fill a recipe. I quickly caught a 1 pound largemouth, and I told myself that I could get off a cup and freeze the rest of it. Well, a fillet off the bass didn't even start to fill the cup up, and the second fillet came to the halfway mark. I took a fork and flaked the meat off the backbone, picked the ribs clean, and even got the meat off the head. Still, I came up a little short.

Exact yields per pound of fish are impossible simply because each kind of fish will be different. I suspect also that the size of the fish will make a difference, in that the larger fish may have a higher average yield. Also, a "cup of fish flakes" can be loose or packed, with a considerable difference in weight. But, as a rule of thumb, you can figure on 1 cup of flakes per 1 ½ pounds of undressed fish. Also, 1 cup of fish flakes weighs from 6 to 8 ounces; therefore, 1 pound of boneless fillets should make at least two cups when flaked.

Melt "butter" in a frying pan on medium heat. Brown fish flakes slightly. Beat eggs slightly in a separate bowl and pour into frying pan with fish. Add parsley, chives, salt, and pepper. Scramble until done. *Serves 4 or 5.*

Variations: Try adding a few chopped green onions, green tops and and all. Or add a cup or so of finely chopped ham and, instead of scrambling, cook the mixture like an omelet. Also remember that a peeled and diced tomato goes nicely in omelets.

Fish Flake Soft Loaf

2 cups of bass flakes
16 crackers
¼ cup of milk
¼ cup sautérne
1 tablespoon Worcestershire sauce
garlic powder
grated cheese
melted butter
salt and pepper to taste

Preheat oven to 350 degrees. Roll or beat crackers into fine crumbs. Mix crumbs with ¼ cup of melted butter and ¼ cup of milk. Mix in fish flakes. Add wine. Season with the Worcestershire sauce, garlic powder, salt, and pepper. Form mixture into a loaf in an oblong 1½-quart casserole dish. Pour 1 tablespoon of melted butter over loaf and top with grated cheese. Bake for 35 minutes. *Serves 4.*

Note: this recipe was a little difficult to name because it is really not firm enough to

Rx for Fish Bones

The time to look for fish bones is before a dish is cooked, and certainly before it is eaten. This is especially true of fish used in fish flake cookery. The bones can be taken care of by anyone who is careful when dressing the fish, and who understands where the trouble spots are with a particular species of fish.

But everybody who eats lots of fish is likely to tangle with a bone or two at one time or another. Usually, this is not serious. I've never known anyone who had to be taken to a doctor because of a fish bone. But I'm sure it can happen, and having even a tiny bone stuck in your throat can scare the hell out of you. Usually, swallowing a large blob of bread will dislodge such a bone and it will go on down with the bread, where it is easily digested by stomach juices. But if two or three swallows of bread don't clear the bone, head for a doctor or an emergency room.

be called a "loaf" and not gooey enough to be called a "casserole." It's in-between and mouth-watering. Try it.

Sweet 'n Sour Fish Balls

For many years I mealed and fried most of the fish that I ate. There was a rather sharp turning point—and this recipe was it. I made it first with largemouth bass flakes, but any good fish will do nicely:

The Fish
- 2 cups of fish flakes
- ½ cup of peanut oil
- ½ cup water chestnuts, minced
- ¼ cup dry bread crumbs
- 2 tablespoons soy sauce
- 1 teaspoon ground ginger root

The Sauce
- 1 can pineapple chunks and liquid (20-ounce size)
- 1 bell pepper, diced
- ½ cup apple cider vinegar
- ¼ cup brown sugar
- 2 tablespoons cornstarch

Heat peanut oil in a large frying pan. Mix fish, water chestnuts, bread crumbs, soy sauce, and ginger. Shape mixture into about 25 small balls. Fry and stir fish balls in hot oil until brown on all sides. Drain on absorbent paper. (I use flattened grocery bags.)

To make the sauce, drain the juice from the pineapple can and add a enough water to make 1 ½ cups of liquid. Put the liquid into a large saucepan. Heat and add vinegar, brown sugar, and cornstarch. Stir until well mixed and the liquid thickens. Add pineapple chunks and green pepper. Stir and cook 6 or 7 minutes. Remove from heat and gently stir in fish balls. Serve over rice. *Serves 4 or 5.*

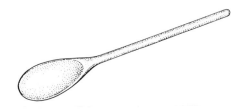

5

BROILING FISH

Broiling is one of my favorite ways to cook fish, especially fatty species such as king mackerel. Usually, a fatty fish doesn't need much on it except a little salt to make a good meal. Lean fish, on the other hand, tend to be dry if broiled for very long, and these should be basted frequently with butter or sauce.

Like "roasting" and "grilling," the term "broiling" has several meanings in cookery, depending on who you are talking to. What I mean by the term is to put fish or meat *directly under* the heat source, and not touching it. Moreover, the best results are usually obtained by putting the meat or fish very close to the heat source, although there are some variations from one recipe to another.

I usually prefer to broil fillets instead of whole fish, but this often presents a problem because tender fillets are difficult to turn over

without breaking them apart. A double rack will work, and I often use two small portable racks placed atop the main oven rack; of course, the fish is sandwiched between the two racks so that it can be flipped over instead of turned. Also, I have included several recipes that are designed so that you won't have to turn the fish. Start with:

Broiled Crappie Fillets Paprika

Here's a dish that is half fried and half broiled. I cook it in a flat iron skillet or griddle, using the stovetop first, then switch to the broiler. By using this procedure, I avoid having to turn the fillets. It works nicely on delicate fillets, such as those from crappie.

> **1 pound skinless fillets**
> **1 tablespoon bacon drippings or**
>   **butter**
> **salt**
> **paprika**
> **lemon juice**

Turn on the stove. Turn on the broiler. Brush fillets with bacon drippings, then salt them to taste. Sauté them on one side on a flat griddle for 5 minutes (or less if griddle is hot to begin with). Then, without turning or moving the fillets, squeeze a little lemon juice on each and sprinkle liberally with paprika. Put the whole griddle in the broiler very close to the heat source for four minutes, or until the fish flakes easily when tested with a fork. *Serves 2.*

Note: This technique will not work for large amounts of fish, unless you want to cook them in several batches.

Marinated Shark Kabobs

Here's a recipe that I got from Nova Scotia Department of Fisheries. It calls for northern shark, but amberjack and similar fish of rather firm flesh can be used.

> **1 pound northern shark fillets, cut**
>   **into 1-inch cubes**
> **4 ounces fresh mushrooms**
> **15 cherry tomatoes**

Northern Shark

For many years, northern shark has been in high demand in Europe, especially Great Britian where it is widely used in the traditional English fish 'n chips. Northern shark has a white flesh containing some dark meat that provides a unique sweet, delicate flavor. Sharks do not have a skeletal structure, therefore there are no bones to contend with. Shark, when properly handled, gives off a slight ammonia odor due to a natural chemical occurrence. This odor dissipates during cooking; however, to remove the odor completely, you can marinate shark in an acidic solution such as lemon juice or vinegar/water solution. Northern shark is excellent for barbecuing as the flesh will not fall apart.

—Nova Scotia Department of Fisheries

> **½ cup lemon juice**
> **½ cup vegetable oil**
> **2 tablespoons chopped parsley**
> **1 teaspoon dry mustard**
> **1 clove garlic, minced**
> **½ teaspoon salt**
> **¼ teaspoon pepper**

Mix oil, lemon juice, parsley, mustard, garlic, salt, and pepper in a large bowl. Stir. Add fish chunks and toss. Refrigerate for an hour. Just before cooking, add the mushrooms and tomatoes to the fish and toss. Be sure to reserve the marinade.

Turn the oven broiler on, break out the kabob skewers, and grease a broiling rack.

Place rack so that kabobs will be 4 inches from the heat source. Make kabobs by threading on a cherry tomato, fish chunk, and mushroom, in that order. Start and end with a cherry tomato. Broil four inches from heat for 3 minutes. Baste. Broil 3 minutes. Baste and turn. Broil for another 3 minutes. Baste and broil for 2 minutes, or until fish flakes easily when tested with a fork. *Serves 2.*

Broiled Fillets with Tangerine Sauce

Because I currently live in Alabama, it strikes me as being somewhat ironic that the following recipe from *Alabama Conservation*, a state publication, was sent to me from Florida! The Alabama people gave credit for the recipe to the National Marine Fisheries Service, Consumer Affairs Division. I don't know exactly who to thank, but I suspect that the Florida citrus folks had something to do with it. Anyhow, somebody, somewhere, came up with a good one, which (of course!) I have improved on somewhat:

The Fish
  2 pounds fillets
  2 tablespoons butter, melted
  2 tablespoons tangerine or orange juice
  ½ teaspoon salt
  ⅛ teaspoon pepper
The Sauce
  ¼ cup butter
  ½ cup sliced almonds, sautéed (see below)

2 tablespoons cornstarch
1 cup tangerine or orange juice
¼ cup white wine
¼ cup apple jelly
¼ cup lemon juice
1 teaspoon grated tangerine or orange peeling
1 tangerine or orange, cut into chunks (see note below)
¼ teaspoon Louisiana hot sauce (or Tabasco sauce)
⅛ teaspoon salt

Turn broiler on so that it will be ready. Combine melted butter and tangerine juice. Place fish in a well-greased baking pan of suitable size. (Fish should not overlap.) Brush fish with butter and tangerine sauce. Sprinkle with salt and pepper. Broil 4 inches from heat for 8 minutes, or until fish flakes easily when tested with a fork. Baste while cooking. Carefully remove the fish and arrange on a warm serving platter. Keep it warm while making the sauce.

Melt margarine in a saucepan. Add the almonds and sauté until they are browned a bit. In a bowl or other container, mix the cornstarch with ¼ cup of tangerine juice; set the bowl aside. To the sautéed almonds, add the rest of the tangerine juice, wine, jelly, and lemon juice. Bring to a quick boil. Stir in the cornstarch mixture. Cook, stirring, until the mixture thickens. Reduce heat. Stir in the hot sauce, salt, grated rind, and tangerine pieces. Remove from heat and serve sauce hot over the fish fillets. *Serves 4 to 6.*

Note: Sections of orange or tangerine, cut into bite size chunks, will be satisfactory in the recipe above. Neither the Alabama nor the Florida sharps mentioned it, but if you want the ultimate in flavor and texture, take the trouble to peel the thin skin off each section of the orange or tangerine. For peeling each section, I prefer to work with rather thick-skinned navel oranges.

Lemon Broiled Walleye

walleye fillets, skinless (or other
    suitable fish)
salt
pepper
½ cup melted butter
½ cup white wine Worcestershire sauce
juice from 1 lemon

Melt butter in saucepan and stir in lemon juice and Worcestershire sauce. Turn on broiler. Salt and pepper fillets. Arrange on a broiling pan and baste with lemon sauce. Put under preheated broiler. Turn after 4 minutes, and baste again with lemon sauce. Baste again after two or three minutes. Fish is done when it flakes easily with a fork. Exact times are difficult to establish and depend on the

thickness of the fish, distance to heat source, and intensity of heat. I normally cook mine about 3 inches from the heat source for a total of about 8 minutes, then I raise the broiling pan or rack closer to the heat source to brown the fillets slightly.

Broiled White Perch Fillets

I developed this recipe with crappie, which yielded a rather flat fillet about the size of a man's hand. At the time, crappie were called white perch where I lived. Hence, the name. Actually, it will be good with any suitable mild fish. It is especially suited for flatfish such as flounder. With long fish such as trout or bass, the recipe works better if you pound the fillet flat before cooking. Merely put the fillet between sheets of wax paper and pound it with a mallet (or the bottom of a small skillet) until it flattens to about ⅜ inch. Here's what you need:

boneless fillets
butter
garlic juice
Creole mustard (or Dijon)
salt
crackers

For two small fillets, melt ¼ cup of butter in a small pan and add ¼ teaspoon garlic juice in it. (Increase measures for more fish.) Swab a little of the butter onto the surface of a shallow skillet and cook fillets on high heat

---

Northern Pike

These fish grow to be quite large, but the fish of under 6 pounds make better table fare. Of medium oil content, the pike can be cooked by several methods. Baking or broiling is recommended. They are quite bony.

for 2 minutes. Transfer fillets, without turning, to a piece of aluminum foil and turn oven on broil. Swab a little butter and sprinkle a little salt on top of fillets. Then spread a tablespoon of Creole mustard on each fillet. Crumble four crackers into a saucer and pour the rest of the butter on them. Spread buttered crackers evenly on top of fillets.

Broil fillets, close to heat source, for about 5 minutes, or until crackers are browned. Watch carefully so that crackers won't burn. (It's not necessary to turn fillets because the bottom part was cooked in the skillet.) When the fillets are browned on top, slide them off the aluminum foil directly onto the serving plate. (The purpose of the aluminum foil in this recipe is to facilitate handling the thin fillets without breaking them up.)

Easy Broiled Bluefish

Some of the best recipes for fish are also often quite simple. Here's one designed for bluefish fillets, but it's also good with other fillets and fish steaks:

> 2 pounds bluefish fillets
> 2 tablespoons of prepared Creole
>   mustard (or Dijon)
> juice of 1 lime
> ¼ cup butter
> salt and pepper
> 1 lime (for garnish)

Dress the bluefish and fillet them. Line a broiling pan of suitable size (it should hold the fish in a single layer) with aluminum foil

---

Sauger

This excellent freshwater fish, a smaller cousin of the walleye, is very good table fare when cooked by any method. It has medium oil content. It's a fish of big waters, and the large impoundments on the Tennessee and other rivers have greatly expanded its habitat.

---

and turn on the broiler heating unit so that the oven will be ready. Adjust the rack so that the fish will be 5 inches from the heat source. Grease the foil with a little butter. Salt and pepper fillets and arrange them, skin side down, in the pan. Mix the melted butter with 2 tablespoons of Creole mustard and the juice of one lime. Spread the mixture evenly over the fillets. Broil for 15 minutes, or until the fish flakes easily when tested with a fork. Baste several times with pan drippings. Serve hot with lime wedges. *Serves 4 to 6.*

Saucy Parmesan Fillets

The following dish should be made in a large skillet that has an oven-proof handle.

> 2 pounds boneless fish fillets, skinned
> butter or margerine
> 1 medium onion, diced
> salt
> pepper

1 can cream of shrimp soup (10 ¾
　ounce)
¼ cup sherry
¼ cup cream (half and half)
Parmesan cheese, grated

In a saucepan, heat shrimp soup. Stir in sherry and cream. Set aside. Turn on broiler so that it will be ready.

Heat butter in skillet and sauté onion. Add fish fillets and cook about 4 minutes. Pour in soup sauce. Sprinkle top with cheese and put the frying pan under the broiler for 5 or 6 minutes, or until the cheese is melted and fish flakes easily. *Serves 4 to 6.*

Fish Lea & Perrins

If I could pronounce the name without twisting my tongue, I would no doubt give more word-of-mouth advertising for Worcestershire sauce. (A contributor to *The South Carolina Wildlife Cookbook,* Ben McC. Moise, called it "wurster sauce.") I'm fond of the flavor, and it goes nicely with some red-meat dishes. I was therefore excited in the local supermarket when a bottle of new white wine Worcestershire sauce caught my eye. Quickly I bought a bottle. Eagerly I tried their recipe for broiled fish. It's good.

　2 pounds boneless fish fillets
　4 tablespoons white wine
　　Worcestershire sauce
　juice of 1 lime
　salt
　pepper

Salt and pepper fillets to taste. Combine lime juice and white wine Worcestershire sauce. Broil fish, basting frequently with sauce, until the flesh flakes easily with a fork. Do not overcook. *Serves 4 to 6.*

Lemon-Glazed Lake Trout

The following recipe came from a booklet that was distributed by the Manitoba Export Corporation in Canada. Be sure to try it the next time you've got lake trout. Also, try it with catfish or bullhead:

　2 pounds lake trout fillets
　¾ tablespoon prepared mustard
　juice of 1 large lemon
　¼ teaspoon grated lemon rind
　¼ cup brown sugar
　salt
　thin lemon slices

Cut the fillets into serving size pieces. Mix the mustard, lemon juice, lemon rind, and brown sugar. Marinate fillets in the lemon

---

Rock Bass

This little fish gets excellent ratings in other books, but, frankly, I rate them as inferior to bluegill or black bass. The rock bass, and similar sunfish such as warmouth perch and Roanoke bass, are often called goggle-eyes. To me, they have a somewhat muddy flavor.

mixture for half an hour. Preheat broiler. Salt the fillets to taste. Place on a greased rack within 3 or 4 inches from heat source. Brown fish on one side. Turn, baste, and brown the other side. Top with thin lemon slices, then cook for another two minutes. The glaze should bubble and brown. *Serves 4 to 6*.

Broiled Flatfish for Beginners

This recipe, at once simple and quite tasty, makes an excellent starter for people who haven't broiled fish before.

> **fillets from thin fish (flounder, crappie, etc.)**
> salt
> pepper
> 1 cup good mayonnaise
> 1 tablespoon crushed dried dill weed
> ¼ cup minced onion
> 1 teaspoon of grated lemon peel
> paprika
> lemon wedges

The fillets for this dish should be no more than ½ inch thick so that they will cook through without being turned. (Turning fillets can tear them apart and is often a problem with broiled fish, as well as grilled fish.) If you don't have flatfish, try putting a bass or catfish fillet between wax paper and pounding it down a bit.

Several hours before cooking, mix mayonnaise, dill weed, onion, and lemon peel.

When you're ready to cook, turn on the oven broiler unit so that it will be ready. Place fish fillets on a well-greased oven-proof serving platter. Salt and pepper to taste, then spread mayonnaise mixture evenly over fish. Broil very close to heat source for 4 or 5 minutes, or until the fish is browned on top. If fish flakes easily when tested with a fork, take it out. If the fish isn't quite ready, turn off the broiler and close the oven door for a few minutes. Sprinkle each serving with paprika and garnish with lemon wedges.

Note: If I have no more than 4 people to serve, I normally broil the fish on small, oven-proof ceramic plates about 10 inches in diameter. I bought some of these from Corning Ware some years ago, when I was something of an authority on the spin-off benefits of space research (such as the high modulus graphite that we now use in fishing rod blanks and the aluminum oxide that we now use in fishing rod guides). Anyhow, these small plates have served me well, and I can get four of them under my broiler. Remember, however, that this ceramic material, which I

Mackerel

The king mackerel, the Spanish mackerel, the Pacific mackerel, chub mackerel, cero, sierra, and other mackerels are all high in oil content. They can be very good when broiled or grilled, but I do not recommend that they be fried. It's best to eat them fresh, simply because they do not freeze well. They have a smooth, finely scaled skin that should be scraped and washed.

understand came from research on missile nose cones, holds heat very well, and stays hot for some time. It will help finish cooking marginal fillets, but remember that it will also burn your guests or maybe damage the finish on your table. So, don't put them on the table until they have cooled down a bit.

Gulf Coast Trout Amandine

Along the American coast of the Gulf of Mexico, the weakfish is called a "trout" or "speckled trout" or "spec." By whatever name, it is an excellent table fish, and this is an excellent way to prepare it:

The Fish
   2 pounds of spec fillets (or fillets of other mild fish)
   2 tablespoons of melted butter
   ¼ cup flour
   1 teaspoon salt
   ¼ teaspoon white pepper
   1 teaspoon paprika
The Sauce
   2 tablespoons melted butter
   2 tablespoons freshly squeezed lemon juice
   ½ cup sliced almonds
   1 tablespoon chopped parsley
   Louisiana hot sauce (or Tabasco sauce)

Preheat the broiler. Mix flour, salt, pepper, and paprika. Roll fish fillets in the flour mixture and place, skin down, in a well-greased

Mullet

This fish is very high in iodine and mineral content. Usually, those mullet that are caught by sportsmen are taken with cast-nets, but more and more anglers are going for them with tiny bait and salmon egg hooks. They should be dressed quickly and put on ice. Although they are high in oil content, they are very good fried, broiled, grilled, or smoked. For best results, dress a mullet soon after catching it and ice it down.

"If you plan to freeze mullet for more than a month," according to UNC Sea Grant, "remove the strip of dark meat that runs along the lateral line. You'll lose as much as a third of the meat, but it will be worth it because it will improve the taste of the meat when you pull it from the freezer. This dark meat is high in fatty acids, and it impairs freezer shelf life. The remaining white meat can be frozen for up to six months."

baking pan or dish. (The fillets should not overlap.) Spread melted butter equally on the fillets. Broil about 4 inches from heat source for 10 to 15 minutes, or until fish flakes easily when tested with a fork.

Meanwhile, sauté almonds in 2 tablespoons of butter; stir until almonds are golden brown. Remove from heat. Add lemon juice, parsley, and a few drops of hot sauce, to taste. Pour sauce over fish fillets and serve hot. *Serves 4 or 5 people of moderate appetite.*

6

BOILED, POACHED, and STEAMED FISH

If you enjoy the subtleties of French cooking or the mysteries of the Chinese, poached or steamed fish is for you. True Chinese or even French cooking is difficult in most parts of America because you can't get all the ingredients. But I think the recipes in this chapter will satisfy almost all tastes, and anyone who thinks that poached, steamed, or boiled fish are too delicate should try the following hearty country recipe:

Sheepshead

This fish has good white flesh of medium oil content. They can be prepared by most any method. *The Frank Davis Seafood Notebook* suggests that the sheepshead can be poached, then used in recipes that call for crab meat.

Puppy Drum and Potatoes

It might surprise many people to learn that the recently famous "blackened redfish" of Cajun cookery is really a drum. Most of the people up the Atlantic coast know the fish as a channel bass. But the people who live along the Outer Banks of North Carolina call a small one (less than 10 pounds) a "puppy drum."

The following recipe for puppy drum is from *Coastal Carolina Cooking*. It came from Elizabeth Howard, who was born and raised on the island of Ocracoker, one of the more remote areas of the Outer Banks. Before the highway was built in 1957, the people on such islands as Ocracoker branded their hogs, cows, pigs, and horses and allowed them to roam free. Most of the homes were fenced in, and one islander commented that Ocracoker was one of the few places where the people were fenced in and the animals roamed free! Anyhow, several recipes in this fine regional book are similar to Puppy Drum and Potatoes, and it is a dish that I highly recommend. It's better, in my opinion, than burned "redfish."

1 4- to 6-pound drum, filleted and diced*
1 teaspoon salt
6 medium potatoes, peeled and diced
2 slices salt pork, diced
1 to 2 medium onions, diced
2 hard-boiled eggs, sliced

*In the recipe that I read, Elizabeth Howard specified fillets. But I prefer that the fish be diced like the potatoes.

Hardboil the eggs and let them cool. Dice the onions and chill them. Boil the diced potatoes until they are tender. Panfry the salt pork until it is crisp, then let it sit in its own grease. Poach the fish pieces (or fillets if you prefer) for about 10 minutes, or until it flakes easily with a fork.

Take up the potatoes and fish in separate serving bowls. Mix the servings on each plate. Sprinkle with salt pork and grease. Top with chilled onions and serve sliced egg to the side. *The above measures serve 4 to 6.*

Note: The size of "puppy drum" seems to vary somewhat in the strong-willed minds of the folks who people *Coastal Carolina Cooking*. Here's a rundown on one named Lucille Truitt: "Lucille is a fisherman. She can smell a school of fish on the air and read the weather in the sky. Born at Paw Cats Creek in Goosetail Swamp, Lucille says, 'Fishing was born to me. I spent the first six years of my life on the river [Neuse]. We lived on an old flat my father pulled up and down the river. He fished for shad, and my mother dried the fish and picked the fatbacks. Lucille says there are three types of drum: puppy drum, yearling, and old drum. Using her hands, she shows that a puppy drum measures about 10 to 12 inches in length, a yearling about 18 to 20 inches, and an old drum 28 to 30 inches. . . . To clean the large fish, she nails their tails to a board and scales them with a hoe."

Cold Dilled Fish

fish fillets
dill weed
½ cup sour cream
1 tablsepoon lemon juice
salt and pepper

Poach fish fillets for 4 or 5 minutes in 1 quart of boiling water with 1 teaspoon of crushed dill weed added. Do not overcook; fillets are done when they flake easily when tested with a fork. Drain fillets, salt and pepper to taste, and refrigerate for at least 30 minutes.

Make a sauce by mixing ½ cup of sour cream, 1 tablespoon of lemon juice, ½ teaspoon salt, and ¼ teaspoon crushed dill weed. Pour over chilled fish. Garnish with sprigs of parsley. I like this dish with French bread—and with ice cold green onions, served directly from ice water in a tall glass or similar container.

Tweed Kettle

Here's an old Scotch recipe from Edinburgh, where, I understand, the tail end of the salmon was considered to be the best. (I too have noticed that the tail part of some fish, such as the larger catfish, seems to be much better than the larger end, at least for some recipes.)

3-pound fresh salmon (undressed
   weight)
2 chopped green onions
1 cup of fish stock (obtained from
   salmon)
1 cup of white wine
salt and pepper
⅛ teaspoon mace
2 tablespoons of chopped parsley

Put the fish into a pot, cover with water, bring to quick boil, reduce heat, and simmer for 5 minutes. Remove the fish. Retain at least 1 cup of the liquid. Remove the skin from the salmon and bone it. Cut the meat into 2-inch cubes and season with salt, pepper, and mace. Put the fish into a suitable pan, add 1 cup of the fish stock, 1 cup of

Freshwater Drum

This fish is quite plentiful, but unfortunately it is not highly prized as table fare. It is of medium oil content, but it tends to get dry and tough when it is cooked. Try a good poaching recipe.

white wine, and the green onions. Bring to heat, reduce, cover, and simmer for 10 minutes. Add the chopped parsley. *Serves 3 or 4.*

Easy Fish Newburg

2 pounds boneless fish fillets
salt
pepper
1 can cream of shrimp soup (10¾-
    ounce)
¼ cup sherry
¼ cup cream

Poach fillets until done. Salt and pepper to taste. In a saucepan, heat soup slowly. Stir in cream and sherry. Serve sauce over fish. It's easy. It's good. *Serves 4 or 5.*

Cold Fish with Avocado Mayonnaise

Here's an excellent dish for a hot summer's day. It might well be my favorite recipe for poached fish, and for salmon steaks, but remember that I am especially fond of the avocado. The recipe below has been adapted from Bert Greene's excellent book *Greene on Greens.*

The Fish
    2 pounds of fish fillets or steaks
    3 cups water

½ cup dy white wine
1 small onion
1 stalk of celery
1 bay leaf
juice of ½ large lemon (or lime)
6 peppercorns
1 teaspoon salt
Avocado Mayonnaise
    1 large avocado
    1 cup mayonnaise
    juice of ½ large lime (or lemon)
    salt and ground white pepper
Garnish
    1 lime peel, finely grated
    lime slices or wedges (optional)
    sprigs of fresh parsley (optional)

Pour about 3 cups of water into a large skillet, Dutch oven, or other container suitable for poaching. Bring to boil. Cut the stalk of celery into several large pieces and put them, along with the green tops, into the water. Cut onion in half and add it to the liquid, along with bay leaf, lemon juice, peppercorns, and salt. Let liquid simmer for 5

Salmon

There are several kinds of salmon, and all are quite good. Typically, they are high in oil content, but their flesh has a good flavor, texture, and color. Frying is not recommended for most salmon, although the coho and the sockeye are often cooked by the method. Usually, the salmon is best when grilled, broiled, smoked, or baked. Also, it is excellent when poached.

Weakfish

Often called seatrout, speckled trout, or specs, the weakfish is quite popular as a gamefish and as table fare. It's meat is lean, white, and flaky. It can be cooked by any method. Several related fish—white trout, sand trout, spotted seatrout, and silver seatrout—are quite good if prepared properly. Their flesh softens quickly, and for this reason many people do not eat them. But it is very good if it is dressed quickly, iced down, and cooked right away.

minutes. Then turn the heat up and add the fish, one piece at the time. Reduce heat and poach for 5 minutes, or until the fish flakes easily when tested with a fork. (Thick fillets or steaks might take longer.) Take the fish up with a spatula and place it, carefully, on a serving platter. Cover the fish and refrigerate for at least an hour.

Cut the avocado in half and scoop out the meat with a spoon. Put it into a blender or food processor. Add the mayonnaise and lime juice. Turn on the blender and puree the mixture until it is a smooth paste. Mix in salt and white pepper, to taste. Put the mixture into a serving bowl, cover, and refrigerate for at least an hour.

When you're ready to eat, grate the lime peeling and sprinkle it evenly over the fish. (Use a fine grate on the outer part of the lime, and avoid cutting into the bitter white part of the inner peeling.) For color, garnish with yellow lemon slices, and with a few sprigs of fresh green parsley. *Serves 4 to 6.*

Low-Salt Poached Fillets in Light Cream Sauce

I usually like quite a bit of seasoning on fish, but the following recipe from Lea & Perrins is good. It's even better with a little salt sprinkled on it, but of course individual servings can be salted to taste—or to low-sodium diet specifications:

2 pounds of fillets
2 tablespoons unsalted butter
1 cup white wine Worcestershire sauce
¼ cup light cream (or half and half)

Melt butter in a saucepan and add Worcestershire sauce. Bring to boil, reduce heat, and simmer for a few minutes. Add cream and keep warm. Poach fillets in water for 4 minutes—or until fish flakes easily. Carefully place fillets on a plate or platter and top with cream sauce.

Grant Avenue Fillets

I've browsed around in a number of Chinese cookbooks over the years, looking for recipes for ducks and fish that can be cooked without special equipment and without all sorts of roots and seaweeds and stuff that I can't get. I finally gave up. But here's an excellent steamed-fish dish from San Francisco's Chinatown. It's good with flounder, mutton snapper, and other mild fish with a low or medium oil content. However, some fish, such as the largemouth bass, are quite flaky and are a little difficult to handle without tearing the fillets apart.

2 pounds of fish fillets
4 fresh green onions (with tops)
2 teaspoons salt
1 tablespoon of grated fresh ginger root (or 1 teaspoon ground ginger)
⅓ cup of salad oil, heated
⅓ cup of soy sauce
½ cup of sliced green onions, including part of tops

Rig for steaming. Fix a rack with legs, or some sort of trivet with legs, into a roasting pan or some suitable container. Your container must hold about a quart of water and your rack must not be submerged. Ideally, the rack should hold all the fillets without overlapping. Also, you must have a cover for the container. When you've got the equipment ready, heat a quart of water to boiling. Arrange fillets on the rack and sprinkle them evenly with salt and ginger. Place whole green onions atop fillets. Bring water to boil. Cover. Steam for 8 to 10 minutes (depending on the thickness of the fillets), or until fish flakes easily.

Dolphin

This popular saltwater game fish, not to be confused with the porpoise, is quite good and can be prepared by any method. For best results, the dolphin should be put on ice as soon as it is caught.

Carefully transfer the fish to a heated serving platter. In a saucepan, heat the salad oil and mix in the soy sauce. Pour over fish. Garnish with sliced green onions, including part of tops. *Serves 4.*

Soused Rainbow Trout

Here's a recipe that I got from the Freshwater Institute in Manitoba, Canada. Be sure to try it, cold, during a hot summer's evening:

several pan-sized rainbow trout
1 quart boiling water
1½ cup white vinegar
1 tablespoon salt
2 peppercorns
3 stalks of celery, thinly sliced
1 medium onion, thinly sliced
1 carrot, thinly sliced
3 tablespoons mixed pickling spice

To make a *court-bouillon* or poaching liquid mix all ingredients except the fish in a suitable pan. Simmer for 15 minutes. Strain and retain the liquid.

Dress and scale the trout. Make diagonal incisions into the skin along each side of the fish. Butter a shallow pan of suitable size and place the fish in it so that they do not touch. Pour enough court bouillon over the fish to almost cover it. Cover the fish with a well-buttered sheet of wax paper. Bring liquid to a boil, reduce heat, and simmer for 7 to 10 minutes, or until fish flakes easily when tested with a fork. Carefully transfer the fish to a serving dish. Pour the poaching liquid over the fish and chill. Serve cold with French bread and good white wine.

Note: If you don't have a pan of suitable size, use two or three smaller pans, or cook in more than one batch.

Poached Fish with Egg Sauce

Some of the recipes for poached fish in many other books may seem simple at first glance, but can lead into a quagmire. References to basic sauces, white sauces, court-bouillons, and so on can lead to references within references—and sometimes it's hard to find your way back to where you started from. So, if the recipe below seems a bit long, remember that it's all there and, I hope, easy to follow:

The Fish
  2 pounds fish steaks (about ¾-inch thick) or fillets
  paprika
The Poaching Liquid
  2 cups water
  juice from 2 lemons
  1 small to medium onion, finely chopped
  1 tablespoon chopped parsley
  1 teaspoon salt
  1 bay leaf
The Egg Sauce
  ¼ cup butter
  1¼ cups milk
  2 hard-boiled eggs, chopped

  2 tablespoons flour
  1 teaspoon powdered mustard
  ½ teaspoon salt
  ⅛ teaspoon pepper
  1 tablespoon chopped parsley

Make the poaching liquid first. Bring two cups of water to boil in a saucepan, then add all other ingredients listed under Poaching Liquid. Let simmer for 5 minutes.

Grease a large frying pan or other pan suitable for poaching the fish. Arrange fish in pan and pour poaching liquid on top. Bring to boil, reduce heat, cover, and let simmer for 6 to 10 minutes, or until fish flakes easily when tested with a fork. Carefully remove the fish to a hot serving platter.

To make the egg sauce: melt the butter in a saucepan. Stir in the flour, mustard, salt, and pepper. Stir in the milk slowly; cook and stir until the sauce is thick and smooth. Add the chopped eggs and parsley. Pour the sauce over the fish, then sprinkle with paprika. Eat while hot. *Serves 4 or 5.*

Fillets in Cream Sauce

  3 pounds boneless and skinned fillets
  1 pint of cream
  1 cup of sliced green onions (stems included)
  1 cup of sliced mushrooms
  ¼ cup of chopped parsley
  ½ cup of dry white wine
  salt and pepper

Mix onions, mushrooms, and parsley. Spread evenly over the bottom of a large

Paddlefish

Paddlefish are delicious and can be prepared in a variety of ways. When smoked, the meat is moist and delicious. Fried, it resembles catfish. The roe can be salted and dried for caviar, or fried in butter with a few minced shallots and served on toast.

To clean a paddlefish, hang it by the paddle, then cut the skin around the tail. Twist sharply on the tail to remove it, and pull out the attached notochord. Skin from the head down using pliers, and remove the entrails and head. The meat can be cut into fillets or steaks, but many people recommend trimming off the dark, reddish outer meat and using only the light-colored inner flesh.
—Keith Sutton in *Arkansas Game and Fish*,
March/April 1987

frying pan. Place fillets over vegetables. (The fillets shouldn't overlap. If your frying pan isn't big enough, use two pans or cook in two separate batches.) Pour in wine. Bring to a quick boil, then cover pan, reduce heat, and simmer for 5 to 8 minutes, or until fish flakes easily when tested with a fork. Carefully remove fillets with a spatula and place them in a serving dish. Salt and pepper the fillets to taste and keep warm.

To make a sauce, add 1 pint of cream to the frying pan and bring to a slow boil. Reduce the heat a little—but keep the sauce boiling lightly until it turns a slightly golden color. Be careful; cooking the sauce too long will scorch it; constant stirring helps. Pour the sauce over the fillets and eat while hot. *Serves 5 or 6.*

Walleye Veronique

This is an excellent dish, both tasty and attractive, to serve for special occasions. Break out your best china and polish up the silverware. In addition to walleye, other mild fish can also be used for this dish.

**2 pounds walleye fillets, skinned
3 tablespoons of butter
1 tablespoon flour
juice from 1 large lemon
2 teaspoons salt
⅛ teaspoon white pepper
⅛ teaspoon ground cinnamon
⅛ teaspoon ground ginger
⅛ teaspoon dry mustard
1 cup of seedless white grapes
1 cup dry white wine
paprika**

Grease a large frying pan (or use no-stick spray) and arrange fillets in it, preferably in one layer. Sprinkle fish with lemon juice. In a small saucepan, mix and heat wine, grapes, white pepper, salt, cinnamon, ginger, and mustard. Pour the sauce over the fish fillets and bring to simmer. Cover pan and poach for 5 minutes.

Retain liquids and grapes. Move fish very carefully to an oven-proof serving platter. (I prefer two long spatulas to transfer; one slipped under the fillet, and the other placed on top to hold it.) Preheat the broiler so that it will be ready. In a clean pan, melt the butter over medium heat. Blend in flour. Add liquid (but not the grapes) from frying pan and cook, stirring constantly, until sauce is smooth. Pour sauce over the fish fillets. Put under a hot broiler, very close to heat source, and cook until the fillets are brown. Remove from heat, sprinkle with paprika, and garnish with the grapes. *Serves 4 or 5*.

Norm Lee's Steamed Fish Egg Rolls

Here's a recipe that I received from Mr. George Nelson, Sport Fishing Representative of Manitoba. In a letter, Nelson said, "Norm Lee's Fish Egg Rolls are excellent served hot with sweet and sour sauce and sesame seeds on top. They can be sliced like pinwheel sandwiches and served as hors d'ouvres or whole to each guest as an entree to a Chinese dinner. I usually used sucker for this dish as the grinding of the fish eliminates the intermuscular bones."

In a note attached to the recipe, Nelson added, "Norm Lee is a well known angler and chef from Northern Manitoba. He is Chinese and all his cooking is slanted that way. Norm is in his 70's now . . . but he still wets a line and cooks his catch."

Unfortunately, Norm Lee neglected to write down the measures in his recipe for fish egg roll—or else he wanted to hold them secret. Thus, I exerimented, like a chemist, and hashed this one out with my wife until we came up with the following mix. Since the recipe came from Canada, I first assumed that a blended whiskey was in order. But it wasn't quite right. Later I met a Chinaman from Memphis, and promptly switched to Tennessee sour mash bourbon. Anyhow:

The Rolls
   2 medium eggs
   1 cup minced fish
   1 tablespoon butter
   ½ cup green onions, tops and all
   ½ bell pepper, green or red
   1 tablespoon whiskey
   1 tablespoon soy bean sauce
   salt and pepper to taste
   ½ teaspoon garlic powder or, better, 1 clove garlic, minced
   ¼ teaspoon Mei den (monosodium glutamate)

Melt 1 tablespoon butter in a frying pan on low heat. Beat the eggs and pour into pan with the butter. While cooking, shake and jiggle the pan to keep the eggs from sticking. The eggs should have a large pancake shape.

Black Bass

The largemouth, smallmouth, spotted bass, and red-eye are all very good eating, and I personally don't believe that there is any difference in the taste of these fish. To be sure, the smallmouth has the better reputation—but this is probably because it is usually taken from better water. The fish are medium-low in oil content and have white, flaky flesh.

Slide out of pan onto a flat surface and cool.

Heat water in a steamer. Mix fish and all other ingredients into a paste. Spread the paste on the egg pattie and roll it up. Secure with toothpicks or skewers. Steam the roll for 20 minutes. Slice and serve with sweet and sour sauce, prepared as follows:

The Sauce
    3 cups of water
    1 cup white vinegar
    2½ cups brown sugar

cornstarch
Chinese mixed pickle juice

Add water, vinegar, and sugar to a saucepan. Bring to boil, reduce heat, and thicken with cornstarch. When sauce becomes clear, add pickle juice. Pour sauce over fish rolls. Serves 5 or 6 as a side dish.

Alternate Sauce: If you don't have a jar of Chinese pickles for juice, try using ordinary catsup, mixed with white sugar instead of brown. Prepare as set forth above.

7

FISH CHOWDERS, STEWS, and SOUPS

Once I knew a school teacher, a very learned fellow, who had eight or nine children to feed and a wife who seemed to be perpetually pregnant. Money was his biggest problem. His salary simply wasn't large enough to go around. To class he wore combat boots and World War II khaki trousers and shirts, with a many-colored civilian tie for color and decorum. He wasn't ashamed of what he wore. Rather, he enjoyed people's reaction to it.

Of necessity, he and his good wife were students of nutritional values, and he had decided that collard greens and fish were the ticket. He caught his own fish, and raised stalks of collards in his flower bed. The pot licker from the collards (or from other cooked vegetables) was always saved for the fish stews, and I've even seen him break up leftover corn bread and put it into a pot of stew, adding a good thickness of texture, flavor, and nutrition.

I don't have any of his recipes to report, and I doubt that he ever made a fish stew the same way twice. But from this philosophic fellow I absorbed an attitude toward fish stews that goes beyond mere ingredients. I can only hope that some of his teachings are reflected in the following recipes.

Poor Boy's Gumbo

There are a lot of good gumbo recipes, most of which call for shrimp, crab meat, and so on. It's simply not a poor man's dish anymore. In short, these ingredients can get quite expensive if you have to purchase them at today's prices. I have come up with a fish recipe that does quite well in taste as well as in texture. The trick is in cutting the fish into chunks, strips, and small diced pieces, as well as using flakes. Other than bony species such as pickerel, almost any kind of fish will work with this recipe, but a fish that isn't too soft or flaky works best. And, yes, a mixed catch also works.

½ **pound of fish fingers (2 inches long, ¾ inch thick)**
½ **pound fish chunks, 1 inch**
½ **pound diced fish, ¼ inch**
1 **cup (or less) of fish flakes**
juice from 1 lemon
1 **cup of chopped okra**
1 **cup of chopped onions**
2 **cups of chopped tomatoes (peeled)**
1 **cup of chopped celery**
1 **tablespoon parsley**
½ **cup of cooking oil**
2 **cloves of garlic, minced**
2 **bay leaves**
2 **tablespoons flour**
salt and pepper
file (optional)
rice (optional)

Skin the fish, fillet it, and cut it into fingers, chunks, and dice. Boil the head, backbone, and rib cage and flake off the meat with a fork. Sprinkle fish with a little lemon juice and refrigerate.

Heat 1 quart of water in a sauce pan. Heat ½ cup of cooking oil in a frying pan and sauté onion, garlic, and celery for 4 or 5 minutes. Stir in flour. Transfer to a large Dutch oven and add tomato, okra, and 1 quart of hot water. Bring to heat while stirring in parsley and flour. Salt and pepper to taste. Add bay leaves. Cover, reduce heat, and simmer for an hour. Then add the fish, cover, and simmer for 15 minutes. Taste and adjust for seasoning if necessary, then simmer for another 15 minutes. If you want a thick gumbo, add a little file to individual servings. (Do not add file to whole pot while cooking gumbo or any other dish.) Thus thickened, I like this gumbo over rice. *Serves 6 to 8.*

Quick Chowder

I wouldn't call this one a recipe because it's so easy. I like it from time to time to "use up" a small amount of fish.

fish flakes
clam chowder soup
chopped mushrooms, if readily available
salt and pepper

Reasonable measures above would be 1 cup of fish flakes to 1 can of soup, but exactness isn't required. If the fish is cooked, flake it or dice it. If raw, poach it a few minutes or sauté it in a pan with tad of butter, then flake it or dice it. Heat soup. Add fish and mushrooms. Salt and pepper to taste. My personal taste calls for quite a bit of black pepper, and I sprinkle it onto the chowder after I have put it into serving bowls.

Most of the canned chowders that I have

sampled had a good flavor—but were a little short in meat. Fish flakes will fix that.

Florida Cracker Fish Chowder

Here's a favorite of mine. I adapted it from Marjorie Kinnan Rawlings' book *Cross Creek Cookery*. Mrs. Rawlings called it Ed Hopkins' Fish Chowder, saying that "Ed was of the great amateur cooks of the world, and with the simplest Florida backwoods ingredients and a Dutch oven, turned out dishes so superlative that when I now prepare one, I grieve that Ed is not here to partake.

"In *Cross Creek* I described his fish chowder, 'uncorrupted by alien elements such as peas and tomatoes, that makes a poor thing of any New England chowder.' I thought that I had started another War between the States, for half of New England, it seemed to me, descended on me with disturbed and sometimes virulent letters, crying that no true New England chowder used peas and tomatoes. Somewhere in my past I had eaten Manhattan chowder, and had been misinformed as to its background. Let me here make amends, and proclaim that Ed's fish chowder is almost identical with the best New England chowder—EXCEPT that New Englanders who tried his recipe from *Cross Creek* wrote me humbly that his was as good or better. One generous soul wrote me that her elderly mother, a New Englander from days of the *Mayflower*, sighed on partaking of Ed's recipe and said, 'Daughter, this is it. Don't ever bother again with Grandfather's recipe.' Another New Englander, marooned in California, tried it and wrote that passing cars slowed down by their gate

Try Lake Whitefish in Winter

Long valued by Indians and Eskimos, lake whitefish has only in the past few years been recognized by anglers and consumers for the fine fish that it is. . . . According to northern Indians, it is the perfect food. On a diet of whitefish, all goes well. Without it, ailments.

Lake whitefish has always been important as dog food in the North, where the Indians partially dry or 'hang' it to make light work for the dogs who must carry it. A ten-day requirement for six dogs being 120 fish, weight is a consideration when the whitefish up there run to 8 pounds, of which 90 percent is water. . . .

The recent recognition of the lake whitefish is in measure due to the increasing popularity of ice-fishing, for the whitefish is a winter fish. In summer the bottom-feeding whitefish is fat and sluggish and as a fresh food and angling item it is best ignored.

Winter-caught whitefish is another matter. The post-spawning fish is leaner and hungrier and provides a good sport and tasty flesh.
—Frances MacIlquham, *Fish Cookery of North America*

as the aroma was wafted on the air, and a multi-motored bomber overhead 'dipped its wings in salute.'"

I have fished Cross Creek, which joins Orange Lake and Lake Lochloosa in Central Florida. I've lived on the outskirts of the Big Scrub. I've read some of Mrs. Rawlings' writings, and I enjoyed the recent movie about Cross Creek. In fact, Rip Torn, who portrayed Marsh in the movie, did one of the best acting jobs that I've ever seen, and, I fear, it's his image that I see when I cook the following version of Mrs. Rawlings' version of Ed Hopkins' Fish Chowder:

  4 pounds fish fillets, skinned and boneless
  ½ pound salt pork bacon
  3 potatoes
  3 medium onions
  oyster crackers
  light cream (half and half)
  butter
  salt
  pepper
  water

Put some water on to heat. Dice salt pork. Slice potatoes and onions thinly. Place salt pork in bottom of a large Dutch oven. Then add a layer of fish, a layer of onion, a layer of potatoes, a layer of crackers, a few small pieces of butter, salt, and pepper. Repeat layers in above order until everything is in the Dutch oven. Try to add ingredients in proportion for three complete layers of everything. Put the Dutch oven on high heat. Add enough hot water to bring the level to within two inches of the top of ingredients. Reduce heat to low and cover tightly.

Cook for 45 minutes, at which time the water should be almost gone and the top layer of potatoes should be tender and ready to eat. Heat cream and pour it over the chowder. Let it sit a few minutes off heat. If all goes well, the bottom should be browned, but not burned. *Serves 6 to 8.*

Note: Do not stir this dish, and serve it so that layers remain intact as much as possible.

Texas Shark Chili

If you don't believe this one, I've got proof. The recipe below was sent to me, in a news release packet, by the Texas Parks and Wildlife Department on August 11, 1976, dateline Austin. I've still got the paper, complete with the Texas lone-star logo. After pointing out that Texas cooking has been called a potpourri of many cultures, they claim that this chili is a "fine example of the blending of foods and flavors that represent Mexican, Indian, and Spanish tastes." They go on, "It is rich in the onion and garlic the Spaniards used so well, the chili and oregano of the Aztecs, and our native beans and seafoods."

Anyhow, here's the recipe:

  2 pounds shark fillets (or other fresh fish)
  2 cups of sliced onions
  1 cup diced green pepper
  2 cloves garlic, minced
  2 tablespoons margarine or cooking oil
  1½ teaspoons chili powder
  2 teaspoons salt

¼ teaspoon pepper
½ teaspoon oregano
1 can red kidney beans, undrained (16-
    ounce size)
1 can tomatoes, undrained (16-ounce
    size)
1 can tomato paste (6-ounce size)

Cut skinned and boneless fillets into 1½-inch chunks. Heat margarine in a large frying pan or Dutch oven. Sauté onions, green pepper, and garlic for a few minutes. Stir in chili powder, salt, pepper, and oregano. Add kidney beans, tomatoes, and tomato paste. Bring to heat, then reduce and simmer for 15 minutes. Add fish. Cover and simmer for about 10 minutes, or until the fish flakes easily. Do not overcook.

Eat with corn bread and a tossed salad. *Serves 6 to 8.*

Tennessee Cioppino

This dish clearly has attachments to California, and one report suggests that it was invented in San Francisco by an Italian. Another says that it came to California from Portugal. If you aren't familiar with cioppino but think that you want the real stuff, I suggest that first you boil a whole blue crab, put it into a bowl of catsup, and then try to eat it. Unless you chew the crab shell-and-all, you're clearly bound to have a mess, and if you feed your guests such a dish they will need bibs and towels and finger bowls, or buckets, at the table. With the right partner, of course, it could be fun, like mud-wrestling after all of the children have gone to bed.

Anyhow, the traditional dish has a tomato base and contains crabs, prawns in the shell, clams in the shell, and so on, as well as fish. I have nothing against such fare, and I'm not all that opposed to shucking or picking at the table. I love to peel and eat boiled shrimp, for example, and of course I eat fried chicken with my fingers. But picking crab in tomato soup? Anyhow, some years ago I came up with a sensible and very inexpensive cioppino made from bass that I caught from the Elk River in Tennessee. (If you've got sophisticated guests coming to eat Tennessee cioppino, however, be sure to save the rib cages and the backbones to throw in for pickings.)

3 pounds boneless bass fillets cut into
    easy-to-find chunks
½ cup butter
2 pounds tomatoes, peeled and
    chopped
1 large onion, sliced
1 bell pepper, chopped
6 scallions, chopped, tops and all
2 cloves garlic, minced
2 tablespoons parsley, chopped
8 ounces mushrooms, whole
    (optional)
salt and pepper
⅛ teaspoon Tabasco sauce, if desired
1 cup dry wine

Yellow Perch

This is an excellent panfish of medium low oil content. It is good cooked most any way, and it is very good when fried.

Heat the butter in a Dutch oven or suitable pot and sauté onions, scallions, bell pepper, and garlic for about 5 minutes. Add tomatoes, mushrooms, Tabasco sauce, parsley, seasonings, and wine. Bring to a boil. Add fish chunks, cover, and simmer for 20 minutes.

Serve in large soup bowls, along with sourdough bread and a hearty salad. *Serves 6 to 8.*

Fish Spaghetti Stew

2 pounds boneless and skinless fish chunks
1 cup chopped onion
1 cup chopped celery
1 cup chopped mushrooms
1 clove minced garlic
½ cup butter or margarine
1 can stewed tomatoes (14½ ounce size)
1 can tomato sauce (8-ounce size)
2 teaspoons salt
½ teaspoon black pepper
7 ounces uncooked spaghetti
water
Parmesan cheese

In a large frying pan (with cover) or a Dutch oven, melt ½ cup of butter or margarine. Add onion, celery, mushrooms, and garlic and cook, stirring, until tender. Add the tomatoes, tomato sauce, salt, and pepper. Bring to a boil, reduce heat, cover, and simmer for 20 minutes.

Put 2 cups of water into a pan and bring it to a boil. Add 7 ounces of spaghetti to vegetables, increase heat, and add 2 cups of boiling water. Reduce heat, cover, and cook for 10 minutes. Add fish chunks, cover, and cook for another 10 minutes. Sprinkle Parmesan cheese over individual servings. *Serves 4 to 6.*

Carteret County 'Conch' Chowder

Bill and Eloise Pigott, according to *Coastal Carolina Cooking*, often cook together in their kitchen, and for the recipe below Bill makes the chowder and Eloise makes the dumplings. The result is said to be a Carteret Country Classic, and, according to the book, "There is even a saying that goes along with the dish: 'If you ever eat conch chowder in Carteret County, you'll never want to leave.' Bill says that cleaning and tenderizing this abundant mollusk is time-consuming, but, he adds, the results are worth the effort. He admits that the conch, which is more accu-

Muskellunge

The muskie can make good eating, especially when it is baked or broiled. Usually, fish of 10 pounds or less are considered to be better than larger ones. Remember that the fish are quite bony, so be careful, especially if you put them into stews and chowders.

Striped Bass, White Bass—and Hybrids

The small white bass, a freshwater fish, is low in oil content and can be cooked by any method. The larger striped bass, or rockfish, is a salt water fish that runs up rivers to spawn—and sometimes becomes landlocked in large man-made impoundments. Much larger than the white bass, the striper has rather dry flesh with low oil content. The larger stripers, over 10 pounds, have coarse flesh that is better when cooked in liquid instead of being fried, broiled, baked, or grilled. The literature of angling and fish cookery rates the striped bass quite highly, with a history going all the way back to Captain John Smith. I don't argue—but personally I'll take a black bass any day over any sort of striper.

The small white bass and the large striped bass are related, and have been crossed in the laboratory, producing a hybrid that is being stocked in the nation's waters. These hybrids are called sunshine bass in Florida. My experience in eating hybrids is quite limited, and the opinion of my friends varies. But one thing is certain: an 8-pound hybrid is fun to catch.

rately a whelk, has a strong flavor for which many folks have to acquire a taste."

The Chowder
   7 to 8 whelks, in the shell
   1 quart water
   1 to 2 thin slices salt pork
   2 tablespoons butter
   ½ teaspoon salt
   ½ teaspoon pepper
   2 to 3 potatoes, diced
   1 small onion, diced
   1 teaspoon thyme
   cornmeal dumplings (see ingredients
      below)
Cornmeal Dumplings
   2 cups cornmeal
   1 teaspoon salt
   ½ to 1 cup of water

"For easy removal of the whelk from the shell, Bill recommends freezing the mollusks first. Then thaw the whelks and the meat can be easily pulled out. . . . Once the meat is extracted from the shell, keep only the cream-colored foot. Brush away the black coating with a stiff brush. To tenderise the meat, either pound or cook for 10 minutes in pressure cooker.

"After tenderising, chop whelk into small pieces. In a large saucepan, add whelk, water, salt pork, and butter. Salt and pepper. Bring to a boil, reduce heat, and simmer 2 hours. Add potatoes, onions, and thyme 40 minutes prior to serving."

To make the dumplings, merely combine cornmeal and salt in a mixing bowl. Stir in just enough water to bind the mixture. Shape into small patties. About 15 minutes before serving, drop the corn dumplings around the edge of the chowder.

Note: Up on the Outer Banks, there is considerable controversy over how to make the "best" cornmeal dumplings. First you've got to agree on what texture and taste is best, then you've got to decide on how to achieve these qualities. There are dozens of variations in the method of preparation and in the ingredients, but the recipe above is, in my opinion, not only the easiest but also the best. But it's not really a dumpling. It's an ordinary Alabama corndodger!

Bouillabaisse Louisiane

This is one of my favorites. I've eaten a number of variations, and some sources advise that small fish, such as smelt, be used in the dish. But I prefer boneless fillets, or chunks of fish, because I don't want any bones to slow me down. My recipe is based on the *Heritage Cook Book*. According to this text, the French, who settled Louisiana, had made the dish with a fish called *rascasse*. In their new home, the French had used red snapper. I normally use largemouth bass— or any other good fish that I can catch:

> 2 pounds of fillets, skinned and
>   boneless
> 2 tablespoons fresh parsley, chopped
> 2 cloves garlic, minced
> 1 bay leaf, crumbled
> 1 teaspoon dried thyme, crumbled
> 1 teaspoon salt
> ¼ teaspoon ground allspice
> cooking oil
> 4 or 5 cups of tomatoes, peeled and
>   diced (or a 16-ounce can)
> ½ lemon, sliced
> 1 cup of chicken broth (or fish stock)

> ¼ teaspoon ground hot red pepper
> ⅛ teaspoon ground saffron (optional)
> cooked rice

Lay fillets out on a table or counter. Mix parsley, garlic, bay leaf, thyme, salt, and all allspice with 1 teaspoon oil. Stir. Spread mixture over fillets and let sit.

In a large frying pan or Dutch oven, heat a tablespoon of cooking oil and sauté onion. Add tomatoes, lemon slices, chicken broth, red pepper, and saffron. Add fish fillets. Bring to boil, reduce heat, cover, and simmer for 10 minutes, or until fish fillets flake easily when tested with a fork. Remove lemon slices. Eat with rice. *Serves 5 or 6.*

Note: I normally leave the saffron out of this recipe. It was probably a North African influence on the basic French recipe. Also note that most of the French recipes for this dish call for all manner of liquids made from boiling fish heads and tails. This is fine if you're working with fresh fish, but often frozen fillets are used and getting up the makings for proper French stocks is just not practical. As stated above, I normally use canned chicken stock—and the *Heritage Cook Book* specified instant chicken bouillon granules.

Redear

This sunfish, often called shellcracker, has white flesh of low oil content. It is often fried. This fish is difficult to take with a fly, and it is usually caught with earthworms instead of crickets.

New England Fish Chowder

There must be a thousand published variations of this chowder—and ten thousand unpublished versions. Here's my favorite:

2 pounds boneless fillets, skinned, or
   2-inch cubes
¼ pound salt pork, diced
3 medium potatoes, diced
1 medium onion, diced
½ small green bell pepper, diced
½ small red bell pepper, diced

1 large stalk celery, tops and all, diced
1 carrot, diced
4 cups of milk
4 cups of fish stock or water
flour
butter
2 bay leaves
2 teaspoons of salt
1 teaspoon black pepper (or to taste)
½ teaspoon tarragon

In a bowl, mix 1 tablespoon butter with 1 tablespoon flour. Mix more and more flour, mashing with a fork, until the butter will take up no more. Then work in even more flour

A Failure to Communicate

My father, when a dapper young man, owned and operated a grocery store, advertising plain foods and fancy. He even offered delivery service. A new young school teacher (later to be my mother) moved to town, called his store, said that she wanted 3 pounds of mullet, and that she wanted them dressed and delivered. Well, my father picked out three of the best looking 1-pound fish he had, dressed them nicely, and sent them to her right away. She sent a message back by the delivery boy that the package contained only 1 ½ pounds of fish whereas the bill showed 3 pounds. In short, she wanted what she paid for. My father wrapped up 1½ pounds of mullet heads, guts, scales, and bones, and had them delivered to her!

There was clearly a failure to communicate, and the same thing can happen in recipes if both writer and reader aren't careful. Sometimes, a simple error can ruin a recipe. For example, a teaspoon of salt can be written or read as a tablespoon, a difference that can ruin some dishes. (Such mistakes are more likely to happen when abbreviations are used, and more such mistakes can be made by writer, reader, and typesetter. For this reason, I have written out "tablespoon" and "teaspoon" instead using abbreviations.) Another error of this type can occur when the writer calls for "1 cup of cornflakes, finely crushed" and the reader proceeds with "1 cup of finely crushed cornflakes." By weight, "1 cup of finely crushed cornflakes" can have ten times as many grams as "1 cup of cornflakes, finely crushed." Such a difference can make some dishes far too dry.

with your fingers. Form into small balls and set aside to thicken the chowder when needed.

Put the water or fish stock into a small pan and heat to boiling. Cut the fish into 2-inch cubes. In a Dutch oven or suitable pot, sauté the salt pork. Remove the pork, but leave the pan drippings. Sauté the onions. Add potatoes, peppers, celery, and carrots. Pour in the boiling water or stock. Add salt, black pepper, tarragon, and bay leaves. Bring to boil, cover, reduce heat, and simmer for 20 minutes. Adds the fish chunks, cover, and simmer for 20 minutes. Taste and adjust salt and pepper, if desired. Add the milk and let heat to smoking—but do not boil. Add about half of the flour balls, continue heating for 5 minutes, and blend. Add more flour balls if a thicker chowder is desired. Stir in the salt pork. *Serves 6 to 8.*

Daddy's Oyster Stew

My father cooked three dishes. One, he took care of squirrels that he figured were too tough for mother to handle; two, he fried salt mullet; and, three, he always cooked oyster stew on Christmas eve. I don't know how the exact date was set, but he always bought a burlap bag of oysters for the holidays, and the Christmas eve oyster stew followed. Anyhow, his recipe is almost exactly like one that I found in *Coastal Carolina Cooking*.

According to that work, Sneads Ferry folks say that oyster stew is a 'cure-all' for illnesses. Percy and Loraine Jenkins ran a cafe there for a number of years, and Percy's cooking won him a reputation of being an 'angel of mercy.' Often he took jars of his oyster stew to the sick, and some local folks believe the stew to be better than medicine. Loraine Jenkins said, "If you get so sick you can't eat oyster stew, you're really sick."

> **1 quart of oysters (not washed after shucking)**
> **½ cup water**
> **½ cup milk**
> **¼ cup of butter**
> **salt to taste**
> **½ teaspoon black pepper, freshly ground**
> **saltine crackers, very fresh**

For best results, shuck your own oysters and drop them one by one into a quart jar until it is filled. Usually, "bucket" oysters bought already shucked have been washed, which takes away much of the salty flavor. Also, get some fresh, crisp saltines. If what you have is stale, put them in a slow oven for a few minutes.

Put the oysters, butter, water, and pepper into a pot and bring to boil. Cook until the oysters start to curl on the edges. Reduce the heat, salt to taste, and stir in the milk. Heat to smoking, but do not boil. Serve in bowls,

and have plenty of crackers at hand. Also, have a pepper mill for those who want lots of pepper, which, freshly ground, adds both taste and aroma to this dish. *Serves 6 to 8.*

Minnesota Style Chowder

I got this basic recipe from a booklet on eelpout (burbot) that was published by the University of Minnesota Sea Grant Extension Program. I tried it with channel catfish, and found it to be very good. The recipe in the booklet did not call for pepper, but I took the liberty of adding some. (I also changed the directions somewhat.)

1½ pounds boneless fish, cut into
    chunks
1 large onion, chopped
1 clove garlic, minced
1 cup diced celery
¼ cup butter (used in two batches)
2 tablespoons flour
½ cup dry white wine
2 cups of half and half
1 cup milk
2 cans chicken broth (13¾-ounce size)
2 cans cream corn (17-ounce size)
1½ teaspoon salt
1 teaspoon black pepper
1 teaspoon margarine

Melt 2 tablespoons of the butter a small sauce pan, then sauté onion, garlic, and celery. Melt the rest of the butter in a Dutch oven and stir in the flour until it is blended. Stir in the wine and simmer for 1 minute. Stir in the half and half, and the milk. After the mixture starts to thicken, stir in the chicken broth, corn, salt, pepper, and margarine. Add the sautéed onions, celery, and garlic. Simmer for 10 minutes—but don't bring to boil. Add fish chunks and simmer for 10 minutes, or until fish flakes. *Serves 6 to 8.*

Variation: Try the above recipe with fish flakes (or leftover fish) instead of chunks.

8

APPETIZERS, SNACKS,
and
SANDWICHES

A number of the recipes set forth under other topics in this book could fit nicely into this chapter. A gourmet looking for hors d'oeuvres in the Table of Contents would surely turn to the chapter on fish roe, for example. The truth is that fish and seafood offer such variety that a whole book could easily be filled without exhausting the appetizer possibilities. If the recipes that follow whet the palate for a few dishes that can be used on occasion, fine. If they inspire the imagination or trigger the urge to experiment, so much the better.

Fish Paté

Here is an inexpensive paté, which can be made from any mild fish. I sometimes make it from fish flakes obtained from the backbone and rib cage left from filleting.

> 2 cups fish flakes
> ½ cup butter
> 2 tablespoons white wine
>   Worcestershire sauce
> juice from small lemon (1 tablespoon)
> 1 tablespoon of onion, grated

⅛ teaspoon white pepper
⅛ teaspoon cayenne
¼ teaspoon dry mustard
¼ teaspoon ground mace

Set butter out of refrigerator. Poach fish until done, then flake and mash with a fork. Put butter in a mixer and cream. Add Worcestershire sauce, lemon juice, onion, white pepper, cayenne, mustard, and mace. Mix. Add fish. Mix until smooth. Put in an oblong serving dish or mold and refrigerate. Slice as needed and serve on crackers.

Note: We like the above recipe for lunch, eaten with crackers, along with chilled V-8 juice. It's also good as a sandwich spread when mixed with a little mayonnaise. *Serves 4 or 5 for lunch.*

Walleye Cocktail

This dish, which can be made with any mild fish, is good as an appetizer, to be eaten before getting to a heavy meal.

The Fish
  2 cups fish flakes (cooked)
  ½ cup celery, very finely chopped
  ½ cup green onions, very finely chopped
  ¼ cup green pepper, very finely chopped
  ¼ cup fresh garden radishes, very finely chopped
  2 tablespoons capers
  salt and pepper to taste

Cocktail Sauce
  1 cup of catsup
  ⅛ cup prepared horseradish
  juice from ½ lemon (make garnish slices with other half)
  ⅛ teaspoon Louisiana hot sauce (or Tabasco sauce)

Mix fish, celery, pepper, onions, radishes, and capers. Salt and pepper to taste. Chill. Serve on lettuce. Have plenty of thin crackers and cocktail sauce at hand. To make sauce, mix catsup, horseradish, lemon juice, and hot sauce. Refrigerate until ready to use. *Serves 6 or 7 as an appetizer.*

Smoked Fish Spread

  2 cups of smoked fish (cooked)
  1 cup mayonnaise
  2 tablespoons minced onion
  2 tablespoons celery, finely chopped
  2 tablespoons parsley, chopped
  1 clove of garlic, minced
  2 tablespoons pickle relish (or finely chopped sweet pickles)
  1 tablespoon prepared mustard
  ¼ teaspoon Worcestershire sauce

How Good Is It?

This dish of meat is too good for any but Anglers, or very Honest Men.
—Izaak Walton, *The Compleat Angler*

Flake hot-smoked cooked fish (leftovers are fine.) Mix all ingredients and refrigerate or chill for 2 hours. Spread on crackers. Or add a little more mayonnaise and use the mixture as a dip.

Hot Fish Sandwich

I prefer this sandwich made with fish fillets that have been sautéed without batter on them. Putting heavily battered fish between bread is a bit much of a good thing, in my opinion. (But of course any of the fried fish recipes in Chapter 1 can be used.)

fish fillets
butter
salt and pepper
lemon juice
mayonnaise (or thin tartar sauce)
loaf bread

Salt and pepper fillets to taste, then sauté them in butter. Squeeze a little lemon juice on the fillets. Spread mayonnaise on bread rather generously, then sandwich fillets. For best results, the fillets should be hot and the bread soft. For these "batterless" sandwiches, I prefer regular white bread instead of the thinly sliced sandwich bread.

Variations: Also try broiled and grilled fish fillets.

Fish and Avocado Purée

It would be incorrect for me to call this dish a snack. It's an appetizer. The more I eat of it, the more I want, as long as it lasts!

2 very ripe avocados
1 cup fish flakes (cooked)
¼ cup of mayonnaise
salt
pepper

Cut the avocados in half and scoop out the meat. Mash with a fork. Mix in fish, mayonnaise, salt, and pepper. Serve at room temperature, and eat on thin wheat crackers. *Serves 4 to 6 as an appetizer.*

Zesty Spot Canapes

Here's a recipe that I got from the state of South Carolina some years ago, as published in *Saltwater Conservation*. It calls for spot, a saltwater panfish, but any good fish will do nicely.

1 cup spot flakes, cooked
3 tablespoons mayonnaise
½ cup finely chopped celery
2 tablespoons finely chopped parsley
½ cup butter or margarine, softened
3 tablespoons prepared horseradish
30 Melba toast rounds or toast points
chopped parsley

Mix fish flakes, mayonnaise, and celery. In another bowl, mix margarine and horseradish. Spread the margarine mixture over the toast, then top with the fish mixture. Garnish with chopped parsley. *Makes 30 canapes.*

Stuffed Cherry Tomatoes

The idea for this recipe, but not the exact ingredients, came from the Nova Scotia Department of Fisheries. I tried it with leftover baked bass, flaked, whereas the original calls for snow crab meat. (The snow crab, by the way, is found in the waters off Labrador to the Gulf of Maine.)

1 to 1½ cups of fish flakes, cooked
36 cherry tomatoes
¼ cup good mayonnaise
¼ cup finely chopped celery
¼ teaspoon thyme
2 tablespoons freshly squeezed lemon
 juice
salt (optional)
Parmesan cheese

Slice the tops off the cherry tomatoes, then scoop out the pulp and seeds with a spoon. (A grapefruit spoon with a cutting edge is great for this purpose.) Put the tomatoes upside down on absorbent paper to drain. Leave for at least 20 minutes. Mix flaked fish with mayonnaise, lemon juice, salt, and thyme. Stuff this mixture into the cherry tomatoes. Before serving, sprinkle the tops with Parmesan cheese. *Serve as hors d'oeuvres.*

Fish Bowl

This dish is a tasty appetizer, but I can make a whole meal of it if I've got some ordinary saltine crackers to put the fish chunks on.

2 pounds fish fillets (or chunks),
 skinned and boneless
1 bay leaf
½ cup minced green onions, including
 part of the tops
½ cup minced parsley
½ cup red wine vinegar
½ cup olive oil
2 tablespoons coarse, Creole style
 mustard, or Dijon
2 tablespoons good mayonnaise
1 teaspoon salt
¼ teaspoon black pepper, freshly
 ground, if available

Boil the fish for a few minutes in water with a bay leaf. Refrigerate fish in a serving bowl. Mix onions, parsley, vinegar, oil, mustard, mayonnaise, salt, and pepper. Pour the mixture over fish and refrigerate for several hours before serving. Eat with toothpicks. *Serves 8 as an appetizer.*

Catfish Bleu Appetizers

The recipe below, I understand, took third prize at the 11th Annual National Farm-Raised Catfish Cooking Contest. I got the recipe from the UNC Sea Grant Program.

The Fish
  2 pounds catfish fillets
  1 cup finely crushed cheese crackers
  ½ cup grated Parmesan cheese
  ¼ cup sesame seeds
  ½ teaspoon salt
  ¼ teaspoon black pepper
  ½ cup butter or margarine, melted
  salt
  pepper
The Dip
  1 cup sour cream
  ¼ cup crumbled bleu cheese
  ½ cup finely chopped onion
  ¼ teaspoon salt
  chopped parsley

To make the dip, combine sour cream, bleu cheese, onion, and salt. Garnish with chopped parsley. Refrigerate while fish are cooking.

Preheat oven to 400 degrees. Salt and pepper fillets, then cut them into 1-inch cubes. Mix cracker crumbs, Parmesan cheese, and sesame seeds. Dip fish cubes in the melted margarine and roll in cracker crumb mixture.

Carefully place the catfish cubes about a half an inch apart on well-greased (or foil lined) baking sheets. Bake for 20 minutes or until fish is golden brown. Serve with dip. *Makes about 6 dozen appetizers.*

Low Calorie Sandwich Snacks

  1 to 2 cups of fish flakes (cooked)
  plain yogurt
  finely chopped watermelon rind
    pickles
  very fresh white bread

Mix fish flakes and pickles. Stir in yogurt until the desired consistency is reached. Trim edges from bread. Make sandwiches, then quarter by cutting from corner to corner.

Fish Strips

Fried fish is of course a favorite for a meal, and it can also make a good appetizer. The trick is to use thin fish, cook it very quickly, and serve it very hot. It is best to eat fish strips as soon as they come out of the frying pan, or deep fryer, instead of keeping them warm on a heated platter. (For best results, the fish should be on the firm side. The fillets will be cut into thin strips, and fish that flakes easily may tend to come apart on you.)

fish fillets
peanut oil
buttermilk
fine ground white cornmeal
salt and pepper

Cut boneless fillets into strips that are ¼ inch thick and ½ inch wide. (Partly frozen fillets will slice easier.) Put the fish strips in a suitable glass container and soak in buttermilk for 30 minutes under refrigeration.

Heat peanut oil in a frying pan or deep fryer. Drain the fish strips, salt and pepper them to taste, and shake them in a bag with cornmeal. Fry the strips, a handful at the time, in very hot oil until the strips are golden brown—only two or three minutes if your oil is hot. Drain on absorbent paper.

Fish Spread on Water Chestnuts

The Chinese and some other Oriental peoples often employ the principle of opposites in the their daily life, as in sweet and sour foods. Here's one that's hot and cold, soft and crunchy:

fish flakes (precooked)
butter
garlic salt
canned whole water chestnuts

Split the water chestnuts in half, making two wheels. Chill. Melt a little butter in a small fying pan, add fish flakes, and sprinkle

---

Dolly Varden
This fish, a char, is oily with pinkish red meat. It can be baked, broiled, or grilled. When smoked, it is a delicacy. If you use it as an appetizer, remember the following trivia for conversation. The fish was named for Miss Dolly Varden, a character in Charles Dickens' *Barnaby Rudge*, who wore a spotted pink dress.

with garlic salt to taste. Stir and bring to heat. Drain any excess butter. Put fish in a serving dish that can be heated. Keep hot until ready to eat. Line a bowl with ice and put the water chestnuts on it. With a spread knife, put a little of the hot buttered fish onto the cold water chestnuts (one at the time) and eat on the spot.

Fish Flake & Egg Sandwich

1 pound boneless fish
3 hard-boiled eggs, chopped
½ cup black olives, chopped
½ cup mayonnaise
1 tablespoon prepared horseradish
salt and pepper
1 teaspoon dill weed

Add a teaspoon of dill weed to a quart of water and poach fish until it flakes easily with a fork (five or six minutes). Flake fish. Mix with mayonnaise, olives, horseradish, and eggs. Salt and pepper to taste. Spread generously on rye bread. *Makes 4 to 6 sandwiches.*

Bacon 'n Fish

boneless fish (preferably low-fat and mild of flavor)
bacon
salt and pepper
lemon

Cut boneless, skinned fish into 1-inch pieces. Squeeze a little lemon juice on fish and refrigerate for an hour. Turn on broiler heat. Wrap each piece of fish with ½ strip of bacon and pin with a toothpick. Broil until bacon is crisp on both sides.

Toasted Cream Cheese and Fish Sandwich

Once, long ago, I took a swivel stool at a sandwich counter in Norfolk, Virginia. On the next stool sat Gary Cooper, eating a toasted cream cheese sandwich. I ordered one myself, and I've been a cream cheese fan ever since. Here's my favorite:

1 cup of fish flakes
8 ounces of cream cheese, room temperature
1 tablespoon mayonnaise
1 tablespoon finely chopped olives
white sandwich bread
butter

Mix fish, cream cheese, and mayonnaise. Spread on bread and put two halves together. Butter the outside of one piece of bread lightly, then toast it under the broiler

River Cats Taste Better

Although pond-raised catfish for the masses might be better than none at all, the old-time connoisseurs and many fishermen know that the best cats still come from clean, free-flowing streams. Part of the reason (I believe) has as much to do with texture as with flavor. All catfish have fine-grained flesh, and those raised in ponds tend to be downright mushy. Swiftwater fish are firmer simply because they swim more. They have to work to find crayfish and other natural food, whereas many of the pond fish are fed pellets daily. In fact, some of the "cultured" catfish aren't even free to roam the length and breadth of the pond; they are penned up in cages or baskets. Not long ago a farmer told me that he raised 2,000 channel cat in a basket only 8 feet long by 4 feet wide. He was a hefty fellow with a large mortgage at the bank, so I didn't tell him that somebody ought to poke him in there with the catfish.

until brown. Turn, butter the outside of the other piece of bread, and broil until brown.

Variation: Use smoked fish flakes instead of regular flakes and omit the chopped olives in the mixture.

Mushrooms Stuffed with Fish

12 ounces large mushrooms
1 cup of fish flakes (precooked)
½ cup butter (used in two operations)
1 tablespoon flour
⅓ cup of milk
½ teaspoon powdered mustard
1 teaspoons white wine Worcestershire sauce
¼ teaspoon salt
⅛ teaspoon pepper
1 egg yolk, beaten
1 tablespoon chopped parsley
½ teaspoon of lemon juice
grated Parmesan cheese

Remove the stems from mushrooms and mince them. Melt ¼ cup of butter in a pan. Sauté mushroom stems for a few minutes. Carefully stir in flour, salt, pepper, Worcestershire, and mustard. Add the milk and stir constantly until the mixture thickens. Remove from heat. Stir in fish flakes, egg yolks, parsley, and ½ teaspoon lemon juice. Set aside.

Preheat oven to 400 degrees. Melt ¼ cup of butter in a frying pan. Sauté mushroom caps for about 5 minutes. Drain. Stuff caps

Stone Roller

This small fish, often called a hornyhead, is very good when it is rolled in cornmeal and fried. A minnow, it seldom grows over 7 or 8 inches long, although it can reach 11 inches or more. In parts of Tennessee, the horneyhead is highly prized as table fare; some anglers fish for and catch it with tiny wet flies, although a small hook baited with a piece of earthworm is more commonly used. The stone roller's range is quite wide, and it can be taken in many other states from Texas up to Canada and east to the Carolinas. Catch some and try them as appetizers.

with fish mixture. Sprinkle tops with cheese. Place in a pan and bake for about 15 minutes.

Fish Spread

I'm fond of eating various kinds of spreads on crackers, and here's one of my favorites:

1 cup finely flaked fish
6 ounces of cream cheese
1 golf-ball size onion, grated
¼ teaspoon salt
2 tablespoons white wine Worcestershire sauce
juice from ½ lemon

Mix all ingredients and chill. Spread on crackers. Eat.

Variation: If you are having a party and want a little color on your appetizers, put the spread into a small serving platter and sprinkle with paprika.

Variation: Substitute 4 ounces of grated cheddar for the cream cheese and omit the lemon juice.

Fish Dogs

Here's a dish that children think is "neat." It should be made from fairly large fish, and *must* be boneless. What you need are large fingers, about the size and length of jumbo weiners.

large fish
mayonnaise
salt and pepper to taste
hotdog buns
chopped onions (optional)

Cut fingers from large fillets. Poach the fish fingers for a few minutes, until the meat flakes easily when tested with a fork. Drain. Salt and pepper to taste. Spread mayonnaise in a hotdog bun, then put a fish stick into it. Spread more mayonnaise on top. I like plenty of chopped onions on mine, but many children prefer to leave them off. Be sure that the bun is fresh and soft. Also, many people may want to try this one with tartar sauce, catsup, and so on instead of the mayonnaise. In any case, it's best to have a hot piece of fish topped with cold sauce.

9

FISH GIBLETS
and
ODD CUTS

Once my quick-thinking wife was the guest of honor at a feast in the deserts of the Middle East. The main fare was goat, and, as was the tribal custom, the guest of honor was offered one of the eyes. She thanked the company profusely, but said that, being young and female, she was unworthy of the honor and would give the eye to the elder male of the family. This seemed to please everyone—especially my wife!

If she had been in the the far east, the offering might well have been a fish eye. She wouldn't have eaten it either. Nor would I. I'll eat most anything, but with fish eyes and goat eyes I'll have to draw the line. But I am fond of other fish "giblets," if that's the word,

and I recommend the recipes and comments below for those readers who are game to try them. Actually, many of the entries below are suitable for anyone who likes fish.

Fish Throats

Some people who are knowledgeable about seafood won't pass up such offbeat but choice cuts as grouper or red snapper throats, and I read somewhere that the fishermen (or the fishmongers) kept these pieces for themselves. Almost any fish has a

Watch Out for Puffer's Gall

Puffers are believed to be at their most toxic just before spawning, in late spring or early summer, but they are poisonous enough at any time for the old-time Japanese to have eaten them as a method of committing suicide. In Hawaii, where the word for puffer is *maki-maki* (deadly death), warriors used to use the gall of the fish to poison their spears. If you have a craving to live dangerously and can't wait to taste puffer, go to a first-class restaurant in Japan where there is a licensed 'fugu cook.' The meat is a delicacy there—but blowfish will be left strictly out of *my* pot.

—Janet H. Alexander, *Sports Afield*,
February 1968

"throat," and I have eaten quite a few off largemouth bass and red snapper.

Throats are almost V shaped. They are cut from the front part of the fish, where the belly joins the gills. Usually, when most people behead a fish they cut behind the collarbone and pectoral fin down to the backbone on both sides, then snap the backbone and pull off the head. This leaves the pectoral fins attached to the head, and the meat holding the fins is the throat. Skin it, cut if off from the head, remove the fins, and you've got a good piece of fish. It can be sautéed, fried, baked, or whatever. String them onto a skewer, kabob-style, and cook them over coals. If you've got just a few, cook them along with the rest of the fish. If you've got

enough for a mess, try them broiled, as follows:

> 1 pound of fish throats
> juice of 1 lemon
> ½ cup melted butter
> salt
> pepper

Combine lemon juice and melted butter; pour over fish and marinate for a while. Heat up broiler. Arrange throats on a rack in a broiler pan. Baste with lemon-butter mixture. Salt and pepper to taste. Put the rack close to heat and broil quickly, until fish flakes easily. Feeds two.

Sautéed Mullet Gizzards

Here's some information from *The South Carolina Wildlife Cookbook*: "The common striped mullet (*Mugil cephalus*) consumes large amounts of plant matter. To facilitate the digestive process of this food substrate, mullet possess a pyloric stomach not unlike the gizzard of a chicken. When obtained in quantities, mullet 'gizzards' offer a splendid change for the adventurous appetite." The book then sets forth the following recipe, which was contributed by James M. Bishop of Charleston:

> mullet gizzards
> butter
> chopped parsley
> lemon twist

"To prepare, simply clean the gizzards and sauté in butter. Seasonings may include chopped parsley and a twist of lemon slice."

Students of judicial trivia might also be interested in a bit that I found deep inside *McClane's New Standard Fishing Encyclopedia*. In the state of Florida, a commercial fisherman was charged with taking mullet out of season. The slick defense lawyer got a biologist to testify that only birds have gizzards. Because mullet have gizzards they are birds. Birds are not covered by fishing seasons in the State of Florida. Case closed.

Sautéed Fish Liver with Mushrooms

I haven't specified any measurements for the ingredients in this recipe because I always eyeball the liver, onions, and mushrooms. Equal parts, by volume, of liver, onions, and mushrooms would be about right.

fish liver
oil
vinegar
onion
mushrooms
bacon
salt
pepper

Mix a little oil and vinegar, in equal parts, and marinate the liver in the mixture for several hours under refrigeration.

Fry the bacon until crisp. Remove bacon

and break pieces into three or four pieces. Sauté liver for five minutes, turning. Add onions, mushrooms, salt, and pepper. Cook until tender, then drain off grease and add bacon strips.

Fish Liver and Eggs

Anyone who has a taste for liver but might be a little squeamish about trying *fish* liver might consider starting with the following recipe from the Middle East:

¼ **pound fish livers**
6 eggs
6 strips bacon
salt and pepper
1 tablespoon parsley, chopped
½ **teaspoon ground cinnamon**

Fry the bacon until crisp. Remove bacon, crumble it, and set aside. Sauté the fish liver

All Aboard for Whale Tongue

Whale meat was not greatly esteemed by our grandfathers, but they did set some store by the tongue of the animal, usually salted, and Ambroise Pare says that 'it is tender and delicious.' They also appreciated whale fat which they ate 'during Lent, with peas.'

—*Larousse Gastronomique*

Heads or Tails?

A New York banker's daughter, who fished from the backwoods of Maine to the hills of West Virginia, argued with the son of a Utah Mormon, who fished from upper Baja to lower British Columbia, about whether to leave the heads on trout when you fry them. The one had no good reason for leaving the head on. Nor, on the other hand, did the other have good reason for taking the head off. Does it matter?

Before long, both of them turned on me, although I set forth good reason for leaving the *tails* on fish. For flavor and crunch, nothing beats fresh, properly fried tails of yearling size largemouth and smallmouth bass, and the tails as well as the fins of bluegills and crappie are truly great.

I don't care much for large fish tails, or fins, but note that the Chinese rate shark fins highly.

---

in the bacon drippings for 4 or 5 minutes. (Tiny livers require only a couple of minutes if the oil is quite hot.) Do not overcook. Pour off excess oil. Add the bacon to the liver, sprinkle with cinnamon, and mix quickly. Break the eggs over the liver and bacon mixture. Fry until the eggs set. Season with salt and pepper, then sprinkle with parsley. Eat while hot. *Serves 3 or 4.*

fine-ground white cornmeal
peanut oil

Cut the sounds loose when you dress the fish. Wash them and drain. Salt and pepper to taste, then shake in meal. Fry in hot grease for a few minutes, until they begin to brown.

Fried Fish Sounds

Some fish don't have sounds, but many do. This is, of course, the air or swim bladder. I often save these when I am dressing fish to fry, but I've never eaten them as a main dish. Usually, I add them more or less as a conversation item. They are good, however.

sounds
salt and pepper

Scandinavian-style Fish Tongues

I got this idea from George Leonard Herter and Berthe E. Herter's *Bull Cook and Authentic Historical Recipes and Practices*. Try a few fish tongues cooked this way, and then prepare some for your guests the next time you need a variety of snacks.

Add a teaspoon of salt to a pint of water. Boil the tongues for 5 or 6 minutes if they are from fish no larger than 2 pounds; tongues from larger fish will take up to 15 minutes. Drain the tongues, then put them on a plate or serving platter with mustard on the side. (I prefer coarse, Creole-style mustard.) The Herters also recommend a sauce made by mixing catsup and horseradish.

Newfoundland-Style Tongues and Sounds

The following recipe has been adapted from Frances MacIlquham's *Fish Cookery of North America*. Codfish is plentiful off the coast of Newfoundland, and it is the fish that was recommended in the recipe. Of course, other fish can also be used.

  1 pound of tongues and sounds
  milk
  ¼ pound salt pork
  1 medium onion, minced
  1 cup of egg sauce
  parsley (for garnish)

Wash the tongues and sounds in several waters, then put them in a glass container and soak them (under refrigeration) overnight in a mixture of half milk and half water. Simmer tongues and sounds in a mixture of half milk and half water until they are tender. Drain. Cut the sounds into strips and slice the tongues open (especially from large fish). While the tongues and sounds simmer, dice the salt pork and sauté it with the minced onion. Put sounds, tongues, pork, and onion into a warm serving dish and mix.

Heat egg sauce and pour it over the dish. Garnish with parsley. *Serves 3 or 4.*

Fish Cheeks

Old farm boys like myself know that a chicken has got two choice pieces of meat on it, each about the size of the end of your thumb. They are located in the small of the back, one on either side. But you have to cut up your own chicken to get it. I've looked at a thousand chicken backs in various meat markets, thinking that I could luck into a whole package of backs with the choice bits. But they are never there. Somebody gets them at the packing house. Anyhow, to compare these choice bits to the rest of the chicken is similar to comparing tenderloin to the rest of the beef.

Fish also have two choice pieces of meat— one on either side of the head. They are often difficult to get at, however, and may not be

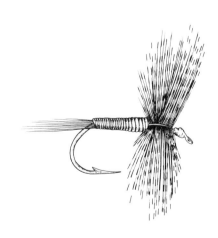

worth the trouble on smaller fish. I normally skin the head partly, then cut the meat out carefully with a sharp knife. Once you have the cheek, cook it in any way you see fit. Fry it, as in the recipe for fried throat above, or sauté it. If you've got only a few fish, of course, it is best to mix throats, tongues, and cheeks.

If you don't want to take the trouble to gouge out the cheeks, cook the whole head, as in the recipe below.

Indian-Style Fish Heads

Here's one from Ted Trueblood, as published in *Field & Steam*, May 1967. "Once when I was camped with Bill McDonald and several Ojibway Indians on Lake Nipigon, in On-tario, I noticed that the Indians were eating the heads of the fish we caught. We had an abundance of big 'coaster' brook trout and northern pike, too, so this was strictly their choice. They would take several heads, put them into a kettle of salted boiling water, let them boil about ten minutes, then fish them out and nibble off the goodies with obvious gusto.

"Bill and I contined to eat fried and broiled trout throughout the trip, but later I got to thinking that maybe the Ojibways had something here. I tried it with the result that I now enjoy both boiled fish and fish heads. Wrap the head of a big, fat fish, such as a 10-pound salmon or lake trout, in foil and let it roast in the coals while you're broiling the remainder. Or give the same treatment to half a dozen trout heads in a single foil package. The result is strictly a nibbling job, but delicious."

Need Vitamins?

Burbot livers, like cod livers, are very large and high in vitamins. Burbot were harvested in Minnesota in the 1930s just for their livers. Rowell Laboratories of Baudette extracted the oil from the livers for a vitamin A and D supplement similar to cod liver oil. The oil was also used in the preparation of an ointment to promote wound healing. Scandinavians even consider burbot livers a delicacy. If you care to try it, boil the liver first to remove some of the oil, then fry it.

—"Eelpout(Burbot): The Fish Minnesotans Love to Hate," University of Minnesota Sea Grant Extension Program

10

FROGS

I've always heard that frog legs would jump about in the frying pan, and even out of the frying pan. And it's all true, up to a point. An old issue of *Sunset* magazine (March 1961), for example, says that chilling the legs in the refrigerator for a few hours will prevent them from twitching. Going further, the article cites one expert cook as saying that soaking them in cold milk will not only take the kick out of them but will also make them as tender as butter.

Well, I've eaten some river-swamp frogs of unbelievable size that could stand a little tenderizing, but I've also been in situations where I didn't want the kick taken out of them. In fact, I've been known to *help* a huge frog kick its way out of the frying pan. Let me explain.

Once I went night fishing in the swamps of the Choctawhatchee River, not too far from a place called Crackerneck. With me was the best football player, for his size, that I've ever known. Later, he got a PhD and wound up being athletic director at a college. Anyhow, we had gone fishing, and had agreed to take only frying pan, grease, a little meal, and salt for food. In other words, we had to catch fish to eat. At two in the morning, we hadn't caught a single fish. We hadn't even had a bite. Neither of us had eaten since noon the previous day, and we thought we were about to starve to death. Finally, we took our only flashlight, which was growing weak, and tried to shine fish or crayfish along the bank, hoping I could dip them up with a net or hack them with a sheath knife. No luck. Finally, I heard a huge bullfrog bellow from a slough downstream. I knew where he was, and ever so carefully I stalked and caught him with my hands. I held him while the football player stabbed him in the head with the knife, which didn't immediately stop him from kicking.

Right off, the football player wanted to know if it was true that bullfrogs could jump out of a frying pan. The guy had already seemed a bit cautious about our potential fare, asking, for example, whether I thought we would have to eat any eels. I knew that I had a tough tenderfoot, so I started working on him, knowing by now that the frog was all the meat that we were going to get that night.

"If this frog ain't enough to fill us up," I said, while we were sloshing back to our campfire, "We'll head home come daylight and get Pa to cook us up a big mess of eggs and hog brains."

He didn't want any hog brains for breakfast. Or any other time. Or chitterlings.

"We won't find a rattlesnake tonight," I said, "but we may run up on a mess of cottonmouth." He didn't want any snakes to eat, either.

By campfire, I carefully skinned the frog from head to toe, literally. After gutting it, I held it up by the lower lip. It was big. The flesh was deathly white in the red glow of the campfire. It looked like a little man, with arms, legs, fingers, and long, long little toes with several joints. Silence came over the swamp, it seemed. Way off, a hoot owl hollered. I pretended to wash the frog while I picked carefully at the tendons in it's back, near the hind legs. I was getting them ready for my trick.

"I . . . I thought you ate just the back legs," he said, finally.

"Oh, no, you eat the whole frog," I said. "As hungry as we are, we can't waste *any* of it. Except maybe the head. Frog brains ain't really big enough to fool with."

"They tell me those things will jump right out of the frying pan," the football player said.

"Awh, there's nothing to that," I said, heating up the grease. Keeping the whole frog intact, I put a little salt on it and shook it in the sack of white meal for quite some time, waiting until I thought the grease was just right. "Here, I'll show you. He won't jump." Carefully, I held the frog by the lip with my left hand and grasped the leaders in its back between my right finger and thumb. Carefully, I lowered the frog's hing-leg toes into the hot grease, then jerked on the leaders in its back. The legs didn't merely twitch; they jumped up, and I helped lift the frog a bit with my left hand.

"Damn," he said.

"Let's try that again," I said, repeating the procedure. It jumped again as soon as its toes touched the hot grease. "We'd better stab this son-of-a-bitch again," I said, lowering his toes into the hot grease once more. He jumped again, but not as violently now. Maybe the leaders were pulling out.

"I don't want any frog," he said, turning his head. "You can have the whole thing!"

A year later, the guy got a football scholarship and went off to a small college somewhere in Louisiana. I don't think he went there because of the excellent frogging in that Sportsman's Paradise!

Anyhow, if you're short of meat and want your frogs to jump, leave the tendons intact and learn to work them properly. If you've got plenty of meat to go around, pull the leaders out before cooking the frogs. Salting the meat may cause it to twitch a bit, but the legs will stay in the frying pan when the leaders are removed.

Here are a few recipes to try:

Dr. Stowell's Advice (or Dr. Wolfe's)

I suppose that bullfrogs remind me of Mark Twain, who could well have been talking about the recipe below when he said, with mock indignation, "It's un-American. It's un-British. It's French." (Or maybe it was Hal Holbrook who said that Twain said it.)

During the best of my frogging days, I worked for NASA in Huntsville, Alabama. While trying to figure out how to get to the moon ahead of the Russians, I sometimes had occasion to talk of good food to a German named Dr. Walter Wolfe, who lived at the local Y.M.C.A. I never did quite figure that one out, and I often wondered how he cooked Swedish meatballs and such at the Y. Anyhow, I made a bunch of notes on cooking and rocketry. Most of these notes were written on a green NASA memo form that had routing instructions, spaces or boxes for codes, boxes to check for action to be taken, and so on. My frog leg recipe is noted on

Dressing Frogs

Frogs are easy to dress. If you want to keep only the hind legs, make a cut across the top of the lower part of the back. Loosen the skin a bit and grasp it, using pliers or your fingers. Pull the skin off. Cut off the hind legs at the joint (I prefer to separate them.) The feet can be trimmed, or you can leave them on.

If you want to dress out the whole frog, make your initial cut on the back just behind the head. Skin the frog as described above. Remove the innards and cut off the head. Cut off the two hind legs, then cut the back just behind the two front legs. This method will give you four pieces: two hind legs, one segment of back, and one piece containing both front legs.

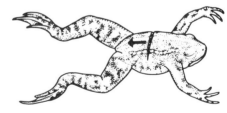

Skinning a frog for only the legs.

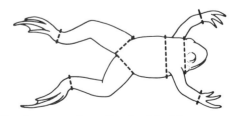

Cutting up a frog for the hind legs, segment of back, and front legs.

such a green paper, MSFC - Form 183 (Rev. February 1961). I suppose that the form worked pretty well. We got to the moon, and I've still got the recipe. But I failed to note whether the information came from Dr. Wolfe or another friend of mine, Dr. Marion Stowell.

I suspect that Dr. Stowell should get the credit. She's from Quitman, Georgia, she studied French in college, and she spent a good deal of time in France. She didn't live at the Huntsville Y. And, to be brief, I'm almost certain that the recipe below is based on her advice. I remember that once I talked with her at some length about my larger frog legs getting a little stringy when they were fried, and I think that on the spot she gave me a list of ingredients used in the recipe below. Although I have no notes on the measures, groups of ingredients are included in

brackets that indicated cooking times. Anyhow, I cooked the recipe several times back then, but after we got to the moon I slacked off somewhat on my frog gigging. Thus, over the years, I forgot some of the details. But I've recently put the recipe back together, and it's as good now as it ever was. Here goes:

> **2 pounds of dressed frog, cut up (hind legs, front legs, back)**
> **¼ cup butter**
> **1 medium onion, diced**
> **8 ounces mushrooms, sliced**
> **flour**
> **salt and pepper**
> **2 tablespoons parsley**
> **¼ cup white wine**
> **juice 1 lemon**
> **½ cup cream**

Frogging Laws

Some years ago, during the great race for the moon, I did a nationwide survey of the game and fish laws for taking frogs. It was bewildering. Some states had no laws at all, and others had some surprises. Louisiana, for example, one of the very best frogging states, did not allow the use of a gig or spear or anything that pierced or punctured the skin or discolored the meat. They did allow some sort of mechanical frog grabbers!

So . . . check your laws carefully. Some states have frogs that are now on the endangered list, and of course it is illegal to take

them. In some states, you'll need a hunting license; in others, a fishing license. And in a few states you'll need either a hunting licence or a fishing license, or both, depending on how you go after the frogs.

I've even got an old news release from Land Between the Lakes which states that gigging is not permitted after midnight! I've seen some rules that allowed the use of firearms, blowguns, nets, bow-and-arrows, clubs, and fishhooks. In short, frogs can provide some mighty good eating, but check local laws before catching them by any means.

Heat the butter in a frying pan and sauté the frogs on low heat for 10 minutes. Add the onions and mushrooms. Salt and pepper to taste. Sauté for another five minutes. Sprinkle with a little flour. Add the wine and parsley. Cook for another 10 minutes. Reduce heat, add lemon juice and cream. Stir. Let simmer for 5 minutes. *Serves 4 or 5*.

Broiled Frog Legs

Frog legs can be very good when broiled, but remember that they tend to dry out unless they are either marinated in oil or basted frequently. Here's what I recommend:

> **frog legs**
> **salt and pepper**
> **paprika**
> **½ cup peanut oil**
> **½ cup lemon juice (freshly squeezed)**
> **1 tablespoon white wine**
>   **Worcestershire sauce**
> **1 tablespoon grated onion**
> **1 tablespoon minced parsley**

Dress the frogs and put into a glass container. Make a marinade of peanut oil, lemon juice, Worcestershire sauce, grated onion, and parsley. Pour over frogs and refrigerate for 4 hours. Preheat broiler. Drain frog legs, salt and pepper to taste, and put on a rack very close to the broiler. Cook for 4 or 5 minutes, then baste and turn. Cook for 4 or 5 minutes, then baste, turn, sprinkle with a little paprika, and broil for 2 to 4 additional minutes, until tender. (Large legs may require more cooking time.)

Easy Sautéed Frog Legs

If you've got a few small frogs that you want to cook up without going to lots of trouble, try this:

> **frog legs**
> **butter**
> **salt and pepper**
> **lemon**

Salt and pepper frog legs. Heat butter in a frying pan and sauté frog legs for 6 to 8 minutes, until golden brown and tender. Reduce heat, sprinkle a little lemon juice over the legs, and simmer for a few more minutes. Serve hot with hot French bread.

Note: Don't let the simplicity of this recipe fool you. It can be very good, if you've got good, fresh frogs to work with. If you are using this dish as an appetizer, garnish the frog legs with a few sprigs of parsley before serving.

Fried Bullfrogs, Legs and All

It's really no joke. All of the frogs large enough to eat have some good meat on the front legs and along the backbone. The front legs and the back contain the best meat, really, on the very large bullfrogs.

Although most frogs are fried by merely dipping them into flour or batter and then plopping them into hot oil until brown, I really can't recommend this method. But let

Bullfrogs

Bullfrogs eat a great variety of foods, but require moving objects. Provision for moving food is one of the many difficulties in frog farming, which is not economically feasible. Crayfish and insects are important foods. Bullfrogs are opportunists, and sometimes gorge themselves on cicadas, grasshoppers, and meadow mice when these animals are locally abundant. Food items occasionally taken include young snapping turtles and fledgling redwinged blackbirds.

—*Frogs and Toads of Missouri*, Missouri Department of Conservation

Frog fishermen sometimes use the frogs' love for live insects to an advantage. An artificial fly dangled or cast near a frog will sometimes get action.

—Texas Parks and Wildlife Department

me quickly add that I've probably eaten a hundred pounds of frogs fried exactly that way. They have a good flavor, but sometimes the texture isn't quite right. The meat can be stringy, and tends to get bigger when you chew it. This usually happens with very large frog legs, and I highly recommend that all very large frogs be soaked for a while in lemon juice before frying, as in the following recipe:

frogs
lemons
butter

salt and pepper
flour

Skin the frogs, then cut off the hind legs and separate them. Cut off the front legs as a unit, and trim the belly flab from the back section. Put the meat into a glass container and squeeze lemon juice on it. (Use 1 large lemon per pound of meat.) Refrigerate for several hours.

Rinse the meat and let it drain. Heat butter in a frying pan. Salt and pepper the meat to taste, then dip, roll, or shake it in flour. Fry in hot butter until golden brown.

Variation: In Florida, I've eaten good frogs that were first rolled in flour, then dipped in beaten egg and rolled in fine bread crumbs before frying in butter.

Grilled Frogs

Frogs tend to dry out quickly, so don't grill them too long. It's best, in my opinion, to cook them quickly over hot coals. Frequent basting will also help. Here's all you need:

frogs
oil
salt
lemon juice, freshly squeezed

Build a hot charcoal fire in your grill. Grease a rack and put it close to hot coals. Salt the frogs and put them on the rack. Cook for a few minutes, then baste frequently with a mixture of half oil and half lemon juice. Cook until frogs have a golden brown color and are tender. Exact cooking times vary, depending on the size of the frogs. Try not to overcook. On an average, small frog legs should be cooked for a total of 15 minutes over medium-hot coals, and very large frog legs may require as long as 25 minutes over the same coals.

Smoked Frogs

frogs
salt
bacon drippings

Build a charcoal fire in your smoker, and have hickory chips (or other wood) ready. Soak the dressed frogs in bacon drippings while the smoker gets hot. Salt legs to taste, then put on a greased rack in the smoker. Add hickory chips, cover, and smoke at about 200 degrees for 30 minutes or so. Baste frequently with bacon drippings.

Frog Leg Omelet

Here's a good recipe when you want something quite unusual but have only a few frogs. I got the idea from an article by Marjorie Latham Masselin in the July 1968 edition of *Virginia Wildlife*:

frog legs
eggs
green onions

How Big Is It?

Too many recipes, especially those influenced by the French, call for a certain number of legs from frogs without giving any indication of what exactly they are talking about. Edible frogs vary greatly in size. The highly prized red-legged frogs found west of the Sierra Cascade mountains attains a maximum head-to-toe length of only 4½ inches. A full grown American bullfrog, by comparison, can measure in excess of 12 inches. I've heard that they attain a weight of 7 pounds and can have as much edible meat as a small chicken. I've never seen one that big, but one night I gigged a huge bullfrog that had swallowed a full-grown sparrow! Other edible species, such as the leopard frog, fall somewhere in between the bullfrog and the red-legged frog. Obviously, any recipe that calls merely for a number of legs leaves a lot of room for miscalculation. The best bet is to go by pounds of meat, but I don't think I've ever seen a recipe that went this far. I'll eat half a pound or more.

butter
salt and pepper

As the article said of frog leg omelets, "To make one you need at least two pair of frog legs per person. Skin and bone them and cut them in small pieces. Beat up one egg for each pair with a not-too-full teaspoon of water for each egg. For every four legs (two pair) mince the white part of a spring onion. Heat plenty of butter in a heavy frying pan and sauté the onion and cut-up frog legs for five to ten minutes, depending on how

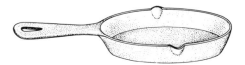

tender the frogs were and how full the pan is. Sprinkle on a little salt and pepper and pour on the eggs.

"Reduce the heat and let this cook gently, lifting it from time to time with a spatula so that the uncooked part runs underneath and keeps the part that is cooked first from getting overly dry. Turn one half over the other and slip it onto a hot platter."

11

TURTLES and GATORS

I must have eaten as many kinds of turtles, cooked in more different ways, as any man alive. In addition to sea turtle steaks (which are no longer legal), I have eaten alligator snapping turtles, loggerheads, ordinary terrepins, Suwanee terrepins, several kinds of softshell turtle, and the delicious dry-land gopher tortoise. All of them were very good, but note that the gopher tortoise is now a protected critter throughout most of its range. I can remember when they were quite plentiful in rolling sandy scrub lands. In any case, I could fill up a whole book up about turtles and ways to cook them. (I have, for example, dressed out "roasts" from the hind part of hugh Florida softshells, some of which weigh as much as 40 pounds.) But, unfortunately, there isn't enough room in a book like this, covering a number of edible

wild creatures, to do full justice to the turtle.

Or to such tasty wild meat as yearling alligator. Actually, I didn't know whether to cover the alligator in the fish section of this book, or in the game section. I put it here because it comes from the water, or water's edge, and because I have caught more than I've shot. That's right. I have caught them with topwater plugs attached with a wire leader to 50-pound dacron line! Also, some people catch them with baited shark hooks suspended just above the water from tree limbs.

But I suspect that most of the alligators are shot. In fact, I helped eat one that my brother got with the aid of a slingshot loaded with a hunk of lead. I told him that he couldn't kill a gator with a slingshot. He said that he knew it didn't *kill* the gator; he shot the thing right between the eyes and just *stunned* it. "And what if it had come to while you were dressing it out?" I asked. "Well," he said, "I reckon it would have been me and the gator!"

Anyhow, if you are lucky enough to live in an area where gators are legal game, try the following recipes. (Note also that gator meat can be purchased by mail.)

Fried Gator Fingers

If I had to choose one wild meat over all the others, I think I would take a yearling gator about 5 feet long. And I would cook it as follows:

> gator meat fingers, ½ inch wide
> buttermilk
> flour
> peanut oil
> salt and pepper

Soak the gator fingers in buttermilk for several hours. Drain, then salt and pepper to taste. Heat an inch or so of peanut oil in a frying pan. Shake the gator fingers in the flour, then fry on medium-high heat for several minutes, turning, until all sides are browned.

Alligator Sauce Piquante

This is a sort of traditional recipe from down in Louisiana, and it is indeed a very good way to cook gator. It calls for cubed gator meat, which can be from the tail, front legs, or anywhere you can get it.

The Meat
> 2 pounds cubed gator, cut about 1 inch square
> 2 cups dry white wine
> salt and pepper

The Sauce
> ½ cup cooking oil
> 2 cups chopped onions
> ½ large bell pepper, chopped

Dressing a Gator

Alligators of reasonable size aren't too difficult to dress out. Start by cutting the hide under the bottom from the throat to the tail. Next, cut from the the bottom side of all the legs out to the paws. Then pull and work the skin back any way you can manage, using pliers and a skinning knife if you have them at hand.

After you have skinned the gator, you can fillet meat off the tail or you can cut the tail, across the grain, into steaks. Also, the tail can be boned, then sliced into steaks. The rest of the gator meat can be cut off the bone and cubed. Just don't throw any of it away!

Note: If your primary purpose in skinning the gator is to get the hide for sale, be sure to check for instructions with market hunters or with dealers who traffic in such things. Also check the local game laws before taking an alligator for hide or meat.

1 stalk celery, chopped
16 ounces canned tomato sauce
1 can Rotel (10-ounce) or Mexican-
style stewed tomatoes
8 ounces of fresh mushrooms, sliced
2 tablespoons Worcestershire sauce
¼ teaspoon oregano
¼ teaspoon basil
1 bay leaf
Late Additions
½ cup chopped green onions, tops and
all
¼ cup fresh parsley, chopped
salt and pepper
rice (cooked separately)

Cube the gator meat, then salt and pepper it. Put the meat into a glass container, pour the wine over it, cover, and refrigerate for an hour or longer.

Heat the oil, then sauté the onion until it is golden. Add the bell pepper and celery and cook until tender. Stir in the tomato sauce and Rotel. Add the basil, bay leaf, Worcestershire sauce, and oregano. Bring to boil, cover, reduce heat, and simmer for 10 minutes. Drain the gator meat and add to the sauce. Add the mushrooms. Cover and cook for an hour, or until the gator is tender. Then add the parsley and green onions. Stirring, add salt and pepper to taste. Simmer uncovered for 10 minutes. Spoon over rice. *Serves 4 or 5.*

Broiled Gator Tail Steaks

Alligator tail steak can be excellent when it is broiled. All manner of fancy marinades and basting sauces are used, as well as barbecue sauce. But I like the following simple recipe, with more emphasis on technique than on ingredients.

gator tail steaks (or fillets) about ½
inch thick
Zesty Italian dressing (store bought)
salt and pepper
paprika

Put the steaks in a suitable glass container and pour some Zesty Italian Dressing over

Gator Ribs

I suppose that the term alligator's tail, like frog's legs, leaves the impression that the rest of the gator is no good. This is not the case, and I have eaten the whole thing.

A friend of mine who worked with a civil engineering firm had his survey party sloshing around amongst the alligators in a Florida swamp. Deciding to take one for tail steaks, they tied a shark hook on a rope, baited up, and secured it to a tree limb. After catching a good sized gator, they shot it, sawed off its tail section, and quickly buried the rest before the game warden came. Word got out, and the next day a Florida cracker came to dig up the rest of the gator, saying that he wanted the ribs.

"How do you cook gator ribs?" my friend asked.

"There ain't but one way to cook ribs," the Florida cracker said. "And you fix gator ribs that way."

them. Put them in the refrigerator for several hours. When you're ready to cook, drain the steaks but do not wash. Salt and pepper them to taste. Turn the broiler on and arrange a rack so that the steaks will be very close to the heat source—about two inches or so. At the last minute, sprinkle one side of the steaks with paprika. Put them on the rack, paprika side up, and broil for 3 or 4 minutes. Turn the steaks over, sprinkle the other side with paprika, and broil 3 or 4 mintues, or until done. Note that broiling is more of an art than a science, and exact cooking times will depend on the heat source, thickness of the meat, and so on.

Note that alligator should not be cooked too long. Usually, it is best when cooked very quickly at high heat—or for a long time at low heat. Avoid anything between these extremes. A fellow in Florida told me this long ago, and my experience confirms his advice.

Variation: The above recipe can also be used for cooking on an outdoor grill. For best results, put the rack close to the fire—and watch the meat closely.

Variation: If you are using a smoker/cooker, reverse your thinking. Use the same marinade and so on, but put the rack a good ways above the heat (using coals for low heat), add some green hardwood chips, and cook the meat for about 3 hours.

Shankle's Turtle Stew

Here's a recipe from Terry Shankle, Division of Conservation Education, North Carolina Wildlife Resources Commission:

5 pounds of turtle meat
1 pound pork chops
1 pound stew meat or venison
2 or 3 pounds chicken
1 pound onions
3 large cans tomato juice
½ gallon milk
2 tablespoons ground red pepper
1 small bottle A-1 steak sauce
salt and pepper to taste

Put all of the meat into a pot, cover it with water, and boil until tender. Then pick the meat off the bones. Combine the meat and all of the other ingredients. Simmer for at least two hours before eating. *Serves 18 or 20.*

Suggestion: This recipe makes a very good "game" stew if you use bear, javelina, or armadillo instead of pork chops; and rabbit, pheasant, or wild turkey instead of chicken.

Fried Soft-Shell Turtle

A fried soft-shell turtle of reasonable age is about as tasty as meat can get. I somehow have the impression that very old turtles may be tough, but, on the other hand, I have fried soft-shells of up to 30 pounds (Florida soft-shell, which grows larger than other kinds of soft-shells) and found them to be quite good. The best ones, however, are not much larger than an ordinary plate, cooked as follows:

turtle, cut into serving pieces
peanut oil
salt and pepper
flour

Dressing a Turtle

I'll be honest about it. I've never found a good way to skin and dress a turtle, and I don't believe that anyone else has. I've tried various "easy" directions that I've found in magazines and books, but they simply don't work for me. Many of these involve dipping the whole turtle into boiling water, which is said to make the skin easier to get off. Then, after you've got the skin off, you've got to disjoint the limbs, somehow. In my opinion, it is best to dress the turtle without half cooking it.

The first step is to behead the turtle and give the muscles an hour or so to quit moving. When you get ready to dress the turtle, turn it upside down and try to fix the shell so that it doesn't move about. Pushing the turtle partly into sand or dirt might help to hold it still. Then cut through the flat bottom shell on either side, close to where it joins the rounded top shell. But of course cutting through the shell is easier said than done. An ordinary knife is not satisfactory. At one time or another, I have tried a meat clever, a hatchet, an ax, and a chisel.

But the best thing I've found to get through a turtle shell is a portable electric circular saw. I have one with an old, dull blade, and this is what is needed simply because a shell is not wood and a large turtle will ruin a good blade. You also need to be very, very careful while using a saw in this manner. Also, adjust your blade so that it makes shallow cuts.

After I cut through the shell, I cut the skin away from the bottom shell and work it toward the outer rim of the top shell. After the two shells are separated, I cut the bottom shell

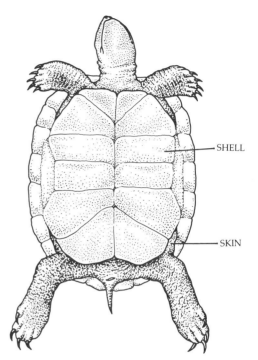

Bottom view of turtle, showing where cut should be made through flat bottom shell on both sides.

free with a sharp fillet knife. This leaves all the meat and innards exposed. Next, I remove the liver, which is very good. Then I twist and turn the legs until I can determine where to start cutting. The two front quarters can be removed separately, but I usually take the hind part out in one piece. In fact, I often trim off the small part of the legs, then make a roast of the hind quarter.

Turtle joints have a physical layout all their own, and by much twisting and turning and a little slicing, you can usually get them apart without using the saw again.

Heat at least 1 inch of peanut oil in a frying pan. Salt and pepper turtle pieces, then shake in flour, put into the hot oil and fry until golden brown. The oil should be very hot, and, for this reason, I prefer peanut oil, which has a high smoke point. I turn the heat on high heat, then reduce it to medium-high after the meat starts cooking; then I turn it back to high when another batch of meat is added, and reduce it to medium high after a few minutes.

Turtleburger Steak for Four

This recipe should be cooked in a large frying pan or, much better, on a flat grill.

    1½ pounds ground turtle meat
    ½ pound fresh ground pork
    1 tablespoon butter
    onion
    fresh mushrooms
    salt
    pepper
    water

Dice an onion, slice a few mushrooms, and leave within easy reach. Draw half a cup of water; set aside, handy to your grill. Heat the grill. Combine ground meat and shape into a "steak" about 1 inch thick. Melt butter on grill and add steak. Put steak onto melted butter. Cook on high heat for 5 minutes. Turn carefully and cook for 4 minutes. With a spatula, divide steak into quarters (if you are serving 4 people). Check center for doneness. Do not overcook, but steak should be done. Separate steaks to gain working room and pour a little water onto the grill. Add onions and mushrooms. Salt and pepper steak to taste while onions and mushrooms sauté. Add a little more water, then add a pinch or two of flour, stirring, until you have a gravy. Serve steak quarters onto plates and top with gravy.

Add to or reduce measures as required. Be sure to allow half a pound of meat per person—or more for big eaters.

Ground Turtle Meat

Some of the most tasty spaghetti sauce I've ever eaten was made with ground turtle meat, with a little pork mixed in. Ground turtle can be used to advantage in meatloafs, chili, and so on. Also be sure to try my famous turtleburger steak.

12

COOKING
FISH on the PATIO

D an Webster changed my mind on two counts. I was brought up to believe that (1) fish ought to be cooked either in the house or along the water's edge, and (2) the saltwater amberjack isn't fit to eat. I was therefore surprised to learn that Dan proposed to cook an amberjack outside the house. He invited me to try it. So, I did. And now I know beyond a shadow of a doubt that accomplished outdoor chefs can work piscatory wonders over wood or charcoal.

Moreover, patio cooking gets easier and easier as better and more convenient equipment is developed. The newer gas or electric grills with reusable lava rock give us better control of heat, and packaged wood chips are now available in a variety of interesting flavors, from mesquite to sassafras. Even Jack Daniel whiskey barrel chips are on the market for cooking.

Dan Webster's Electric Grill Amberjack

Dan says to allow four ounces of amberjack per person. I don't want to argue with him, but I advise him to serve me a little more than that.

The Marinade
  2 tablespoons Worcestershire sauce
  1 tablespoon lemon juice
  1 clove garlic, minced
The Fish
  amberjack steak or fillets
  lemon pepper
  salt

Mix the marinade. Put amberjack into a suitable glass container and pour marinade over it. Let it set for 15 or 20 minutes.

Turn the electric grill on and get the coals hot. Brush the amberjack on both sides with melted butter. Sprinkle with lemon pepper and salt to taste. Grill close to hot coals for 3 minutes. Turn and grill the other side for 3 minutes, or until the meat flakes easily when tested with a fork. Serve hot with vinegar cole slaw, corn on the cob, and garlic bread.

Grilled Fish with Caper Sauce

Here's a dish that I got from California. It specified catfish, but I cooked it with fillets from other fish and found them to be very good. The dish has a fine flavor, and the color is good, too. Make the sauce first.

The Sauce
- ½ cup cooking oil
- ⅓ cup lemon juice
- ¼ cup onion, finely chopped
- 2 cloves garlic, finely chopped
- 2 tablespoons catsup
- 2 tablespoons capers (and juice)
- 1 tablespoon salt
- 2 teaspoons sugar
- 2 teaspooons Worcestershire sauce
- ¼ teaspoon pepper
- 4 bay leaves, crushed

The Fish
- 2 pounds fish fillets, skinned
- paprika

Mix all sauce ingredients and let stand for

an hour. Put the fillets in a suitable container and pour the sauce over them. Let stand for 30 minutes or longer, turning at least once.

Fire up the outdoor grill with charcoal, and grease your hinged wire rack. Remove fish fillets from marinade and arrange in hinged wire rack. Sprinkle fish with paprika and place about 4 inches from the coals. (Use medium hot coals.) Cook for 7 or 8 minutes. Turn. Baste with sauce. Sprinkle with paprika. Cook for another 7 to 10 minutes, or until the fish flakes easily when tested with a fork. *Serves 4 to 6.*

Note: I like to sprinkle on extra paprika, giving this dish a deep reddish color.

Catfish and Bullheads

All of the freshwater catfish and bullheads are good to eat, but of course some are better than the others. In my opinion, a good deal depends on the water they come from. These fish are of medium oil content, and they can be cooked by most any method. Generally, the catfish (channel cat, blue cat, flathead cat, yellow cat, white cat, etc.) are better than the bullheads (yellow, spotted, speckled, brown, black, etc.). The bullhead, however, can be very good table fare if it is dressed quickly and eaten fresh. Some bullheads do not freeze well. With the catfish, I much prefer the smaller size.

In saltwater, the gafftopsail catfish is very similar to the better freshwater cats of similar size. The sea catfish, on the other hand, is not very good, though it is edible.

Grilled Mullet Fillets

Here's a great recipe for grilling rather fatty fish such as mullet and mackerel.

2 pounds mullet fillets
¼ cup bottled French dressing
1 tablespoon grated onion
juice of 1 lemon
salt and pepper to taste

Prepare grill for hot coals. In a pan, mix French dressing, onion, lemon juice, salt, and pepper. Dip fish fillets in the sauce, then put them in a hinged wire grill. Cook 4 inches above coals for 5 to 7 minutes. Baste, turn, and cook for another 5 to 7 minutes, or until fish flakes easily when tested with a fork. *Serves four.*

Lemon Rice Haddock

The following recipe came to me from the Nova Scotia Department of Fisheries. At first, I had doubts about cooking a stuffed fish over the coals. But I tried it, following the instructions carefully, and I'm happy to report a success!

1 whole haddock, 3 to 8 pounds (or
use salmon, trout, etc.)
1 cup sliced celery
1 medium onion, chopped
6 ounces sliced mushrooms
1 small grapefruit, thinly sliced
2 teaspoons grated lemon peeling

Pompano and Permit

The pompano is high in oil and should not be fried. It is usually baked or broiled, but it can also be cooked on a charcoal grill or smoked. The meat is firm and rich. For maximum enjoyment, catch a pompano in the surf with a live sandflea for bait, dress it, and grill it over charcoal on the beach.

The permit, cousin to the pompano, is medium high in oil content and should be smoked, grilled, broiled, or baked. The smaller permit are better, as a rule, than the larger specimens.

¼ cup lemon juice
6 tablespoons butter (two batches)
2 tablespoons melted butter (for
   basting)
2 ½ cups water
1¼ cup long grain white rice
1 teaspoon salt
⅛ teaspoon pepper
¼ teaspoon basil

Scale the fish and clean it, leaving it whole. Melt 3 tablespoons of the butter in a saucepan. Sauté onion and celery until tender. Add basil, lemon peeling, lemon juice, and water. Bring to a boil and add rice. Bring to boil again, reduce heat, cover tightly, and cook for 20 minutes.

Outside, start the coals burning in the grill so that you'll be ready to cook.

Inside, melt another 3 tablespoons of butter in a small skillet. Add the mushrooms and cook until tender. Mix with the rice mixture. Add salt and pepper. Put the stuffing into the fish.

Grease your hinged fish rack. Place half the grapefruit slices onto the rack, stringing them out to approximate the shape of the fish. Then put the fish on top. Put the other half of the grapefruit slice on the fish. Cook it over coals until the fish flakes easily with a fork; 10 minutes *for each inch of thickness* will be about right. Turn several times and baste with melted butter. *Serves 4 to 6.*

Grilled Striper or Hybrid Bass

4-pound striper or hybrid bass, whole
3 teaspoons garlic salt
1 teaspoon pepper
1 tablespoon grated lemon peel
½ cup oil
½ cup lemon juice

Scale the fish, dress it, and remove the head. Score both sides with slashes about ½ inch deep. In a bowl, mix garlic salt, lemon peeling, and pepper. Rub the fish with this mixture, then put fish on a platter and refrigerate for 8 hours or longer.

When you are ready to cook, prepare a medium coal fire in the grill. Mix ½ cup of oil and ½ cup of lemon juice. Place the fish over medium coals and cook for 15 minutes, basting several times with oil mixture. Turn fish carefully and cook for another 15 minutes,

basting several times, or until fish flakes easily when tested with a fork. (Test the thickest part of the fish.) *Serves 4 or 5.*

Grilled Crappie

Being soft and tender, crappie are not normally recommended for cooking over charcoal. But here's a recipe that works nicely if you have a hinged wire grill.

3 pounds of pan-dressed crappie
  (dressed weight)
sliced bacon
1 stick of butter
1 envelope of onion soup mix
¼ teaspoon of pepper
salt to taste

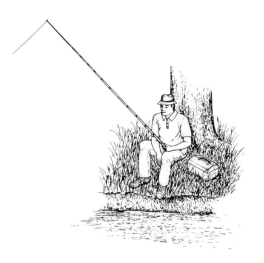

Dress the fish and light the charcoal.

Pulverize the soup mix in a food processor or with a mortar and pestle. Or put it between fine cloth and beat it with the smooth side of a meat mallet or a hammer. Make a sauce by melting the butter and stirring in the soup mix, pepper, and salt. Baste fish inside and out with the sauce. Wrap a strip of bacon around each crappie. Grease a hinged grill and place the fish in it. Cook over moderate coals for about 15 minutes. Baste, flip grill over, and cook the other side of the fish for another 10 to 15 minutes, or until the bacon is crisp and the fish flakes easily when tested with a fork. *Serves 4 to 6.*

Barbecued Pike Steaks

This recipe works well with northern pike, lake trout, and other fish that weigh in the 10- or 12-pound class. It's best to cut the fish into steaks that are 1-inch thick.

    pike, about 12 pounds, steaked
       (undressed weight)
    ¼ cup olive oil
    ½ cup soy sauce
    ¼ cup catsup
    ½ cup orange juice
    juice of 1 large lemon
    ¼ cup chopped parsley
    2 cloves garlic, minced
    2 teaspoons salt
    1 teaspoon pepper

Mix olive oil, soy sauce, catsup, orange juice, lemon juice, parsley, garlic, salt, and

---

Lake Trout

This large char is oily and does not fry very well. But it can be very good when cooked on a grill or under smoke. It can also be broiled and baked successfully. In any case, lake trout should be dressed quickly and refrigerated.

---

pepper. Put the fish steaks into a suitable glass container and pour the sauce over it. Marinate for several hours under refrigeration. Turn once or twice.

Bring coals to heat in the outdoor grill, and break out the hinged racks. Arrange fish steaks in the racks and cook for about 10 minutes on each side over medium hot coals, turning once. Baste with marinade sauce. Fish is done when it flakes easily when tested with a fork. *Serves 8 to 10.*

Oysters, Clams, & Mussels over the Coals

Such shellfish as oysters, clams, and mussels can be cooked, or "roasted," over the coals for a few minutes until they pop open. (They can also be cooked in this manner in an oven, but this can be a messy business and is best handled outside.) As soon as they open, they can be grasped in a heavy gloved hand and "cut" with a suitable knife held in the other hand. Shellfish cooked in this manner are ideal for serving and eating while cooking red meat (or smoking fish) for a longer period of time. The idea is to stand around the grill, on a cool night, and wait for an oyster or clam to pop open, then remove it and replace it with another. It's fun—and it's good.

Note, however, that shellfish eaten in this manner must be suitable for eating raw and should therefore be taken from clean waters. I often purchase fresh Apalachicola oysters by the burlap bagful, and I've eaten thousands of them without ill effect. But unless I know where oysters, clams, or mussels are coming from, I'll fry them or cook them in chowder.

In any case, "roasted" oysters are usually eaten with some sort of sauce, and I recommend one that I got from the Nova Scotia Department of Fisheries:

½ **cup melted butter**
juice of 1 lemon
½ **teaspoon sweet basil**
1 **teaspoon dill seed**
½ **teaspoon salt**
¼ **teaspoon cayenne**

Mix all ingredients and refrigerate for several hours. Before serving, melt the sauce and keep it warm near the roasted shellfish.

Mother Hubbard's Secret

I'll have to admit that the 1978 Edition of the California Department of Fish and Game's *The Catfish Manual and Cookbook* rather surprised me. Before then I had considered the catfish to be a southern speciality. But I'll also have to admit that at least some of those California folks know what they are doing. They've got recipes called "Southern Rapscallion," "The Colonel's Favorite," "Doyle's Dixieland Delight," "Calhoun's Sauté, Meunier" (named, I'm sure, for Calhoun, Georgia—Bert Lance's stomping grounds), "General Longstreet's Victory Dinner," "Pat's Plantation Party," and "Chicamauga Hush Puppies." But regardless of whether you live in the North, South, East, or West, be sure to try the recipe below:

3 **pounds of catfish fillets, skinned**
1 **gallon of water**
1 **cup salt**
½ **cup beer or ale**
½ **cup prepared mustard**
2 **cloves finely minced garlic**
½ **teaspoon Worcestershire sauce**
¼ **cup Louisiana hot sauce (or Tabasco**
    sauce)
½ **cup sesame seeds, toasted (used in**
    two batches)
2 **tablespoons chopped parsley**
paprika

Dissolve the salt in the gallon of water. Put fish into a glass container and pour the salted water over it. Let stand for 30 minutes. Drain fish. Mix beer, mustard, garlic, Worcestershire sauce, Louisiana hot sauce, ¼ cup of sesame seeds, and parsley.

Fire up a covered grill so that it will be ready. Note that the fish will be cooked on low heat, 250 degrees, so that not much charcoal will be required. Dip the catfish fillets into the mustard sauce and sprinkle with the remaining sesame seeds. Put fillets on well-greased rack in the grill. Close the hood and cook for an hour, or until the fish flakes easily when tested with a fork. (Try to keep the temperature at about 250 degrees.) *Serves 5 or 6.*

Smoked Fish with Hot Sauce

This recipe is often used in Florida and around the Gulf Coast to prepare mullet. It can also be used with most any other fish, but the sauce seems to go better with the fatty species, such as mullet or spanish mackerel.

The Fish
   6 whole fish, about 1 pound each
   1 cup salt
   1 gallon water
   ¼ cup of cooking oil
The Hot Sauce
   ½ cup honey
   ½ cup apple cider vinegar
   ½ cup prepared mustard
   ¼ cup Worcestershire sauce
   2 teaspoons Louisiana hot sauce (or
      Tabasco sauce)
   1 teaspoon salt
   1 tablespoon chopped parsley

Do not scale the fish. Remove the head just below the collarbone, then cut along the backbone almost to the tail—but do not cut through the belly. The fish should fold out flat, in one piece. Make a brine with 1 gallon of water and 1 cup of salt. Pour the brine over the fish, in a suitable container, and refrigerate for 30 minutes. Take the fish out of the brine and rinse in cold water. Dry the fish.

While the fish is soaking in the brine, ready a charcoal fire in the smoker. Close the hood and let the coals burn down until they are covered by white ash. Then cover with wet (soaked) hickory chips or fresh hardwood (without any bark). I prefer fresh wood.

Grease the grill and place the fish on it, skin side down. The grill should be from 4 to 6 inches from fire. Close the hood, let cook a while, then baste with cooking oil. Do not turn the fish. Baste often. Cook, under closed hood, for about an hour and a half, or until the fish flakes easily. Add more wood if needed to keep the smoke coming.

Make a sauce while the fish is smoking. In a small pan, blend honey, mustard, and vinegar. Stir in the other ingredients, bring to boil, then let cool a bit.

Serve fish whole, skin side down, on individual plates with hot sauce. Pull the meat off the skin with fork and fingers. Any way you can get it. But don't cut through the fish's skin; remember that they have not been scaled. *Serves 6.*

Smoked Fish with Wild Rice

Fish that are flaky and low in oil content, such as cod, tend to dry out during the hot-smoking process. But here's a recipe that I highly recommend.

The Fish
1 dressed fish, about 4 pounds (dressed weight)
6 slices of bacon
½ cup sliced green onions (including part of tops)
salt and pepper

Wild Rice Stuffing
4 ounces of uncooked wild rice

bacon drippings
½ cup chopped onion
½ cup chopped celery
½ cup chopped mushrooms
¼ cup chopped parsley
salt and pepper

Fire up smoker so that it will be ready. (You'll need a slow fire, 200 degrees, for an hour and a half.)

On stovetop, fry bacon and drain. Retain drippings. To make stuffing, cook wild rice

The Great Cajun Pot Plot

Ever since the Cajuns were booted out of Nova Scotia by the British, they've been trying to get even with the rest of the world. Take, for example, their plot to corner the market on cast-iron skillets.

Recently I was shopping for a Dutch oven and discovered a set of cast-iron cookware in a large department store. The box containing the utensils was labeled 'Cajun Cookware.'

It struck me as odd that a frying pan could be Acadian. Those who have fended for themselves for very long know what cast-iron does for fried chicken, pork chops, and beans, but that saucy foods are better relegated to stainless-steel. What were those Cajuns up to? I bought the pots anyway and took them home—that's when I discovered the scheme.

Inside the skillet was a recipe for blackened redfish.

It all started to click. I recalled that last year [1986], offshore of Louisiana, millions of

spawning size redfish were caught by a small fleet of purse-seiners, who then were able to sell the fish to a market hungry for the main ingredient to chef Paul Prudhomme's gastronomical creation. . . . Then chef Prudhomme told the media that the big specimens such as were being netted aren't fit to be blackened. About that time, cooks started blackening everything they could find—catfish, flounder, prime rib—possibly even ducks. . . .

Blackening calls for an almost white-hot skillet, and nothing but cast-iron will do. All of a sudden, people were thronging in stores to buy vessels in which they could blacken things. I have no proof that the redfish rhubarb was the result of marketing genius by Cajun members of the pot-and-pan industry, but it's almost for certain that the skillet-makers are in the black.

—Larry Teague, *Southern Outdoors*

according to the directions on the package. Sauté onions, celery, and mushrooms in bacon drippings until they are tender. Add parsley and cooked wild rice. Salt and pepper to taste. Set aside.

Sprinkle fish inside and out with salt and pepper. Stuff fish and close openings with toothpicks or skewers. Place bacon on top of fish, then sprinkle with the chopped onion. Place fish on well-greased grill in smoker and cook for 1 ½ hours at 200 degrees, then test for doneness. If the fish flakes easily with a fork, it's ready. Be sure that your test is made on the larger portion of the fish. *Serves 7 or 8*.

Small Fish Smoke

Smoking small fish, such as stunted bluegill and three-finger crappie and cigar-sized smelt, can be done easily by putting them between hardware cloth. You need two sheets of hardware cloth of the same size, and some wire to sew the edges of the sheets together. Merely put the fish on one sheet, cover with the second sheet, baste, put on the grill, and turn the sheets over instead of trying to flip individual little fish. It's faster, and doesn't tear up the fish. This method works best when you've got a rather large smoker, such as one made from a 55-gallon drum. Of course, any good smoker will work, but small fish take lots of room and not many can be cooked at one time in a very small unit. Anyhow:

panfish, dressed
1 stick of margarine or butter

2 garlic cloves, mashed
juice of 1 large lemon
salt and pepper to taste

Melt the butter in a saucepan, heat, and add juice from lemon and garlic. (If you don't have a garlic press, crush or mash the cloves.) Ready a slow fire in your smoker and let coals form a white ash. Salt and pepper the fish inside and out; then arrange the fish in the hardware cloth and secure. Put over slow coals and cook for a few minutes. Baste lightly, and add green (or wet) hickory chips or other good wood. (I use green pecan without any bark.) Lower the hood on fish and smoke for 30 minutes or so, or until fish flakes easily when tested with a fork. Turn fish and baste every 10 minutes.

Note: The measures for the basting sauce should be increased if you've got a large batch of fish to smoke. But I highly recommend that you cook a moderate batch first, simply because no recipe can pin down exact cooking and smoking periods for fish. Too much depends on who is doing it on what and to which kind—or size—of fish.

Smoke Barbecued Arctic Grayling

Here's a recipe that I adapted from an article by Nelson R. Lewis, which was published in *Outdoor Canada*. The original called for two arctic grayling and chopped alder. I tested it with two redeye bass and South Alabama pecan wood. If I thought grayling and alder would taste much better, I would head for Canada.

> **2 grayling or bass, about 1 pound each, split but not skinned**
> **1 tablespoon coarse salt**
> **1 clove of garlic, chopped finely**
> **2 tablespoons brown sugar**
> **1 teaspoon Dijon mustard**
> **1 to 2 teaspoons maple syrup**
> **1 teaspoon sweet basil**
> **1 teaspoon chopped fresh parsley**
> **1 lemon, sliced thinly**

Split the fish down the back and remove innards. Do not scale. Place the fish, scales down, on a rack and sprinkle with salt. After two hours, rinse the fish with cold water. Pat dry with absorbent paper. Put the fish back on the rack, skin side down.

Mix the garlic, maple syrup, mustard, brown sugar, basil, and parsley. Coat the fish with this mixture. Place lemon slices on top of fish. Put the rack over a shallow pan and let sit for two hours. (Retain the drippings in the pan.)

Build a small fire with charcoal let it burn down. Add a handlful of chopped adler, pecan, or other good hard wood. When the smoke builds up, place the rack over fire, a good distance from the heat, and cover it with a large piece of heavy duty aluminum foil. Let smoke for about an hour, basting several times with the sauce from the pan. Mend the fire from time to time, keeping it smouldering.

After smoking for an hour, turn the fish over and cook 4 inches from the fire for 10 minutes. Serve up the fish scale side down and eat with forks. *Serves 2.*

Note: When preparing fish in this manner, many people "butterfly" the fish when spliting it. I really prefer that the fish be filleted with two cuts, thereby getting rid of the backbone. This makes it easier to eat with a fork.

Skewered Shark Oriental

Usually, such soft fish as crappie, smallmouth bass, or walleye won't stay on a skewer. But some fish, such as sharks and sailfish, have tougher flesh and stay on much better. Moreover, they are delicious if they are prepared as follows:

The Marinade
> **¼ cup pineapple juice**
> **½ cup soy sauce**
> **¼ cup sherry**
> **2 tablespoons brown sugar**
> **1 teaspoon ground ginger**
> **1 teaspoon powdered mustard**
> **2 cloves of garlic, minced**

For Skewers
> **2 pounds of fresh shark, ray, or other tough fish**
> **1 can pineapple chunks (16-ounce size)**
> **2 green peppers, cut into 1-inch squares**
> **salt and pepper to taste**

Cut fish into 1-inch chunks and put into a glass or ceramic container. Mix all ingredients listed under marinade above. Pour over fish and refrigerate for at least 4 hours. Retain liquid.

Prepare grill for hot coals. String up shark, pepper squares, and pineapple chunks on skewers (preferably bamboo, for an oriental touch). Cook 4 inches above very hot coals for 5 or 6 minutes. Baste with marinade liquid. Turn. Baste. Cook the other side for 5 or 6 minutes, or until fish flakes when tested with a fork. *Serves 4 or 5.*

Variations: Add cherry tomatoes, mushroom caps, or onion wedges if you prefer more vegetables or if you have lots of people to feed on a small shark. This same dish can be broiled in an oven or cooked in a rotisserie.

Flounder with Crab Stuffing

At first I called this recipe Tax Payer's Flounder because I got it from a booklet called "Fish and Shellfish over the Coals," which I ordered from the Superintendent of Documents. The U.S. Government Printing Office in Washington published it. But, looking further, I'm not quite sure who footed the bill. I found that it was "issued" by the National Marine Fisheries Service as a part of its continuing "Consumer Educational Program" in cooperation with the Commercial Fishing Industry, and it was "developed" at the National Marketing Services Office in Chicago. In short, I don't know exactly who should get credit for the recipe, but I think it is pretty safe to say that, ultimately, the bill was footed, at least once, by "We the People." So . . . here's *your* recipe:

The Fish
  6 flounder, about ¾ pound each
  ¾ cup of butter or margarine, melted
  ⅓ cup lemon juice (freshly squeezed)
  2 teaspoons salt
  paprika
The Stuffing
  1 pound crab meat
  2 cups soft bread crumbs
  ½ cup chopped onion
  ½ cup chopped celery
  ⅓ cup chopped green pepper
  2 cloves garlic, minced
  ⅓ cup cooking oil
  3 eggs, beaten
  1 tablespoon chopped parsley
  2 teaspoons salt
  ½ teaspoon pepper

Make the stuffing first. Clean a pound of fresh crab meat, or use frozen crab meat. Also, canned crab meat can be used. In a large frying pan, heat the oil and sauté the onion, celery, green pepper, and garlic for a few minutes. Mix in bread crumbs, eggs, parsley, salt, pepper, and crab meat. Set the stuffing aside.

Dress the flounder, leaving the head on. As the booklet explained. "To make a pocket for the stuffing, lay the fish flat on a cutting board, light side down. With a sharp knife cut down the center of the fish along the backbone fron the tail to about 1 inch from the head end. Turn the knife flat and cut the flesh along both sides of the backbone to the tail, allowing the knife to run over the rib bones."

Start the charcoal in the grill so that it will be ready.

Stuff the fish. Note that the stuffing will be

exposed, and can be piled up a little above the fish. Mix melted butter, lemon juice, and salt. Cut and grease an 18- by 18-inch sheet of heavy-duty aluminum foil for each fish. Place 2 tablespoons of butter and lemon sauce on each piece of foil and smear it out, flounder-shaped. Place a fish atop the sauce, then top the fish and stuffing with 1 tablespoon of sauce. Sprinkle the fish lightly with paprika. Bring the foil over the fish and close all edges tightly with double folds.

Place each package of fish on your grill, which should be about 6 inches from the coals. Cook for 25 to 30 minutes. *Serves 6.*

Note: Crab meat does make an excellent stuffing, but it can get expensive if you have to buy canned or frozen meat, and it can be time consuming if you have to catch and dress your own. In either case, you can substitute fish flakes for crab meat. Or try diced shrimp or crayfish if you've got them.

Sea Island Snapper

Here's a recipe that I sort of put together from a booklet called "How to Catch your Fish and Eat It Too," which was handed out many years ago by the Georgia Department of Industry and Trade.

The Fish
  2 pounds of fish fillets
  salt and pepper
  cooking oil
The Marinade
  1 cup wine vinegar
  2 bay leaves
  ½ teaspoon thyme

To make the marinade, heat the wine vinegar; add bay leaves and thyme and simmer a few minutes. Let cool. Put fish fillets into a glass container and pour marinade over them. Cover and let stand for at least half an hour.

Prepare charcoal fire. Drain fillets, salt and pepper to taste, then brush with cooking oil. Place on well greased grill and position 3 inches above medium-hot coals. Cook for 7 minutes on one side, then turn and cook for 5 minutes on the other side. The fish is done when it flakes easily when tested with a fork. *Serves 4.*

Note: Flakey fish, such as largemouth bass, will be easier to turn if you put them in a hinged rack.

Oriental Fish Kabobs

This interesting recipe from the Canadian Department of Fisheries and Oceans in Ottawa makes use of two kinds of fish, but, unlike most "kabob" recipes, it doesn't have chunks of vegetables or fruit.

  ½ pound haddock fillets (see note below)
  ½ pound salmon fillets (see note below)
  ¼ cup soya sauce
  ¼ cup vegetable oil
  2 tablespoons sake or dry sherry
  1 garlic clove, crushed
  ¼ teaspoon ground ginger
  1 tablespoon brown sugar
  1½ teaspoons grated orange rind

Cut fillets into cubes of correct size for kabobs and put them into a glass container. Mix all other ingredients and pour over the fish. Marinate in the refrigrator for 3 hours, or at room temperature for 1 hour. Retain marinade.

Build a charcoal fire in the grill. Thread the fish chunks, alternating the types, onto well greased skewers. Place the skewers about 4 inches above hot coals. Grill for 4 minutes, baste, and turn. Baste several times, and cook until fish flakes easily. Do not overcook. *Serves 2 or 3.*

Note: The Canadian fishery folks say that cod, turbot, Boston bluefish, or halibut can be substituted for haddock; and that Arctic char or trout can be substituted for the salmon. I say that Kentucky spotted bass or Gulf of Mexico red snapper will also taste good. And try eel. In any case, try to use two different fish, at least for the sake of comparison and conversation. Note, however, that rather tough fish work better for any grill recipe.

Grilled Salmon Steaks

Fresh or fresh-frozen salmon steaks, cut about ¾ inch thick, can be very good when cooked correctly over coals. It helps to have a hinged wire grill.

2 pounds salmon steaks
1 cup dry vermouth
¾ cup cooking oil
⅓ cup lemon juice (freshly squeezed)
2 tablespoons chopped chives
1 clove garlic, minced
2 teaspoons salt
¼ teaspoon pepper
¼ teaspoon marjoram
¼ teaspoon thyme
⅛ teaspoon sage
⅛ teaspoon Louisiana hot sauce (or Tabasco sauce)

If steaks are frozen, thaw them out very slowly. Put the steaks into a glass container. To make marinade, mix wine, oil, lemon juice, garlic, chives, salt, pepper, marjoram, thyme, sage, and Louisiana hot sauce. Pour marinade over the fish and refrigerate for at least four hours. Retain the marinade.

Get coals ready for moderate heat and grease your grill racks (preferably hinged). Place fish on rack and place 4 inches over coals. Cook for about 10 minutes. Baste with marinade liquid. Turn and cook on the other side until fish flakes easily when tested with a fork. This should take 7 or 8 minutes. Baste several times. *Serves 4 or 5.*

13

COOKING FISH in CAMP

Some of the best fish I've ever eaten were cooked on a portable two-burner gas stove in the wilds of the Wacissa River in Florida, near where some of the Tarzan movies were made, and over oak coal fires on the banks of the Choctawhatchee River in Alabama. But the cooking process was exactly the same as was described in the first recipe in this book. (Note, however, that *frying* fish, or anything else, is more difficult in camp than in a kitchen, primarily because of limited equipment and problems with temperature control.) Nonetheless, most of the recipes in this book can be cooked in camp—if you've got the equipment and ingredients. Obviously, I don't want to repeat all these recipes in this chapter, and I will concentrate on a few that I consider to be especially appropriate for the fisherman—who will have enough trouble taking all his angling gear along, let alone elaborate cooking gear.

Also, please note that this chapter, if fully developed, would have to be a whole book unto itself. Such books already exist, such as *Trail Cooking* by John Weiss and *Complete Book of Outdoor Cookery* by Mel Marshall. Both were published by Outdoor Life Books. Be sure to read them. Also, I am working toward such a book myself, and maybe I'll complete it one of these days. Meanwhile, try the following recipes:

Bacon and Whatever You Catch

This recipe, or method, is a great way to prepare a few fish along a stream or in camp. Note that it does not require a lot of stuff to be packed along. Also, the bacon specified below can be eaten without any fish, just in case you don't catch any. The "seasoning mix" can be made at home, in the correct porportions, and taken along in one small bottle or plastic bag.

> **fish fillets**
> **bacon**
> **white, finely ground cornmeal**
> **seasoning mix**

Prepare the seasoning mix with 1 tablespoon salt, 1 teaspoon black pepper, 2 teaspoons dried and crumbled oregano (or thyme) and put it into a small container. Pack the container with your tackle or gear, along with bacon slices wrapped in aluminum foil and some cornmeal. (Make sure that grease won't leak out of the bacon package.)

If you don't catch fish, mix some cornmeal and some seasoned salt in water. You'll need a rather mushy texture. (It is at the right consistency when you put a spoonful of "mush" into the hot frying pan and it flattens out into a pattie.) Fry bacon and set aside. Cook corn bread in hot bacon drippings. If you don't have fish, eat corn bread with the bacon.

If you've got fish, dress them, then roll them in cornmeal mixed with seasoned salt. Fry quickly in bacon drippings. Eat with corn bread and bacon. If you see any watercress along the way, get some for salad.

Variation: You can sauté trout and other fish in a pat of butter or a small amount of oil. Flour or meal is not essential. A little salt helps, but isn't necessary. Small fish, such as brook trout, can be cooked whole, but larger fish will be easier to sauté if they are filleted or cut into small pieces. A large or heavy frying pan is not necessary to sauté fish. Many memorable meals have been cooked up with nothing more elaborate than a mess kit!

Wader's Fish Lunch

If you wade a stream all day, as, for example, between two bridges, you may not want to lug around a frying pan. Even if you are on a canoe, a frying pan, cooking oil, and so on is a bit much. Take along a few squares of heavy aluminum foil, folded compactly and stuck into your pocket or tacklebox. Also, bring along a few tiny packs of salt and pepper; these can be folded up into the aluminum

foil—along with a sealed pat of butter or two. Ironically, these fast-food conveniences are quite helpful for wilderness hikes!

An hour or so before eating time, keep a sharp eye out for a good supply of dry wood. Also, if you are knowledgeable about natural foods and have already caught a fish for your meal, keep a sharp eye out for cattails, edible mushrooms, arrowwood, and so on. Build a good fire, being aware that it should burn down into coals before cooking will be ideal. While the fire is getting ready, dress the fish that you have saved.

When the coals burn down, open up a square of aluminum foil and carefully press it flat. With the pat of butter, grease part of the foil that will be in contact with the fish. Salt and pepper the fish, then place it (either whole or filleted) in the center of the greased portion of the foil. Wrap the fish, folding seam and ends of the aluminum foil tightly. Rake out a bed of coals and lay the aluminum foil on top. Leave small fish in coals for 10 minutes. Large fish require more time.

cooking fish, a suggestion for the summer camp or picnic:

"The general is spending the summer in Sapphire, N. C. He is a good fisherman and knows how to cook fish. Here is the way, says a friend:

"The instant the fish was landed, it was dressed, and a chunk of sweet fresh butter, a pinch of salt, a shower of pepper, and a diminutive rasher of breakfast bacon were placed inside. A fresh shuck, out of which the roasting ear had just been taken, was procured, and the trout, thus prepared, put in place of the ear. The shuck was smoothed down and tied at the silk end. Then this shuck with its precious cargo was put in the embers and covered with live coals until the fish was done to an exact turn; the roasting ear was toasted before the fire, and corn hoecake was brought into requisition. The fish must swim in the water before he is caught, and again in butter after he is roasted.'"

—*The Progressive Farmer's Southern Cookbook*

Fish and Shucks

I've read a dozen tips on how to wrap fish in green corn shucks and cook them in a campfire. I've always wanted to try it, but somehow I have never had fish, campfire, and green corn shucks all at the same time. But if you want to try it, consider the following quote from an old text:

"From a 50-year-old scrapbook comes Gen. Wade Hampton's unique recipe for

Fish and Elder Bloom Fritters

Here's a recipe that I prefer to prepare in camp by lake or stream when the elder is in bloom. But I've eaten it more than several times in a house, and it's good there, too. (Once we lived on an island in a Florida lake, and the elders around our house bloomed all year! It was a nice spot, but I had to leave it because of lack of will power. I worked at

Flatfish

There are hundreds of flatfish, similar to flounder, that make very good eating. These range in size from panfish to huge halibut. Most of these fish have low oil content and good white, flaky flesh, regardless of size.

Each year sportsmen take many thousands of flukes and other flatfish by hook and line by day and by spear at night. Some of the common coastal flounders move into shallow water after dark, and they usually prefer a sand bottom to mud. Thus, they can be spotted with a strong light and speared.

home, or was supposed to, and had my office in the boathouse. What angler can concentrate on office work while lunker bass slosh around after frogs in the boat slip?) Anyhow, be sure to try this recipe. In flavor, it hints slightly of fried oysters, which I love. Here's what you need:

2 cups of fish flakes
2 cups of elder blooms
2 eggs
¼ cup of milk
⅓ cup of flour
⅓ cup of fine-ground white cornmeal
cooking oil
salt and pepper to taste

Mix milk, flour, and meal. Pour over fish flakes and mix in eggs, elder blooms, salt, and pepper. Form into patties and fry in hot cooking oil until fritters are brown on both sides. Eat while hot. *Serves 4.*

Planked Fish

I have seen recipes for placing fish on a plank and then putting the whole thing into a kitchen oven. I see no point in this unless you don't have any baking pans or broiling racks. Nor do I see any need, or advantage, in using a plank in camp if you have other cooking aids. I do admit that planked fish can be tasty, but note that too often the fish ends up dropping off the plank and into the fire, coals, or dirt. Then what do you do?

I concede that, on first thought, planked fish might be a good way to cook fish in camp or in an emergency situation. Of course, finding a suitable driftwood plank is entirely possible along ocean beaches, lake shores, and even stream banks. But finding such a plank in the deep woods often presents problems. Some people, writing for Boy Scouts and such, recommend that a log be split. But splitting a log is easier said than done. If you've got an ax, your best bet is to heat the blade in your fire and cook the fish on it instead of trying to split a log.

Even if you get a plank or a log, attaching the fish to it is not always easy. Most people recommend nails, but often nails are not readily available. If you've got a knife, try cutting pegs and boring suitable holes into the plank.

Many people recommend that the plank, with the fish attached to it, be put on one side of the fire and a reflector oven, or some such aid, be put on the other side. The reflector can be a piece of aluminum foil—but note that it might be better to wrap the fish in the aluminum foil (if you've got plenty of it) and put it under a few coals for cooking.

But nonetheless planks can be used to cook good fish. It's best to "butterfly" the fish; that is, cut the fish down the back and almost through the bottom, then use the belly skin as a hinge and spread the fish open. Nail or otherwise secure the fish skin side down to the plank. Note that it is not necessary, or desirable, to scale or skin the fish. Eat it off the plank, pulling the meat from the skin with fork or fingers. Salt and pepper helps, and a little butter or bacon swabbed onto the fish from time to time works wonders.

Notes: Planks from pine trees and other conifers may impart an unpleasant taste to the fish, and may even ooze a tarlike substance. Also, using a boat paddle to plank fish may seem to be a good idea, but think twice about using one if it has any sort of varnish on it.

Further Notes: This chapter deals mostly with cooking in camp, but note that planked fish is sometimes cooked in the home kitchen. My copy of an old *Progressive Farmer* cookbook, for example, advises that the plank be oiled well and heated while the oven preheats. Arrange the fish on the plank, season it (the fish), and bake at 400 degrees for 35 to 45 minutes. Then remove the plank from the oven and serve the fish surrounded with mashed potatoes and other cooked vegetables. Remember that the mashed potatoes surround the fish and all other vegetables, thereby building a dam to hold the juices off the tablecloth. Such a dam is essential when serving this planked fish at a table with a cloth on it.

Country-Boy Treat

Here's a method of cooking fish that almost every outdoorsman has heard about, but not enough of us have actually tried it. The following quote from an *Outdoor Life* column by C.B. Colby gives some good directions: "Have you ever tried trout cooked in clay packs? If not, you've missed a real country-boy treat. Dig under the gravel of a stream bed and you'll find clay. Clean your fish, and enclose it, head and all, in an envelope of clay. Some folks like to salt and pepper the cavity and put in a slice of onion. Put the clay-covered trout into a bed of coals, and dig them out 45 minutes later if the fish are small or an hour later if they're large.

"If you can't find clay, use mud. If you do,

Crappie

Both the white crappie and the black crappie are very good table fare, low in oil, and can be prepared by a variety of ways. To me, their flesh is a little on the soft side. For best results, dress the fish quickly and keep them on ice or under refrigeration. Crappie fillets freeze well in water. Of course, crappie have a number of local names, including white perch and sacalait.

Flatrock Fish?

It is entirely possible to cook fish on a flat rock that has been heated in or over a fire. But be careful. Rocks that contain moisture may pop or explode. Note also that a number of other flat surfaces can be used in a pinch. The blades of axes, hoes, and machete come readily to mind. In fact, the term "hoecake" for a certain kind of bread might have arisen from the practice of cooking hand-sized pones of corn bread on a hoe handle.

however, first wrap the fish in green corn husks, which will protect the meat from the mud. Clay bakes hard and so doesn't dirty the fish."

Camp Grilled Fish

Split unscaled fish on the underside from throat to tail. Cut so that only the top skin holds the two halves together. (Cut out the backbone, if you want to do so.) Salt to taste. Put the fish skin side down on a rack or screen and place over hot coals. Baste with a little oil (if available). For more smoke flavor, reduce the coals and add green hardwood chips from oak, hickory, mesquite, etc. To get more smoke flavor, make a tent with aluminum foil and put it over the fish. Cook until the fish flakes easily from the skin. Put the fish flat on a plate, or other surface, and eat it with a fork, pulling the meat off the skin side. Remember that the fish is never scaled.

Note that some fish, such as catfish and eels, can also be cooked in this manner without skinning them. In fact, some people prefer to leave the skin on them so that the meat won't dry out. Note further that the skin on small fish of this sort can be eaten without having to pull it off after cooking. The Indians of the northeast, I understand, were especially fond of unskinned eels cooked over the coals.

Easy Bacon n' Fish

Here's a good recipe for the campfire, and it works nicely on canoe float trips where extensive cooking gear isn't feasible. All you need is a folding wire broiler, fish, and a few strips of bacon wrapped in foil or plastic. Clean the fish, wrap with bacon, and put into a folding wire broiler, which will facilitate turning without tearing up the fish. Cook over wood coals until the bacon is crispy.

14

FISH ROE

"Are you going to eat *that*?" my son Bill asked, peeping into the frying pan when I had my soft roe dish about half done.

Well, yes. If there is anything better than scrambled brains and eggs, it is soft roe and eggs. My wife loves the combination. But the boys won't touch it because it doesn't *look* right, and I usually fry ordinary roe for them to eat. But of course I know better than to fry roe that is too large and dry. Bluegill roe is my favorite for frying, and the boys always search for it when they dress the stunted "bream" that they bring home by the dozens from a nearby farm pond.

Everyone knows about caviar made from sturgeon roe, and of course a lot of coastal anglers already have favorite recipes for shad roe. But anyone who fishes at all should be aware that some other species have very, very good roe. One dangerous exception is the roe of the various garfish, which is toxic to man. I understand also that the innards from the puffer can be deadly, and I therefore stay clear of their roe. But I've eaten excellent roe from a number of other fish, including largemouth bass, carp, and bullheads.

One of my favorites is "white" roe from mullet, which is, of course, another name for

---

Tarpon

Although tarpon provide lots of protein for the peoples of Central America, it is not normally eaten in this country. The flesh is quite oily, tough, and not good. The roe, on the other hand, is quite tasty.

soft roe, or milt. In addition to being good, it's also highly nutritious and is easily digested. White roe from mullet, which is available around the Gulf of Mexico in the fall of the year, is one of my personal favorites, but carp, mackerel, shad, and other fish also have good white roe.

In any case, here are some of my favorite recipes for fish roe:

Roe 'n Eggs

If you don't have any soft roe to cook the recipe above, or don't care for soft roe, then try this one with regular roe. Again, I haven't given any measures for the ingredients. Often this is a practical matter of putting whatever fish roe you have in with enough eggs to feed everybody. If you've got plenty of roe, however, use about half roe and half egg.

roe
eggs
butter
salt
pepper
4 cups water
2 tablespoons vinegar

Put water and vinegar into a pan and heat. Add fish roe. Bring to boil, then reduce heat.

Warning

None of the fish and game cookbooks that I have seen, or any other book that I know about, give fish roe the coverage that it deserves. Typically, they set forth a recipe or two for shad roe, then indicate that other roe can be used. Don't believe it. *The roe of puffers and gars can be toxic. In fact, gar roe can have extremely dangerous stuff in it.*

Consider the following quote, which is from Dr. Donn E. Rosen, Curator of the Department of Ichthyology at New York's Museum of Natural History. (The quote was published in a sidebar to an article by Janet H. Alexander in *Sports Afield*, February 1968.) "The roe of a species of fresh-water garfish is so dangerous to eat that the slightest taste on the tongue can be fatal. In its death-dealing qualities, it's similar to cyanide—no one ever survives."

But don't throw away your gar roe. It's one of the best bluegill baits that you can put onto a hook. (Apparently bluegill have become immune to the roe so that they can feed on it. Bluegill are, more than people realize, roe eaters and nest robbers.) When baiting up, use tiny salmon-egg hooks, or, since the gar eggs are quite sticky, bait with a gob of 'em. Gar eggs can be frozen and used later for bait—but be sure that you mark the package properly before freezing. Draw a skull and crossbones on it.

While roe is cooking, break the sacs and scatter roe. Simmer for about 10 minutes. (If you are cooking a large batch of roe, increase the measures of water and vinegar. Or add more water as needed. Note that roe will absorb water while cooking and will expand to about twice its original volume.)

Strain roe and put into a bowl with eggs. Whisk until mixed. Heat butter in a skillet and scramble egg/roe mixture. Salt and pepper to taste.

If you want a delicious breakfast, serve this dish with buttered toast and sliced tomatoes.

Scrambled Soft Roe and Eggs

    soft roe
    eggs
    green onions
    butter
    salt and pepper

Remove eggs from the refrigerator before starting. After the eggs have reached room temperature, break them into a bowl and whisk them lightly. Melt a little butter in a frying pan. Chop up some green onions, including about half the tops, and sauté them for a few minutes in the butter. Add the soft roe, heat, and stir. Break up the roe, chopping it with a fork, as it cooks. Add the eggs and scramble everything, stirring constantly. Salt and pepper to taste. Freshly ground pepper is best. Serve hot with toast, bacon, and very cold tomatoes. Exact amounts of eggs

and soft roe aren't critical but, as a rule, try about half egg and half roe by volume.

Bonus Small Fry

My boys are very, very fond of tiny roe of bluegills and other small panfish. If we are frying panfish, we normally cook the bonus roe right along with the fish, in which case we use the same oil, batter, and seasoning.

The recipe that follows is pretty much our standard recipe for fried fish, but note that I prefer bacon drippings for pan frying a mess of small roe alone. The point that I want to make here is that this technique works best for small roe with sacs no longer than 3 inches. Some larger roe tend to be far too dry when cooked by this method.

    small roe
    fine-ground cornmeal
    salt
    pepper
    bacon drippings or other cooking oil.

Salt and pepper the roe, then shake or roll it in cornmeal. Pour ⅛ inch of bacon drippings in a skillet and heat. Pan fry roe on each side over medium heat for 5 to 10 minutes, depending on size. Some roe pop violently, so be careful if you fry on high heat; stand back and turn with a long fork. Do not overcook. Usually, a breaded or floured roe is done when the outside takes on a golden brown color. If you feel that you need to check inside, cut off a slice and look for any variation in color. The middle should look pretty much like the edges in color and texture.

Shad Roe with Sweet Potatoes

This is an unusual combination that I got from *Coastal Carolina Cooking,* which attributes it to Jessie Savage of Morehead City, North Carolina:

> 4 shad roe (or a total of about 1 pound)
> ½ cup cornmeal
> ½ teaspoon salt
> ½ teaspoon black pepper
> vegetable oil for deep frying
> ½ cup vegetable oil or shortening (for sweet potatoes)
> 2 large sweet potatoes, peeled and sliced

Rig for both deep frying and pan frying. Season the cornmeal with the salt and pep-per, then roll or shake the fish roe carefully in the meal mixture. Deep fry the roe until it is golden brown. Meanwhile, heat a little vegetable oil in a skillet, then pan fry the sweet potatoes over medium heat until they are browned on both sides. Serve the roe and potatoes together. Serves 4.

Fried Roe

I tend to be both easily amused and highly argumentative, and in a book like this it's hard to avoid Herter's *Bull Cook and Authentic Historical Recipes and Practices.* Herter says that he has never happened upon anything as bad as fried fish roe. He probably got hold of some rather large roe that were cooked too long, which, I admit, can be dry, hard, grainy, and even difficult to swallow.

Small roe, as stated in another recipe, can be fried deliciously as it is. But the larger roe should be poached for a few minutes before frying. Poaching expands the eggs, making them more fluffy and moist. The poaching liquid is a mixture of 1 pint of water, ½ teaspoon salt, and juice of 1 lemon. Expand these measures if you've got lots of roe to cook.

After poaching, roll the roe in flour and fry it in cooking oil. Avoid high heat, which causes the roe to pop too much. (In fact, it's best to use a cover on the frying pan.) Don't overcook. If in doubt, cut into a roe and look at the cross section. If it is done, the center will be the same color and texture as the edges.

Variations: Use other batters, dip in egg,

Shad

The bony American shad is highly touted as table fare in some quarters. The hickory shad is also edible, but it is best when smoked. Threadfin shad and gizzard shad are seldom eaten.

Fish Roe

Some say the best caviar is the roe of the sturgeon. Coastal Carolinians are sure to disagree. When prepared correctly, the fish eggs of mullet, menhaden, shad, and herring are just as tasty, they say.

The roe usually consist of two elongated sacklike ovaries, covered with a connective membrane. The color varies according to species, ranging from yellow to orange to black.

The eggs of each species have a distinctive taste and texture. Descriptions of the variations in flavor will not suffice; you must try the roe for yourself. And even roe-lovers warn that it is a taste you have to acquire.

Most roe are good fried, baked, dried, or scrambled with eggs. If roe are plentiful, cooks often serve them alone as the main dish.

—*Coastal Carolina Cooking*

buttermilk, or whatever you prefer. Roe can also be deep fried successfully, or it can be sautéed in butter.

Pan Fried Soft Roe

soft roe
cooking oil
salt
flour

Salt the soft roe to taste and roll it in flour. Fry in medium-hot cooking oil until the outside is golden. Handle carefully. Overcooking, within reason, doesn't seem to hurt the quality very much. But soft roe does tend to shrink as it is cooked.

Variation: Forget the flour and oil. Salt roe to taste and sauté in a little hot butter. Sprinkle with lemon juice and dust lightly with paprika.

Broiled Roe

I first became acquainted with broiled roe during 1968 at a rather elegant eating house on the Gulf Coast of Mississippi, near Pascagoula. My waiter told me how it was done.

roe
butter
lemon juice
salt

Paddlefish

In the late 1800s, paddlefish were important commercially in the Mississippi Valley, valued for their tasty flesh and their eggs that sold as caviar. Around 2,500,000 pounds were harvested in 1899.

—*Arkansas Game and Fish Department*

Steam the roe for five minutes. Make a basting sauce from butter, lemon juice, and salt. Broil roe 2 inches from heat source until done, turning once and basting. Carefully remove roe from broiling rack and place on a plate. With a sharp, thin knife slice the roe in half (long way) and brush some of the basting sauce lightly from one end to the other. Garnish with parsley.

Variations: The roe can be poached or boiled instead of steamed, and very small roe can be broiled without prior preparation.

Roe and Bacon

Fish roe and bacon compliment each other, no matter whether you cook them together or separately. I prefer to cook mine together, usually by wrapping the bacon around the roe or, with smallish roe, by folding the bacon over the roe longways. Bacon and roe are good fried without any other ingredients added, but I prefer a little salt and pepper with them. The combo can also be broiled, or put into a folding wire rack and grilled over coals.

Cod's Roe Ramekins

Here's an old Irish dish, *eochrai truis*, that I got from George L. Thomson's *Traditional Irish Recipes*.

½ **pound boiled cod roe**
4 ounces bread crumbs
1 egg
1 cup milk
2 teaspoons chopped parsley
pepper
salt

Preheat the oven to 400 degrees. Mash the roe and mix it with the parsley, salt, and pepper. Add the bread crumbs. Beat the egg yoke, stir in the milk, and pour over the bread crumbs. Let the mixture sit for about ten minutes. Beat the egg white until it stands, and then fold it into the bread mixture. Grease some ramekins and spoon them nearly full of the bread mixture. Bake for about 15 minutes, or until golden brown.

Caring for Roe

For best results, roe should be removed from the fish as soon as possible and put on ice. Remove the roe slowly, being careful not to break or puncture the egg sac. Far too many good roe are cut with a knife when gutting the fish, thereby making the roe much more difficult to handle, store, cook, and eat. Usually, if you have experience and a good eye, you can tell before you dress a fish whether or not it is fat with roe.

If the fish aren't dressed soon after catching, then, needless to say, keeping them alive or quite cold will yield better roe.

Fresh roe can be kept in a refrigerator for several days. They can also be frozen. I prefer to freeze them in small containers of water, being careful to completely cover the roe. They can also be wrapped like cigars. Wrap them first with plastic film, then with aluminum foil.

Small roe can be fried, broiled, or grilled between bacon without any prior cooking, but large roe tend to be too dry unless they are first poached for a few minutes. If they are poached, add a little salt and lemon juice to the water.

Warning: If you fry roe, even with bacon wrapped around it, watch out for violent popping. Cook on medium heat instead of high—or use a lid on the frying pan.

If you choose to fry the bacon separately, then be sure to use the drippings to cook the roe.

Roe on Toast

Here's a recipe that I like to use with roe that I consider too large for cooking in the sac. My own guideline in this matter is that the eggs must be a good deal smaller than ⅛ inch—the size of the beads on a two-bladed spinnerbait.

> **roe (medium to large)**
> **2 lemons**
> **salt**
> **butter**
> **bread slices**
> **bread crumbs**
> **radish and parsley for garnish**

Heat a pan of water and add lemon juice and salt. Break egg sacs and squeeze fish eggs into water. Boil lightly for 4 or 5 minutes. Strain and drain. Preheat oven to 400 degrees. Fry bread and bread crumbs in butter.

Spread roe over bread and sprinkle with fried bread crumbs. Sprinkle with lemon juice. Put bread on a baking sheet and bake for a few minutes, being careful not to burn bread crumbs. Garnish with sliced red radish and parsley. If you don't have any parsley, try the radish tops.

Soft Roe Surprise

Here's a tasty dish that depends, in part, on a crispy outside and a soft inside.

> **soft roe**
> **juice of lemon**
> **water**
> **salt**
> **butter**
> **egg**
> **fine bread crumbs**

Poach roe on low heat for a few minutes in a mixture of water, lemon juice, and salt. (Exact measures for the poaching liquid aren't too important, but try about 1 pint of water with the juice of one lemon and ½ teaspoon salt. Increase measures if you have lots of roe to cook.) Carefully drain roe, carefully dip in beaten egg, carefully roll in bread crumbs, and carefully pan fry in hot butter until outside is golden. Eat these with your fingers so that you have full awareness of texture, crunch, and softness.

Note: If you've got lots of folks to feed, deep fry the roe in a basket instead of pan frying. Drain on absorbent paper before serving.

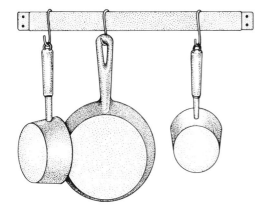

Variation: If you want to surprise your guests with a mystery appetizer, make "balls" of this dish. After poaching, cut the roe into sections with a sharp, thin knive. Dip, roll, and fry as above. Serve hot or warm.

Soft Roe 'n Bacon

This is a good dish to introduce somewhat skeptical folks to soft roe. If they are downright squeamish, change the name to bacon 'n white roe. Here's all you need:

soft roe
bacon

Heat a frying pan. Fold a strip of bacon over roe longways and secure with a round toothpick. (Roe can also be wrapped with a spiral of bacon, but this is a little harder to wrap and cook.) Fry on one side, then turn carefully and fry the other side.

Other possibilities: Broil the roe and bacon instead of frying it. Handle carefully. Also, put the roe and bacon units into a hinged rack and grill over coals.

Baked Roe

This recipe (and this cooking technique) works best with medium to large roe, with sacs about 6 inches long.

roe
bacon
salt
pepper
lemon wedges

Preheat oven to 350 degrees. Salt and pepper roe, then place them close together (but not touching) on a shallow baking pan or sheet. Cross hatch with bacon strips. Bake for about 30 minutes, or until bacon begins to crispen. Serve with lemon wedges for those who prefer a little juice on their roe.

Caviar and Cheese

Most people eat caviar on dainty crackers or thinly sliced bread, maybe with a little lemon juice squeezed on top. I prefer mine with a slice of ordinary "hoop" cheese, which I usually buy unrefrigerated from a country grocery store. (It's the kind with a red rind around it, and is cut in wedges from a large wheel-shaped hoop.) The cheese can be put on crackers, and the caviar put atop the cheese. But of course all true connoisseurs know that the caviar, instead of being canned, must have been held at a temperature somewhere between 28 and 32 degrees for at least 5 months. Further, hoop cheese must be served at room temperature and, indeed, must not have been refrigerated at all.

Just as true wine must be made from grapes, not blackberries or elderberries, true cavier must be made from sturgeon roe, not carp roe or whitefish roe. Also like fine wine, good cavier is too difficult to perfect in home kitchens without special equipment. But I may be wrong, and you may want to consider the following opinion:

According to Herter's *Bull Cook and Authentic Historical Recipes and Practices,* caviar was originally made in China from carp eggs. Genghis Khan, Herter said, took it to Russia, where sturgeon roe became popular because of its color. Herter says that sturgeon roe tastes no different, when prepared "in the same manner," from the roe of bluegill, walleye, and such. Carp, he says, still make the best caviar. Here is what he recommends:

carp eggs
1 gallon water
2½ cups salt
⅙ ounce sodium nitrate
1/32 ounce sodium nitrite
1 teaspoon powdered ginger
1 teaspoon powdered mustard

Stir the salt into the water. Put an egg into the solution. If it floats, fine. If it sinks, add more salt until it does float. Stir the sodium nitrate, sodium nitrite, ginger, and mustard into the water. Cut the end off the roe sacs and carefully squeeze the eggs into the salt-water solution. Leave the eggs in the salt solution, at room temperature, for 5 days. Strain the eggs and put them into glass jars. Keep them under refrigeration (or frozen, he says) until you are ready to eat them.

Note: Herter says that sodium nitrate and sodium nitrite are available at drug stores. Check with your pharmacist before proceeding with the above recipe.

Salt-Cured Roe—or Outer Banks Caviar

I've always felt that the Russians had the best of the caviar trade, but I have definitely acquired a taste for *batarekh*, which is an ancient treat that was enjoyed on the Nile long before Anthony and Cleopatra came barging along. Today the secret is known to a few gourmets in New York, Paris, and elsewhere,

Anyone for Sturgeon Marrow?

Just about everyone knows that the Russians make great caviar from the roe of large sturgeon, which can grow up to 2,500 pounds. But did you know that *vesiga*, made by drying the spinal marrow of the sturgeon, is also used in Russian cookery?

while the old salts on the Gulf Coast of Mexico and along the Outer Banks of North Carolina walk around with salt roe in their pockets!

The delicacy is usually made from the roe of mullet or cod, both of which are widely available. Get some very fresh roe, wash it, and drain, being careful not to tear the sacs. Roll the roe in salt, then place it on absorbent paper (I use brown grocery bags). Sprinkle more salt on it. Within a few minutes, the salt will start drawing the moisture from the roe, and the paper must be changed every few hours. At each change, turn the roe over and sprinkle with more salt. Continue this for several days, or until no more moisture is coming out and the paper doesn't have to be changed. Then hang the roe in a cool, airy place for several days, or put it on a well ventilated rack. When it becomes dry and rather hard, it's ready to eat. Slice it very thinly, put it atop a small wheat cracker, and put one drop of fresh lemon juice on it.

To store *batarekh*, wrap each roe individually and refrigerate until you are ready to eat them. Dried salt roe will keep for several weeks.

Be warned that the dish does have a strong flavor, like caviar, and it may be an acquired taste. I loved it from the start. But, to be honest, my wife still doesn't care too much for it, and I can't even get my son Bill to taste the stuff.

"It doesn't *look* good," Bill said, staring at one of the skin sacs, which was dry and salt-coated.

Patiently I explained that *batarekh* is a delicacy from ancient Egypt—food for the Pharaohs.

"I don't want any," he said, quickly turning his head, not looking so good himself right now. "They look like . . . little mummies!"

Even for the sake of culinary research, I didn't ask Bill what he thought my famous scrambled soft roe and eggs looked like.

15

CRAWDADS, GARFISH, PEA-CRABS, etc.

Once I drove through Louisiana while headed for Texas. Feeling hunger pains, I stopped in a small cafe in a small town and took a seat at an old wooden table. There were some fellows sitting at stools along what looked like an oyster bar. But they were eating crawfish.

There wasn't a printed menu at the table, so I ordered some sort of crawfish dish from a chalkboard menu on the wall. It was delicious. On into Texas I drove—but I kept thinking about the crawfish. Finally, I turned around and headed back to Louisiana for another helping!

I've been a crawfish fan ever since, and I never pass up a chance to eat them whenever they are available commercially. The market crawfish are a special variety, or varieties, that seem to have more meat in their tails in proportion to the size of their body. By contast, I've eaten some big black crawfish out of rocky streams in Tennessee that were almost all head. But there must be a hundred kinds of crawfish in North America. They are available in just about all streams, lakes, and ponds—and lots of'em—all good to eat!

Since this book is supposed to be about cooking fish, game, and fowl that are taken in the name of hunting and fishing, I have included only a few recipes for shrimp, which most folks buy in a fish market. Of course, a few sportsmen do catch their own shrimp, and a good many more catch crabs by one means or another. This chapter does contain what I consider to be some important culinary information on both shrimp and crabs, along with some suggestions for cooking other tasty creatures.

Moreover, I have included recipes and advice for cooking such fish as carp that are widely available and frequently caught. A number of people are reconsidering the term "game fish," and this statement applies to the table as well to stream, lake, or ocean. Hopefully, the recipes in this chapter will help fill a real need in this area.

Crawfish Salad

Crawfish tails can be used in almost any salad that calls for boiled shrimp or lobster. If you don't have a favorite recipe, try this:

    1 pound crawfish tails (about 4 pounds whole crawfish)
    4 bay leaves
    juice of one lemon
    1½ tablespoons mayonnaise
    1½ tablespoons sour cream
    3 stalks celery, sliced crossways
    ½ cup onion, finely chopped
    1 teaspoon celery seeds
    1 tablespoon dry dill weed, crushed
    salt to taste
    white pepper to taste
    paprika
    lettuce leaves
    2 cups cooked macaroni

Bring water to boil in a large pot with bay leaves. Boil crawfish for 6 about 6 minutes,

more or less, depending on the size. Discard the water and bay leaves. Let crawfish cool, then shell and devein the meat. Sprinkle with lemon juice, toss, and refrigerate until you are ready to proceed.

In a large boil, mix crawfish tails with mayonnaise, sour cream, macaroni, celery, celery seeds, dill weed, salt, and white pepper. Fix individual servings on lettuce leaves and sprinkle lightly with paprika. Eat with crackers. *Serves 4 for a light lunch.*

Crawfish and Mushroom Bisque

Here's a dish—often made with shrimp, crab meat, or lobster—that can be purely excellent when prepared with freshwater crawfish. The natural fat from the crawfish adds a little something extra to a bisque.

    4 pounds whole crawfish
    4 bay leaves
    2 tablespoons butter
    1½ tablespoons crawfish fat (see text below)
    ¼ cup green onions, finely chopped
    1 tablespoon fresh parsley, minced
    2 tablespoons flour
    2 cups whole milk
    ¼ cup heavy whipping cream
    salt to taste
    white pepper to taste
    ¼ cup sherry

Boil the crawfish tails in water with bay leaves for 4 to 7 minutes, depending on size.

Discard water and bay leaves. Peel the crawfish. Devein the tails and cut into ½-inch pieces. Remove 1½ tablespoons of fat from the heads. (When you remove the tails from the heads, look at one and you'll see the fat inside. Scoop it out with a teaspoon or baby spoon, depending on the size of crawfish.)

In a small saucepan, melt a ½ tablespoon of the butter and add the crawfish fat to it. Sauté the onion and parsley until the onion is clear. Stir in salt and white pepper to taste. Set aside.

In a pot of suitable size, melt 1½ tablespoons butter and stir the flour into it. Heat and stir for about 5 minutes, then add the milk, whisking briskly while you pour slowly. Allow the mixture to heat up, but do not boil. Add crawfish and cook for 2 minutes. Do not boil. Reduce heat and stir in the cream. Add onions and parsley from the saucepan and stir in the sherry. Eat the bisque with toast. *Serves 4 or 5.*

Sautéed and Fried Crawfish Tails

Crawfish tails are just as good if you call them crayfish or crawdads. The problem is not in cooking these but in having the patience to catch and clean enough to feed everybody.

If you've got only a few crawfish tails, just for yourself or maybe one other person, try sautéeing them in butter. Peel the tails off the meat, sprinkle them with a little salt and pepper, and cook in hot butter for 3 or 4 minutes, or a little longer for large tails.

Sprinkle the meat with a very small amount of lemon juice, if you've got it at hand.

If you've got a big batch of crawfish, you might want to dress them all, salt and pepper them to taste, shake them in flour, and fry them quickly in hot oil. Don't cook them too long.

Crawfish and Eggs

If you've got only a few crawfish, try the following recipe for breakfast or brunch.

crawfish tails
eggs
green onions
salt and pepper
butter

Peel the crawfish tails and dice the meat finely. Mince a couple of green onions, including part of the tops, and sauté them in butter in a frying pan. Add the crawfish tails and cook for 3 minutes. Break the eggs into a bowl and whisk them for scrambling. Pour the eggs into the frying pan and stir until they are ready to eat. Salt and pepper to taste. Serve with toast.

Short Measure Gumbo

Here's a dish designed to feed lots of people on a small amount of shrimp, crawdad tails, crabs, or lobster. Any combination of these shellfish can be used, or fish flakes can be used to fill in. I always try to cook a batch of this gumbo a day or two following a shrimp or crab boil, thereby using up leftovers:

1 pound shrimp or crab, cooked and
    peeled
½ cup cooking oil
2 cups okra, sliced crossways
5 medium tomatoes, peeled and
    chopped
½ cup chopped celery
½ cup chopped onion
½ cup chopped green pepper
½ cup chopped red pepper
2 cloves garlic, minced
2 cups beef boullion (can be made
    from cubes)
2 teaspoons salt
¼ teaspoon pepper
¼ teaspoon thyme
1 bay leaf
⅛ teaspoon Louisiana hot sauce (or
    Tabasco sauce)
rice, cooked separately
filé (optional)

Heat the oil in a large skillet (or Dutch oven) and sauté the onion, garlic, celery, green pepper, and red pepper. Add the beef boullion, okra, tomato, salt, pepper, thyme, bay leaf, and hot sauce. Cover and simmer for 30 minutes. Add the shellfish. Cover and simmer for 10 to15 minutes. Put about a cup of rice into individual soup bowls, then fill with hot gumbo. Have filé at hand in case anyone wants to thicken their gumbo a bit—but it's best not to put filé into the main pot. It's tricky stuff and should be used cautiously. *Serves 7 or 8.*

Boiling Shrimp, Crabs, and Lobster

Whenever I head through Florida, I'll drive a hundred miles out of my way to eat at a little cafe at Salt Springs, in the Big Scrub or Ocala National Forest. They have a special blue crab that grows there (many miles from the ocean) but I think that the real secret is that the people in the Scrub know how to cook them! And it's easy. It's very easy. It's too easy, perhaps. Nonetheless, it is the best way to cook any kind of crab from any part of the country.

Boil the crabs for 10 minutes. If you want to get fancy, add a little salt to the boiling water. (Add 1 cup of salt per gallon or water; better, use seawater if you've got it nearby.) Pile the crabs onto a platter in the middle of the table. Get the meat out the best way you can. Dip the meat in a mixture of half melted butter and half lemon juice.

Of course, when boiling you can add all manner of New Orleans spices to the crabs (or shrimp), or you can buy a commercial crab boil mix, which is usually sold packaged

in easy-to-use cloth bags. But I prefer mine simple. Note that no matter how much spice you put in them, crabs will not be good if you boil them too long. Of course, my "ten minute" rule of thumb will have to be modified for cooking very large crabs or stone crab claws. Also, note that, for best results, there should be lots of water in the pot in relation to the number of crabs. If you add too many crabs, the water will cool and cease to boil, giving your pot an unconstant temperature and making a guessing game out of cooking crabs. Note also that some adjustment will have to be made at high elevations. If in doubt, remember that the crab is "done" when the "apron" starts to rise.

Pea Crab

You may find more inside an oyster shell than just the oyster. Many oysters serve as host for the tiny pea crab, or oyster crab. The small crabs take up residence as larvae. The females live permanently with their host, but the males are free-moving. At maturity, the females are pink, one inch in diameter, and soft-shelled. They neither hurt nor help their host, the oyster, but merely share its food.

Fishermen have long recognized the pea crab as a seafood delicacy. Many a fisherman will demonstrate his or her fondness for the tiny crabs by consuming them alive. Others eat the crab steamed along with their oysters or sautéed in butter.

—*Coastal Carolina Cooking*

For shrimp in the shell, use the method set forth above, but boil for only five minutes for normal shrimp. Don't put too many into the pot. Jumbo shrimp may take a little longer. The shells will turn pink when they are ready to eat. If in doubt, try one.

Personally, I prefer to boil the whole shrimp and clean them at the table, as they are eaten. I also like them with the head removed, but with the shell still on. Again, I prefer mine cooked plain, with a little salt in the boiling water, and with a dipping sauce made of half melted butter and half lemon juice. Leftovers (if any) can be refrigerated and eaten cold, possibly with a little red cocktail sauce. It's best to shuck and devein the shrimp when eating them cold.

Lobster and "saltwater crawfish" can be boiled by exactly the same method described above. Just use more water and increase the cooking time. Normally, a lobster of regular size will require about 15 minutes, but of course a huge 30-pound granddaddy will take longer. In any case, the lobster will turn bright red when it is ready.

Many recipes for shrimp, crab, and lobster salad and so on call for boiled meat. All these recipes will be better if you do not cook the shrimp, crab, or lobster too long.

Deep Fried Crab Patties

This is a very tasty dish, which can be prepared with pure crab meat or with a combination of crab meat, fish flakes, finely diced shrimp, and so on. It should, however, contain at least half crab meat.

½ pound cooked crab meat
oil for deep frying
½ cup dry Italian bread crumbs
2 tablespoons finely diced onions
2 tablespoons mayonnaise
salt and pepper
½ teaspoon powdered mustard
½ teaspoon white wine Worcestershire
  sauce

Drain the crab meat well, then mix it with bread crumbs, mustard, mayonnaise, salt and pepper to taste, and Worcestershire sauce. Shape it into patties of between ½ and ¾ inch thick. Heat oil for deep frying and cook until they are golden brown. *Serves 2 or 3.*

Eels and Lampreys

The culinary history of eels and lampreys goes back thousands of years. Over the centuries they have been held in high regard in France and England. It was the annual custom for the City of Gloucester to present a lamprey pie to the British monarch. The importance of the eel to an Englishman has been such that even when England and Holland were at war the eel trade carried on uninterrupted, and the Dutch eel barges, holds bulging with the slithering live fish, ploughed up the Thames to the London markets.

—Frances MacIlquham,
Fish Cookery of North America

Fried Eel

I've eaten some fried eel that was good, and some that wasn't. It is best to have small or medium-sized eels, no heavier than 1 pound each. Skin the eels, bone them, and cut them into 4-inch pieces. Salt and pepper the pieces, shake them in cornmeal, and pan fry each piece in very hot oil until it is brown on both sides. Always eat eel shortly after it has been caught—and eat it hot.

Smoked Eel

Many people regard hot smoking as the very best way to prepare eels, and of course there are dozens of variations. Here's a basic recipe

that I adapted from *Home Book of Smoke-Cooking Meat, Fish & Game*. First, prepare a brine with:

4 gallons water
8 cups salt
1 pound dark brown sugar
1½ cups lemon juice
2 tablespoons liquid garlic
2 tablespons liquid onion

Dissolve the salt in the water, then mix in the other ingredients. (Note that you can reduce the above measures proportionally if you don't have many eels to smoke.) Skin and gut the eels while they are very fresh. Soak them in the brine for one hour. Rinse.

Have a pot of boiling water ready. Dip the eels for a few seconds in the boiling water, which will make the cavity open up. Then smoke the eels over your favorite green hardwood at 140 degrees. Small eels will be ready to eat in 2 hours, but large eels may take up to 4 hours.

a fork and bake for 10 minutes, until browned slightly. Mix flaked eel and cheese. Spread evenly in pie shell. Mix eggs and cream. Pour on flaked eel and cheeses. Place in oven, reduce heat to 325 degrees, and bake for an hour. *Serves 4.*

Baked Eel

Here's an interesting recipe from the Maine Department of Marine Resources: "Clean and skin eels and cut in 3-inch pieces without splitting open. Twist out intestines with a knife, fork or piece of wood. Lay pieces of fat salt pork in a baking pan and add the pieces of eel. Bake in 350-degree oven until well done."

Eel Quiche

If you've got a small eel and don't know what else to do with it, try this:

½ pound of dressed eel
1 pie shell, unbaked (9-inch)
6 ounces Swiss cheese, grated
1 cup light cream (or half-and-half)
2 eggs
1 tablespoon flour
salt
pepper

Preheat oven to 450 degrees. Poach the eel for 20 minutes and flake it with a fork; salt and pepper meat to taste. Prick pie shell with

Frying a Carp

Here's a method that I got from Euell Gibbons, and I've seen variations of it printed in other sources. Get a very fresh carp. Skin it and, using your fingers and thumb, tear pieces of flesh from the backbone. Salt these pieces and fry them in very hot peanut oil for a few minutes. Use nothing but salt on the fish. Eat while quite hot. Too easy? Try it. We've got a lot of carp in our waters that need eating!

Carp for a King?

I base the recipe below (and the title above) on a column in *Outdoor Life* by C.B. Colby. It's good, but I've never felt quite right about eating carp at home. Or at least not in my home. Of course, I know that in some lands, such as China, the carp is highly regarded as table fare. It's often steamed.

My problem is that I never feel that I am getting the very best that the fish has to offer. The foreign masters of carp cookery, I understand, keep these bottom feeders in special tanks for several days before cooking them, thereby flushing out the flavor of mud. I could catch carp and get them home alive, but I personally have no carp holding tank on my premises, and I haven't yet figured out a good way to keep them. My wife raised hell about two dozen little crappie minnows that I kept in the bathtub for a day or two, and I'm not going to test our bonds with a couple of 5-pound carp nosing about in the tub!

But . . . the following recipe is a good one when cooked with or without the aid of a carp holding tank. If you don't have a tank, it's best to dress the carp soon after catching it, then ice it down as soon as possible. Skinning the fish helps.

> **2 pounds of carp fillets, skinned and**
> **   boneless**
> **1 medium onion, chopped**
> **1 cup of dry bread crumbs**
> **1 teaspoon salt**
> **¼ teaspoon pepper**
> **½ teaspoon paprika**
> **⅛ teaspoon thyme**
> **⅛ teaspoon celery salt**
> **1 bay leaf, powdered**
> **1 tablespoon chopped parsley**
> **butter**
> **water**
> **6 tablespoons of fresh lemon juice**
> **   (used in two batches)**

Turn oven to 300 degrees. Butter an oblong baking dish of suitable size and sprinkle the onions on the bottom. Arrange carp fillets on onion bed. Mix the breadcrumbs, 1 teaspoon salt, pepper, paprika, thyme, celery salt, powered bay leaf, and parsley. Sprinkle this mixture over the fillets, then dot with pieces of butter. Next, mix 3 tablespoons of lemon juice with ½ cup of water, then sprinkle it evenly over the fish. Bake for 15 minutes in preheated 300-degree oven. Mix the remaining 3 tablespoons of lemon juice with ½ cup of water and sprinkle it evenly over the fish. Bake for another 15 minutes, or until the breadcrumbs are browned. Remove from oven and let it sit for a few minutes before eating. *Serves 4 to 6.*

Gar Balls Toogoodoo

Here's a recipe that has been adapted from *The South Carolina Wildlife Cookbook*. The original was submitted to that publication by James M. Bishop of Charleston.

> **2 pounds garfish meat, flaked**
> **1 pound potatoes, mashed**
> **2 large onions, chopped fine**
> **1 cup (or more) of mixed parsley,**
> **   green onions, and celery tops,**
> **   chopped**
> **½ cup prepared yellow mustard**
> **½ cup vinegar**
> **flour**
> **cooking oil**

First, mix a sauce of yellow mustard and vinegar. Then mix fish, potatoes, onions, and vegetables. Shape fish mixture into balls about 1½ inches in diameter. Roll in mustard sauce and flour, then deep fry. *Serves 6 or 7.*

Sautéed Bay Scallops

If you see people wading about with a long-handled dip net in a shallow saltwater bay, they may be after scallops, especially if there is some eelgrass growing in the area. Unlike the oyster, the adult scallop constantly moves about in the water by opening and closing its shell. In so doing, it develops a muscle, and this is what we normally eat. When you "shuck" a scallop, the muscle should be cut on either end very close to the shell.

The small bay scallop makes better table fare than the other species, and it is the one more often taken by sportsmen. The flavor is quite delicate, and I cook it delicately.

fresh scallops, dressed
butter
salt

Heat some butter in a frying pan and add a little salt to it. Sauté the scallops for a few minutes, until they start to brown. Do not overcook. Drain on absorbent paper, but don't let them get cold.

A Better Scallop

The amateur can obtain scallops of better quality than those commonly marketed. Because they are somewhat difficult to produce in quantity, commercial distributors often put scallops through a process of "soaking," which depletes the delicate flavor of a fresh bivalve. The small cream-colored eye, or adductor muscle, which is the part that goes to market, is placed in freshwater for several hours until the meat has absorbed enough water to increase the bulk by about one-third. Actually, this improves the appearance of the scallop in that it becomes very white, but, from an epicurean standpoint, the flavor is inferior.

—*McClane's New Standard Fishing Encyclopedia*

Squid and Octopus

If you tie into a squid or octopus, remember that they can be cooked in a number of ways. The body as well as the tentacles are eaten. Sometimes the body is stuffed, but more often the meat is cut into thin strips and pounded to tenderize it. The larger specimens are especially tough. Use any good deep frying recipe for squid or octopus.

The orientals hold the octopus in high esteem as table fare, and the peoples around the Mediterranean region consider the squid to be a delicacy. Some of the French even stuff squid bodies with chopped tentacles and *spinach*!

Fried Bowfin or Mudfish

Here is a fish that fights harder than anything that swims, and it terrorizes bass anglers in the south and up the Mississippi drainage system. It covers mid-America, and is as game as a fish can be. Some people call them mudfish, grindle, cypress trout, blackfish, and so on.

In any case, the bowfin is eaten in some areas. First, start by bleeding the fish as soon as it is caught. This is accomplished by making a cut on both sides just above the tail. Skin the fish and fillet it. Salt and pepper to taste, shake in flour, and fry quickly in very hot peanut oil. *Eat it very hot.* If it cools, the flesh is spongy, like cotton. Note that the end of the fillet toward the tail is better than the the other end.

This same method can be used to fry other fish that are not noted for taste and texture.

Clam Fritters

I love raw clams, but I am very uncomfortable about eating them because of water pollution. I therefore recommend that they be cooked in a good chowder recipe, or as follows:

> **2 cups chopped clams**
> **1 egg, beaten**
> **¼ cup flour**
> **¼ cup white cornmeal**
> **salt and pepper**
> **¼ cup green onions, tops and all, very**
> **finely diced**

Mix all the ingredients in a bowl. Heat oil in a frying pan and test one spoonful of fritter mixture. If it doesn't hold together well when you turn it with a spatula, add a little more flour to mixture. If the texture is right, continue to cook patties on both sides until they are golden brown. *Serves 4 or 5.*

Fried Oysters

Fried oysters happen to be one of my very favorite foods, and I've tried all manner of egg dips and batters. I much prefer to have them freshly shucked than in a bucket. Fresh oysters have more taste, and, if they are taken on low tide in the fall of the year, they require no seasoning. If I've got fresh oysters, and shuck them myself, here's all I want:

> **oysters**
> **saltine crackers**
> **oil**

Crush some fresh crackers quite finely with a rolling pin. Heat at least ½ inch of oil in a frying pan. Shuck the oysters—but do not wash or drain them. Drop the oysters one by one into the cracker crumbs, then roll or shake. Fry the oysters in hot oil for three or four minutes, or until browned.

Note: If you cook many oysters by this method, you'll need to change oil and clean the burnt cracker crumbs from the bottom of your frying pan. Have two pans ready if you've got lots of folks to feed.

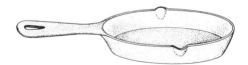

Steamed Periwinkles

These are small snail-like molluscs that cling to rocks and pilings and other structures in and around saltwater. There are over a hundred species—all good to eat. Steam them over boiling water for 10 minutes, or until their "cap" can be lifted. Stick the steamed periwinkle with a toothpick and pull it out of the shell. Dip it into a bowl of melted, lightly salted butter and eat directly from the toothpick.

Conch, Whelk, and Abalone

There are several kinds of conch and whelks, all of which are a sort of marine snail. I don't have any sort of scientific breakdown, but my rule of thumb to separate them from the periwinkle is size. Conch and whelks are big enough to take more seriously. They are all edible saltwater mollusks—and all are tough.

There are several ways to separate the meat from the shell, but the most widely used method is to boil the whole thing for about 15 minutes, then pull the meat from the shell. Use only the muscular foot part, which must be cut away from the rest. Often, the meat is pounded with a mallet, chopped up finely, ground up, and steamed in a pressure cooker before it is used in recipes. It can be made into fritters, or sliced thinly and fried. Usually, however, the meat is used in a chowder. (See the recipe in Chapter 7.)

Abalone is a sort of large California version of conch and is also tough. The meat (or foot) can be tenderized by pounding it with the edge of a plate or with a meat mallet. The meat is usually cooked in a chowder, but of course it can also be cooked in other ways, including baking. Try cutting it into thin strips (about ⅛ inch thick), salting and peppering to taste, shaking in flour, and frying it in butter. Abalone does not keep well and should be eaten right away or kept quite cold.

Skates & Rays

In case you tangle with a big skate or ray, here's some good information from UNC Sea Grant's brochure, *Skates and Rays*:

"Unfrozen or uncooked skate and ray meat will not keep as long as bony fish. Once a skate dies it spoils rapidly because it contains urea. This fluid is broken down quickly by surface bacteria, forming ammonia which gives the meat a strong odor and bitter taste. The animal must be dressed within 15 to 20 minutes after it is caught. The most usable portion of the skate or ray is the wings, although roasts from the back section can be obtained from large rays. After you've pulled in your catch, cut off the pectoral fin (wings) on each side of the fish, and rinse thoroughly to remove any excess blood. . . . Discard the head and body. If the fish is large, wings can be skinned, but this is difficult and not necessary. To skin a skate or ray, peel away the hide. Make a cut under the skin to get a skin flap big enough to grip. Grip the skin with one hand, then use the other to cut back with a sharp fillet knife. It will be easier and quicker to leave about one-fourth of an inch of meat attached to the skin. Skinned meat can be cut into chunks and sautéed or pan fried. If you choose not to skin, skates and rays can be cooked or frozen with the skin on. The skin is easily removed after poaching.

"Before cooking or freezing, it is important to soak the fish in a brine or acidic solution to remove any excess urea. Salt, vinegar, milk or lemon juice can be used for this. A standard salt or vinegar solution is one cup of salt or half cup of white vinegar to one gallon of water. Since the meat becomes firmer in vinegar than in salt, it is recommended that the fish be placed in a cool area (refrigerator) for four to eight hours in brine and four hours in vinegar. Skates and rays can be left in lemon juice or milk for up to 24 hours. Milk soaking is often used when the skate will be deep fried, while lemon soaking is recommended for broiling recipes. After brining, the skin should be scraped with a knife and rinsed.

"Skates and rays become very dry if overcooked. They can be prepared by steaming, broiling, baking, boiling, or barbecuing. Frying is probably the most difficult method, because skate meat contains a lot of mositure that causes the grease or oil to splatter. Cooked fish flakes when brushed with a fork. The cooking period is short: five to eight minutes for steaming, 10 minutes for broiling, and 10 to 20 minutes for baking."

16

RAW, SMOKED, and PRESERVED FISH

One reason that I moved back to the small town where I was raised is that oysters from Apalachicola Bay are available in cafe bars. During my lifetime, I must have eaten a bargeload of these oysters. But I won't eat them from just anywhere, and not in just any oyster bar.

A few years ago, Lew Childre landed a large airplane near my home and unloaded a bunch of people. He came on business with me, and to see a little boat that my nephew, David Livingston, was making. Among the company was a very important fishing tackle fellow from Japan, the vice president of a large reel manufacturing company. Also with them was a guy from Arkansas who made his way in the world by selling fishing tackle to underdeveloped countries, and he had some good stories about unloading half a million dollars worth of leadhead jigs to Saudi Arabia. This fellow got interested in a local hot-dog, which was billed as the World's Best. He must have thought so because he ate enough to kill a normal man. Maybe he was thinking on getting the franchise for Iceland or somewhere.

Anyhow, everyone ate a lot—but the Japanese businessman really stole the show and became the talk of our town. He ate only oysters. Raw. Oysters only. No crackers. No sauce. Nothing. He picked up the half shell and slurped the oyster, swallowing it without chewing. After the rest of us had filled up and were smoking and talking good fishing, this guy kept eating Apalachicola oysters. It was unbelievable, what with him being so little. More than once the waitress had to clean the shells off the table. Recalling this event later, David Livingston said that it was probably the only home cooked meal that the guy had eaten since he left Japan!

In addition to oysters, I've also eaten various dishes made with raw meat and fowl, and, of course, I have eaten sushi. Frankly, I like these dishes, but I'm uncomfortable about eating them these days. The main risk involves various kinds of food poisoning and such diseases as hepatitis, as well as anisakis worms. (I might add, however, that I don't like to trust supermarkets, either, and I usually cook store bought chicken until I'm sure that it is well done.) So . . . if you want to eat raw fish, that's up to you. But if you do it is usually best to catch your own from a clean steam, dress it out yourself, and store it properly until you are ready to eat.

In addition to a few recipes for raw fish, I am also including in this chapter some recipes for fish that have been smoked, canned, salted, or pickled at home. Remember that some pickled and cold smoked fish aren't really cooked.

California Yellowtail

This ocean fish, an amberjack, is quite popular in California and Baja California waters. The fish is high in oil content, and it is best when grilled, broiled, or smoked. It is also canned. Some anglers rate it highly as a food fish.

Ceviche

Here's a tasty dish, from Mexico, that can be served as an appetizer, a salad, or as a lunch or light meal. But it has to be made several days ahead of time. I make it with bass and other such fish, but the Mexicans use most anything that swims in fresh or salt water, including conch, clams, and oysters.

1 pound fish fillets
5 limes
1 lemon
dry wine
2 medium onions, finely chopped
5 green onions and tops, finely
  chopped
1 can tomatoes (16-ounce size)
1 can tomato sauce (8-ounce size)
½ cup bell peppers, finely chopped
2 fresh hot peppers, minced
2 tablespoons capers
1 teaspoon sweet basil
1 teaspoon oregano
1 teaspoon coriander
2 tablespoons cilantro leaves, finely
  chopped (or 1 tablespoon
  dried cilantro leaves)
1 tablespoon Tabasco sauce
olive oil

Dice the fish (or other seafood) and put into a glass container. Add the juice from five limes and one lemon. Then pour in enough wine to cover fish. Refrigerate for at least 24 hours.

After 24 hours, add chopped onion, green onions, tomatoes (remove the hard core and chop the rest), tomato sauce, capers, bell pepper, hot pepper, oregano, basil, coriander, cilantro, and Tabasco sauce. Stir and refrigerate for at least a few hours. (Ceviche will keep for about ten days.)

Add a little olive oil on individual helpings before serving. I serve it up in salad bowls, then pour on ½ teaspoon oil. Crisp wheat crackers go nicely with ceviche. *Serves 4 or 5 for a light lunch.*

SALT CURED FISH

Curing fish with salt is easy, and the results are good, at least to me, although many people on a low-sodium diet will of course stay clear of such fare. Traditionally, fish are salted and stored in a wooden barrel or wooden box. Other containers can also be used, but avoid anything with metal. The fish I've salted were in a large styrofoam ice chest, and it's rectangular shape worked nicely.

Buy a *large* bag of pickling or noniodized salt. It's cheap in large quantities, and you'll need lots of it anyway.

Cut the fish in half. Remove the innards and the head, but do *not* scale or skin. Sprinkle a layer of salt on the bottom of your container. Add a layer of fish, skin side down. Then put another layer of salt and another layer of fish, etc. Put the top layer of fish skin side up, then top with a thick layer of salt. Cover and leave for a week. A "pickle" or brine will form as the salt draws the moisture from the fish. The fish, in turn, will shrink in size and the flesh will become firmer. Pour off this brine and remove the fish.

Prepare a fresh brine by first boiling some water and then adding salt to it until it will float a raw egg. Make enough of this brine to half fill your container. Then put the fish back into it, and add some crushed peppercorns. Cover with a cloth and leave in a dark, cool place for two weeks. The fish can be stored for several months in the brine, or it can be packaged and frozen. Note also that salt fish can be removed from the brine and smoked without much ado.

It's a good idea to keep the top layer of fish under salt or brine at all times. Putting a weighted plate or platter over the fish helps, and some people cut a wooden board for this purpose. For a rectangular ice chest, I recommend one or more pyrex baking dishes partly filled with water for weight.

I've eaten salted fish *raw*. I rinsed it, re-

Ciguatoxin

Some tropical and subtropical reef fish can carry ciguatoxin. It is produced by microalgae, and it can accumulate in the flesh of fish that eat it. Also, it can accumulate to dangerous levels in predator fish, such as as barracuda, amberjack, and jack crevalle. Although ciguatoxin is seldom fatal, it can produce some frightening short term effects.

The chances of a fish from American waters having dangerous amounts of ciguatoxin are slim. The danger is limited to waters around deep reefs, and usually involve the larger fish. Small barracuda and jacks from coastal flats are usually safe.

moved the skin, sliced it very thinly, and ate it atop crackers. It was good, but I recommend that you try one of the following recipes:

Oyette Taylor's Salt Crappie

Here's a good one from my barber, who salts fish and then freezes them. Put the salt-cured crappie into a glass container with water. Soak for 18 hours, changing water several times. Wash fish with a pressure hose, then scale. Heat oil in a skillet. Dry fish, shake in cornmeal, and fry until browned.

Oyette says that salting the crappie firms up the flesh without making it strong, resulting in a good-tasting fish that is like no other.

Salt Fish Balls

 1 cup salt fish, finely flaked
 3 medium potatoes, diced (about 4
   cups)
 1 egg, separated
 2 tablespoons margarine or butter
 ⅛ teaspoon black pepper
 flour
 cooking oil

Put fish and potatoes into a small saucepan and cover with hot water. Cook until potatoes are tender. Drain, let cool, and put into blender container. Add butter, pepper, and

---

Rainbow Trout

Although it is medium to high in oil, the rainbow fries well and can be cooked by any other method. As a rule, fish from free-flowing streams are better than commercially raised trout.

---

yolk of egg. Blend on high for half a minute. Beat egg white slightly by hand, then add to mixture and blend on medium speed for half a minute.

Let mixture cool in refrigerator for an hour or so, then shape it into balls and roll in flour. Heat cooking oil in a deep fryer. When oil is hot, fry fish balls until they are golden brown. Serves 4 or 5.

Note: These fish balls tend to soak up lots of grease and should be used only as an appetizer. If you like the flavor, however, and want to serve something similar for a lunch or for a dinner, try making small patties from the balls. Then cook them on a sparsely greased hot griddle.

Gulf Coast Breakfast

During the great Depression some fifty or sixty years ago, most of the southern towns had electricity, but many of the rural sections did not. The folk who peopled these areas relied partly on salt fish, trucked up from the Gulf of Mexico in barrels or wooden boxes, as a sort of staple food. The markets in every country town, and every crossroads store, as well as all the rolling stores, had at least one barrel of fish delivered weekly. The widespread availability of electricity and ready refrigeration has all but eliminated the barrels and wooden boxes, but salt fish, wrapped in plastic now, are still available in some supermarkets and fish markets.

Anyhow, here's the way that my father and grandfather ate, and liked, mullet for breakfast:

> **2 pounds salt mullet**
> **cooking oil**
> **fine white cornmeal**
> **grits**
> **biscuits from scratch**
> **butter**
> **pepper**

Soak mullet overnight in cold water. An hour before dawn, get up and build a fire in the wood stove. Draw a bucket of water out of the well. Put on the coffee and heat up the oven for cooking biscuits. Prepare dough, roll it, and cut out the biscuits. Put biscuits into the oven. Drain fish. Heat oil in frying pan. Shake fish in fine cornmeal and fry until done. Cook grits while fish are frying. If your timing is right, everything will hit the plates while hot. Dish out grits and top with butter. Butter the biscuits. Break up the fish and stir in with the grits. Pepper to taste. Eat with a fork, using a biscuit half to help get a good mouthful. (Hard or lumpy grits "ain't fit to eat" and grits that are too soupy won't work with a fork.) The procedure is made easier by placing both elbows firmly on the table and lowering the head directly over the plate. *Serves 5 or 6 for breakfast.*

Cod Cakes Nova Scotia

I must have caught, or snatched, a ton of cod somewhere north of Halifax, using some sort of heavy lead fowl-hooking jig that I bought from an enterprising Eskimo. The cod is a fine fish in abundant supply, and is often salted, just as mullet are salted around the Gulf Coast. The following recipe came from the Home Economist section of the Nova Scotia Department of Fisheries—folks who know that they are talking about.

> **1 pound salt cod or other salt fish**
> **2 cups cooked mashed potatoes**
> **¼ cup of finely chopped onion**
> **¼ cup of finely chopped parsley**
> **¼ cup grated cheddar cheese**
> **1 teaspoon black pepper**
> **cooking oil**
> **dry bread crumbs**

Soak the salt fish overnight in cold water. Change water once if convenient. When you're ready to cook, simmer the fish for 10 or 15 minutes, or until it flakes easily when tested with a fork. Drain the fish and flake it, being careful to remove all bones. Mix fish flakes, mashed potatoes, onion, parsley, cheese, and pepper. Form the mixture into patties, like small pancakes. Roll in bread crumbs, coating lightly. Heat a little oil (very little) and fry the cakes for 2 or 3 minutes on each side, or until golden brown. *Serves 4.*

PS: The last time I saw a cod-snatching jig was in Columbus, Mississippi, home of an Air Force SAC base. It's a wierd looking thing, about 5 inches long, made of solid lead, and weighs about 2 pounds. The thing curves around a little, like a banana, only it is flat and has a huge hook sticking out of one end. The line is tied to the other end, and the heavy jig is dropped to the bottom in deep water, then snatched up. It's shape makes it curve up, causing the hook to arc around and stick into a low-lying cod's belly. Anyhow, I saw one in a tackle shop in Columbus, Mississippi. It no doubt came from one of the Air Force boys who had spent some time in Tuhle.

I asked the guy in the tackle shop how much it costs. He laughed and asked what in the world I wanted with it. To his surprise, I told him that I was going cod snatching in the Tombigbee!

Rougaille of Salted Fish

Here's a recipe from Mauritius Island that I found in *The Africa News Cookbook*. After cooking the dish several times, it has become one of my favorite ways of preparing salted fish. Remember that salt fish goes a long way, and the measures listed below will *serve 3 or 4*.

1 pound dried salted fish
¼ cup cooking oil
2 cups chopped onions
2 sprigs parsley, chopped
6 green onions with tops, chopped
2 cups cherry tomatoes, halved
2 cloves garlic, minced
**2 teaspoons fresh ginger, grated, or 1
   teaspoon ground ginger**
rice (cooked separately)

Put the salted fish in a crockery or glass container, cover with plenty of water, and soak overnight in the refrigerator. Changing the water once or twice will help.

Heat the oil in a frying pan and sauté the fish for 5 or 6 minutes. Add onions, garlic, parsley, green onions, and tomatoes. Stir un-

---

Rackling

This product was introduced to this country by Scandinavian fishermen who prepare it for home use. Large flounder, halibut, pollock, cust, hake, rock cod, or similar fish with a fat content of about 2 per cent are suitable. The head is removed, leaving the collarbone. The fish is split into two sides and the backbone removed. then the sides are cut in long, narrow strips about an inch in width, left joined together at the collarbone. They are soaked in saturated salt brine for 1 hour. They are hung out to dry, preferably in a shady place where they will not be exposed to direct sunlight. Drying requires from 1 to 2 weeks. When wanted for use, the rackling may be soaked for a few hours, and steamed and made into fish cakes, fish loaf, or creamed fish. It is most often eaten like jerked meat, however, without any preliminary preparation.

—Frank G. Ashbrook,
*Butchering, Processing
and Preservation of Meat*

til onions are soft. Stir in ginger. Simmer for 15 to 20 minutes. Serve over rice.

SMOKED FISH

I have heard that my grandfather, Jefferson Livingston, had the first bathtub in our part of the country. He put it in the smokehouse. But this was logical, logistically speaking.

They had no running water inside the house. Nor did the smokehouse have running water, but it was next to the well and it did contain a large iron pot for boiling water. The reason they had no running water was that there was no electricity to run a pump, and of course there was no "city" water. I don't want to give the impression that my grandfather was in any way backward. He was, in fact, ahead of his times. (Who else had a bathtub in the smokehouse?) He even had gas lighting inside the house, whereas most of the few folks

THREE BASIC SMOKERS

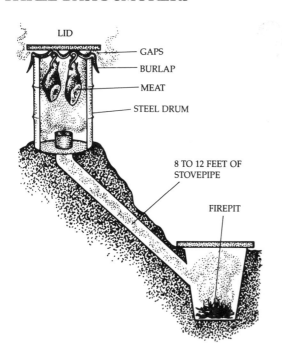

Typical cold smoker handmade from a steel drum and stovepipe.

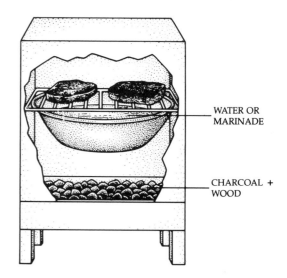

Commercial hot smoker.

in this part of the country had kerosene lamps. There are, in fact, still copper pipes running all over the attic of my house (I bought the old homeplace). They led out to a gas "generator," which was also in the smokehouse.

I can remember my father smoking hams and sausage in the smokehouse, but it was torn down a few years ago and, like most other modern men, I have to make do with a portable cold smoker and a hinged-top "smoke" oven. I keep thinking that I'll make

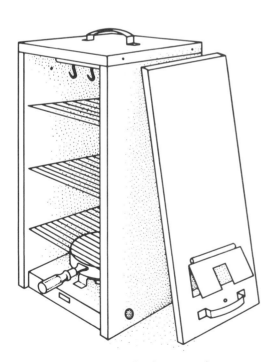

Commercial portable (hot) smoker.

a larger facility for smoking, and I've saved both an old refrigerator and a heavy-duty metal barrel. I've even saved old magazine articles and book chapters about making larger smokers. But I don't think I'll ever actually build one—and I doubt that many readers of this book will either. It's just too easy to buy good portable smokers these days.

Smoking is, of course, an aid in preserving food, but modern refrigerators and freezers alleviate many of the needs for smoking, salting, canning, and pickling. Usually, modern chefs use smoke primarily for flavor. There are three basic types of smoking: cold, hot, and that done on a smoker/cooker. Most of the really hot smoking these days is done in the smoker/cooker units, and is covered in the chapter on patio cooking.

Cold-smoking, as the name implies, does not cook the meat. It will help preserve meat, but it's the flavor that most people are after. To me, it is by far the best way to smoke fish. Cold-smoked fish has a flavor like no other. If flavor is the only consideration, I much prefer to eat cold smoked fish without cooking it—but I must smoke it myself and I must catch and dress the fish myself. Thus, I will know that I have healthy fish from good water, fresh fish properly cared for, and correctly smoked. I strongly advise other people to be equally fussy. In any case, true cold smoking must take place at temperatures of around 90 degrees, and this usually must be accomplished by having a firebox and green hardwood some distance from the meat racks. Obviously, most people will not often practice this method.

Usually, *heat-smoking* will be used, and this method sort of splits the difference between the patio "smoker/cookers" and true cold smoking. Most of the small home smoking units, converted refrigerators, and so on fall into this category. For heat smoking, the temperature is usually between 110 and 120 degrees.

Before cold smoking or heat smoking, the meat must first be "cured" with salt, sugar, and pepper. Sometimes spices or herbs are also added. Here is a basic brine:

> 1 gallon of water
> pickling salt
> ¼ cup brown sugar or molasses
> 1 tablespoon black pepper

Mix salt in the water until the solution will float a raw egg. Then stir in brown sugar and pepper. Soak small fish or fillets for 8 to 10 hours in the brine. Larger fish will take longer, and a 4-pound whole fish will take two days or so. When you are ready to smoke the fish, hang it in a cool, shady place until a pellicle forms. Then hang them in the smoker, or place them on racks, and smoke at about 120 degrees for several hours. Thin fillets may be ready in an hour, and small whole fish may be ready in 2 hours. Larger fish may take 4 hours or longer. Smoking is influenced by too many factors to be pinned down exactly in a book like this. Until much experience is gained, the taste and wait method is the best way to proceed. It also helps to keep careful notes on the kind of fish you smoke, times, temperatures, and so on.

If you have purchased a commercial smoker, be sure to read the instructions carefully.

In any case, I am not certain whether *heat-smoked* fish is cooked or not. Nor am I certain how long it can be stored in the refrigerator. Yet, I am very, very fond of the flavor of such fish, and I love to eat it on crackers. But, as I said above, the process is not exact, and many people will want to cook the fish some more, as in the next recipe.

Smoked Fish Patties

> 2 cups cold- or heat-smoked fish,
>   flaked or diced
> 2 cups mashed potatoes
> ½ cup bread crumbs
> ½ cup finely chopped onions
> ¼ cup parsley flakes
> 2 eggs
> cooking oil
> salt and pepper to taste
> lemon

Sauté onion in 2 tablespoons of cooking oil. Whisk two eggs. Then mix all ingredients except lemon. Shape into patties. Brown

Smoke Big Minnows

The Northern squawfish, a true minnow, often weighs 10 pounds, and a related fish, the Colorado squawfish, can weigh up to 80 pounds! The fish are bony, but they can be quite tasty when smoked properly. Other methods of preparing the squawfish are not highly recommended.

both sides in cooking oil, turning carefully. Drain on absorbent paper before placing on serving platters or plates. Garnish with lemon slices or wedges. In fact, a little lemon juice squeezed atop each pattie really enhances the flavor of this dish. *Serves 4 to 6.*

them to the bowl, along with the fish. Combine thoroughly but gently.

Just before serving, cut the avocados in half, remove pits, and fill cavities with the fish mixture. Garnish with pepper or pimento, and pass around the remaining lime juice to sprinkle on individual servings. *Serves 2 for lunch, or 4 as a side dish.*

Avocado with Smoked Fish

If you are as fond as I am of both avocado and smoked fish, you'll welcome a recipe that puts them together. It's from Ghana, and I got it from *The Africa News Cookbook.*

½ **pound smoked fish**
4 **eggs, hard-boiled, with whites**
   separated from yolks
¼ **cup milk**
¼ **cup lime juice**
¼ **teaspoon sugar**
½ **teaspoon salt**
⅓ **cup light cooking oil**
2 **tablespoons olive oil**
2 **large ripe avocados**
1 **large red bell pepper, or a dozen**
   pimentos from a can or jar

Remove the skin and bones from the fish and flake the flesh with a fork. In a deep bowl, mash the egg yolks with the milk until they form a smooth paste. Add sugar, salt, and 1 tablespoon of the lime juice. Then beat in the vegetable oil, a teaspoon or so at a time. Add the olive oil in the same gradual manner. Chop egg whites finely and add

Potato Salad with Smoked Fish

Cold-smoked fish is very, very good in this recipe. But unless you know the fish came from clean waters and was properly prepared, you might want to hot smoke it instead.

1 **pound smoked fish, flaked**
2 **cups of diced potatoes, cooked**
1 **stalk of celery, chopped**
¼ **cup sliced olives**
½ **cup diced onion**
1 **tablespoon chopped parsley**
juice from ½ lemon
¼ **cup good mayonnaise**
1 **tablespoon prepared mustard**
1 **teaspoon wine vinegar**
salt and pepper to taste
¼ **teaspoon celery seed**
1 **small jar chopped pimento**
   (optional)

Flake the fish and toss with potatoes, celery, onion, parsley, olives, and chopped pimento (for color). In a separate bowl, mix mayonnaise, mustard, vinegar, and celery seed. Mix with fish and vegetables. Salt and pepper to taste. Chill for an hour or so before eating. *Serves 4 or 5.*

Variation: if you've got plenty of ripe tomatoes, chill one for each person, core, and stuff with potato salad. Serve on a lettuce leaf.

Smoked Fish Quiche

This recipe can be used with either cold-smoked or heat-smoked fish. Also try it with leftover fish from a patio smoker/cooker.

 1 cup smoked fish, flaked
 1 cup grated Swiss cheese
 1 ready-to-bake pie shell (9-inch)
 4 eggs
 2 cups cream
 2 tablespoons parsley, chopped
 ½ teaspoon salt
 ⅛ teaspoon white pepper (or a pinch of cayenne)

Preheat oven to 425 degrees. Mix fish and cheese, then sprinkle into the pie shell. Mix other ingredients and spoon into pie shell. Bake for 10 minutes; reduce heat to 300 degrees and bake for another 40 minutes, or until done. (To test: insert a kitchen knife blade into the center of the quiche; if the blade comes out clean, the dish is done.) Let it cool a few minutes, then cut into wedges. *Serves 4 to 6.*

CANNING FISH

One of my favorite lunches during a day-long fishing trip is a can of sardines, salmon, or tuna eaten on crackers, along with a little cheese and a big cola drink. Often I have wanted to can fish myself to eat on such trips, but I never do it. The art of home canning has been on the decline for a number of years, with the advent of the home freezer. Of course I have canned fish—but I don't feel good about eating it without recooking the meat.

The instructions below apply only to fish that is intended to be boiled or recooked thoroughly after it is removed from the jars. If you want to try canning, I highly recommend a pressure cooker and some good jars, with good seals, that were made especially for canning and will withstand heat and pressure.

Skin the fish and gut it. Cut the fish into chunks or fingers. (Canning will soften the bones, so that even the backbone can be left in small fish.) Put the fish into a brine solution—a cup of salt to a gallon of water—for 1 hour. Rinse the fish well.

Pack the fish into hot wide-mouthed jars, leaving an inch of room at the top. (Do not use jars that have cracked or nicked rims.) If you have cut the fish into fingers, stand them so that the skin side is against the glass. Add ¼ teaspoon of salt to pint jars, or ½ teaspoon to quart jars. Do not add oil or liquid.

Put the lids on the jars. Most lids are made in two pieces: a screw band and a flat sealing element with a gasket-type sealing compound. (The sealing element should not be reused for canning purposes, and may not be interchangeable with all brands of screw bands.) To be sure, buy new lids and follow the manufacturer's directions. Tighten the lids and place the jars into your pressure cooker. Process at 10 pounds for 100 minutes. (If you live at high altitude, you'll have to adjust the pressure. Use 15 pounds above 2,000 feet.) Be sure to follow the directions that came with your pressure cooker—and be careful.

Store the jars in a dark place. Before eating or even tasting the contents, it is best to boil the fish for 10 minutes.

Note on canning tuna: Follow the directions above, but use only the light colored meat. Also, add ½ teaspoon vegetable oil to pint jars, or 1 teaspoon vegetable oil to quart jars. After storage, do not eat without cooking.

PICKLED FISH

Pickled fish is one of my favorite foods, and I've never tried a recipe for it that I didn't like. My favorite recipe is for fish that is pickled by a cold process. In other words, the fish is uncooked. It's raw. But most of the recipes in this section are cooked, and can be enjoyed by squeamish folk.

Pickled Bullheads

After finding this recipe in Illinois' *Outdoor Highlights,* I tried it with bullheads out of the

Chattachoochee River, and I can recommend it highly for that species, provided they are fresh, not frozen. The recipe is quite heavy on the bay leaf, but I like it.

1 to 2 pounds bullhead fillets, skinned
4 medium onions, sliced
5 or 6 bay leaves
1 tablespoon whole pickling spice
1 ½ cups water
1 ½ cups vinegar
1 tablespoon salt
⅛ teaspoon pepper

Choose a suitable container to hold the fish and layer the onions in the bottom. Add the bay leaves and pickling spice. Lay the bullheads on top. In a separate container, mix vinegar, water, salt, and pepper. Cover the

Potting

Basically, potting involves the semi-dehydration of fish by dry-heat cooking, and pounding it with a mixture of fats, sugar, and spices into an elegant little product not far removed from the Indians' pemmican.

The Cree Indians make a fish pemmican by pounding dried fish to a powder and mixing in lard, goose, or bear fat to a thick paste. Berries and brown sugar may be added. The mixture is formed into little cakes which may be coated in fat.

—Frances MacIlquham,
Fish Cookery of North America

fish with this mixture. Bring to boil, cover, reduce heat, and simmer for 8 to 10 minutes, or until the fish are done. Let fish cool in the pan. Refrigerate and serve cold.

Variation: Throw in a little dill weed. Cut the fish into bite size chunks and eat, chilled, on crackers. I also like the onions from this dish.

Pickled Herrings

The recipe below comes from Scotland, where herrings (or kippers) have been traditional for a good many years. The recipe can also be used for other small fish, such as 8- or 9-inch brook trout or horneyheads. I've even used it for small catfish, skinned.

> 8 small herrings (fresh) or other small
>   fish
> ½ cup white vinegar
> ½ cup water
> 1 medium onion, diced
> 4 bay leaves
> 1 teaspoon peppercorns
> ½ teaspoon pickling spice
> salt and pepper

Preheat the oven to 325 degrees. Fillet the fish. Salt and pepper to taste. Roll the fillets, working from the tail toward the head. Crush the bay leaves and sprinkle evenly on the bottom of a baking dish of suitable size. Place the rolled fillets on top of the bay leaves. The rolled fillets should be packed rather tightly so that they won't unroll. Crush the peppercorns and sprinkle them

over the fillets, along with the diced onion. Mix the water and vinegar, then pour the mixture over the fillets. Cover with foil and bake for 40 minutes. Let fish cool in the liquid. Save the liquid, strain it, and pour a little of it over each fish just before eating. *Serves 4 or 5.*

Pickled Pickerel

Smaller pikes and pickerel are good eating but the fillets have too many troublesome bones. Here's a perfect answer: dissolve the bones in vinegar, then pickle the fillets.

> 2 pounds fillets of pickerel or similar
>   bony fish
> vinegar
> water
> 2 tablespoons of pickling spices
>   (available mixed)
> ½ teaspoon pepper
> 1 lemon, sliced
> 1 medium onion, sliced

Cut skinless fillets into 1-inch chunks and put into a glass container. Cover with a mixture of ½ white vinegar and ½ water. Refrigerate for 24 hours. The vinegar, an acid, will dissolve or soften the bones.

Drain the fish. In a pan of suitable size, prepare a solution of 3 cups of vinegar and 1 cup of water. Add 2 tablespoons pickling spices, ½ teaspoon pepper, and 1 sliced lemon. Bring to a boil. Put about half of the the pickerel chunks into the boiling mixture and simmer for 6 minutes, or until the fish is done. Put the chunks in a sterilized large-mouth jar and add a layer of sliced onions. Boil another batch of fish until done and put them atop the sliced onions. Cover second batch with onions. Repeat until all the fish are gone, ending with onions. Bring the pan to boil again and fill the jar with the liquid. Seal. Refrigerate. Serve cold fish pickles with crackers and beer. Eat within a week or so.

Gourmet Pickles

I don't know what this recipe should be called, but note that the fish is not cooked. I enjoy the recipe very much as a snack, and I take care to cut each piece of fish so that it will sit just right atop a cracker. I normally use skinned fillets for this dish. In fact, I got it

from the late Euell Gibbons, who developed it for bluegill fillets.

Soak fillets in a brine made with 1 cup of salt per ½ gallon of water for 2 days. Wash thoroughly and drain.

Obtain a bag of crab or shrimp boil at the grocery, or tie up two tablespoons of mixed pickling spices in a piece of cloth. Put the spice bag into the bottom of a 1 quart wide-mouth glass jar. Cover the bag with a layer of thinly sliced onions. Top the onions with a layer of fish. Alternate onions and fish until the jar is full, being sure to top it off with a good layer of onions. Make a mixture of ½ water and ½ red wine vinegar and pour it into the jar, filling all the way up. Let it settle, tapping to dislodge the bubbles from the fish, onion, and spices. Cover and refrigerate for 3 weeks before eating.

Save a few of these pickles, chop them finely, and put them into pheasant or turkey salad instead of pickle relish.

17

FISH SAUCES

The fish came from Elk River in Tennessee. I thought it was an ordinary 7-pound largemouth, but the guests that I had invited for dinner convinced me otherwise. At the time, I lived in a rented farmhouse atop Pea Ridge, near Skin'um, Tennessee, home of the Big Mac Chicken Coop Factory. A local chamber of commerce in the county wanted to change the name from Pea Ridge to Highland Rim, but the folks around Skin'um weren't too hot for that idea.

Anyhow, I set out to cook this Elk River bass by a fancy French recipe, which, I figured, would interest my guests. One of these came from England, one from Germany, one from Japan, and another one from Indianapolis. Highland Rim folks, for sure. They all worked in America's space program in Huntsville, Alabama, located on red clay lands just across the state line off the south slope of Pea Ridge.

The big cookbook that I was trying to use, a sort of encyclopedia that had been translated from the French, must have weighed 10 pounds more than the bass. I had to clear all my jig-tying stuff off the kitchen table just to spread the thing open.

I found an interesting recipe, but was referred right off to a section on *court-bouillons*. At that entry, I read that I needed *fumets* in order to make *court-bouillon*. So, I turned to *fumets*, where I found out that I had to have the bass head, skin, and bones—all of which I had already buried out beside my tomato plant. But I had put these French ingredients into a plastic bag for convenience of handling, and when I dug them up I found them to be in good shape and not yet fuming too badly. So, I decided that I could indeed handle both the *fumets* and the *court-bouillon*.

Back to the main recipe, which called for *Hollandaise* sauce. Well, the book contained entries for several hundred sauces, and there were no less than three recipes for *Hollandaise*. The first one called for a *bain-marie*, or double boiler. I couldn't find the top half of my *bain-marie*, so I went on to the second *Hollandaise* sauce. This recipe called for Isigny butter. While trying to find out what Isigny butter is, I got interested in the Izard, a wild goat of the Pyrenees. Not finding any Izard recipes that I thought would do justice to Henry (a rogue goat who lived on Pea Ridge and always seemed to show up when I had invited guests who sported cars with tasty vinyl tops), I went on to *Hollandaise* number three.

It called for 2 tablespoons of *Allemande* sauce. Four kinds of *Allemande* sauce were listed, and I started on the first one, which called for another *bain-marie*. I found the missing part of my double boiler and proceeded. The recipe required 2½ cups of *Veloute* sauce. (Remember that I needed only 2 tablespoons of *Allemande* sauce in the first place.) So, I looked up *Veloute* sauce and found out that I needed ½ cup of *Allemande* in order to make it. In other words, I needed ½ cup of *Allemande* in order to make 2 tablespoons of *Allemande*! At first I jumped to the conclusion that some French writer or fancy chef was pulling my leg, but then I decided that it was merely a typographical mistake or an error of literary translation instead of intercontinental hanky-panky.

By now, I had forgotten the name of the fish recipe that I had set out to prepare in the first place, and I couldn't find my way back to it. So, I said to hell with it and buried the *fumets* again under Henry's watchful eye.

The sun was already setting west of Pea Ridge, and I didn't have time now to prepare a fancy dish; so I filleted the bass closely and cut it into fish fingers about the size of New Hampshire brook trout. Out came the old cast iron frying pan, peanut oil, salt, water-ground white south Alabama cornmeal, and catsup.

In short, I fried the damn fish and served it up on ordinary brown grocery bags along with catsup, lemon wedges, and hush puppies. Of course, I put the catsup in my *bain maire* to heat it enough to get it out of the

Risky Sauces Omitted

Some of the best sauces, such as homemade mayonnaise and hollandaise, are made with raw eggs. Such sauces have been omitted from this book because, at the time of writing, several people died from a disease that was traced to homemade mayonnaise. The mayonnaise had salmonella bacteria in it, which in turn was traced to raw eggs purchased at market.

The eggs are no doubt contanimated from the chicken (which came before the egg) and could, I feel, be safely used if they were washed and contained no cracks. But to be on the safe side, I'm not including sauces or dishes that call for uncooked eggs. Anyone who feels that homemade mayonnaise and hollandaise are worth the risk will have to look elsewhere for recipes.

sauces is required, simply because many people want, for example, tartar sauce even with fried fish. If you are one of these, you should know that you can usually make a better sauce than you can buy. Try the following:

Lemon Butter Sauce

I prefer this sauce for dipping boiled shrimp, and we usually use the Easy Method. It's also quite good when used as a baste. When the sauce is to be poured over poached fish, try the Fancy Method.

bottle, then I served it in a puddle on a little platter. Any robust red sauce like my Highlander's *Rimpearidge Rouge*, I told my guests, should be served at room temperature in order to bring forth its full flavor. Ordinary sauces, like *Allemande* or *Veloute* are, of course, a different ball game, I claimed.

They loved it and wanted recipes.

The inspiration for this quaint dish, I said, pushing my luck, came upon me while I was camped out in the Appalachians, where I was at the time hunting for the *azard*, a rare wild goat of the region, the ancestral home of Henry. More Highlander's *Rimpearidge Rouge* sauce, anyone?

If not, maybe one of the following sauces will fill the bill. In any case, I use the above story to illustrate a point. Far too many cookbooks have far too many references in them, and references within references, so that its just too hard to use them. Perhaps I have erred in the other direction, in that most of the recipes in this book are pretty much self-contained. But I believe that a chapter on

Eulachon: The Candlefish

The importance of the eulachon to the economy of the Indians of the northwest coast of North America goes far back, with great value placed on the little fish as food, a source of cooking oil, of light, and as a medium of barter.

The eulachon is a very oily fish, and when dried and fitted with a wick from the inner bark of the cedar, burns like a candle. Hence the name "candlefish."

. . . A very perishable little fish, eulachon is superb with broiled fresh from the water, over hot coals. It is highly esteemed by Indians from California to Alaska.

—Frances MacIlquham,
Fish Cookery of North America

Easy Method
 ½ **cup melted butter**
 ½ **cup lemon juice (freshly squeezed)**
Fancy Method
 ½ **cup melted butter**
 ½ **cup lemon juice (freshly squeezed)**
 ⅛ **teaspoon salt**
 ⅛ **teaspoon white pepper**
 ⅛ **teaspoon paprika**
 1 **tablespoon white wine**
  Worcestershire sauce
 1 **tablespoon minced parsley**

Mix everything in a suitable bowl shortly before using, keep it a little warm, and serve at room temperature.

Cocktail Sauce

Many people like some sort of cocktail sauce for dipping shrimp, fish fingers, and so on. For hot shrimp, I prefer a simple lemon butter sauce as set forth above, but for cold shrimp and cold poached fish, it's hard to beat the following:

 1 **teaspoon olive oil**
 1 **large garlic clove**
 1 **cup catsup**
 juice of 1 large lemon
 2 **tablespoons red wine**
 1 **teaspoon fresh horseradish**
 ¼ **teaspoon Tabasco sauce**
 ⅛ **teaspoon salt**

Crush a garlic clove and let it steep in 1 teaspoon of olive oil for several days. Pour oil off garlic (or strain) into a small mixing bowl. Add catsup, lemon juice, wine, horseradish, Tabasco sauce, and salt. Chill until ready to serve.

Hot Egg Sauce

 2 **hard-boiled eggs, sliced**
 4 **tablespoons butter**
 2 **tablespoons flour**
 1 **cup boiling water**
 salt and pepper to taste

Melt butter in a saucepan and slowly mix in the flour. Add boiling water while stirring. Cook until mixture thickens. Salt and pepper to taste. Add eggs and serve hot over boiled, baked, or poached fish.

Catsup

If the truth be known, more people dunk more pounds of fish into more gallons of catsup than all other sauces combined. I too could be a catsup man, but for two reasons. First, I don't have the patience to shake the bottle to get out a sufficient amount. Second, I don't like the feeling of being ripped off by catsup bottlers. They keep coming out with various kinds of squirt bottles, but none of these that I've tried work any better than bottlenecks. After studying this situation for a number of years, my conclusion is that *they*

Walleye

The popular walleye is one of the best fish that swims, and they can be cooked in any way. They are medium-low in oil content, and their flesh is firm, white, and flaky. Walleye are also called jack salmon, pike, dore, and opal eye.

don't want a better bottle. Why? Because they want you to throw away from 5 to 20 percent of the catsup so that you'll buy more quicker. I know how to package catsup—thick catsup. Put it into big-mouth jars. Like mayonnaise. I can get all the mayonnaise I want out of a jar, then I can clean off the sides with a spoon. So . . . if you want to try the following recipe, be sure to save a big-mouthed mayonnaise jar. I prefer the 1-pint size. You'll also need:

2 gallons of ripe tomatoes
5 large onions
1 tablespoon black pepper (or less)
2 or 3 hot pepper pods (whole)
2 tablespoons powdered mustard
2 cups white vinegar
½ cup sugar
2 tablespoons salt

Quarter the tomatoes and put them into a large pot. Bring to boil. Peel the onions, quarter them, and add to tomato pot. Simmer for 1 hour. Strain out the tomato and onion pulp.

Return the liquid to the pot. Add 1 table-spoon black pepper, 3 hot pepper pods (whole), 2 tablespoons powdered mustard, 2 cups white vinegar, ½ cup sugar, and 2 table-spoons of salt. Bring to boil and cook down until sauce thickens. (This will take some time because more than half the liquid must be boiled out, depending on how thick you want the catsup.) Stir the liquid from time to time.

Take the pot off the heat and discard the pepper pods. Using a ladle, spoon the catsup into a sterilized big-mouth jar. Refrigerate.

Billfish

These are large, big-game ocean fish, including sailfish, swordfish, marlins, and spearfish. All of these are high in oil content, but they are quite tasty if they are properly handled and appropriately cooked. The marlins and swordfish are especially good when grilled or broiled, and they are often eaten raw in sashimi dishes. The sailfish and spearfish tend to be a little tough. They are often smoked or cooked over charcoal. Frying is not normally recommended for billfish.

But remember that the term "billfish" is quite broad and includes dozens of different fish. The black marlin, for example, is of moderate oil content whereas the blue marlin is high in oil content.

In any case, billfish for the table should be dressed out and iced down as soon as they are caught. Saving the fish for dockside snapshots is a waste of good meat.

Fish Finger Dip

I seldom use anything on fried fish, except perhaps for a little lemon juice, but I do enjoy tartar sauce and such when it is available. If we have guests to feed, I almost always whip up some sort of sauce or dip, just in case they aren't too fond of fish and want to cover it up. Here's one of my favorites in color and taste:

> 1 cup of sour cream
> ¼ cup catsup
> 1 tablespoon white wine
>   Worcestershire sauce
> 2 tablespoons grated onion
> juice of ½ lemon
> juice of 1 clove of garlic
> 1 teaspoon Tabasco sauce
> ⅛ teaspoon pepper

Mix all ingredients. Let chill in the refrigerator for several hours before serving.

Easy Tartar Sauce

Some cookbook authors tend to make fun of tartar sauce, but it would not be so popular if it were not easy to make *and* good. Here's all you need:

> 1 cup good mayonnaise
> 1 teaspoon prepared mustard
> 2 tablespoons sweet pickle relish (or
>   finely chopped pickle)
> 2 tablespoons chopped green onions
>   (including part of tops)

Mix mayonnaise and anchovy. Stir in onions, pickle, capers, parsley, tarragon, chervil, and mustard. Stir in cream and lemon juice. Taste. Add salt and white pepper, if desired, and mix. Refrigerate until ready to serve. Spoon into individual serving bowls and garnish with a sprig or two of parsley.

Sauce Tartare

If you want sauce a little more sophisticated than the Tartar Sauce recipe above, change the name to *Sauce Tartare* and add more ingredients.

> 1½ cups mayonnaise
> 2 teaspoons anchovy paste (or two
>   mashed anchovies halves)

Redfish (Red Drum)

Blackened or not, the redfish is one of the more popular sport fish along the Gulf of Mexico and other coastal areas. The smaller fish are good fried or baked, but the larger ones tend to be rather coarse. There is a considerable range of opinion on exactly how small redfish should be for table fare. Some say 15 pounds. Others say 10. Just the other day, a fellow told me that a redfish over a foot long "ain't fit to eat." In some areas, these fish are called channel bass.

4 green onions, finely chopped
    (including part of the tops)
⅓ cup of dill pickle, finely chopped
1 tablespoon chopped capers
1 tablespoon chopped parsley
1 tablespoon chopped tarragon
1 tablespoon chervil
1 teaspoon powered mustard
½ cup cream
juice from ½ small lemon
salt
white pepper

1 tablespoon chopped parsley
½ teaspoon garlic powder

Mix all ingredients in a suitable bowl, then put it into the refrigerator for at least an hour before serving.

Molho Cru

Here's an excellent sauce from Angola. Serve over poached fish fillets or other seafood. Also try it as a dip for fried fish fingers.

1 cup diced green onions, including
    part of tops
¼ cup chopped parsley
3 cloves garlic, minced
2 tablespoons ground cumin
½ teaspoon salt
½ cup vinegar
½ cup water

Mix everything and zap it good in a food processor or blender until it forms a paste. Put the paste into the refrigerator, or put on ice, before serving.

18

FISH SALADS

At one time, I toyed with the notion of putting a fish salad chapter at the front of this book, just to whet the reader's appetite. But then I remembered the problem that my son Bill had when we took him to a large seafood restaurant. We had driven some distance to get to the place, and, getting hungrier and hungrier by the mile, Bill had visions of red lobsters and piles of pink shrimp and platters of golden brown fried fish and lots of hush puppies and so on. Before ordering, we all went to a salad bar, which was quite long and might well have been the most complete selection that I've ever seen in one place. Bill wasn't much more than waist high and he walked up and down this spread, craning his neck to look at the lettuce and tomatoes and so forth. Suddenly

he broke into tears. He thought this was it!

Bill is taller than I am now, and maybe even he will read on.

Bluegill Stuffed Tomatoes

Few foods are better, in hot weather, than chilled tomatoes, and when they are in season I tend to eat too many of them. Also, during the same season, fish are quite plentiful because this is the season when bluegills hit topwater bugs and flies with abandon. Of course, any good fish can be used in this recipe, but bluegill is highly recommended. First scale the bluegill with a spoon, then gut

Bluegill and Other Bream

A number of panfish similar to the bluegill make purely excellent eating. These include the redbreast and the pumpkinseed. Most of these fish, except the redear, can be taken on flies, bugs, or tiny spinners as well as on worms, crickets, and other natural bait. These fish have delicate white flesh, of low oil content, and are very good when fried. They can be poached, flaked, and used in various salads, or they can be filleted, sliced into mock shrimp, and fried or poached.

it. Boil until the fish flakes easily, then remove and let cool. Scrape the skin off the bluegills and discard. Then flake off the meat with a fork.

2 cups bluegill flakes
½ stalk of finely sliced celery
½ cup of good mayonnaise
1 tablespoon of grated onion
½ teaspoon black pepper
4 large tomatoes, chilled
2 slices of bacon
a little grated cheese (optional)
salt to taste

To make a stuffing, mix all ingredients except tomatoes, bacon, and cheese. Add salt to taste for stuffing only, then a little more will be added to each tomato. Chill the stuffing. Fry bacon until crisp. Crumble bacon and set aside.

Peel the tomatoes. Cut off the top part, about ½ inch from the stem. Scoop out the "pulp" and save for later use—or eat now. Sprinkle a little salt on the inside of the tomatoes. Spoon in the stuffing salad, top with grated cheese and bacon bits. Serve on lettuce leaves. *Makes 4 servings.*

Fish Flake Salad

Here's a recipe that my mother used for canned tuna fish. I fix it with any flaked fish.

1 cup fish flakes (cooked)
½ cup celery, thinly sliced
juice from 1 lemon
2 tablespoons olive oil
1 tablespoon parsley, chopped

Mix all ingredients. Chill. This salad can be served on lettuce, but I confess that I spread it on bread just as often, or scoop it up on crackers. *As a salad, this recipe makes about 4 servings.*

Marinated Fish Salad

Salad
2 cups fish flakes (cooked)
½ cup bell pepper, diced finely
½ cup celery, diced finely
2 hard-boiled eggs, diced
Marinade
½ cup olive oil
juice of 1 lemon
1 teaspoon onion juice

Squeeze chopped onion in a garlic press until you have a teaspoonful of juice. Mix with ½ cup olive oil and the juice of 1 lemon. Pour this mixture over the fish flakes, toss lightly, and refrigerate for 2 hours. Then combine the fish flakes with bell pepper, celery, and mayonnaise. Mix in the eggs. Salt and pepper to taste. *Makes 6 to 8 servings.*

solve the gelatin over boiling water. Stir the mayonnaise into the dissolved gelatin. Add sour cream, onion, salt, lemon juice, and parsley. Combine this mixture with contents of fish bowl and stir, then transfer to a ring mold. Chill until firm. Before serving, unmold over lettuce leaves. Fill center with tomatoes, green peppers, and onion. Top with mayonnaise. *Makes 8 to 10 servings.*

Ring-Mold Salad

If you want a pretty salad on your table, as well as a tasty one, try the following:

2 cups fish flakes
2 hard boiled eggs, chopped
½ cup almond slivers, toasted
½ cup ripe black olives, chopped
¼ cup water
1 tablespoon unflavored gelatin
1 cup mayonnaise
1 cup sour cream
1 tablespoon grated onion
2 tablespoons lemon juice
½ cup chopped parsley
1 teaspoon salt
3 tomatoes, quartered
¼ cup chopped green pepper
¼ cup chopped onion (mild purple
  onions if available)
mayonnaise

Mix fish, eggs, olives, and almonds in a bowl. Set aside. In the top part of a double boiler, put gelatin in ¼ cup of cold water and soak for 5 minutes. Heat water to boiling in the lower part of double boiler. Then dis-

Molded Fish Salad

2 cups fish flakes
2 envelopes gelatin, unflavored
1 cup cold water
2 hard boiled eggs, chopped
1 cup sour cream
¼ cup French dressing
¼ cup white wine
½ cup chopped celery
¼ cup chopped bell pepper
¼ cup sliced black olives
¼ cup chopped cucumber
¼ teaspoon dry mustard
salt and pepper
lettuce or watercress (for garnish)

Put 1 cup water into a saucepan and soak gelatin for 5 minutes. Then heat gelatin until it dissolves. Pour it into a large mixing bowl and let it cool. Stir in wine, French dressing, sour cream, and mustard. Then stir in celery, bell pepper, olives, cucumber, fish flakes and eggs. Salt and pepper to taste. Grease a salad mold, preferably fish-shaped, and place mixture into it. Chill until salad is firm. Serve surrounded with lettuce or watercress. *6 to 8 servings.*

Cold Potato Salad With Fish

1 cup flaked fish
2 slices bacon
1 cup cooked potatoes, diced
¼ cup onion, chopped
1 stalk celery, chopped
1 tablespoon green bell pepper, diced
2 tablespoons mayonnaise
salt and pepper to taste
paprika

Cook the bacon and crumble it. Mix all ingredients except paprika. Put into a serving bowl, sprinkle lightly with paprika for color, and chill until ready to eat. *Makes 4 or 5 servings.*

Hawaiian Fish Salad

4 cups boneless fish chunks (about 2 pounds of fillets)
salt
1 can pineapple chunks (20-ounce)
1 small can water chestnuts, sliced
1 stalk celery, diced
½ cup toasted almonds, sliced
½ green bell pepper, diced
¼ cup shredded coconut
1 cup mayonnaise
1 teaspoon curry powder

Mix mayonnaise and curry powder in a small bowl. In a large bowl, mix fish with pineapple, water chestnuts, celery, almonds, and pepper. Then stir in mayonnaise mixture. Sprinkle top with coconut. Chill before eating. *Serves 5 or 6 for lunch.*

Fish-Stuffed Eggs

8 large eggs
½ cup fish flakes
¼ cup good mayonnaise
juice of ½ lemon
1 tablespoon white wine Worcestershire sauce
¼ teaspoon salt
⅛ teaspoon pepper
paprika

Hard boil the eggs, cool, and carefully cut in half lengthwise. Scoop out the yolks. Place yolks in a bowl and mash with mayonnaise. Add lemon juice, Worcestershire sauce, salt, and pepper. Mix well and spoon into the center of the egg whites. Refrigerate. Sprinkle lightly with paprika before serving. *Makes 8 servings, allowing 2 stuffed egg halves per serving.*

Bass Salad

2 cups of bass flakes (or other flaked fish)
2 tablespoons salad pickles (or finely chopped sweet pickles)
1 large hard-boiled egg, chopped

1 medium onion, chopped
1 tablespoon fresh parsley, chopped
1 tablespoon pimento, chopped
1 stalk celery, chopped
1 teaspoon paprika
1½ tablespoons mayonnaise
½ lemon
salt and pepper to taste

Poach fish and flake two cupsful. Combine with salad pickles, egg, onion, parsley, pimento, celery, and paprika. Add mayonnaise and juice of ½ lemon while tossing lightly. Chill. Serve cold as dinner salad, cracker snack, or hors d'oeuvres garnish. Try it served on whole lettuce leaves for a light lunch, to be eaten on crisp crackers. *As a salad, this recipe makes about 6 servings.*

1 cup cabbage, shredded
1 cup red cabbage, shredded
salt
lettuce leaves
lemon wedges

Bring water to boil, adding salt and pickling spices. Put fillets into water, cover, and simmer for 8 to 10 minutes, until the meat flakes easily with a fork. Drain fish and cut into chunks.

In a large salad bowl, combine fish chunks, salad dressing, onion, lemon juice, and pickle relish. Salt to taste. Cover and chill for several hours. Shortly before serving, add cabbage and toss. Make "cups" from lettuce leaves and spoon slaw into them. Garnish with lemon wedges. *Serves 5 or 6.*

Fish Slaw

Here's a dish that is not only good, especially during hot weather, but is also good for you. It's also pretty, what with red cabbage and yellow lemon wedges.

2 pounds skinless and boneless fish
   fillets
1 quart of water
1 tablespoon pickling spice mix
1 tablespoon salt
¼ cup low calorie mayonnaise-style
   salad dressing
2 tablespoons pickle relish or chopped
   sweet pickles
2 tablespoons finely chopped onion
juice from 1 lemon

Hot Fish-Stuffed Tomatoes

1½ cups fish flakes
4 strips of bacon
4 large tomatoes
1 tablespoon chopped parsley
1 teaspoon lemon juice
1 tablespoon melted butter
salt and pepper to taste

Preheat oven to 350 degrees. Mix fish flakes, melted butter, parsley, lemon juice, salt, and pepper. Form a cavity in each tomato by removing the stem end and spooning out the centers. Stuff with fish-flake mixture and bake for 20 minutes. While stuffed tomatoes are in oven, fry bacon until crisp and drain on absorbent paper. Crumble bacon and sprinkle over tops of stuffed tomatoes. For lunch, we like stuffed tomatoes served with cheese toast. *Serves 4.*

Hot Potato Salad with Fish Chunks

If you like potato salad, be sure to try this German-style dish with chunks of good fresh fish:

> **1 pound of boneless fish, cut into 1-inch chunks**
> **6 slices of bacon**
> **3 cups of cooked potatoes, sliced**
> **½ cup of onion, diced**
> **½ cup of celery, chopped**
> **3 tablespoons of sugar**
> **1 tablespoon flour**
> **½ teaspoon paprika**
> **salt to taste**
> **¼ teaspoon celery seed**
> **1 cup of water**
> **½ cup white wine vinegar**
> **chopped parsley**

Fry bacon, crumble, and set aside. In bacon drippings, sauté onion and celery. In a small container, mix sugar, flour, paprika, salt, and celery seed, then stir this into the onions and celery. Pour vinegar into the water, then add it slowly to the pan. Stir constantly and cook until the sauce thickens. Add bacon crumbs, fish chunks, and pota-

---

Eat More Fish

The American Heart Association recommends two meals of fish per week for preventive measures against heart disease. Two recent studies reported in the *New England Journal of Medicine* show that the polyunsaturated fatty acids of fish have metabolic effects that differ substantially from other polyunsaturated fatty acids and may reduce the incidence of cononary heart disease. Oily fish such as bonito have higher levels of polyunsaturated fatty acids than leaner fish such as flounder and grouper.

　　　　　　　　　　　—*Atlantic Bonito,*
　　　　　　　　　　　　UNC Sea Grant

---

toes. Stir carefully. Cover pan and cook on low heat for 10 minutes, or until the fish flakes easily. Sprinkle with parsley. *Makes 5 or 6 servings.*

Ambrosia with Fish Chunks

Ambrosia was one of my mother's favorite dishes, and I have eaten enough of it to establish criteria. The flavor is almost always good in any reasonable recipe, but it's the texture that really distinguishes one batch of ambrosia from another. A good deal depends on the oranges.

1 pound skinless fish fillets (mild and
  low fat)
½ cup mayonnaise
1 cup orange chunks (see instructions
  below)
1 grated orange rind
juice of 1 lemon
2 teaspoons sugar
1 stalk celery, thinly sliced
¼ cup sliced olives
½ cup green onions and tops, sliced
¼ cup shredded coconut
1 bay leaf

Select mild, low-fat fish, such as flounder.
Fillet, skin, and cut into 1-inch chunks. Boil a
bay leaf in a quart of water for a few minutes.
Remove bay leaf and poach fish chunks for 5
or 6 minutes, or until it flakes easily. Do not
overcook. Drain carefully and chill.

Peel a large navel orange. Grate 1 tablespoon of the rind and set aside. (For best
results, do not have much of the inner pulp in
the grated rind.) Section the orange and peel
the sections. Then cut sections into 1-inch
pieces. Thus, you will have a juicy orange
chunk without any skin or pith. Set orange
chunks aside.

Make a sauce by mixing the mayonnaise,
lemon juice, orange rind, and sugar. Set
aside. In a large bowl, mix chilled fish,
orange chunks, celery, olives, green onions,
and coconut. Add sauce and toss carefully.
Serve on lettuce leaves. *Makes 7 or 8 servings.*

Avocado Stuffed with Fish

1 cup fish flakes
1 large avocado
2 small lemons
1 tablespoon melted buter
salt and pepper to taste

Cut chilled avocado in half, lengthwise.
Remove pit. Stuff fish flakes into cavities.
Mix juice of 1 lemon in melted butter and
pour over fish. Cut the other lemon into
slices and use as garnish. My wife and I like
this dish for a light lunch in hot weather.
Serves 2.

Variations: Reduce lemon juice and top
with mayonnaise or other suitable sauce.

Egg and Fish Chunk Salad

1 pound fish fillets, mild
10 large eggs
½ cup mayonnaise
1 stalk celery, diced
½ cup chopped onions
1 teaspoon salt

Cutthroat Trout

The cutthroat is an excellent fish of fine
flavor and medium oil content. The color of
its flesh ranges from white to red. It can be
cooked by any method.

½ teaspoon pepper
2 teaspoons of dill weed
lettuce leaves
paprika

Heat a quart of water and add 2 teaspoons of dill weed. Add fillets and cook for 5 minutes, or until fish flakes easily. Remove fillets, drain, and sprinkle with a little salt. Put the eggs in water, bring to boil, reduce heat, and cook for 15 minutes. Peel and quarter with a sharp knife.

In a bowl, combine mayonnaise, onions, salt, and pepper. Mix in onions and celery. Add fish and eggs, "tossing" carefully by hand to keep from flaking. Serve on lettuce leaves, and sprinkle top lightly with paprika. *Makes about 8 servings.*

19

DRESSING FISH

Before you start dressing fish, give some thought to how you are going to cook and eat them. Then proceed with the easiest way to get what you want. In my opinion, anyone who fillets small fish is not only a glutton for self punishment but is also quite wasteful. I have therefore decided to explain first how to *eat* fish, and how to use the whole thing, before getting into filleting, steaking, and so on.

At the end of the chapter, I'll have a few words on caring for the catch while you're fishing or coming home, as well as tips on freezing fish.

The Livingston Edge

If anyone has plenty of panfish and the time to fillet them, fine. I'll certainly help eat them. But filleting isn't necessary and may not even be desirable. It wastes not only a lot of time but also a lot of good meat.

For several years my family lived on an island in a Florida lake. Just about every Saturday night, and sometimes during the week, we fried up 40 or 50 hand-sized bluegills or shellcrackers or crappies. I enjoyed catching them on a flyrod. But I didn't enjoy filleting them—and I flatly refused to do so, even for guests. Once we served a batch of crappies to a PhD from Quitman, Georgia, the home of Carl Barber; a brain cell specialists of some sort from England; and a school teacher from Scotland. Before the fish ran out, they were eating "specs" and licking their fingers like old time Florida Crackers!

There is a method for eating such whole-fried fish. First, forget about a knife and fork. Pick up the fish whole, then bite off the tail and the tips of the fins. Gently pull on what is left of the dorsal fin. Pull carefully so that all the bones come out. Then do the pectrol fin the same way. It is most important that *all* the related bones come out with the fins; leaving a single fin bone in the fish destroys confidence, without which this method simply won't work. After the fins and fin bones are removed, hold the fish by both ends. Hold it upright, so that the back points up. Start eating just behind the head. Bite down to the rib cage, but stop and hold when you reach bone. Then pull meat off both sides of the backbone. Work toward the tail. Then

turn fish over and start on the tail end. Work forward until you reach the rib cage.

Working on each rib cage separately, the expert will hold both sides of the ribs between his teeth, then pull on the backbone with both hands. This strips the meat off the bones of the rib cage. However, I don't advise inexperienced or young people to practice this rib cage technique at the beginning of the meal. It's best for them to save the rib cages until last, thus assuring that they get a fair share of fish. My brother Jim and his son David, as well as my son Bill, a true Livingston, are past masters of this method of eating fish, and together they will clean up a whole platter of bluegills while an unsuspecting guest picks at one little rib cage.

Warning: The method above works best if you leave the fins on the fish when you clean them, thereby giving you something to hold onto while pulling out the fin bones. Do *not*, as some cookbooks instruct, cut the fins off with scissors or shears. This practice can leave numerous tiny bones embedded in the flesh.

An Ice Fishing Problem

Ice fishermen sometime have a problem with their fish freezing before they are ready to dress them. If this happens, it's best to leave the fish frozen, then transfer them, whole, to a suitable bag or box and put them into the freezer without ever letting them thaw out. When you are ready to cook, take out the fish, let them thaw, and dress them at that time. Ice fishermen can also glaze these fish easily by dipping them in water and letting it freeze on the fish. Glazing will help, but it isn't necessary unless the fish will be frozen for more than a week or so.

I hate to admit it, but while living in sunny Florida I have frozen whole fish for a few days without even dressing them simply because I was too tired or lazy to do the job when I came in from fishing. But I do not recommend this practice.

Scaling Fish

I've used all manner of devices to scale fish, including ordinary knives, electric knives, store bought scalers with alligator teeth, knives with saw-teeth scalers on one side of the blade, scalers made at home by nailing bottle caps to wood handles, and so on. But the scaler that I use more often than any other is an ordinary large kitchen spoon. I suppose that I use spoons so often for two reasons: (1) they do a good job, and (2) I can usually find one in my kitchen. Once I had a knife, made by Case, I believe, that had a spoon scaler on one end, and this worked very well while I had it. Somehow, knives have a way of leaving my possession.

I might add, however, that the best place to scale and dress fish is not at home but at the stream or lake. There may be other opinions on this matter, but I always felt that the turtles and crayfish appreciate whatever is left of the fish if you'll throw it back into the water. (I don't, however, recommend that you clean fish at a crowded public boat ramp.) In any case, the sooner the fish are dressed and scaled, the better—and the easier.

Never try to scale dry fish. If they do dry out for some reason, I soak them in water before proceeding.

The scaling process should start at the tail of the fish and move toward the head.

Small fish usually are easier to scale than large fish of the same species. For this reason, I usually scale smaller fish, such as

largemouth or smallmouth bass under 2 pounds. I also scale larger fish, especially if I want to bake them whole. There are other opinions on this matter, however, and some people believe in skinning *all* bass and most other fish. Suit yourself. Large fish can be difficult to scale. I heard of a woman who lived along the Outer Banks of North Carolina who uses a garden hoe to scale large drum.

Longnose Gar

The longnose garfish (*Lepisoteus osseus*) is a common denizen of the state's coastal waters and an unused resource. Commonly considered trash fish, there is no commercial market for this species. When properly prepared, however, the flesh is mild, boneless, and can be obtained in large quantities for social gatherings. Gar are the bane of shad fishermen, who are more than happpy to pass these net tanglers on to anyone willing to accept them.

Cleaning garfish involves some effort, but this lessens with experience. Beginning at the head, split the shell (armored scales) open down the back with a hatchet or suitable instrument. Remove head and tail, separate shell from meat along sides with a knife. Scrape exposed meat from carcass with a large spoon, fork, or serrated fish scaler. Gar meat is permeated with tendons and fascia, and this procedure leaves most gristle behind. Grind meat if necessary.

—*South Carolina Wildlife Cookbook*

Scaling a fish with a spoon.

Skinning Fish

I always use special fish skinning pliers for this job, if I have them. There are several brands on the market, but the more expensive models (sometimes called commercial grade) are usually better. You can get by with regular pliers, but fish skin and slime, especially from catfish and eels, will quickly clog these up and prevent you from maintaining a good hold. I've also skinned catfish by grasping the skin between my thumb and a knife blade, but this is not recommended if you've got pliers.

Regardless of the kind of pliers I have, I

SKINNING A FISH

1. With a sharp knife, make a shallow cut on both sides above the gills. Loosen enough skin to grasp with pliers.

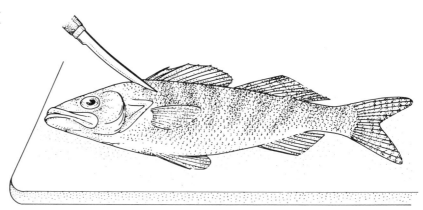

2. Often the skin will pull off evenly until it splits about halfway down the head; then it will taper off, leaving a triangle of skin on the belly, just under the gills. Grasp the end with pliers and pull it toward the tail.

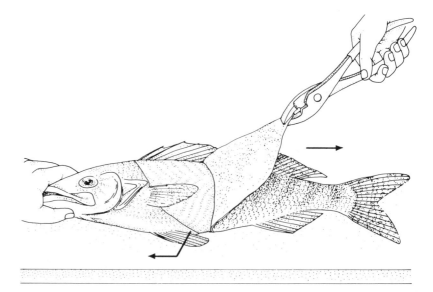

always skin fish by first making a cut behind the head. Then I loosen the skin a bit with my knife blade, just to get things started. Next, I grasp the head with my left hand and the skinning pliers with the other and pull. Often, the whole skin will come off, except for a triangluar patch under the throat. This patch of skin can usually be pulled back toward the head without much effort.

This is the basic method that I use for any fish that I skin, as well as for eels, lampreys, and frogs. Large fish are often more difficult to skin than smaller fish of the same species. Many people nail catfish and eels to a tree trunk or to a barn wall so they can get a better pull, and I'll admit to having done that with large catfish. I've also hung them up with a rope.

Note: Skinning fillets of fish with scales on them is covered later in this chapter. In my opinion, catfish and other such fish should be skinned before filleting them.

I've read about a number of other ways to get the skin off scale fish and catfish, but I've never tried one that was more satisfactory than the method above. Some of these recommend scalding the whole fish or fillet and then pulling or scraping the skin off. I've tried scalding, but I don't think that it saves any time, if you know how to skin a fish the old fashioned way.

Beheading Fish

After you have skinned or scaled the fish, the next step is to behead it. The object here, of course, is to remove the foreward fins and gills along with the head, while at the same time saving as much meat as possible. This usually requires a slightly diagonal cut.

Normally, I lay the fish flat a make a cut with a sharp knife, going down to the backbone. To make the cut, I snug the knife blade,

---

BEHEADING A FISH

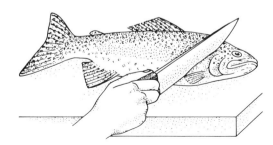

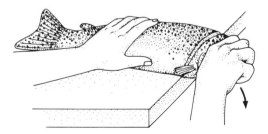

1. Make a diagonal cut to the backbone on both sides of the fish.

2. Snap the backbone off the side of the table.

at an angle, up against the base of the fin. Then I flip the fish over and make a similar cut on the other side. Next, I cut from the top down to the backbone. After that cut, the backbone can usually be snapped with a slight bending pressure from hands, holding the fish head in one hand and the body of the fish in the other. Thus, the fish can be beheaded without having to cut through the bones. Exceptions are very large fish and very small fish. The smaller ones can easily be cut through with a good knife, and the larger ones may require some hacking with a large knife. This method will leave some meat on the throat, attached to the head. If you want to fool with it, cut this part out and skin it.

You can fillet a fish, as discussed later in this chapter, without having to behead it. But you'll lose some good meat.

Gutting Fish

After you have either skinned or scaled the fish and have removed the head, the next step is to remove the innards. This is easily accomplished by making a cut at the vent, inserting the knife a bit, and cutting toward the head. Some trout fishermen will take issue with this text, claiming rather loudly that this species is usually gutted before beheading; others will claim, even louder, that you neither behead, skin, or scale trout. But a good deal depends on what sort of trout they are, how big they are, and what part of the country the anglers comes from.

In any case, avoid cutting into the organs when the fish is gutted. After you have made the cut, remove everything with your hand.

GUTTING A FISH

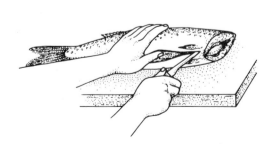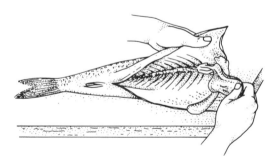

After beheading the fish, insert knife point into the vent and make a shallow cut forward. Remove the entrails.

Be careful with roe, lest you cut the sac. The liver and air bladder can be removed if you want to keep them. Be very careful with the liver, and remove the gall bladder without bursting or puncturing it.

It is possible to fillet a fish without having to gut it, as will be discussed later in this chapter.

large fish of about 10 pounds or so. Steaks are traditional cuts for broiling and grilling. While you can steak fish with a knife, making uniform cuts is sometimes difficult and it isn't easy to get through the backbone. A meat clever or a butcher's saw will help, but your best bet is to find a good commercial butcher who will steak the fish for you.

Making Fish Steaks

There is a little confusion about fish steaks, and some people call a fillet a steak. What I call a fish steak is a cross-section of the fish that contains a segment of the backbone. Also, very large fish are sometimes cut into slabs that are called steaks.

Usually, fish steaks are made from fairly

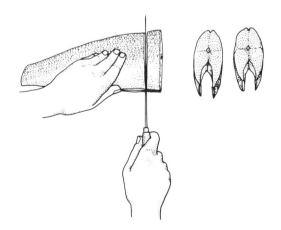

Cutting fish steaks requires a strong knife or a cleaver. Usual thickness is about 1 inch.

Filleting Fish

Method I
There are several ways to fillet a fish. Many of my friends use an electric fillet knife and start with a cut behind the head. They go in, and down the backbone, cutting right through the ribs. At the tail, they don't cut all the way though the skin. Instead, they flop the fillet over and separate the fillet flesh from the skin by a combination of cutting and pulling. They do the opposite side of the fish the same way. When they get the fillets out, all the rest of the fish, including the skin, is still attached. With this method, the rib bones are still attached to the fillets. They can be removed, but many people leave them in the fish.

Method II
Most people, including myself, start filleting a fish at the tail, then cut up through the rib cage and out at the head. Then the other side is done the same way. Usually, but not always, this method is used when the fish has been scaled but not skinned. In a variation on this method, some people behead the fish before making the cut on either side. The rib

FILLETING (I)

1. Lay fish flat and make
a diagonal cut close to
the fins and gills. Cut down
to, but not through,
the backbone.

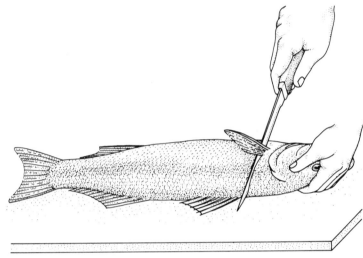

3. Work toward the tail,
keeping the blade close to
the backbone.

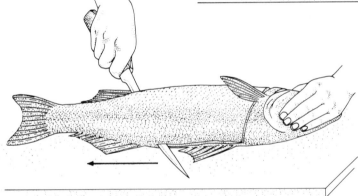

2. Turn the fillet over and
cut carefully through
the thin layer of meat
down to the skin; then
cut the fillet from the skin.
Cut the other fillet
in the same way.

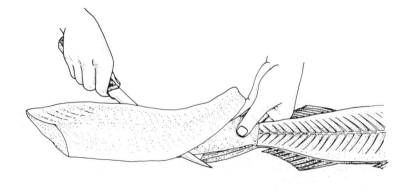

FILLETING (II)

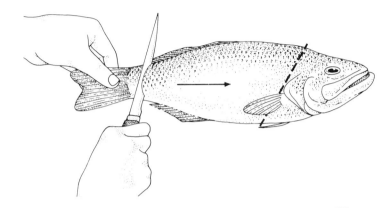

1. Start at the tail; cut along the backbone and through the ribs.

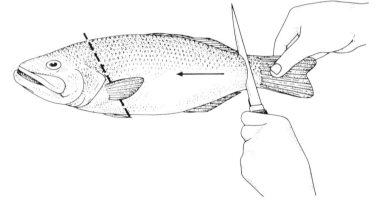

2. Turn the fish over and repeat the procedure on the other side.

FILLETING (III)

Start behind head and cut toward tail, taking all the meat off the rib cage as well as the backbone.

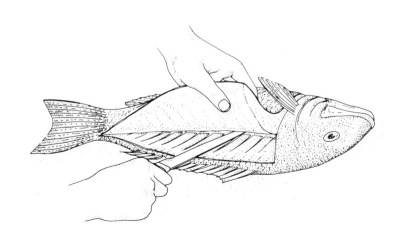

cage is sometimes left in the fillet, or it is removed entirely, without attempting to debone it. If you want to save this "rib cage" meat intact with fillets, use the next method.

Method III

This method is sometimes used to produce a boneless and skinless fillet. It works best with larger fish, and it saves the boneless flesh between the rib cage and the skin. Start cutting behind the head, working down the backbone and along the edge of the rib cage. The idea is to cut all the meat off the rib cage as well as the backbone. After you've cleaned the rib cage, it's easy to work on toward the tail.

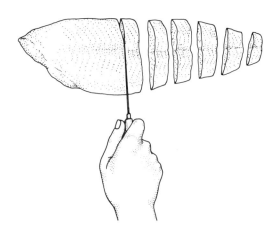

Cutting fish fingers from a fillet.

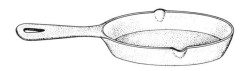

Fish Fingers

Fish fingers are nothing more than strips of fish flesh 3 or 4 inches long and no thicker and wider than an inch. Usually, fish fingers are cut from the fillets of larger fish, such as 100-pound jewfish. I also get fish fingers from along the backbone of medium sized fish when making my "family" cut, as described elsewhere in this chapter. Usually fish fingers are boneless and skinless, and are excellent for deep frying. For some reason, children love this cut.

Pan Dressing Fish

This term is rather vague, but in general it means getting fish ready for the frying pan. A small bluegill that has been scaled, beheaded, and gutted is considered to be pan dressed. On the other hand, a very large bluegill, weighing 2 pounds, should be halved lengthwise and might even be reduced to smaller size, depending on individual taste and the size of the pan.

A 1-pound bullhead and similar fish might be pan dressed by first cutting it in half, then cutting each strip into two pieces, as shown in the illustration. Note from the illustration that I recommend leaving the tail and fins on the fish. If you do remove the fins, be sure to get all the associated bones from the flesh. As I stated earlier in this chapter, *never* use scis-

PAN DRESSING SMALL FISH

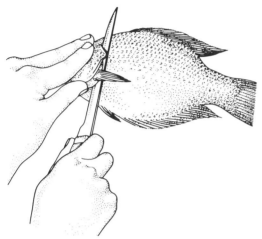

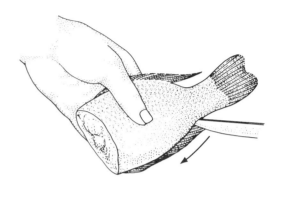

1. Remove head with a diagonal cut just behind the gill.

2. Cut from vent forward and remove entrails to make ready for pan.

PAN DRESSING A 1-POUND FISH

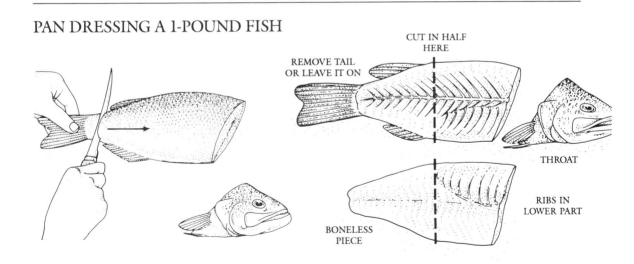

CUT IN HALF HERE

REMOVE TAIL OR LEAVE IT ON

THROAT

RIBS IN LOWER PART

BONELESS PIECE

1. Behead the fish; then cut it in half starting at the tail.

2. Cut both parts of the fish in half again.

sors or shears for trimming off the fins because they leave small bones embedded in the flesh.

The Livingston Pan Dressing Plan

Larger fish, such as a 3-pound bass, can of course be filleted—but I like to use *all* the fish. At the same time, I realize that many families who have small children may want to have some boneless fillets. Thus, I have developed a method of giving a maximum of boneless pieces of fish and, at the same time, minimizing waste. The method works nicely for fish in the 3- or 4-pound class, but I also use it for 1-pound fish if I've got children to feed. Of course, it's up to the cook to keep the boneless pieces seprate from the rest.

The dotted lines in the illustration indicate that the fillets from the small end of the fish can be cut in half. Usually, fillets from fish of 2 or 3 pounds should be so divided. Larger fish can also be divided into smaller pieces, or cut into fingers.

Also, the two pieces of boneless fish that I get from the thicker part of the fish, right

NO-WASTE METHOD

Fillet the fish, then cut each fillet in half. Remove tail and cut remaining piece in half as shown. This produces six boneless pieces and three pieces with bones.

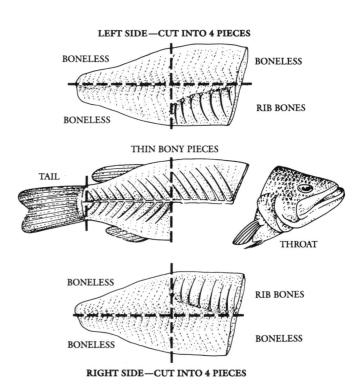

LEFT SIDE—CUT INTO 4 PIECES

BONELESS

BONELESS

RIB BONES

BONELESS

THIN BONY PIECES

TAIL

THROAT

BONELESS

RIB BONES

BONELESS

BONELESS

RIGHT SIDE—CUT INTO 4 PIECES

behind the head, can also be cut into strips. I normally dress out the throat from fish that are a pound or larger. But I confess that I usually throw out the head without bothering with the cheeks.

Boning Fish

A few recipes call for boned fish, but I don't recommend the method. I like the recipes, but I'll let somebody else do the boning. Once I read an article in one of my wife's magazines that called for boned fish. It said the process was easy, and recommended that you ask your butcher to bone the fish for you. Well, I told the meat man at my local Piggly Piggly store that I wanted six boned mullet. He didn't know what I was talking about. When I explained how to do it, he didn't even answer me! Maybe he thought I was joking.

If you want to give it a try, start with a scaled fish that weighs at least 5 or 6 pounds. Smaller fish can be boned, but they are more difficult. Usually, a fish to be boned must be *scaled*, not skinned.

Start by cutting out the top fin and associated bones. Insert a very sharp, small knife blade into the fish on the side of the fin, then make a shallow gash the entire length of the fin. Make a similar gash on the other side. Pull out the fin. If it won't come easily, you haven't cut the gash quite deep enough. Now extend the gash to the head, and then to the tail. Carefully work the knife down to the backbone. You'll have to make a cut on either side of the backbone, extending from the tail to the rib cage. Next, carefully cut along the rib cage on either side. But don't cut all the way through to the belly of the fish. Your objective will be to lift the backbone and the rib cage out of the fish, leaving the belly flesh intact. At some point, you'll have to cut the backbone next to the tail, and next to the head. After you cut both ends, you'll be able to work your knife down far enough to completely free the bones from the flesh. You must be very careful when cutting along the rib cage, lest you cut through the flesh and skin. The larger the fish, the greater the margin for error.

If you perform the boning properly, you'll end up with a whole fish without bones. It will have a slit in the top, and it is usually stuffed.

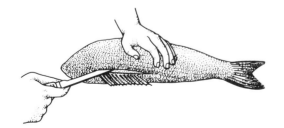 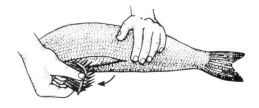

To remove dorsal fin, make two shallow cuts on either side and pull it out.

Refrigerating Fish

I don't like to keep fish in the refrigerator or on ice longer than three days after they are caught. Always dress the fish, or at least gut them, before refrigerating. Personally, I like to dress mine all the way and keep them in water. But some people maintain that they should not be kept in water. Instead, they recommend putting the fish in a suitable container, or on a platter, and wrapping the top with cling paper, aluminum foil, or such. Do not wrap the individual fish.

Keep the fish in the coldest part of your refrigerator, preferably at a temperature between 32 and 35 degrees.

If you plan to keep fish longer than two or three days, freeze it.

Freezing Fish

By far the most satisfactory way to freeze fish with ordinary home equipment is to cover them completely with water. I like to fillet or pan dress the fish, put the pieces into plastic milk cartons or similar containers, cover the meat with water, and freeze the whole thing. But suitable containers are not always at hand, in which case I cut up the fish into pieces and wrap as tightly as I can, first in plastic film and then in freezer paper.

I seldom attempt to freeze large fish without reducing them to fillets or other pieces. You can wrap a whole 10-pound bass and freeze it, but I don't recommend this. I've done it, though, and will probably do it again. Some people recommend that you first dip a whole fish in water, then freeze it. After it is frozen, dip it again in *very* cold ice water, then put it immediately back into the freezer. Dip several times, building up a layer of ice. The success of the method depends in part on how hard frozen the fish is and on how cold the water is. I don't recommend freezing skinned fish in this manner, and, in fact, it's best to leave the scales on them. Again, I think it is best to cut the fish up and freeze it in a block of water.

If you've got a lot of fish to freeze and not much room in the freezer, of course you must fillet the fish or otherwise reduce the volume. The most compact method is to boil or steam the fish, then make fish flakes and freeze them in small plastic cartons or zip bags.

Dressing Sharks

Shark is an excellent food fish that has suffered because many fishermen do not know how to take care of it. It must be immediately bled by chopping off the head and caudal (tail) fin. This should be done within a few minutes of boarding. If you wait to get back to the dock to take pictures, it's too late. Next, eviscerate, or gut, the shark as soon as possible. Then flush out the main artery with saltwater. Do not use iodized salt for shark; it will turn the flesh black and cause it to spoil more quickly. Last, thoroughly rinse the fish and put it on ice. If you use crushed ice, the fish should be packed inside and out to reduce the core temperature as rapidly as possible. Slush ice, using saltwater, however, is the best alternative, because you obtain maximum cooling and the slush acts as a brine solution. Keep the fish out of the sunlight.

To dress the fish, first cut off the fins. This is best done on the vessel since it allows for an easier fit in the cooler. Skinning is difficult and not necessary. But if you choose to skin the whole fish, use a sharp knife. Begin by making an incision through the skin down the middle of the back. Do not cut deeply into the meat. Make a cut underneath the skin and begin to peel it back until removed. Next remove the belly flaps. They can be smoked or used for jerky.

Next, cut the fish into usable portions by slicing steaks at least one inch thick. Because of their anatomical structure, sharks can be filleted by cutting from the edges of the sinews, called *skeletogenous septa*, lengthwise to produce long strips of meat. This meat can then be chunked, or cut into fillets and roasts.

As a general rule, the more mature a shark is, the tougher and chewier its meat. A more mature shark is usually a larger shark. Flavor and color, however, do not change with the size and maturity of a fish.

—UNC Sea Grant brochure, "Sharks."

In any case, be sure to mark your packages carefully, noting the kind of fish, how they are dressed, the approximate weight, and the date that you froze them.

Some fish don't keep very well when frozen. I've kept small bass for over a year, but they were very fresh to start with and they were frozen in a block of ice. Usually, lean fish keep better than fatty fish, but again there is quite a difference between one species and another. I've frozen channel and blue catfish with very good results, while bullheads in the same batch didn't fare too well.

As a rule, I don't freeze fatty fish unless I have to. Some people recommend that fatty fish should first be soaked for a few minutes in a solution of water and ascorbic acid, mixed in the proportions of 1 teaspoon of acid to 1 cup of water.

Thawing Out Frozen Fish

According to the experts, fish should be thawed by taking them out of the freezer and putting them into the refrigerator. I don't do this, and I doubt that many people do it more than once. It takes too long. I usually thaw mine at room temperature, putting them out a few hours before time to cook. More often than not, I'll end up running cold water over fish that have been frozen in a block of ice. The results are good, provided that you had good properly handled fish to start with.

I'll have to admit that on more than one occasion I've dropped partly thawed small fish into a deep fryer. The cooking time increased a bit, but the fish was good. I don't make a habit of this, however, and would never attempt to cook solidly frozen large fish, except in a real emergency.

Once a fish has been thawed, do not refreeze it—unless it has been cooked. Leftovers can be frozen again, if necessary. If I have to thaw out more fish that I need, I usually boil part of them for flaking and refreezing. They can be used in the recipes that call for flaked fish (Chapter 4).

Caring for the Catch

The best possible course is to dress your fish and cook them on the spot, and some oriental people go to great pains to keep fish and eels alive until they are ready to cook them. The next best course of action is to *dress the fish and put them on ice immediately after catching them.* But few anglers will do this, especially if the fish are biting well. If you're on a boat, a good live well is nice to have, but too many people let the fish die from overcrowding or lack of oxygen. In my opinion, having a good ice chest with plenty of ice in it is usually more satisfactory than a live well.

I'm not one to talk, as I've strung up several thousand fish during my lifetime, but one of the worst things you can do with fish is to put too many of them on a stringer, or in a creel. But both methods are sometimes necessary, especially when you're wading a stream, a lake, or the salt flats.

My brother came up with a solution to part of the problem. Once he was wade fishing Lake Ockeechobee, in Florida, catching bluegills on a flyrod and stringing them up behind him, when he discovered that a huge cottonmouth was tugging at the other end of the stringer. He said that on the spot he invented the Ockeechobee Jig. After that he

started pulling a little plastic boat behind him. The craft, or toy, I suppose, was about 2 ½ feet long—just big enough to hold a small ice chest, a little spare tackle, and a .410 scattergun pistol for snakes! I've never seen another minature boat quite like it, but I have noted that some flounder giggers and frog giggers, as well as people after bay scallops, pull a small wash tub behind them. In any case, putting the fish on ice when they are caught is usually better than putting them on a stringer or in a creel.

Part Two

GAME BIRDS

20

DOVES

Regardless of what other cookbooks say, allow at least two doves per adult. I prefer three. And four isn't too many, for me, if doves make up all the meat that is to be served during the meal. But on the other hand I am inordinately fond of doves. I like their tender, somewhat dark meat with a hint of the wild. It's perfect, at least for my taste.

I suspect that some of the contributors to other books confused doves with pigeons, and that this confusion was compounded by having multiple authors or contributors. One cookbook, for example, has a tabular guide to bird servings and allows 1 to 1½ doves per person. Yet, a few pages later the author says that he has gone hungry at "boards" where the cook served up only 1 dove per hunter.

Moreover, another cookbook, in a table of approximate weights, lists the dove as weighing ¾ of a pound (12 ounces) and the quail as weighing 6 ounces. Thus, they are telling the world that the dove is twice as big as the quail. In truth, adult quail are quite a bit larger than any adult doves that can be legally hunted in this country. Of course, there are several kinds of quail and several kinds of doves, and there are some size variations—but none that will put the largest quail only half the size of the largest dove. (I'm talking about game doves with legal hunting seasons, not fat Central Park pigeons.)

In the United States, only two species of doves are widely hunted legally: the mourning dove and the whitewing dove—and the whitewing is limited to selected areas of the Southwest. Another species, which I call the ground dove, is quite small and is not hunted legally in most states. In any case, the recipes that follow can be used on either mourning dove or whitewings.

Baked Doves

If I had to choose one method of cooking doves, I'd have to consider this recipe carefully. It has a certain flavor that complements the taste of wild dove—and the gravy is supurb! Be sure to try it.

8 to 10 doves
1 can chicken broth (10 ¾ ounce)
1 tablespoon Worcestershire sauce
1 teaspoon onion juice
¼ teaspoon garlic juice
½ stick of margarine or butter
flour
salt
pepper

Preheat oven to 350 degrees. Salt and pepper doves, then shake them in a sack that contains a cup or so of flour. Heat the margarine (or butter) in a frying pan and brown the birds. Remove birds and set aside. Stir 1 tablespoon of flour into a cup of cold water and add to pan drippings. Stir, mixing thoroughly. Increase heat until gravy starts to bubble. Add chicken stock and Worcestershire sauce. Stir in the onion and garlic juice. Cook for a few minutes. Arrange doves, breast up, in a baking pan or casserole dish. Pour gravy over birds and bake for 30 minutes. Baste several times with liquid from pan. *Serves 3 or 4.*

Fried Dove

doves or dove breasts
oil
flour
salt
pepper

Heat oil for frying doves. Deep frying works best, but this method isn't very practical for cooking only a few birds. So, use a small frying pan for 4 or 5 birds, a larger pan or deep fryer for a large dove supper. Salt and pepper birds to taste, then shake in flour. Fry in oil at medium-high heat until browned.

Fried doves will be dry and tough if they are cooked too long. Like duck, dove is best on the rare side.

Doves in Easy Gravy

8 to 10 doves, whole
8 to 10 strips of bacon
1 tablespoon cooking oil
salt
pepper
1 can beef gravy (10½ ounce)
2 green onions
4 ounces mushrooms, sliced
½ cup red wine

Salt and pepper doves. Wrap each bird in a bacon strip and pin. Heat oil in the frying pan, brown doves, and set aside. Chop the onions (including part of the green tops). Brown onions and mushrooms in pan drippings, then stir in gravy. Add doves. Simmer for 30 minutes. Add wine and simmer for another 15 minutes. *Serves 3 or 4.*

Dove Fricassee

It's true that some recipes work best with dove breasts, which leaves a lot of backs, wings, and legs. Although many people throw these parts away, I highly recommend that they be used to make some sort of pie or a dove fricassee. Of course, the recipe below is so good that you will find yourself making fricassee of the whole birds!

2 cups dove meat, chopped
1 tablespoon butter
salt
pepper
¾ cup diced onion
¾ cup sliced mushrooms

Boil the doves in a little water until meat pulls easily from the bones. Retain the water from boiling. Drain birds and pull meat with a fork. (If you use whole birds, the breasts should be chopped.) Heat butter in a frying pan and sauté the onion and mushrooms. Add dove meat. Cover with some of the water that was used to boil the doves. Salt and pepper to taste. (I prefer to go a little heavy on the pepper in this dish.) Bring to quick boil, then reduce heat. Cover and simmer for an hour. Add flour to thicken gravy, if desired. Serve over rice. *Serves 4.*

Note: If whole doves are used to make this dish, allow 2 birds for a cup of meat.

Charcoal Grilled Doves

doves, plucked and halved
olive oil
lemon juice
salt
pepper

While the charcoal briquets get hot, mix a basting sauce with ½ olive oil and ½ lemon juice. Marinate birds in sauce until ready to cook. Salt and pepper birds to taste, then lay out on grill over coals. Cook for about 15 minutes on each side, or until done. (Much depends, of course, on how hot your fire is, and on the distance from birds to coals.) Baste several times during cooking.

Dove, Rainwater, and Joel Vance Spice

Here's a good recipe from Jan Phillips' *Wild Edibles of Missouri*. One of the merits of this dish is that you have to go duck hunting before you can cook it!

dove breasts (emergency substitute:
  quail, chicken, turkey)
10 cups rainwater
2 tablespoons butter
8 chicken bouillon cubes
2 cups hot rainwater
4 teaspoons salt
¼ teaspoon pepper
8 tablespoons chopped onion

1 teaspoon thyme
1 teaspoon rosemary

"Gather rainwater on the day you go duck hunting!

"Brown dove breasts in butter for 10 minutes. Add all ingredients from bouillon cubes down through rosemary and simmer for 20 minutes. Remove doves and add the following ingredients:

4 cups sour cream
2 cups white wine
¼ cup flour to thicken

"Heat, add doves and serve with either wild rice and mushrooms or noodles and mushrooms (cooked in the remaining cups of rainwater, of course!)."

"Why Not" Doves

My original recipe for this dish called for white wine vinegar. But when I started to cook, I had only red wine vinegar, which, if used, would have to be mixed with white wine Worcestershire sauce, thereby committing some sort of French culinary sin. Well . . . why not?

12 doves
cooking oil
1 medium onion, chopped
flour
salt
pepper
1 cup white wine Worcestershire sauce

⅓ cup red wine vinegar
water

Stand back a bit, hold your nose, and close your eyes while you mix the red wine vinegar and the white wine Worcestershire sauce. Pour the mixture over the doves, put into your refrigerator, and marinate over night. Save part of the marinade liquid.

Heat oil in large skillet with a tight-fitting cover. Brown chopped onions and set aside. Salt and pepper doves. Cover doves heavily with flour, then brown in skillet. Pour off excess oil. Add 1 cup water and onions. Bring to boil, then reduce heat, cover tightly, and simmer for 30 minutes. The gravy goes well over rice. *Serves 4 to 6.*

Doves n' Deer

I got the idea for this dish from *Cooking the Sportsman's Harvest*, published by the South Dakota Department of Game, Fish, and Parks. But the recipe below is not a quote; I changed it considerably and bear the responsibility for the changes. Try it the first time you've got leftover venison roast and a mess of doves.

12 doves
12 strips bacon
2 cups leftover venison, diced
1 can mushroom soup (10¾ ounce size)
1 cup sour cream
½ cup water
salt

pepper
1 teaspoon garlic juice
1 tablespoon bacon drippings

Select a casserole dish of suitable size and shape for holding 12 doves. Preheat oven to 350 degrees. Wrap each dove in a strip of bacon. Grease the casserole dish with bacon drippings and garlic juice. Spread diced venison on bottom. Arrange doves on top of diced venison. Sprinkle with salt and pepper. Add the can of mushroom soup mixed with ½ can of water and the sour cream. Bake for 3 hours. *Serves 4 to 6.*

Smothered Doves

doves, plucked and halved
butter
green onions with tops, finely minced
salt
pepper
flour
spring water

Heat butter in a frying pan, sauté a few onions in butter and set aside. Salt and pepper dove halves. Shake in flour and brown in butter. Remove birds from frying pan. Add a little more butter and heat. Add green onions and a little water. Bring to quick boil,

then reduce heat. Sprinkle with flour and stir. Put birds back into gravy, cover tightly, and simmer for 30 minutes.

Dove Pie

I cook all the ingredients listed below in a Dutch oven, heated first on a stovetop then transferred to the oven.

8 doves
8 slices bacon
salt
pepper
bay leaf
water
4 medium potatoes, diced
4 carrots, sliced
8 green onions cut into 1-inch
    segments (tops too)
1 cup sherry
pie pastry—or canned (refrigerated)
    biscuits

Cook bacon in a large frying pan with an oven-proof handle and drain. Brown doves in bacon drippings. Return bacon to pot with doves. Salt and pepper to taste. Cover with water, add bay leaf, and bring to a quick boil. Reduce heat, cover, and simmer for an hour. Add carrots, potatoes, and onions. Add wine and enough water to almost cover vegetables. Simmer for 30 minutes.

Preheat oven to 400 degrees. Sprinkle flour on a flat surface and roll out some canned biscuits, making a thin pastry. (Or use a pastry of your choice.) Cut the pastry into strips and criss-cross them across the dove and vegetable mixture. Put the frying pan into the oven and bake for 20 minutes, or until pastry is browned. *Serves 4.*

Variation: put some pastry strips down in the pie to make dumplings.

Dove Breasts and Bacon over Charcoal

    dove breasts
    bacon
    salt
    pepper
    lemon juice

Dress birds and remove breasts. Sprinkle with lemon juice and set aside. Start charcoal briquets. Salt and pepper birds to taste. Wrap each breast with about half a strip of bacon and pin with toothpicks. Grill over medium hot coals. Usually, when the bacon is crisp, the doves will be done—but this rule of thumb won't hold true if the bird breast is held very close to very hot coals.

Variation: Whole birds can be used in the above method, but the problem is that the small legs tend to get done before the interior of the breasts. My solution here is to work in units of two birds. Dress the birds as for stuffing. Next, insert the legs of each bird into the cavity of the other. Then spiral wrap both birds with one strip of bacon.

Variation: Dove and bacon kabobs can be cooked as above if the skewers are loaded as follows: Insert the very end of a strip of

bacon onto the tip of the skewer. Insert top of skewer into a dove breast until the point protrudes. Wrap bacon over dove breast and pierce with point of skewer. Repeat procedure, adding a new strip of bacon if needed. This method works best on a rotisserie.

Crockpot Dove

This dish is quite tasty if prepared with the whole dove, but the legs and wings tend to come apart during long cooking, filling the pot with bones. I therefore recommend that you use only dove breasts (and save the rest of the bird for dove fricassee or other dishes).

    20 dove breasts
    cooking oil
    garlic salt
    pepper
    flour
    4 medium potatoes, sliced
    2 medium onions, sliced
    2 carrots, sliced

2 cans cream of celery soup (10¾-
   ounce size)
1 cup water
1 teaspoon oregano

Salt and pepper dove breasts to taste. Heat cooking oil in a frying pan. Roll dove breasts in flour and brown. Put dove breasts into the crockpot. Add potatoes, onions, carrots, oregano, celery soup, and water. Turn crockpot to low and cook for 9 hours. *Serves 7 or 8.*

What Mattie Cobb Missed

Whenever I cook this dish, I think of my mother. I also remember, with mixed feelings, a little redheaded lady named Miss Mattie Cobb, who, in spite of cronic neuralgia in her arm, tried hard to teach me Latin in high school. No doubt she was among the last of the small-school Latin teachers, having been retained by a staunch principal named J.J. Yarborough, who suffered no neuralgia in his arm. For some reason that I never did understand, mother invited Miss Cobb over for a bird supper. I had bagged lots of doves, quail, and a few snipe during the holidays, and, since we had plenty, and had company to feed, my mother cooked only the breasts.

In spite of the neuralgia in her arm, Miss Cobb consumed, with tiny bites, about ten birds—ten times what I had figured for her. Even so, her feast on my ten birds didn't pull up my Latin grade.

I think that Mother invited Miss Cobb to the wrong meal. Although the bird breasts were mighty good, served with grapes and all, the real finger-licking, table-hunkering feast was yet to come. If you want to try it, proceed as follows:

When dressing the birds, save the heart, liver, and gizzard, along with the legs, back, wings, and neck. It's all right to leave the feet on the birds. Set the livers aside. Boil the bony parts of the bird (along with the gizzard and hearts) in a small amount of water for about an hour. Save the broth for the recipe below. Take a fork and pull the meat from the bones. Mince the hearts and gizzards. Chop up any bird breasts left over from the main meal and add to giblets. Add bird livers. Proceed with:

2 cups bird giblets and pickings
1½ cups bird broth
⅓ cup flour
salt
pepper
1 small onion, minced

FAT AND PROTEIN IN BIRDS

(Based on 100 Gram Edible Portions)

Bird	calories	protein*	fat*
chicken	124	18.6	4.9
wild duck	233	21.1	15.8
pheasant	151	24.3	5.2
quail	168	25.0	6.8

Note: The above table was made up from data published in *The South Carolina Wildlife Cookbook*, which in turn credited the Georgia Extension Service.
*measured in grams

butter
2 eggs, hard boiled, sliced
corn pone

In a thick cast iron frying pan, sauté onions in a little butter. Add the stock to the frying pan and heat quickly. Reduce heat and add flour slowly, stirring constantly, whisking with a fork. (There may be easier methods to do this, but much whisking helps the flavor of the gravy and cures neuralgia.) When all the lumps are gone, stir in giblets and onion. Salt and pepper to taste. Add the eggs, but don't stir. Heat almost to a boil, then quickly reduce heat and simmer for 30 minutes.

Serve with hot corn pone. Be sure to have enough corn pone to feed everybody, then let the gravy stretch as far as it needs to. It's every man for himself. So . . . if you don't

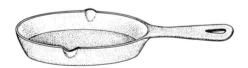

know how to sop gravy with corn pone, just quit the table and wait until Miss Mattie Cobb comes for more proper fare.

Zesty Broiled Doves

8 to 10 doves, halved
salt
pepper
2 tablespoons bacon drippings
2 tablespoons Worcestershire sauce
1 teaspoon onion juice

Cut birds in half and turn on broiler. Salt and pepper birds. Heat bacon drippings in a saucepan, then mix in Worcestershire sauce and onion juice. Dip birds in sauce, then arrange them, breast up, on a rack and baste. (The doves should be about 3 inches from the heat source.) Broil for 3 minutes, then baste and broil for another 3 minutes. Turn birds, baste heavily, and broil for 5 minutes, or until done. *Serves from 3 to 5.*

21

QUAIL

Never go quail hunting with a long-legged barber. They'll walk you to death, unless you've got a horse or a jeep. The reason, I figure, is that they stand up all day long, with their movement being confined to short steps in a circle around the chair. When they get afield, however, they break the circle habit and head on out, straight as a tangent. Sometimes even a pointer has trouble keeping up with them during a day's hunt.

Oyette Taylor is one such barber in my hometown of Headland, Alabama, in the heart of the Wiregrass area. It's quail country, and Taylor's Barber Shop, just off the town square, is a sort of headquarters for local outdoor news. As indicated in the recipe for salt fish elsewhere in this book, the Taylors will tell you not only where the fish are biting, but also exactly how to get there, exactly how to catch the fish, exactly how to dress them, and exactly how to cook them.

But Oyette doesn't talk too much about his favorite quail hunting spots. I think I know why. You'll know, too, when you try his favorite quail recipe.

Quail Oyette Taylor

Allow three birds and two biscuits per person, or two birds and three biscuits.

quail
buttermilk
peanut oil
salt and pepper
flour
fresh mushrooms, sliced
buttermilk biscuits from scratch
   (cooked separately)

Pluck the birds, dress them whole, and remove shot. Put the birds into a glass container, cover with buttermilk, and refrigerate for several hours. Drain. Salt and pepper to taste. Heat an inch of peanut oil in a frying pan, or in a Dutch oven if you've got many birds to cook. Brown the birds on all sides and remove. Pour off most of the grease, and scrape up the pan drippings. Sauté the mushrooms in the pan drippings. Add a little water to the pan and increase heat. Pour in a little buttermilk, stir, and return the birds to the pan. Cover and simmer for 30 minutes. Serve gravy over biscuits.

Polynesian Quail

8 quail
½ stick of margarine or butter
1 can tomato sauce (8-ounce)
1 cup sugar

Four by Twos

Since I usually serve two quail to each person, I find it handy to freeze them by fours in 24-ounce containers. Simply place the quail in the plastic containers, cover them completely with water, put the lid on snugly, and store them upright in your freezer. It pays to mark your container 'quail,' 'dove,' 'woodcock,' etc., so that you will not thaw out the wrong birds.
—Barbara G. Dickey, *Florida Wildlife*

---

1 cup soy sauce
¼ cup cooking sherry
cooked rice

Melt margarine in large frying pan. Cook quail, on medium heat, for 10 minutes, turning once.

While quail are cooking, add soy sauce, sherry, and tomato sauce to a pan. Heat and add sugar. Bring to boil and stir until sugar is melted. Pour sauce over quail in skillet, cover tightly, and cook over low heat for 15 minutes. Put quail on bed of rice and spoon on sauce from frying pan. Serve with vegetables as follows:

1 bell pepper, cut into chunks
1 can water chestnuts (8-ounce)
1 can bamboo shoots (8-ounce)
1 can pineapple chunks (15¼ ounce)
2 tablespoons margarine or butter

Melt margarine in frying pan (or wok). Add bell pepper. Drain pineapple, saving liquid. Add pineapple to frying pan and braise until it browns. Add ½ cup of pineapple juice from can, together with ½ cup of liquid from quail dish. Add water chestnuts and bamboo shoots. Simmer for about five minutes. Drain and serve with quail and rice. *Serves 4.*

Mesquite Quail

If you like the flavor of smoke in your barbecue, here's an easy quail dish that can be prepared in the oven.

8 or more quail
salt
pepper
1 bottle Mesquite barbecue sauce (19-ounce)

Preheat oven to 400 degrees. Salt and pepper quail, then put them into a baking dish. Pour barbecue sauce over birds and bake for about 30 minutes. Baste several times during baking. *Serves 4.*

Golden Honey Quail

Lea and Perrins sent me a booklet called "Light & Elegant," which contained a recipe for chicken wings. It is good, of course. After sneaking a little butter and salt into the recipe, I tried it on quail and can highly recommend it.

The Marinade
  1 cup white wine Worcestershire sauce
  ¼ cup honey
  ¼ cup pineapple juice
  ¼ cup soy sauce
The Quail
  8 to 10 quail
  salt
  pepper
Basting Sauce
  ¼ cup melted butter
  ¼ cup marinade sauce, above

In a marinade bowl, mix white wine Worcestershire sauce, honey, pineapple juice, and soy sauce. Cut quail in halves and put into

bowl, coating all sides. Cover and put in refrigerator for 6 hours, or overnight. Turn several times.

Preheat oven to 350 degrees. Place quail in a well-greased baking dish, baste with butter sauce, and bake for 45 minutes. Turn once and baste often while cooking. *Serves 4 or 5.*

Fried Garlic Quail

quail
cooking oil
flour
garlic powder
salt
pepper

Heat about 1 inch of oil in a frying pan. Cut quail in half and season each side with salt, pepper, and garlic powder. Shake or roll in flour and fry until golden brown. *Allow 2 birds per person.*

Lemon Broiled Quail

8 quail, halved
salt
pepper
juice from 1 lemon
½ cup white wine Worcestershire sauce
¼ cup melted butter

Turn on broiler. Cut birds in half. Salt and pepper to taste. Melt butter in a saucepan, then stir in lemon juice and Worcestershire sauce. Arrange bird halves on broiling rack and baste with sauce. Put under broiler, about 3 inches from heat source. Broil for about 5 minutes, basting once. Turn birds, baste, and broil for another 5 minutes, basting at least once. Test for doneness. *Serves 4.*

Quail Fricassee

Here's a dish that seems to stretch a few quail into a real "mess." It's one of my favorites.

5 or 6 quail
quail stock
2 tablespoons butter
salt
pepper
1 cup diced onion
1 cup sliced mushrooms
1 tablespoon white wine
    Worcestershire sauce
rice

Boil the quail in a little water until meat pulls easily from the bones. Retain the water for use as stock. Drain the birds and pull the meat from the bones with a fork. Chop the breast.

Heat the butter in a frying pan and sauté the onion and mushrooms for a few minutes. Add the quail meat. Salt and pepper to taste. Add Worcestershire sauce, then add enough of the broth to almost cover the meat. Bring to quick boil, then reduce heat. Cover and simmer for an hour. Add flour to thicken

gravy, if desired. Serve over cooked rice. *Serves 5 or 6.*

Variation: Use the juice of ½ lemon instead of the white wine Worcestershire sauce. Also, try this dish on a blend of wild rice and long grain rice.

Oven Barbecued Quail

8 quail
¼ pound bacon
1 cup catsup
½ cup onion, chopped
1 clove garlic, minced
2 tablespoons red wine vinegar
1 teaspoon salt
¼ teaspoon black pepper
2 tablespoons brown sugar

Cook bacon in skillet until well done. Crumble and set aside. Sauté onion and garlic in bacon drippings. Add vinegar, catsup, salt, pepper, bacon, and brown sugar. Simmer for 10 minutes or longer. Place quail in a suitable baking dish and pour sauce over them. Bake at 400 degrees for 30 minutes. *Serves 3 or 4.*

Italian Grilled Quail

Not long ago I took my family to the banks of the Omussee Creek to do a little cane-pole fishing. We went to a sort of family spot, complete with concrete picnic tables, barbecue pits, and so on. I took charcoal and planned to cook whatever fish the boys caught. Just in case the fish weren't biting, I took along some iced-down quail and Italian salad dressing. Fishing proved to be slow, and after eating quail everybody wanted to switch to bird hunting! Here's all you need:

Scaled Quail of the Desert

Often called blue quail, this game bird measures about 11 inches long and weighs an average of 6½ ounces. Scaled quail are easily identified by their overall bluish cast above and light gray to whitish coloring below. Feathers of the breast, neck, and upper back have dark margins, giving birds a scaled appearance. These birds also sport a short, white tuft of feathers atop their heads.

Scaled quail are typically desert or semi-arid species which reside in the southwest United States and northern Mexico. In Oklahoma, they occur in rugged terrain featuring sand, sagebrush, mesquite, juniper, and cactus cover.

In winter, birds gather into coveys that average 30 birds but sometimes exceed 100. . . . Unlike bobwhites, they are more apt to run into dense cover than suddenly take wing when alarmed. While scaled quail will fly for short distances, their advantage clearly lies in their running ability as they can outdistance a sprinting man.

—Oklahoma Wildlife News Service

quail (plucked)
Zesty Italian salad dressing
butter

I prefer plucked quail for cooking over coals, but skinned birds can certainly be used if necessary. Cut dressed quail in half. Get fire started. Melt a little butter and mix with salad dressing. (About 3 parts salad dressing and 1 part butter will be fine.) Marinate quail in salad dressing mixture while fire heats up. Put quail on grill and cook for 30 minutes, or until done. Baste and turn the quail two or three times. *I allow 2 quail per person.*

Fried Quail

Quail can be fried whole, or you can use only the breast. I prefer mine to be plucked instead of skinned, and fried whole.

quail
cooking oil
salt
pepper
flour, all purpose

Put about an inch of oil into a frying pan and heat. (A deep fryer can also be used, if you've got lots of quail to fry.) Salt and pepper birds to taste, inside and out. Shake in flour and fry on medium heat until done. *Allow 2 quail per person.*

Variation: Split birds in half and reduce the depth of oil in frying pan. Or use a little butter on a griddle.

Country Fried Quail with Gravy

Here's a good dish to serve anywhere, anytime. But it is especially good with homemade biscuits for breakfast.

> **quail**
> **cooking oil**
> **salt**
> **pepper**
> **flour**
> **onions, minced**
> **toast**

Heat about 1 inch of oil in a frying pan. Salt and pepper quail to taste, roll or shake in flour, and fry on medium heat until browned. Remove quail, pour off most of the oil, and sauté onions for a few minutes. Add water, bring to a quick boil, and reduce heat. Sprinkle with a little flour and stir. Place quail back in frying pan, cover, reduce heat, and simmer for 20 to 30 minutes. Serve on toast with gravy. *For breakfast or a light lunch, allow 1 bird per person.*

Double Quail 'n Bacon over Charcoal

Quail breasts can be used with this recipe, but I prefer whole birds. The trouble with whole birds over charcoal, however, is that the small legs tend to get done before the inside of the breasts. As was pointed out in a similar recipe for dove, my solution to this problem is to work in units of two birds. (Most people will eat two birds anyway.) Pluck and dress the birds as for stuffing. Next, insert the legs of each bird into the cavity of the other bird. Then spiral wrap both birds with one strip of bacon (have bacon at room temperature). Cook and serve as a unit. Here's all you need:

> **quail (in units of two)**
> **garlic salt**
> **pepper**
> **bacon**
> **lemon juice**

While charcoal briquets heat up, sprinkle quail with lemon juice. Then season with garlic salt and pepper. Wrap with bacon, as discussed above. Grill about 4 inches from medium heat and cook until bacon is crisp. Baste lightly three or four times with lemon juice. *Serve 2 quail per person.*

22

WILD TURKEY

Seldom do I look forward to a dinner of domestic turkey. The way most people cook it, the meat is too dry to suit me. The meat goes down better as leftovers, sliced thinly against the grain and made into sandwiches, with plenty of good mayonnaise.

The wild turkey, on the other hand, is a good deal moister. It is a darker meat, which suits me fine. But, unforunately, the wild turkey is likely to be cooked far too long in most kitchens. For one thing, a wild turkey is usually much smaller than a domestic "market" bird, which means that cooking times for "whole bird" recipes should be reduced drastically. For another thing, many people cook wild meat much too long merely because it is wild. Also, the tricks for testing the doneness of domestic birds don't work as well for wild turkey. The leg doesn't move as easily when it is done, and the meat does not feel as soft when poked with the finger. If in doubt when cooking a wild turkey, use a meat thermometer inserted into the breast (but not touching the bone). The thermometer reading should not exceed 180 degrees. Remember also that baking the bird whole isn't the only way to cook a turkey, as the following recipes show.

Fried Turkey Fingers

If there were enough wild turkeys to go around, this simple recipe could form the basis of another fast food chain, even without a dozen secret spices added to it.

203

turkey breast
cooking oil
salt
pepper
milk
flour

Marinate turkey breast for several hours in milk. Heat cooking oil in frying pan. Cut turkey breasts into fingers. Salt and pepper to taste. Roll or shake in flour. Fry until golden. *Allow ¼ to ⅓ pound of turkey fingers per person.*

Roast Wild Turkey á la Seminole

I've eaten lots of turkey, and this is one of the best recipes I've ever tried. And why not? The wild turkey is a native American, and I got the recipe from a book called *Seminole Indian Recipes* by Marina Polvay.

1 turkey, 8 to 10 pounds
salt and pepper
2 small apples, cut in half
1 medium onion, cut in half
2 stalks celery, sliced
1 teaspoon sage
6 to 8 slices of bacon
cheesecloth soaked in bacon drippings

Preheat oven to 325 degrees. Sprinkle salt and pepper on turkey, inside and out. Put apples, onion, and celery into the cavity. Pull the turkey's legs upward and tie them together with a cotton string. Turn the wings under the bird's back and pin with skewers. Put the bird, breast up, on a rack in a roasting pan. Cover the turkey's breast with bacon slices and with a cheesecloth that has been soaked in bacon fat. Bake for 20 to 25 minutes per pound of bird. Baste several times with pan juices.

Wild Turkey Gumbo

A gumbo is hard to beat when made with anything reasonable, and leftover turkey is perfect!

2 cups chopped turkey meat, cooked
1 quart of turkey stock (or chicken bouillon made with cubes)
4 strips bacon
2 cups fresh or canned tomatoes (including all juice)
1 cup of fresh or frozen okra, sliced crossways
2 stalks of celery, diced
1 medium onion, diced
1 green pepper, diced
2 tablespoons parsley
salt and pepper
1¼ cups uncooked long grain rice
file (optional)

Fry the bacon and set aside. Sauté the okra for 10 minutes in hot bacon drippings, then add the celery, onion, and green pepper. Sauté for another 5 minutes. Transfer the vegetables to a suitable pot, then add crumbled bacon, diced turkey meat, and parsley. Add tomatoes and uncooked rice.

Wild Turkey

There's a saying in Virginia, "Just get a husband who can kill a wild turkey." This sage further advises to catch both man and turkey in their youth, as both are easier to handle while young.

—*Progressive Farmer's Southern Cookbook*

Salt and pepper to taste. Bring to boil, reduce heat, cover, and simmer for 45 minutes. Don't peek. *Serves 8 or 9.*

If you want to thicken this gumbo, sprinkle a little filé on it and stir it in. But don't cook the gumbo after the filé has been added; in fact, if you serve the gumbo in bowls, it's best to stir the filé into individual servings.

Variation: Be sure to try this recipe with smoked turkey.

Pork Skin Turkey with Cranberry Salad

Anyone who believes that roast turkey is too dry should try the following method from the National Wild Turkey Federation.

1 turkey, 10 to 12 pounds, dressed
salt
coarse black pepper
garlic powder to taste
3 ribs celery, with leaves
2 bay leaves
2 pounds pork spare ribs or skin from pork shoulder
1 onion, quartered

"Wash and thoroughly dry turkey. Rub cavity inside and outside with salt, pepper, and garlic powder. Place onion, celery, and bay leaves in cavity. Place bird on rack in roaster, breast side up. Cover with spare ribs or pork skin, which can be ordered from your meat merchant. When meat is done, pork skin will be crisp, and the cracklings can be used in corn bread. If spare ribs are used, you will have a delicious second dish. Roast turkey at 325 degrees for 3 or 4 hours. Remove pork skin or ribs during last half hour of cooking to allow turkey to brown."

Cranberry sauce of one recipe or another always goes nicely with baked fowl. You can get by with a can of ordinary supermarket canned cranberry sauce with Pork Skin Turkey—but if you've got the time and inclination to prepare it, I especially recommend the following recipe.

Cranberry Salad
1 envelope gelatin, unflavored
1 can whole cranberry sauce (16-ounce size)
1 can pineapple chunks (8½ ounce size)
1 apple, peeled and diced
1 cup water
½ cup good mayonnaise
juice of 1 lemon
1 teaspoon grated lemon peeling
2 tablespoons sugar
¼ teaspoon salt (optional)

Mix the gelatin, sugar, and salt in a saucepan. Stir in 1 cup of water and heat, stirring, until the gelatin dissolves. Remove from heat and stir in the mayonnaise, lemon juice, and grated lemon peeling. Beat until well mixed with a blender or a hand-held machine. Pour the mixture into a tray and place it in a freezer for 15 minutes. Remove from tray and beat again in blender until mixture is fluffy. Fold in the pineapple and diced apple. Put the mixture into a suitable mold (to hold about 4 cups) and chill it until it is firm. Unmold onto a serving plate and serve chilled.

Note: The cranberry salad part of the above recipe was adapted from a book called *Treasured Southern Family Recipes*, by Geddings de M. Cushman and Ora Lou O'Hara Cushman.

Turkey Casserole

Here is a good recipe to use for leftover turkey. It makes lots of casserole, but it can be frozen.

3 cups cooked turkey, diced
1 can chicken and rice soup (10¾-ounce size)
1 cup onions, chopped
1 cup celery, chopped
2 hard boiled eggs, chopped
1 cup mayonnaise
½ cup slivered almonds (or pecans)
½ teaspoon salt
¼ teaspoon pepper
juice from ½ lemon

½ tablespoon white wine Worcestershire sauce
2 cups crushed potato chips

Preheat oven to 375 degrees. In a large bowl, mix turkey, soup, onion, celery, almonds, salt, pepper, Worcestershire sauce, and lemon juice. Add mayonnaise, then carefully stir in the chopped boiled eggs. Put mixture into a well-greased casserole dish and sprinkle crushed potato chips on top. Bake for 30 minutes. *Serves 6 to 8.*

Wild Turkey and Country Dressing

The Bird
1 turkey, about 8 pounds, plucked and dressed
salt and pepper
butter
The Dressing
6 cups of corn bread, broken into pieces
2 cups dry biscuit crumbs
2 medium onions, finely chopped
2 stalks celery, finely chopped
3 hard-boiled eggs, chopped
4 raw eggs
¼ teaspoon pepper
1 teaspoon salt
water (if needed)
The Gravy
turkey neck
turkey liver
turkey gizzard

water
2 hard-boiled eggs, sliced
flour
1 teaspoon Kitchen Bouquet
salt and pepper

Preheat oven to 325 degrees and mix the dressing ingredients (except water) while it heats. Put the turkey (plucked and dressed, of course) on a rack in a suitable roasting pan. Add a little water to the pan. Cover the turkey with aluminum foil and bake for 4 hours, or until done. Remove the turkey from the roasting pan. Raise oven to 375 degrees. Put the dressing mixture in the pan, mixing with the pan juices. Add a little water if necessary to make a soft dressing. Bake uncovered until dressing is golden brown.

Make the gravy while the turkey and dressing are baking. Boil the neck, liver, and gizzard in a saucepan until tender. The liver will take about 40 minutes; the neck and gizzard, an hour and a half. Retain the broth.

Talking Turkey

Each turkey has a different voice. They all sound different and other turkeys know who is calling. When I go into the woods, I try to be a turkey. I want to sound like a turkey and act like a turkey. I want to be a bird the other birds don't know, and I want them to be curious enough to come check me out.

—Ray Eye, quoted by Gary Thomas in Illinois' *Outdoor Highlights*.

Bone the neck and dice the meat, along with liver and gizzard. Add chopped meat to the broth, then season with salt and pepper and add Kitchen Bouquet. Thicken with a little flour. Add sliced eggs. Serve gravy over dressing. Eat with sliced turkey.

Wild Turkey Salad with Apple

My wife likes chicken salad made with diced apples, and I asked her to come up with a recipe for wild turkey. She did—and how. The sour cream is better than the mayonnaise that is called for in most recipes of this sort.

3 cups of diced turkey meat (cooked)
lemon juice
1 apple, diced
1 small onion, diced
½ cup (or 3-ounce package) walnuts
  or pecan pieces
4 tablespoons sour cream
2 tablespoons pickle relish
1 teaspoon mustard
2 hard boiled eggs, sliced
salt and pepper

If you've got leftover turkey, dice two cups of it and sprinkle with a little lemon juice and refrigerate it. If you've got raw turkey, simmer part of it for an hour, or until it is tender. Bone and dice the meat. Sprinkle lightly with lemon juice and refrigerate.

Put diced turkey into a large glass bowl. Peel, core, and dice the apple, then peel and dice the onion. Add both to the turkey, then stir in sour cream, mustard, pickle relish, nuts and boiled eggs. Add more sour cream, or mayannoise, if needed. Toss and chill. Serve on lettuce leaves. *Serves 5 or 6.*

Smoked Wild Turkey

Smoked wild turkey is very, very good. And it's easy if you save up some bacon drippings. You'll also need a smoker big enough to hold the bird, and some sort of temperature control is highly desirable.

Fresh Cranberry Sauce

Any reasonable cranberry sauce, canned or otherwise, adds something rather festive to a turkey dinner, and is also good with venison, bear, and other wild game. If you've got access to a cranberry bog, or if you can purchase fresh or frozen berries, you may want to try this easy sauce recipe:

1 pound fresh or frozen cranberries, whole
1 ¼ cups sugar
1 ¼ cups water

Dissolve the sugar into the water and bring to boil. Add cranberries and bring to second boil. Reduce heat and simmer for 10 minutes, stirring several times. Let cool. Pour into a serving dish (or dishes) and refrigerate until you are ready to eat. Leftover sauce can be kept for several days in the refrigerator.

1 turkey, plucked and dressed
1 pint bacon drippings

Bring your smoker to heat and add some green or soaked hickory, oak, or similar wood of your choice. (I use green pecan wood, but my choice is based largely on my having a ready supply of it.) Put the turkey in the smoker and adjust the heat to about 170 degrees. Smoke for an hour and a half for *each pound* of dressed turkey. Baste turkey with bacon drippings every 30 minutes or so. Try to keep temperature at about 170 degrees—or at least somewhere between 160 and 180 degrees.

Pit-Cooked Turkey Tom

If you want a really succulent bird, and have the time, try the recipe below with a wild turkey.

1 large wild turkey, plucked, or two small turkeys
lots of barcecue sauce (at least half a gallon)
lots of good wood
lots of cheesecloth (at least five square yards)
salt and pepper

Dig a pit in the ground about 3 feet deep, 3 feet wide, and 3 feet long. Build a fire and add to it until the pit is ¾ full of coals. Wash the cheesecloth, then soak it in barbecue sauce. Baste the plucked turkey inside and out with barbecue sauce. Wrap turkey with cheesecloth, pinning the legs and wings in tight. Coat the cheesecloth heavily with barbecue sauce. Put the wrapped turkey into the pit, directly onto hot coals. Cover with dirt, and pile dirt on top. (Use all of the dirt that came out of the hole.) Let turkey cook for 12 hours or longer. Timing can be a problem, and it's best to build a bed of coals one afternoon (or night) and cook the turkey during the night.

Warning: Putting meat into a pit can be dangerous, so be very careful; I use a pitchfork to get the turkey over the pit.

Brian Hyder's Wild Turkey Roll in Sauce

Here is an excellent recipe from Brian Hyder of the North Carolina Wildlife Resources Commission. It was published in a booklet called *Wild Game Recipes*, which is currently out of print. The measures lised below will serve 8 people.

8 (6-ounce) pieces of turkey breast
    (boned and skinned)
8 slices bacon
3 ounce package pressed beef
½ pint sour cream
1 can cream of mushroom soup

"Roll bacon slice around piece of turkey breast. Lay breast on 2 slices of beef. Bring edges of beef around breast meat. Hold together with toothpick. Place in greased 9 × 13-inch pan. Mix sour cream and soup and pour over turkey rolls. Bake at 275 degrees for 2 hours uncovered. Serve with wild rice."

Wild Turkey Giblets on Toast

I'm fond of any good giblet gravy, and this is one of my favorites. It'll make a turkey hunter of you!

turkey neck, liver, and gizzard
4 cups of water
bay leaf
salt
pepper
2 hard-boiled eggs, chopped
1 small to medium onion, finely diced
2 strips bacon
flour
toast

Boil the neck, liver, and gizzard in a little salted water with a bay leaf for 30 minutes. Remove the liver and boil the neck and gizzard for another 1½ to 2 hours. Remove bay leaf from the stock, and add a little pepper. Fry the bacon in a small pan. Crumble the bacon and put it into the stock. Sauté the chopped onion in the bacon drippings. Add the onion to the stock and simmer. Chop the liver, gizzard, and meat from the neck. Add the meat to the stock and simmer for 10 minutes. Add a little flour, if needed, to thicken the gravy. Add more salt or pepper, if needed. When the consistency of the gravy is about right, stir in the chopped eggs. Serve over well-browned toast. Or biscuits.

Turkey with Chestnuts

I read not too long ago that spiders would avoid chestnut wood. It may be true. For several years I lived in a house in Tennessee that had been built from wild chestnut wood before a bad blight wiped the trees off the face of that countryside. I never saw a spider, or a spider web, inside the house. In any case, here's a good recipe that calls for chestnuts. I got it from a column by C.B. Colby in the July 1967 issue of *Outdoor Life* magazine—the year in which I lived in the chestnut wood house!

"Use about 3 cups of good, sound chestnuts. Peel the shells from the nuts with a knife, or cut a hole in the shell and soak them overnight to soften and separate the shell from the meat. If you use a knife, cut from side to side over top of nut and peel down and away from cut.

"Boil peeled chestnuts in water until nut meats are tender. Then put meats through a colander or a meat grinder. Add 2 tablespoons butter, and salt and pepper to taste. Other seasoning may be added as desired.

"Into this stuffing base, mix 1 cup of finely crushed cracker crumbs. Moisten the mixture with sweet cream, adding a little at a time until the desired consistency is reached.

"When the chestnut stuffing is ready, fill the bird, packing the stuffing into every part of body cavity. Just before closing the opening, place the pieces of turkey liver with the stuffing. Thrust skewers through the bird's flesh on both sides and across opening. Lace stout twine about both ends of skewers and draw the opening closed.

"Cook the bird in an oven at about 450 degrees, and baste frequently with pan liquid. You may want to add water to the liquid to keep meat moist during cooking. Some cooks baste with butter or add strips of bacon across the breast of the bird to add moisture and help brown the skin. It will take about 2 hours for the turkey to cook properly, depending upon its size. Test about every 30 minutes with a fork. If flesh is too dry, add water to liquid, baste, and turn off oven. If skin is not brown, baste with butter or fat for last few minutes."

Cold Turkey Sandwiches

The best part of the traditional Thanksgiving or Christmas turkey, apart from the giblet gravy, comes several days after the main event. I'm talking about cold turkey sandwiches.

cold turkey (leftovers)
salt and pepper
good mayonnaise
soft white bread

There are tricks to making a good turkey sandwich: Slice the turkey thinly against the grain, then put several slices on very fresh white bread that has been spread generously, top and bottom, with good mayonnaise. Salt and pepper to taste. For some reason, turkey sandwiches seem to taste better if you cut them in half, diagonally. The best bite will be in the very middle of either half.

23

PHEASANT

Both in the field and on the table, the ring-necked pheasant is surely one of the most popular game birds in its range. In the field, its size and the brilliant plumage of the cock no doubt account for much of the bird's appeal. As table fare, the white, mild-flavored meat can easily be compared to chicken, and it therefore makes an excellent bird with which to introduce people to wild game and fowl. But the bird can be disappointing if it isn't properly cooked. The meat is quite lean and tends to be dry, and the older cocks, of course, can be on the tough side. Unless you've got young, tender birds, it is best to be careful with recipes that are fried or baked.

Pheasant Kiev

A Russian dish, Chicken Kiev, is a purely excellent way to prepare pheasant. It is a treat in our family, and it is surely one of my favorites. Try it. But be careful with cooking times, as discussed at the end of the recipe.

breasts from 2 pheasants
salt
pepper (optional)
peanut oil
½ stick of chilled butter
½ tablespoon green onion, chopped
½ tablespoon parsley, chopped
flour

1 tablespoon water
1 beaten egg
fine bread crumbs

Skin the pheasant breasts and carefully cut out the two fillets. Place each fillet, skin side down, between two sheets of plastic wrap. With a large meat mallet, pound the fillets, starting at the center and working out. Continue to pound until the fillets are a uniform ¼ inch thick.

Remove top plastic wrap. Sprinkle fillet with salt, onion, and parsley. (I prefer a little pepper, too.) Cut the butter longways into 4 strips. Place one strip of butter on the larger end of the fillets. Roll each fillet around the piece of butter. Do this neatly, tucking in the sides a bit to hold in the butter. Press the ends well to seal. Coat each fillet roll with flour. Mix the beaten egg with 1 tablespoon water. Dip each fillet into the egg mixture, then roll it in the bread crumbs. Chill for at least an hour.

Prepare for deep frying, heating the oil to 375 degrees. Fry the fillet rolls for about 5 minutes, or until golden brown. Eat while hot. *Serves 2.*

Warning: It is difficult to fry the pheasant rolls so that the center is done exactly right. Once I served this dish to guests, only to find that the center of the pheasant roll wasn't quite done. If this happens, all you can do is cook it some more. It is therefore best to cook an extra roll or two for testing before serving the whole batch.

Pheasant Castillane

This old Spanish-Mexican dish is an excellent way to cook pheasant. It makes an attractive dish, and is quite tasty.

1 large pheasant (3 to 4 pounds) or
    two smaller birds
3 cups water
2 bay leaves
1 teaspoon salt
½ teaspoon pepper
2 tablespoons butter
1 medium onion, diced
½ cup green bell pepper, diced
½ cup red (or orange) bell pepper,
    diced
2 cloves garlic, minced
¼ cup parsley
3 medium tomatoes, peeled and cut
    into 1-inch pieces
¼ cup seedless raisins, chopped
1 cup white wine
3 cups of fluffy cooked rice (cook
    separately)

Young or Old?

A yearling pheasant can be distinguished from an old bird by the first wing-tip feather, which is pointed in a young bird and rounded in an old one. When the upper part of the pheasant's beak is pliable to the touch, then one can be certain that it is a yearling bird.

—*Larousse Gastronomique*

1 small jar chopped pimento (2-ounce size)

Dress the pheasant and cut it into pieces. Boil it in 3 cups of water to which has been added 2 bay leaves, 1 teaspoon salt, and ½ teaspoon pepper. Boil old cocks for an hour, or until a fork sticks into the pheasant at the thickest part. Younger birds will be tender after boiling for only 30 minutes. Remove the pheasant pieces and let cool. (Discard bay leaves, but retain the broth.) When cool, take all the meat from the bones and cut it into bite-size pieces.

Melt the butter in a large frying pan. Sauté the onion, garlic, and pepper until the onion turns transparent. Add 2 cups of the pheasant broth, parsley, tomatoes, pheasant, wine, and raisins. Bring to boil, cover, reduce, and simmer for 15 minutes.

Put the rice into a serving platter and serve the pheasant mixture over it. Sprinkle the top with chopped pimento. Eat while hot. *Serves four.* Make more rice to serve five or six.

Roast Pheasant in Applejack and Cream Sauce

The basics of this recipe came from the *Ducks Unlimited Cookbook*, to which it was submitted by David Lee Wells of North Kansas City, Missouri. Be careful with the applejack.

The Meat
  2 pheasants

salt and pepper
4 slices bacon, cut in half
½ cup applejack (used in two batches)
½ cup chicken stock
¼ cup heavy cream

The Stuffing
  ¼ cup finely chopped onion
  2 pheasant livers, coarsely chopped
  4 tablespoons butter
  1½ cups cubed day-old bread
  ½ cup peeled, chopped apple
  1 tablespoon parsley
  salt and pepper to taste

To make the stuffing, sauté onion and livers in 2 tablespoons of butter in skillet for 3 or 4 minutes, stirring frequently, then dump mixture into a large bowl. Using the same frying pan, sauté the bread in 2 tablespoons butter for 3 or 4 minutes. Add the bread to liver mixture, along with the apple, parsley, salt, and pepper.

Preheat oven to 375 degrees. Rub the pheasant with 2 tablespoons of melted butter. Sprinkle with salt and pepper inside and out. Spoon the stuffing mixture into the cavities. Truss. Carefully arrange the bacon over the breasts and legs. Place the birds breast side up on a rack in a baking pan and bake for 30 minutes.

Pour half of the applejack (¼ cup) into a small saucepan and heat it. Carefully ignite the applejack (I use long kitchen matches) and pour it over the pheasant. Bake for another 15 minutes, or until the pheasant is brown, the bacon crisp. (Note: Ovens vary considerably, and the position of the pheasant in the oven can influence cooking times. Toward the end, be careful that the bacon doesn't burn. You can remove the bacon, or you can retard futher browning by placing a little aluminum foil over it.) When it's done, remove the pheasant from the pan and place it onto a heated serving platter.

Dump the contents of the pan, scraping up the bottom dredges, into a frying pan. Add ½ cup of chicken stock and ¼ cup of applejack. Bring to boil for 3 minutes. Add cream, bring to boil, reduce, and simmer for 3 minutes. Pour this sauce over the pheasant. *Serves 4.*

Pheasant Cock Pilau

This country recipe is suitable for a large cock pheasant. Two smaller birds can also be used.

pheasant
water
salt and pepper
2 cups of rice

Dress pheasant and cut it up. Put the pieces into a pot of suitable size and cover slightly with water. Boil the pheasant until it is tender (the time will vary, depending on how tough the bird is). Remove the pieces, drain, and debone. Set aside. Measure out 6 cups of the broth, or, if there isn't that much left in the pan, add enough water to make 6 cups. Put the broth back into the pot and add the pheasant meat. Salt and pepper to taste. Bring to boil. Add 2 cups of rice, bring to boil again, reduce heat, cover, and cook for 20 minutes, or until rice is done. *Serves 6 to 8.*

Note: I usually include the liver, gizzards,

and hearts in this recipe. To feed more folks, add chicken livers and gizzards.

Variation: Add quite a bit of chopped parsley to the pot along with with the rice.

Zesty Pheasant Fingers

Here is a very tasty dish to be used when you are getting lots of pheasant. This one works best with breasts, but be sure to save the rest of the meat for a casserole, salad, or fricassee.

pheasant breasts
Zesty Italian salad dressing
butter

Fillet the pheasant breast and cut into thin fingers. Marinate old cocks overnight in Italian dressing; younger birds, three or four hours. Drain. Melt butter in a frying pan and sauté pheasant fingers on high heat for 4 or 5 minutes, or until lightly browned. Allow 6 to 8 ounces of meat per person.

Variation: Cook under broiler or over coals. Do not overcook.

Roast Pheasant

I've eaten some baked pheasant that was just too dry to suit me. I think that some people tend to cook "wild" game too long anyhow, and pheasant tends to be dry to start with. The following recipe, from the National Rifle Association, produces some excellent, moist pheasant, if you follow the cooking times and temperatures exactly.

1 pheasant
1 tablespoon flour
½ cup apple cider
salt and pepper
1 tablespoon melted butter
favorite seasoning (see below)
½ apple or orange

This recipe almost got by me because the "favorite seasoning" bit put me off. But my wife saved the day with the following:

1 teaspoon garlic juice
2 teaspoons prepared mustard
⅛ teaspoon Louisiana hot sauce (or Tabasco sauce)

Her thinking was that this batch of seasoning could easily be mixed in with the melted butter. It worked nicely!

Preheat oven to 350 degrees. Shake 1 tablespoon flour in a small 10 × 16-inch oven cooking bag. Place the bag into a 2-inch deep roasting pan. Pour the cider into the bag and use a wooden spoon to stir the flour until smooth. Melt the butter and mix in the "favorite seasonings." Brush the pheasant inside and out with the melted butter and seasonings. Place ½ apple or orange (I prefer apple) inside the body cavity and place pheasant into the bag. Tie off the bag and make six ½-inch slits in the top of the bag. Bake for 1½ hours. If the pheasant isn't brown enough, slit the top of the bag, increase temperature to 400 degrees, and cook for an additional 15 minutes, or until pheasant is browned. Put pheasant on a serving platter and spoon gravy from the bag over it. *Serves 2.*

Creamed Pheasant with Biscuits

Although pheasant tends to be a little dry, this recipe will work wonders for even tough old cocks:

2 cups diced pheasant meat, boiled (see below)
water
bay leaf
2 cups pheasant broth
1 cup cream or half and half
½ cup butter
½ cup flour
1 can mushroom soup (10¾-ounce size)
2-ounce jar diced pimento
1 small to medium onion, finely chopped

salt and pepper to taste
biscuit dough or 1 can ready-to-cook
  biscuits

Boil pheasant in water with 1 bay leaf until tender. Save 2 cups of the broth. Preheat oven to 450 degrees. Let meat cool, then dice about 2 cups of it. Mix butter and flour and shape into small balls. Heat 2 cups of the broth in a pan and stir in the flour balls. Cook until mixture is thick, stirring constantly. Stir in cream. Add chopped pheasant, mushroom soup, pimento, onion, salt, and pepper. Simmer for a few minutes. Pour into a greased baking dish (about 9 by 12 inches) and cover with biscuits spaced about an inch apart. Bake for 10 to 15 minutes, or until biscuits are browned. If the top of the biscuits tend to brown too quickly (leaving the underside and middle too gooey) lay a piece of aluminum foil in the dish so that it touches the biscuit tops. *Serves 4 to 6.*

Note: This dish is also good when it is made with leftover pheasant and turkey.

Oven Fried Pheasant

Here's a recipe for fried pheasant that seals in the juices. I'm not too happy with the title of the recipe—but I can't argue with the results!

  1 frying-size pheasant
  1 stick of butter
  flour
  salt and pepper
  jalapeño potato chips

Pluck pheasant and cut into serving size pieces. Preheat oven to 400 degrees. Salt and pepper the pheasant, then roll or shake the pieces in flour and let sit for a while. Line a baking pan with aluminum foil, then grease it with part of the butter. Melt the rest of the butter. Dip each piece of pheasant in the butter, then roll it in crumbled potato chips and place it into the baking pan. When all the pieces are in the pan, drizzle with any leftover butter and cover with aluminum foil. Bake for 45 minutes. Then remove the aluminum foil and leave in the oven until the pheasant pieces brown. *Serves 2.*

Pheasant Salad

  2 cups cooked pheasant meat, diced
  juice from ½ lemon
  1 stick of celery, diced
  1 small apple, diced
  8 ounces of sour cream
  2 eggs, hard-boiled and chopped
  ½ cup chopped pecans (sautéed in
    butter)
  1 tablespoon capers
  salt and pepper to taste

Dress the pheasant, then boil it in water with a bay leaf until the meat is tender. Allow 30 minutes for young birds, or an hour for tough old cocks. Bone the meat and put it into the refrigerator for a while before dicing it.

Sauté the pecans in a little butter and salt; these scorch easily, so be careful. Combine the pheasant, celery, and lemon juice. Chill.

Shortly before serving, mix in 1 ½ cups of sour cream, capers, boiled eggs, pecans, salt, and pepper. *Serves 4 to 6.*

Patio Pheasant

1 pheasant
½ cup olive oil
½ cup sautérne
pepper, freshly ground
salt

Cut the pheasant into serving size pieces. Mix olive oil and sautérne. Pour over pheasant, sprinkle generously with freshly ground black pepper, and marinate for several hours. Drain pheasant; retain marinade. Grill over moderate coals, salting to taste, and basting with marinade mixture. *Serves 2.*

Pheasant Giblet Paté

The following recipe can be used with giblets from doves, quail, turkey, and other game birds, including duck, as well as pheasant. Also try it with blackbirds and crows. If you don't have 2 cups of giblets, either fill in with chicken parts or adjust the recipe measures in proportion to what you do have.

2 cups (about 1 pound) bird livers,
    gizzards, and necks
2 hard boiled eggs
¼ cup butter
½ cup diced onion
1 bay leaf
salt
pepper
1 tablespoon rose wine

Bring a pot of water to boil and add bay leaf. Simmer gizzards and necks for about an hour or so. Remove bay leaf and add liver. Cook for another 20 minutes. Meanwhile, boil two eggs. Bone the necks, trim the gizzards, etc. Put everything except salt, pepper, and wine into food processor or blender and zap it until texture is smooth and creamy. Add salt and pepper to taste. Add wine. Mix. Shape into a loaf on an oblong serving dish, cover, and refrigerate. Serve on crackers or use for sandwiches.

24

PARTRIDGE, GROUSE, and SIMILAR BIRDS

Once I puzzled with a recipe from the corn belt that called for a 4-pound partridge. What the author had in mind was a pheasant—not a partridge or a grouse. In another recipe, this one from Alabama, the author advised cooks to allow two or three partridges per person. He had bobwhite quail in mind. To avoid further confusion, let me say that the game birds in this chapter include grouse, ruffed grouse, sage grouse, sage hen, partridge, chukar partridge, chukar, ptarmigan, prairie chicken, willow ptarmigan, white-tailed ptarmigan, rock ptarmigan, spruce grouse, sharp-tailed grouse, gray partridge, Hungarian partridge, and so on.

All these birds have been grouped together here because they are of similar size, with an average weight (undressed) of about 2 pounds and a range of about 1½ to 2½ pounds. It's true that there is some difference in flavor, but this can also be said of any family of birds; for example, wild turkeys that have fed extensively on acorns in a hammock in Florida will have a different flavor from turkeys that have fed on the edge of corn fields in Indiana.

In spite of variations, all the birds of the

partridge or grouse family are good! But, for the most part, they don't taste as mild as chicken, and, if you object to a gamey flavor, a marinade will be in order. I prefer ordinary milk, in which the birds are soaked, under refrigeration, for several hours—or overnight. Remember also that the flesh of these birds is dark and lean. It will be too dry if you cook it too long. Try the following recipes:

Chatfield Grouse

The recipe below came from Chuck Dixon of the Wildlife Branch of Manitoba Natural Resources. It is heavy on the brandy, but the results are good and I enjoy it (the recipe, that is) on a cold winter's night.

6 ruffed grouse breasts (12 fillets)
¼ cup butter
⅓ cup of flour
½ teaspoon salt
1 teaspoon white pepper
1 medium onion, diced
4 cloves garlic, minced (optional)
1 can cream of mushroom soup (10-ounce size)
4 ounces of good brandy or cognac
2 ounces dry white wine
2 shakes of Tabasco sauce (optional)

Heat the butter in a frying pan. Mix flour, salt, and pepper. Roll bird fillets in flour mixture, then brown in butter. Add onion and garlic and cook for a minute or two. Add mushroom soup, wine, brandy, and Tabasco sauce. Reduce heat, cover, and simmer for 30

minutes. Test for doneness and add more salt if needed. *Serves 6.*

Variations: If available, wild mushrooms and ½ pint of whipping cream can be used instead of canned soup. If you like this recipe, also try it with duck breasts.

Note: The above recipe calls for grouse breast fillets. Save the rest of the birds, boil until tender, bone, and freeze or refrigerate the meat. Use this good meat to cook the last recipe in this chapter.

Creamed Grouse on Toast

The following recipe calls for uncooked birds, but leftovers can be used with good results.

2 or 3 cups of chopped grouse meat
2 tablespoons butter
½ cup onion, finely chopped
½ cup mushrooms, sliced
½ cup bird stock (or chicken broth)
½ cup dry white wine
1 bay leaf
salt
pepper
juice of ½ large lemon
¼ cup heavy cream
toast

Boil 2 grouse in water with a bay leaf. When tender, pull off the meat and chop 2 or 3 cupsful, more or less. In a frying pan, melt butter and sauté onions and mushrooms. Add meat, bird stock, and lemon juice. Heat. Stir. Salt and pepper to taste. Simmer for 20 minutes, then add wine and simmer for another 20 minutes. Add more stock, or water, if needed. Cook for another 20 minutes, then remove from heat. Stir in ¼ cup of heavy cream. Serve over toast. *Serves 4 to 6.*

Note: The first time I concocted this dish, I spilled a pepper box into it. Fortunately, the box was almost empty, but I did get an amount that would normally be considered too much pepper for a dish of this sort. But my wife and I liked it, and we started making it rather hot.

Sharon McPhee's Partridge

Here's a good, easy recipe from *The Maine Way.* It was contributed by Sharon McPhee, of Eagle Lake:

"Cut partridge breasts into slices. Soak all day in refrigerator in milk and beaten egg batter. Before frying, coat slices with cracker crumbs. Fry in deep fat (375 degrees) until golden brown."

This is also an excellent way to fry pheasant breasts.

Dr. Tom's 40 Garlic Chukar—Microwaved

A memorable story always makes a recipe better, in my opinion. I'll never cook this dish without thinking of Dr. Tom, although I personally love lots of garlic. The recipe

came from Paula J. Del Giudice's book *Microwave Game & Fish Cookbook.*

4 chukars
½ onion, cut in half lengthwise and separated into sections
1 teaspoon dried parsley
1 teaspoon thyme
4 bay leaves, whole, plus 1 bay leaf, crumbled
⅔ cup olive oil
1 teaspoon ground sage
1 teaspoon rosemary, crumbled
1 teaspoon dried thyme
salt and pepper
40 unpeeled garlic cloves (about 4 large heads of garlic)
3 tablespoons water

"Separate the onion sections. Keep the four smallest ones. In each of four sections, sprinkle ¼ teaspoon parsley, ¼ teaspoon thyme, and 1 whole bay leaf. Set aside.

"In a heavy stovetop skillet, heat olive oil. Add crumbled bay leaf, sage, rosemary, and dried thyme to oil. Add chukars. Brown chukars on all sides in oil. Remove from oil and dust with salt and pepper.

"Stuff an onion section into each body cavity. Tie legs together with string to hold onion in place. Place small pieces of aluminum foil around ends of legs to keep legs from overcooking. Make sure pieces of foil do not touch each other and are at least 1 inch from oven walls. Place birds in an 8-inch square glass dish. Add garlic cloves around birds. Add water to bottom of dish.

"Cover tightly. Microwave on 60 percent or bake for 18–19 minutes. Remove from the oven. Cover with aluminum foil, shiny side down, for at least 5 minutes before serving."

Note: Dr. Tom Gallager was my childhood dentist and longtime family friend. He can't stand garlic, but he has had to tolerate its notorious odor for many, many years as an innocent bystander—a hazard of his profession. He is also an avid shotgunner and hunter. I raided his freezer to test some of the recipes for this cookbook, including this one for 40 Garlic Chukar.

Just for you, Tom, the garlic won't be missed too much if you leave it out of the recipe.

Traditionally, the garlic cloves are served with the birds. The creamy cooked cloves are pressed out and spread on pieces of toast. In the traditonal recipe, chicken is cooked instead of chukars. But the spices in the recipe work great with the chukars.

In a regular oven, the cloves become browned. This won't happen in the microwave, but for those who like garlic, serve it with pieces of toast anyway. The cooked cloves taste completely different than you would imagine.

Sage Grouse for Two

If you like the flavor of lemon, be sure to try the following recipe. My wife loves it.

> 2 sage grouse, partridge, ptarmigan,
>   or similar birds
> ½ bay leaf
> juice of 1 lemon
> sage grouse stock
> 2 tablespoons butter

> 4 ounces fresh mushrooms
> 1 tablespoon finely chopped onion
> 1 tablespoon of white wine
>   Worcestershire sauce
> salt
> pepper
> cooked rice

Boil the birds in a pan with water and ½ bay leaf until tender. Retain ¼ cup of liquid. Pull the meat from the bones and chop. Sprinkle the boned meat with lemon juice, cover, and refrigerate for an hour or longer.

The Grouse of Europe

The largest bird of this family is the *Capercaillie*, a superb creature, the largest game bird, with very delicate flesh. Quite common in countries of Northern Europe, it is only rarely found in France. It is prepared like pheasant or ordinary grouse.

The *Black grouse*, a bird about the size of the pheasant and cooked in the same way, the French *Gelinotte* (hazel grouse or hen), the English *Red grouse* or *Scotch grouse*, and the *Ganga* or pin-tailed grouse which is found in the South of France and Algeria, all belong to the same family. The latter bird, whose flesh is extremely delicate, is the size of a good partridge. . . .

All these birds have good flesh, but they have a pronounced pine flavour, the leg meat in particular; so normally the legs are not served.

—*Larousse Gastronomique*

In a small frying pan, heat the butter and sauté the mushrooms and onion. Add the bird meat and Worcestershire sauce. Add the ¼ cup of liquid from boiling pan and 1 tablespoon white wine Worcestershire sauce. Season to taste with salt and pepper. Bring to boil, then reduce and simmer for an hour or so. Add a little more sage grouse stock or water as needed. Serve piping hot over rice, along with vegetables of your choice and French bread. *Serves 2.*

Heald Pond Road Partridge

From *The Maine Way* comes a rather curious recipe that was contributed by Mrs. Douglas C. Miner of Hampden. Before starting to write this book, I never thought I would find myself beating cabbage with a wooden spoon, but I did it and I can recommend the results most highly:

"Chop equal parts of onion and crisp cabbage, then beat them with a wooden spoon and blend the two until each attains some of the virtue and flavor of the other. To this, add 1 lightly beaten egg, salt, pepper, a few bread crumbs and enough evaporated milk to make a wet dressing. Fill the small orifices of partridge with the mixture, sew up neatly, then cover the birds with strips of fat bacon. Roast in a 400 degree oven until tender—about 40 minutes. Remove bacon for last 15 minutes, if breast is not browning. The dressing becomes hot and the steam permeats the flesh of the birds; as a result, the meat is juicy and tender, full of rich flavor."

Sage Hens or Pheasants

The following recipe is from *Cooking in Wyoming*, to which it was submitted by Mrs. John C. Pickett of Cheyenne: "The following method is one I use for either sage hens or pheasants. Soak in cold, salted water for several hours. Dry thoroughly. Dip the pieces of meat in a batter of 2 beaten eggs to which has been added a tablespoon of cold water. Remove and roll pieces in flour to which salt and pepper has been added. Dip again in beaten egg and roll in fine, dried bread crumbs. Allow to stand for an hour or so in refrigerator, if possible.

"Brown pieces in hot fat, then place in roaster. Pour rich milk over it and allow to steam in covered roaster for an hour or more at 325 degrees, or until tender. Add more milk if necessary to keep meat moist during the baking."

Camp Partridge

If you're going to camp out during a hunt, take along a few basic ingredients so that you can cook the the following recipe:

**young partridge or grouse
bacon**

lemon
salt and pepper

Clean the birds and quarter. Soak for two hours in water with a little salt added to it. Build a good keyhole fire so that you'll have coals that can be raked away from the blaze. Dry the birds. Salt and pepper them to taste. Take a piece of bacon and grease a rack or grill. Wrap partridge quarters (especially the breasts) with bacon. Put on grill about 4 inches from coals. Two or three times during cooking, squeeze a little lemon juice on the meat. Cook until the bacon is crispy. *Allow one bird per person.*

Note: Bacon grease dripping onto hot coals tends to start a fire, so have a large grill that can be moved easily, or have long tongs at hand to move the meat around as needed.

Easy Grouse Fricassee

Most any of the fricassee recipes given in this book can be used with grouse, and I hesitate to give yet another. If I tend to go overboard, it is because I consider the fricassee, as I cook it, to be one of the best methods for preparing wild meat for folks who are not in the habit of cooking and eating it. Because this recipe requires few ingredients, it is especially suitable for cooking in camp.

Oklahoma Prairie Chickens

Prairie chickens feed mostly on sorghum crops such as milo and maize after a killing frost in the fall, so pass-shooting over feed fields is one of the most popular methods of hunting them. Hunting grasslands over bird dogs is also popular.

—Oklahoma Wildlife News Service

grouse
lemon (1 lemon per grouse)
water and broth
butter
flour
salt and pepper

Skin the grouse, cut it into serving size pieces, and boil it in a little water until it can be pulled easily from the bone. Retain the broth. Pull the meat from the bones, salt and pepper it to taste, and sprinkle the lemon juice over it. (Use one lemon per bird; I like to use quite a bit of freshly ground pepper.) Let the meat sit for an hour or more.

Melt a little butter in a frying pan. Brown the meat on high then add 2 cups of the broth left from boiling the bird. Bring to boil, reduce the heat and sprinkle on a little flour. Simmer for an hour or longer, adding more broth if needed. Serve over crispy toast or rice.

25

WOODCOCK and SNIPE

These two birds do resemble each other and the recipes are pretty much interchangeable, but of course on average the woodcock is a little larger than the snipe. The long bill is probably what links the birds in the mind's eye. This image is further enforced by an old French and English practice of leaving the heads on the birds when they are cooked, and tying the bills to the legs. Some even "hang" the birds for a week and then leave the "high" guts inside when the birds are cooked—and that's not the whole story, either. Personally, I don't care what the French and British do, or how they do it, in the privacy of their own dining room. If your curiosity is now aroused and if you've got a strong stomach, go directly to the mini-article on page 226. Also see the information on "hanging" birds on page 255. Normal red-blooded, weak-stomached Americans can proceed with the following recipes:

Sautéed Birds with Sherry

Here's an excellent bird recipe from Louisiana. The dish is especially good with snipe or woodcock.

8 to 10 snipe
salt and pepper
½ cup of butter
½ cup chopped green onions

¼ cup chopped parsley
1 cup sherry
1 tablespoon lemon juice

Sprinkle the snipe with salt and pepper. Melt butter in a large frying pan and brown the snipe. Add onions and parsley and cook for a couple of minutes. Add sherry and lemon juice. Reduce heat, cover, and let simmer for 20 minutes. *Serves 3 or 4.*

Variation: use 6 to 8 woodcock instead of snipe; or mix the two birds in any reasonable proportions.

Woodcock in Sour Cream

4 woodcock
salt and pepper
flour
½ cup peanut oil
2 slices smoke-cured bacon
½ cup beef stock (or bouillon made
  with cube)
½ cup sour cream

Salt and pepper birds to taste, inside and out, and shake in flour. Let sit for a few minutes. Heat peanut oil very hot in a frying pan and quickly brown the birds (but don't cook fully). Preheat oven to 350 degrees. Grease a small casserole dish and place the bacon slices in the bottom. Place the birds atop the bacon slices. Pour a cup of beef stock over birds and bacon. Cover and bake for an hour. Reduce heat to 200 degrees and pour the sour cream over the birds. Cover and return to oven for 10 minutes. *Serves 2.*

Note: The bacon in the above recipe does not brown nicely, but it does give a distinctive flavor to the gravy and woodcock. I like it.

Woodcock with Grapes

4 woodcock
salt and pepper
¼ cup of butter
¼ cup water
½ cup orange juice, freshly squeezed
1 teaspoon grated orange peeling
1 cup white grapes, whole
¼ cup rose wine

Dress the woodcock, salt and pepper them to taste, and arrange them in a well-greased casserole. Preheat oven to 350 degrees. Heat the water in a saucepan and melt the butter in it. Mix in orange juice, grated orange peeling, wine, and grapes. Bake for 50 minutes, basting several times with pan juices. *Serves 2.*

Woodcock in a Bag

Here's one that you have to try to believe! I got it from *The Maine Way*, to which publication it was submitted by Gennie Peppard of East Holden, Maine.

"Put several birds (number needed) into a Brown & Bake bag. Add about a quarter of a fruit juice glass of wine and 2 packages of onion gravy mixture. Seal bag. Put a small amount of water in an electric fry pan, then put in bag which has been punctured with several fork holes. Cover and simmer about 65 minutes. Add water as needed to fry pan. When tender remove woodcock from bag; pour juices into fry pan and thicken the gravy."

Camp Woodcock

This recipe is good anywhere, but I designed it to be used in camp where staples must make up the diet and ordinary fried foods tend to get old. Apart from the birds, which, I assume, you will bag on the trip, the ingredients are easy to carry and won't spoil. This recipe can also be used for quail.

4 woodcock
2 tablespoons cooking oil or butter
flour
salt and pepper
½ cup Coffee-Mate
hot water
2 chicken bouillon cubes
rice

Pluck and dress the woodcock. Salt and pepper to taste, then roll them in flour. Heat the oil in a frying pan with cover, or in a Dutch oven. Brown the birds. Carefully pour

---

Roast Woodcock—French Style

Truss the woodcock, drawing the head round and running the beak through the legs. Bard it and tie with string. Cook on a spit on a very lively fire, from 18 to 20 minutes, or in the oven from 15 to 18 minutes.

Arrange the woodcock on a canape of bread fried in butter, or fried golden in the dripping pan, or in the roasting pan.

Roast woodcock must always be served with its *rôtie*, i.e. croûton of fried bread spread with the intestines of the bird taken out after cooking. It is prepared in the following manner.

Chop up finely the woodcock's intestines (the gizzard having been removed) with an equal quantity of *foie gras* or fresh grated bacon fat, season with salt and pepper and add a pinch of grated nutmeg and a dash of brandy.

Spread this mixture on pieces of bread, either fried or cooked in the dripping pan. Sprinkle with freshly ground pepper straight from the pepper mill. Put in a very hot oven for a few momemts.

The *rôties*, i.e. pieces of fried bread with the trail on them, can be garnished with peeled grapes. Instead of cognac, the mixture can be flavoured with Armagnac or Calvados.

Finally, we must add that it is customary for making croûtons for serving the trail of woodcock, or other winged game, to use crustless bread, or what is called in France "English bread". These croutons can also be made from home-made bread. The trail is best served on this, in our opinion.

—*Larousse Gastronomique*

off most of the oil. Mix ½ cup of Coffee-Mate in 1 cup of hot water and pour over the birds. Cover the pan and simmer for 1 hour.

Prepare the rice according to the directions on the package. (Usually, two cups of water per cup of rice will be just right. Salt to taste. Bring water to boil, then add rice, bring to boil again, reduce heat, cover, and simmer for 20 minutes without peeping.)

Remove the birds from the pan and let them cool a bit. Add a little water to the pan and stir in 2 chicken bouillon cubes. Let simmer to make gravy. Remove the meat from the birds and put it into the pan with the gravy. Simmer for a while. Serve over rice. *Serves 2.*

Fried Buttermilk Woodcock

This delicious recipe can also be used for snipe and other small game birds that tend to be a little dry. The buttermilk, it seems, keeps all the moisture in. Also, plucking the birds instead of skinning them will help keep them from drying out.

8 to 10 woodcock
cooking oil
2 medium eggs
½ cup of buttermilk
flour
salt and pepper

Pluck the birds and cut them in half. Put the birds in a glass container, then pour the buttermilk over them. Refrigerate for 4 or 5 hours. Drain the birds but do not wash. Retain the buttermilk. Salt and pepper the birds to taste. Beat the eggs in with the buttermilk. Shake or roll the birds in flour, then let sit for a few minutes. Heat cooking oil in a frying pan. Cook the birds on medium high heat until browned and done. *Allow 2 birds per person.*

If you want gravy, pour off part of the grease, add a little water, bring to boil, and thicken with flour.

Gutsy Woodcock or Snipe

Actually, cooking woodcock or snipe without drawing them isn't as gross as it may seem. If you want to try it, here's a recipe from Bradford Angier's *Gourmet Cooking for Free*:

"Another way to cook woodcock without drawing them is by dry-plucking birds shot that day, rubbing them with salt and freshly ground black pepper and perhaps a bit of tarragon, and lowering them carefully into a pot of deep oil that is seething at about 365 degrees. After they have tossed and bobbed for 6 minutes, the viscera will have tightened into a clean hard ball that can be discarded, along with the well-picked bones, while heart, liver, and perfectly cooked meat are enjoyed to the utmost."

I note with considerable interest that Angier specifies birds that have been recently shot instead of those that have been "hung" for a week or so!

Fried Wilson Snipe

It may not be necessary, but I usually marinate snipe before frying them. The recipe below calls for wine vinegar, but you can also use a weak baking soda marinade to good advantage.

12 snipe
1 cup red wine vinegar
water
½ cup cooking oil or butter
1 medium onion, diced
salt and pepper
flour
rice, mashed potatoes, or biscuits to
    go with gravy (optional)

Dress the birds, draw them, and cut them in half. Put into a glass container and marinate in mixture of 1 cup of wine vinegar and 1 cup of water for at least 8 hours, under refrigeration. Drain the birds. Salt and pepper to taste. Put into a sack and shake with flour. Heat the oil in a frying pan and sauté the onion. Remove the onion and fry the birds until browned. Let drain. Pour off most of the grease. Add water and flour, stirring up pan dredges. Return onions to pan. Cook, adjusting water or flour, until you have a gravy of the consistency that you like. The gravy can be poured over the fried birds, or it can be served over rice, mashed potatoes, or biscuits. *Serves 3 or 4.*

Variation: Put the fried snipe back into the gravy and simmer for a few minutes. Make some crisp toast. Serve snipe on toast, topped with lots of gravy.

Woodcock

Never cook woodcock with any other bird unless you want the others to have the flavor of woodcock.

                         —The Maine Way

Crockpot Snipe

Although this recipe calls for snipe, it is also good with dove and other small birds. Mix them up if necessary.

20 snipe
cooking oil

salt and pepper
flour
2 medium onions, diced
½ cup green onion, chopped, tops and
all
mushrooms (optional)
1 tablespoon fresh parsley, chopped
1 can of cream of chicken soup (10¾-
ounce size)
1 can of cream of celery soup (10¾-
ounce size)
¼ cup white wine
rice (cooked separately)

Clean and draw the snipe. Remove the breasts from the birds, then boil the rest in a little water until the meat can be pulled from the bones easily. Chop the meat finely and put it into a crockpot. Add the chicken soup and celery soup. Add onions, parsley, wine, salt, and pepper. If you've got fresh mushrooms, throw in a few. Turn crockpot to low heat.

Salt and pepper the snipe breasts, then shake them in flour. Heat some oil in a frying pan, brown the breasts, and put them into the crockpot. Add wine. Stir. Cook on low

heat for 6 or 7 hours. Serve over rice. *Serves 8 to 10.*

Bradford Angier's Voodoo Snipe

Here's a basic recipe that I adapted from Bradford Angier's book *Gourmet Cooking for Free.* Angier said that the results come close to gastronomical voodoo—and I tend to agree:

snipe
melted butter
salt pork
salt
pepper
thyme

Preheat oven to 400 degrees. Rub the birds inside and out with a little butter, salt, pepper, and thyme. Cut salt pork into thin strips and crisscross them across the breasts of the snipe. Bake for about 25 minutes, basting often with melted butter.

26

DUCKS and GEESE

I've never eaten a duck that I didn't like, but note carefully that the quality of waterfowl depends in part on what they have been feeding on. Ducks that have been eating grain are better, to most people, than those that have been eating water-borne fare. If you suspect that you have "strong" or "fishy" ducks, you may want to choose one of the recipes that call for a marinade. Usually, ducks should be plucked so that they will be moister and more succulent after having been cooked, but, again, consider skinning strong ducks and choose a "wet cooking" method instead of baking them.

Most people who object to the so-called wild or gamey flavor of ducks and geese simply don't like the flavor of the meat. Period. I, for one, happen to love its flavor, texture, and color. But of course you can get too much of a good thing, and I feel that ducks should be

field dressed as soon as possible after they have been killed—even on icy days. A duck is very well insulated because of its feathers, and the body heat simply can't escape quick enough. It's best to draw the bird, and then leave it where air can circulate through the body cavity.

In the following recipes, I have tried to follow a somewhat tempered approach to waterfowl cookery. Many hunters and epicures prefer their duck to be very rare. I don't care how these people eat their own duck, but I feel that they should consider their guests before putting really raw meat on the table. I prefer duck to be on the rare side, but not *too* rare. Ideally, I want freshly sliced meat to be reddish—but without blood oozing from it.

Newcomers to waterfowl cookery might do well to stay away from recipes for cooking whole birds. First acquire a taste for the meat, then try whole birds.

Slow Grilled Duck

2 or 3 ducks, plucked
½ cup melted butter
½ cup lemon juice
½ cup red wine vinegar
1 teaspoon garlic juice
salt and pepper

Fire up the grill, adding enough charcoal for slow heat. Mix a basting sauce of melted butter, lemon juice, and vinegar. Cut the ducks in half, lengthwise, of course, and season on both sides with salt and pepper. Grill over slow heat, basting, for about 30 minutes. Turn, baste, and grill until the duck's skin is crisp and brown. Baste often. *Serves 2 to 4.*

Camp Fried Duck

I'll have to be honest. The best duck I've ever eaten was nothing fancy. We had pitched tents somewhere between the Choctawhatchee River and the Pea in southeast Alabama, and we were after turkey. We got two. We also got some ducks, and a fellow with us cooked them in a frying pan on coals from our campfire.

duck breasts (skinned and filleted)
oil
salt and pepper
flour

Fillet the duck breasts and beat each one thoroughly with the mouth of a bottle. That's right. Each time you pound the meat, you leave a ring impression in it. When all the breast fillets have been thus pounded, salt and pepper them to taste. Go a little heavy on the pepper. Shake the fillets in a bag of flour. Heat the oil in the skillet. Carefully put 3 or 4 fillets into the hot oil. Cook quickly until browned. Don't cook too long—4 or 5 minutes will do, if you've got very hot oil.

Governor's Duck

The following recipe was submitted to *Cooking in Wyoming* by Mrs. Joe Hickey, whose husband was governor from 1959 until 1961. I have reworked the format of the recipe, so the version is *not* a direct quote.

The Meat
2 wild ducks
6 slices of bacon
The Stuffing
2 eggs
6 cups of soft bread crumbs
1 cup celery, chopped
1 cup onion, chopped
1 cup seedless raisins
1 cup pecans, chopped
½ cup heated milk
½ teaspoon salt

Basting Sauce
    1 cup catsup
    ½ cup Worcestershire sauce
    ½ cup A-1 sauce
    ½ cup chili sauce
The Garnish
    orange slices
    candied cranberries

Heat the milk and beat the eggs. Combine both with bread crumbs, celery, onions, raisins, pecans, and salt. Preheat oven to 350 degrees. Fill ducks with stuffing and close. Place in an uncovered roasting pan and cover each duck with 3 strips of bacon. Baste. Roast for 15 to 20 minutes per pound of duck, basting twice.

Serve with orange slices and cranberries. For best results, peel the orange and slice across the wedges. Then pile the cranberries onto each slice. *Serves 2 to 4.*

Teal Stuffed with Rice

Here's a very good recipe that can be used with any duck, but was designed for use with early-season teal.

The Birds
    4 teal or 2 mallards
    bacon drippings
    salt and pepper
The Stuffing
    1 cup rice, cooked
    6 ounces sliced mushrooms
    1 tablespoon parsley, chopped

2 slices bacon
The Sauce
    1 cup fresh orange juice
    ½ cup red wine
    ½ cup butter

Fry two slices of bacon and crumble. Preheat oven to 350 degrees. Rub the ducks inside and out with bacon drippings, then salt and pepper to taste. Mix the cooked rice, mushrooms, parsley, and crumbled bacon. Stuff the ducks, then put them into a baking pan, breast side *down*. Melt ½ cup butter in a saucepan, then add ½ cup of good red wine and 1 cup orange juice. Pour about half of the sauce over the ducks.

Roast the duck for 30 minutes, basting it several times with the remaining sauce. Turn the ducks breast side up and continue to cook until they are browned. (Mallards or larger ducks will take longer than the teal.) If in doubt, cut into one of the breasts to check the color. When it's done, the breast will be pink. Carefully put the duck onto a platter and pour the pan drippings over them before serving. *Serves 4.*

Carolina Version of Kentucky Burgoo (with Duck)

I don't know the history of this recipe, but the version below was adapted from *The South Carolina Wildlife Cookbook*, to which it was submitted by Nancy Ann Coleman of Columbia. I use duck and venison in the recipe, which, I think, go quite well together. There are many ingredients in this recipe, and I have divided them into two batches, as follows:

First Day Batch
   1 or 2 chickens, ducks, or a turkey
      (anyway, 5 pounds of fowl)
   2 pounds of venison
   1½ to 2 pounds venison (or beef)
      bones
   1 stalk celery
   1 carrot, peeled
   1 small onion, peeled
   5 to 6 sprigs parsley
   1 can tomato puree (10-ounce size)
   4 quarts water
   1 red pepper pod
   ¼ cup salt
   1 tablespoon lemon juice
   1 tablespoon Worcestershire sauce
   1 tablespoon sugar
   1½ teaspoon black pepper
   ½ teaspoon cayenne

Combine all above ingredients in a large pot. Bring to boil, cover, and simmer for 4 hours. Let cool. Strain out vegetables and discard. Retain meat and stock. Bone the meat and remove any gristle. Chop the meat finely and put it into the stock. Refrigerate overnight.

Second Day Batch
   meat and stock from first day batch
   6 medium onions, finely chopped
   8 to 10 tomatoes, peeled and chopped
   1 turnip, peeled and finely chopped
   2 cups fresh butterbeans (or baby lima
      beans)
   2 cups thinly sliced celery
   2 cups finely chopped cabbage
   2 cups fresh okra, sliced
   2 cups fresh corn (3 to 4 ears)
   ½ unpeeled lemon, seeded

Remove meat and stock from the refrigerator and skim off fat. In a large pot, combine meat and stock. Bring to boil, then add the rest of the ingredients listed under second day batch. Mix, cover, and simmer for 1 hour. Uncover and simmer for about 2 hours, stirring frequently. This recipe makes about a gallon of thick stew.

Duck Giblet Delight

Traditionally, giblet gravy is served on dressing along with a turkey or other fowl. Duck makes very good giblet gravy, but the meat in main-dish duck is so rich that dressing and gravy really isn't in order. The best bet is to

Wood Duck

One of the most beautiful of American birds, the wood duck is also a great success story. It was almost extinct in 1915, according to the *Louisiana Conservationist*, but today it is the number one duck taken by hunters in the Atlantic Flyway—and number two by hunters in the Mississippi Flyway!

save the giblets for a next-day treat. Modify the term "giblets" in the recipe below to include not only necks, hearts, gizzards, and liver but also any leftover duck meat, including the goodies from inside the back cavity. (Hearts and gizzards should be diced finely. If the neck wasn't cooked along with the duck, it should be boiled until the meat comes off easily. The necks of very small ducks won't have much meat.)

3 cups duck giblets
2 cups broth (duck or chicken)
½ cup flour
salt
pepper
1 medium onion, diced
3 eggs, hard boiled and sliced
rice or biscuits

In a large frying pan, heat ¼ cup of the broth. Add ¼ cup of flour and reduce heat quickly. Stir in 1½ cups of broth and put on low heat. Add salt and pepper to taste. Mix onion, eggs, and diced giblets. Add mixture to broth. Bring to a quick boil, then reduce heat and simmer for 20 or 30 minutes. Serve on rice or hot biscuit halves. Makes six hefty servings—but seconds will surely be requested.

Duck Gizzards with Rice

The recipe below is good with duck gizzards, coot gizzards, or goose gizzards, or a combination of those. If necessary, fill in with chicken, pheasant, or turkey gizzards.

1 to 2 pounds of gizzards, dressed and washed
2 bay leaves
water
1 teaspoon salt
½ teaspoon red pepper flakes
1 small to medium onion, chopped
½ cup butter (used in two batches)
2 cups minute rice
1 small stalk celery, chopped
4 cups chicken stock or bouillon (can be made with cubes)
¼ cup chopped parsley
¼ teaspoon marjoram
¼ teaspoon savory
¼ teaspoon thyme
flour

Put the gizzards into a pot, cover with water, and bring to boil. Add bay leaves, onions, salt, and pepper. Cover, reduce heat, and simmer for an hour.

Melt ¼ cup of butter in a pan large enough to hold the rice. Put the rice into the pan and sauté over low heat until the rice begins to brown, stirring occasionally. In a separate pan, bring the chicken broth to boil. Pour it into the pot with the rice. Add parsley and celery. Bring to boil. Stir in the marjoram, savory, and thyme. Reduce heat, cover tightly, and simmer for 15 minutes without peeking.

While rice is cooking, trim up the gizzards and cut into bite-sized pieces. Melt ¼ cup butter in a frying pan and sauté the gizzards until they brown. Remove gizzards and drain. Add ½ cup of water to the pan liquid, sprinkle with flour, stir, cover, and simmer for 15 minutes. Salt and pepper the gravy to taste. Thicken it with more flour, if needed.

Pile the rice into the center of a serving platter and place the gizzards around the outside. Pour the gravy over the rice. *Serves 4 to 8.*

Day-Lilied Duck

With a definite flair for words held together by reckless grammar, a fellow named Ben McC. Moise, of Charleston, said of his recipe for "prairie oyster" in *The South Carolina Wildlife Cookbook*: "Cures bilious remitting and unremitting fevers, agues, some symptoms of gout and will rid one's self of fleas." Well, the recipe that follows may not be quite so potent, but consider these words: "The Chinese enjoyed the day lily long before the written word, and earliest records tell of the plant's use as food. An herbal from the T'ang Dynasty, about A.D. 650, informs us that "it quiets the five viscera [heart, lungs, kidneys, stomach, and liver], reduces worry and benefits the mind." Anyhow, the above quote and the following recipe are from Leona Woodring Smith's book *The Forgotten Art of Flower Cookery*:

1 duck, cut into serving pieces
4 tablespoons butter
2 tablespoons cornstarch
2 tablespoons soy sauce
3 tablespoons peanut butter
½ teaspoon nutmeg
½ teaspoon ginger
1 tablespoon grated orange rind
salt and pepper
1 cup sliced mushrooms
2 cups day lilies (whole or chopped)

"Place duck in water to cover along with an onion studded with several cloves, a bay leaf, and salt. Simmer for 45 minutes. Drain and dry duck. Strain broth and reserve 2½ cups. Sauté duck in butter until golden brown. Combine cornstarch and soy sauce and add to broth; stir over medium heat until smooth and thickened. Then add peanut butter, nutmeg, ginger, orange rind, and salt and pepper to taste. Continue stirring and when broth starts simmering add mush-

Easy Way to Age Your Ducks and Geese

Waterfowl should be drawn as quickly as possible. In ideal conditions (at home) you should age your field-dressed ducks, with feathers on, in the refrigerator. A normal refrigerator temperature of 38 to 40 degrees, for three or four days, is all that is necessary.

Hunting camp is another story. First, you do not generally have the facilities that you do at home. Second, you may not be in camp for four straight days. In my hunting camp I just reverse the process. I completely clean my field-dressed ducks, put them in heavy freezer bags, and freeze them in containters of water. In thawing the ducks prior to a big dinner, I'll be sure to age them in the fridge for three or four days.

—Billy Joe Cross, Ducks Unlimited

rooms and day lilies and cook for 3-4 minutes. Pour over duck on a heated serving platter."

Wild Duck with Bourbon and Bing Cherries

I don't know exactly where this recipe originated, but I got it from Austin, Nichols Distilling Co., of Lawrenceburg, Kentucky. They make Wild Turkey Kentucky Straight Bourbon Whiskey, and of course specify their own brand in the list of ingredients. It's good stuff all right, but I think that any good bourbon would be satisfactory, as long as it's from a sour mash. Anyhow, thank the Wild Turkey folks for the following:

1 4- or 5-pound duck
1 clove garlic, crushed
½ cup of bourbon
½ cup cranberry juice
2 tablespoons freshly squeezed lemon juice
1 can of Bing cherries (and juice from can)
salt and pepper

Preheat oven to 325 degrees. Rub duck inside and out with salt, pepper, and garlic, then place it on a rack in a shallow pan. Roast for 30 minutes. Drain fat from pan.

Baste duck with a mixture of lemon juice and cranberry juice. Roast for another 2½ hours, basting every 20 minutes. (The Wild Turkey folks say to roast the duck 40 minutes per pound, so the time can be adjusted considerably.) Remove the duck from the pan. Add roasting pan juices to a saucepan, then stir in the bourbon and the juice from the can of cherries. Salt and pepper the sauce to taste. Add cherries, bring to a quick boil, reduce heat, and simmer for 5 minutes. Carve the duck. Pour some sauce over carved meat, and serve the rest in a sauce boat. *Serves 2.*

Note: If you want a pretty dish at the table, put the browned duck on a serving platter, garnish with yellow lemon slices, and pour the cherry sauce over it.

Smoked Duck Breasts

3 duck breasts (6 breast fillets)
6 strips of bacon
1 small bottle Zesty Italian dressing
salt and pepper

Skin the ducks and fillet out the breasts. Put the breasts into a glass container and pour the dressing over them. Cover. Marinate for 8 hours or longer in the refrigerator.

Build a charcoal fire in your grill with smoker hood. When the coals are ready to cook with, put some wet hickory chips (or green hickory wood chips) on top and close the hood.

While smoker is heating up, drain the fillets. Reserve marinade. Salt and pepper to taste. Wrap each fillet with bacon, then place on greased rack in the grill smoker. Cook for a total of 20 minutes, turning and basting with marinade liquid, several times. Do not overcook. *Serves 3 or 4.*

Crockpot Ducks

If your cabin or camp has electric power, consider the crockpot as a possible cooking aid. I got the idea and the following recipe from Chandler S. Cheek's book *Answering the Call to Duck Cookery*: "When at camp, use duck taken the previous day; brown ducks and cut up vegetables the evening before so you can quickly put this together and turn on the pot before you head out the door in the morning. A mouth watering, ready to serve treat will be ready when you return from the hunt in the evening."

  2 ducks, skinned
  4 potatoes
  2 onions, quartered
  2 sticks celery
  2 carrots
  ½ cup sautérne
  oregano
  garlic salt
  lemon pepper
  ½ cup cooking oil

"Trim fat from ducks, rinse and blot dry. Brown in cooking oil over high heat; remove and set aside. Dust birds with oregano, garlic salt, and lemon pepper inside and out. Cut 2 carrots to fit the crock and add to the bottom of the pot to act as a rack for the fowl. Add wine and birds to the pot along with 4 or

more peeled potatoes. Cover and cook on low heat for 8 hours. Remove ducks discarding stuffing and carrot racks. Serve with potatoes."

Caddo Wild Duck

I got the name for this slow-bake recipe from *Southern Living* magazine. I don't know where they got it, but I suspect that it came from Caddo Lake in East Texas.

The Meat
  2 ducks, plucked and singed
  bacon
  salt and pepper
  lemon
  cooking oil
The Stuffing
  1 apple, chopped
  1 teaspoon salt
  2 teaspoons Worcestershire sauce
  ⅛ teaspoon black pepper

⅛ teaspoon cayenne pepper
1 medium onion, chopped
1 stalk celery, chopped

Mix the stuffing and spoon it into the duck cavities. Pin shut with toothpicks or skewers. Preheat oven to 325 degrees. Heat oil in a large frying pan or Dutch oven and brown the ducks. Wrap each duck with bacon and pin it with round toothpicks. Place the ducks close together, breast down, on a rack in a roasting pan of suitable size. Roast for 3 hours, or until tender. *Serves 2 to 4.*

Variations: Try stuffing made only from chopped onions or rutabaga.

Smothered Duck

duck, plucked and cut into serving
   pieces
salt and pepper
butter
flour
1 cup half and half

Salt and pepper the duck pieces to taste, then coat with flour. Set aside for a few minutes. Heat the butter quite hot, then brown the duck pieces. Reduce heat and cook a little longer. Pour off most of the fat, add 1 cup of half and half, cover, and simmer very slowly for an hour.

Duck with Orange

If you dislike the flavor of duck, or if you have a bunch of ducks that you suspect are rather strong from eating fish for a long period of time, you may want a recipe that will take away some of the flavor, yet will be very, very good. Here's one that I adapted from Betty Melville's *The Hunter's Cookbook.*

4 large ducks or 8 small ducks
2 apples, peeled and quartered
salt and pepper to taste
1 clove garlic, minced
½ teaspoon grated orange rind
2 tablespoons orange juice
2 cans cream of chicken soup (10½-
   ounce size)

Put the ducks into a pot along with apples and minced garlic. Cover with water and simmer until the meat comes off the bones easily; this will take about 3 hours for large ducks or 2 hours for small ducks.

Remove the ducks, discard the apples, and let the broth simmer until it is reduced to 1 cup. Skim fat from broth. While the broth is cooking down, remove the skin from the ducks, bone the meat, and cut it into large slices. Place the meat into a chafing dish or some sort of electrically heated pan suitable for serving.

In a bowl, mix chicken soup, broth, orange rind, and orange juice. Salt and pepper to taste. Pour this mixture over the duck and simmer for 10 minutes, or until the gravy thickens to the consistency that you prefer. *Serves 4 to 8.*

Variation: Try 1 can of cream of chicken

soup mixed with 1 can of cream of mushroom, cream of celery, cream of asparagus, etc.

Country Wild Duck with Rice

2 wild ducks
1 cup of butter
salt and pepper
2 cups rice
4 cups of water

Put ducks into a suitable pan and cover with water. Add some salt. Boil until the duck meat is tender. Add 1 cup of butter, 2 cups of long-grained rice, and pepper. Bring to a quick boil, reduce heat, and simmer for 20 minutes, or until the rice is done. Adjust salt and pepper, if desired. *Serves 4 to 6.*

Variations: All sorts of spice and such can be added to this recipe, but I like it plain. If the ducks have eaten a lot of fish, however, a little doctoring might be needed. Two or three bay leaves boiled along with the duck will do wonders.

Roast Teal

Teal are small ducks, so figure on at least 1 bird per person. The recipe below is for 4 birds, but measures can be increased or decreased.

4 teal, plucked
4 slices of bacon
bacon drippings
salt and pepper
3 apples, chopped

Preheat oven to 450 degrees. Rub ducks with bacon drippings, then salt and pepper to taste, inside and out. Stuff the cavities loosely with chopped apple. Place the birds, breast up, on a rack in a roasting pan. Cut the bacon strips in half, then place a piece on each side of each bird's breast. Roast for 15 minutes, then baste with pan drippings. Roast for another 5 minutes, then baste again. Roast for 5 more minutes, or until bacon looks ready to eat.

Note: Teal will be better if they are not cooked too long; however, if you must have well-done meat, then cook longer.

Midgett's Wild Goose

One of the easiest, and best, recipes for baked goose came from the Outer Banks area of North Carolina. It's from Dorothy Treadwell of Grandy, and she was a Midgett before she married. According to that wonderful book *Coastal Carolina Cooking*, "Synonymous with the Midgett family name is the tradition of waterfowl hunting. Dorothy's father, Harrison Midgett, was born in Chicamacomico, now Rodanthe, in 1889, but he moved north to Currituck, where he was a sharecrop farmer by trade and a professional hunting and fishing guide at heart.

"My father could call in the ducks and geese like no other,' says Dorothy. Using his mouth to imitate their calls, Harrison clucked at ducks and honked at geese. Those were the 'market days,' when hunters came from all over to cash in on the abundant waterfowl and shipped them out to northern markets, literally, by the barrel. It was not uncommon for a hunter to kill hundreds of ducks and geese in a day. As word of the waterfowl lode spread northward during the late 1800s, the wealthy of New York and Boston came to isolated Currituck Country to see for themselves. More often than not, they wanted a 'local' to supply the hunting expertise. And like many others, Dorothy's father guided his share of the rich and famous through the grasses of Currituck Sound.

"What does Dorothy remember most about those days with father? 'The good food and good fellowship that went along with the waterfowl tradition.'"

Here's one of her recipes:

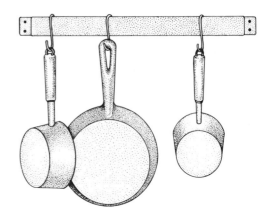

1 dressed wild goose
1 teaspoon salt
1 teaspoon black pepper
1 teaspoon sage
1 apple, potato, or rutabaga
4 cups water
1 bay leaf
cheesecloth to cover bird

"Wash and clean fowl. Rub salt on outside skin and pepper and sage inside the cavity. Place the fruit or vegetable inside the fowl and place fowl in a large roasting pan. Add water and bay leaf. Bake at 350 degrees for 4 hours. More water may be needed as fowl cooks. When tender, remove fowl from pan. Pour off excess juices and save. Return fowl to pan and cover with clean cheesecloth soaked in the excess juices. Turn up oven to 425 degrees and brown fowl with cloth on top. Remove vegetable before serving and discard. *Serves 6 to 8.*"

Goose Breast with Orange Marmalade

If you've been looking for a good, easy recipe for goose, try this one. And you can thank the following: Art Boebinger for the writing; the Kentucky Department of Fish and Wildlife's magazine *Happy Hunting Ground* for publishing it; and Thomas E. Runyan for the goose breast.

"Can anyone hear the call of a flock of

Canada geese without getting excited? To be in a blind when the birds respond to your call is one of the hunter's most thrilling experiences. When this roast goose is presented at the table, the thrill will be relived."

1 large goose breast
1 package brown gravy mix
¼ cup flour
salt
sugar
2 tablespoons orange marmalade
1 can frozen orange juice concentrate
(6-ounce)

"Preheat oven to 375 degrees. Combine all ingredients except goose breast and pour into a large glass casserole or 2-inch-deep roasting pan. Place meat in the pan and turn it so all sides are moistened. Cover pan tightly with aluminum foil and cook 1½ to 2 hours or until the meat is tender. Slice the breast meat and place on a platter. Degrease pan juices and spoon over the meat. Garnish with orange slices."

Goose with Sour Cream and Mushrooms

This is an excellent recipe that I got from *The Official Louisiana Seafood and Wild Game Cookbook*:

5 to 8 pound goose
garlic salt
paprika
1½ stalks of celery, chopped
1 carrot, chopped
1 onion, chopped
fat sufficient for browning
4 tablespoons flour
½ teaspoon rosemary
¼ teaspoon thyme
1¼ teaspoons salt
1 cup thick sour cream
4-ounce can button mushrooms

"Wash and dry goose inside and out. Cut off neck and wing tips. Season inside and out with garlic salt and paprika. Place on rack in shallow pan. Roast uncovered in 325 degree oven for one hour or until browned and fat has cooked off. Simmer giblets, neck, and wing tips in water to cover. Brown chopped celery, carrots, and onion in fat until soft and golden. Stir in 2 tablespoons flour, then blend in liquid from giblets (1 cup stock). Season with rosemary, thyme, and remaining salt. Stir remaining 2 tablespoons flour into sour cream to keep it from curdling during roasting. Blend into gravy. Remove goose from shallow pan and place in roasting pan. Pour gravy and drained mushrooms over it. Cover and continue roasting another 2 hours or until tender." *Serves 4 to 6.*

Apricot Goose

This is an excellent recipe for the wild goose. I don't know its origin, but I got the gist of it from a lady in Florida.

> 1 wild goose
> 6 slices of smoked bacon
> bacon drippings
> liquid smoke (optional)
> juice of 1 lemon
> salt
> pepper
> 1 medium onion, chopped
> 1 tart apple, diced
> 1 cup dried apricots, chopped
> 3 cups soft bread crumbs
> 1 cup boiling water

Set the goose on a flat surface, then sprinkle it with lemon juice, salt, and pepper. Preheat oven to 325 degrees.

To make a stuffing, add a little bacon drippings to a large frying pan. Sauté onion until it is tender. Stir in apple, apricots, bread crumbs, salt, and pepper. Stuff the goose with this mixture and close the opening.

Soak a piece of cheesecloth (enough to wrap the goose with a double thickness) in some bacon drippings. Drape bacon strips across the breast of the goose, then cover with cheesecloth.

Place the goose, breast side up, on a rack in a suitable roasting pan and put in oven. Mix a basting sauce with one part bacon drippings and one part liquid smoke. Baste the bird several times while it cooks. Roast for 20 minutes per pound of *dressed* bird. At the end of the calculated cooking time, pour a cup of boiling water into the pan, cover, and cook for another half hour. *Serves 4 or 5.*

Stir-Fry Snow Goose

If you've got geese and a wok, you may want to try this Chinese dish. It was contributed by Dorothy Donnelly to the North Carolina Wildlife Resources Commission's booklet "Wild Game Recipes."

> 4 goose breast fillets
> 3 green onions
> 4 ounces mushrooms
> 8 ounces water chestnuts
> 8 ounces broccoli
> 2 tablespoons oil
> 1 tablespoon soy sauce
> 1 tablespoon sherry
> 1 tablespoon cornstarch

"Cut goose into thin strips. Slice onions, mushrooms, and water chestnuts thinly.

Wash and trim broccoli into 3-inch lengths. Blend soy sauce, sherry, and cornstarch together until smooth.

"Set wok at 420 degrees (high). Heat 1 tablespoon oil and stir-fry goose until lightly browned (2-3 minutes). Drain and keep hot. Add remaining 1 tablespoon oil to wok. Add broccoli and stir-fry for 2 minutes. Add onions, mushrooms, and water chestnuts and fry for another 2 minutes. Add goose and sauce. Stir all ingredients together and cook on low heat until sauce is thickened. Serve. Goes well with wild grain and brown rice." *Serves 4.*

27

MARSHBIRDS, CROWS, and BLACKBIRDS

I won't call names of person or place. At the time I rented a farm house and pretty much had the run of several hundred acres of pasture and wooded lands. A friend of mine, shouldering a shotgun, knocked on my door one fine Saturday morning in the fall of the year. He wanted to bag some birds for a recipe. He didn't wear a hunting jacket with a game pouch but he did carry a brown paper bag.

"You're welcome to hunt," I said, "but the farm doesn't have any grain, and you're not likely to find any birds." By birds I meant doves and quail.

"I'll find some," he said.

Well, there was much shooting along the creek in front of the house. Then there was much shooting along the creek in back of the house, and along the fencerow that led back to the barn. Standing on the back steps, I saw him drop one of my neighbor's pigeons as it flew over. Perhaps he mistook it for a large dove, I thought.

I met him at the barn gate, asking, "What in the world were you shooting at?"

"Birds," he said, tilting the paper bag so that I could see inside.

The guy had shot blackbirds, meadowlarks, sparrows, blue jays, brown thrush, barnyard pigeons, robins, and I don't know what else.

"My God!" I said, looking up and down the road. "You'd better get those things out of here."

244

"I'd kind of like to dress 'em before I go back to town," he said, looking toward the shed at the barn.

"Man they'll put you in jail for shooting those birds," I said. "And me too."

"Awh?" he said. "Why would they put the birds in a recipe book if it's against the law?"

"What recipe? What book?"

"Birds St. Thomas Aquinas. Bull Cook Book. Or something."

Herter. George Leonard Herter's *Bull Cook and Authentic Historical Recipes*. The guy's sister had given me a copy of the book.

"I don't know what Herter has in the recipe," I said, "but believe me it's against the law to shoot mockingbirds and robins and everything else that you've got except maybe blackbirds and ricebirds. You'd better get those things away from here. Hell, man, look at it from my side. I can see the headlines now. OUTDOOR WRITER CONVICTED OF POACHING ROBINS, MOCKINGBIRDS, BROWN THRUSH, MEADOWLARKS . . ."

"I'm going," he said, heading for his car.

A few months later, I told the story at a dinner party given by the guy's sister. There were several conversations going back and forth across the table, but a young lady from Ireland, with red hair, big blue eyes, and a beautiful brogue, got the gist of my story.

"What *kind* of birds?" she asked with enough intensity to hush the rest of the company.

"Old blackbirds. Ricebirds. Crows. Old blackbirds."

"Robins? You said robins? St. Thomas Aquinas ate robins?"

"Well, that's what the book said," I said, squirming.

"And what," she said, looking upward, "will St. Patrick be saying about that?"

Well, I confess that I ate some of the Birds St. Thomas Aquinas, and I found the birds to be good. Except that my neighbor's pigeon was tough. Of course, I'll never shoot such birds in the name of sport, but I wouldn't hesitate to take them on a survival basis.

Remember that many species of birds can make very good table fare. Just be careful about what you are shooting. But, on the other hand, take full advantage of the very liberal game laws that some states have on ricebirds, blackbirds, and other species. The best bet, of course, is to write your state game and fish department for information concerning such birds. Many farmers will welcome hunters who want to shoot the flocks of blackbirds that are feeding in their grain fields.

Remember also that marsh birds offer good hunting in many areas. These also make excellent eating, as follows:

Sautéed Sora Rails

Here's a good, simple recipe from Don Maris as published in *The Maine Way*: "Pluck rails after cutting off head, feet, and wings. Split up back and clean. Open ('flatten') and sauté in butter, bacon fat, or a little oil. Sprinkle with onion salt or garlic salt if desired. Cook 10 to 15 minutes, splash with white wine or good hard cider, cook a couple more minutes and serve with remaining liquid. Good with dark rice and currant jelly."

Fricassee of Marsh Bird

Some marsh birds tend to have a rather strong flavor, at least as compared to quail. The soda, bay leaf, and lemon juice in the recipe below will help cut any undesirable flavor or odor, and plenty of rice will also help. In any case, this is a good, basic recipe that can be used with rail, gallinule, fish-fed ducks, or even coot.

    marsh birds for approximately 2 cups
        chopped meat
    1 quart of water
    1 teaspoon baking soda
    1 bay leaf
    juice of 1 lemon
    2 tablespoons butter
    chicken broth (or water)

salt
pepper
¾ cup diced onion
¾ cup sliced mushrooms
cooked rice

Dress the birds and marinate them overnight in a quart of water with a tablespoon of baking soda added. Rinse. Boil the birds in a little water, with a bay leaf, until the meat pulls easily from the bones. Drain the birds and pull meat with a fork. (If you use whole birds, the breasts should be chopped.) Sprinkle bird meat with the juice of a lemon and refrigerate for several hours.

Heat butter in a frying pan and sauté the onion and mushrooms. Add marsh bird meat. Add chicken broth to just cover. Salt and pepper to taste. Bring to a quick boil, reduce heat, cover, and simmer for an hour. Add flour to thicken the gravy, if desired. Eat over rice. Serves two or three (or more, depending on how much rice you cook).

Marsh Hens

Hunting for the long, skinny marsh hen (clapper rail or *Rallus longirostris waynei*) requires stamina and good eyesight. The thin, grayish-brown bird with a needle-like beak will scurry through the marshes, duck underwater, and even hold itself under by a weed to avoid hunters. Its slow, low flight has prompted a regulation against the use of a motor in the marsh. But those who cherish the delectable meat in brown gravy with onions will paddle and brave the cold autumn winds at high tide to bring home a clapper rail.

—*The South Carolina Wildlife Cookbook*

Marinated Marsh Hens or Clapper Rails

Marsh hens or clapper rails can be very good, but it is usually safer to marinate these birds before cooking them for company of unknown tastes. The following recipe should suit everybody.

The Birds
    8 or 10 marsh hens or rails, halved
    flour

cooking oil
salt
pepper
water
The Marinade
¼ cup white wine vinegar
¾ white wine Worcestershire sauce

Cut birds in half and put into a suitable container. Mix marinade and pour it over the birds. Cover and refrigerate. Marinate overnight, turning several times.

Salt and pepper birds. Heat oil in skillet. Roll or shake birds in flour, then brown in oil on high heat. Pour off most of oil. Add a cup of water, bring to a quick boil, then reduce heat, cover pan, and simmer for 30 minutes. Eat with French bread and steamed carrots. *Serves 4 or 5.*

Purple Gallinule & Mushrooms

This recipe can be used with rail, gallinule, and other marsh birds. It makes a tasty gravy, which I like to spoon over French bread.

12 purple gallinules or rails
1 cup water
1 cup wine vinegar
12 ounces of mushrooms
1 can cream of mushroom soup (10¾-ounce size)
1 soup can of water
1 medium onion, chopped

Go after Gallinules

There's no reason why gallinules can't support greater hunting pressure, and, according to those who've tried it, the meat is delicious tablefare.
—*Louisiana Conservationist*, March 1984

---

salt
pepper

Mix a cup of wine vinegar and a cup of water. Pour over birds in a glass or crockery container and marinate overnight.

Mix cream of mushroom soup and a soup can of water. Put birds into Dutch over or other suitable container and pour soup mix over them. Add mushrooms, chopped onion, salt, and pepper. Bring to boil, then reduce, cover, and simmer for about 4 hours. *Serves 4 to 6.*

Variations: If you've got a little red wine handy, pour a quarter of cup or so over the birds and simmer for another 15 minutes.

Holiday Sandhill Crane

If you are lucky enough to bag a sandhill crane, here's a recipe that you should try. It's from the Oklahoma Wildlife Federation's *Wildlife Chef.* As the book says, "This dish takes a lot of time to prepare but all the work is well worthwhile."

1 sandhill crane, cleaned, cut into
   serving pieces
8 tablespoons butter
salt
white pepper
¼ cup flour
3 cups sandhill crane stock
bouquet garni, made of 4 parsley
   springs and 1 bay leaf, tied together
½ teaspoon dried thyme
¾ cup chicken stock
24 wild onions, peeled
¾ cup fresh mushrooms, whole
1 teaspoon vinegar
2 egg yokes
½ cup heavy cream
2 tablespoons fresh parsley, finely
   chopped

"Wash the crane pieces thoroughly in cold water. Dry with a damp cloth. In a heavy three-quart heatproof casserole, melt six tablespoons butter over moderate heat. Fry a few pieces of the crane at a time, turning until no longer pink. Remove to a platter and season with salt and pepper.

"Stir the flour into the remaining butter in the casserole and cook over low heat stirring constantly for 2 minutes. Remove from heat. Slowly pour in the crane stock, beating vigorously to blend roux and liquid. Return to heat and, while stirring constantly, let the sauce thicken and come to a boil. Reduce heat and simmer for 2 minutes.

"Return the crane to the casserole together with the juices that have collected on the plate. Add the bouquet garni and thyme.

The sauce should cover the crane. Bring to a boil, reduce heat and simmer for 45 minutes.

"Put chicken stock into a 10-inch skillet over medium heat. Add 2 tablespoons of butter and the onions. Bring to a boil, cover and simmer for 15 minutes or until the onions are tender when pierced. Using a slotted spoon, transfer the onions to the bowl and set aside. Add the vinegar and mushrooms to the remaining stock. Bring to a boil and simmer for 10 minutes. Remove the mushrooms and place them with the onions in the bowl. Boil the remaining liquid until reduced to 2 tablespoons, and pour it over the crane.

"Remove the crane from the casserole and transfer the pieces to a plate. Discard the *bouquet garni*. Skim the fat from the surface

Sandhill Crane

Today, large numbers of sandhill cranes wing over the prairies from Canada into Mexico. Along the way, several states offer hunting seasons on the bird. If you hunt the sandhill, watch out for your eyes when you go after wounded birds. They can stand tall, having both long legs and long necks. Adults are grey with black wing tips. Young birds are somewhat brownish.

The sandhill feeds mostly on grain, and its mild meat can be excellent table fare. An adult bird, well fed, weighs about 4 to 4 ½ pounds when dressed. The sandhill's wide wings contain very little meat, and the long legs are full of tendons.

of the sauce. Blend the egg yolks and cream and whisk into the hot sauce, a few tablespoons at a time, until about half a cup has been added. Bring to a boil, stirring constantly. Boil slowly for one minute. Taste for seasoning. Strain through a fine sieve into a large bowl.

"Clean the casserole, arrange the crane pieces, onions, and mushrooms in it, and pour the sauce over them. Before serving, cover the casserole and simmer it over moderate heat for 10 minutes, or until the crane pieces are hot. Do not let the sauce come to a boil again. Serve directly from the casserole which at the last minute has been sprinkled with chopped fresh parsley."

Note: A full grown sandhill will serve 6 to 8 people.

Chinese Crane with Parsley Rice

Here's an excellent dish that I adapted from Henrietta Goplen's book *Sportsman's Gourmet Guide.*

    1 sandhill crane, breast and thighs
    3 tablespoons cooking oil
    3 tablespoons flour
    ½ teaspoon monosodium glutamate
    1 cup chopped celery
    ½ cup water
    2 tablespoons soy sauce
    1⅓ cups rice (prepare separately)
    2 tablespoons dried parsley

Cook the rice with dried parsley and set aside. Slice the meat thinly. (If the sandhill has been frozen, slice the meat before it completely thaws out.) Heat the oil in a large frying pan and brown the meat. Add water and soy sauce. Bring to boil, reduce heat, cover, and simmer for 15 minutes. Add celery, cover, and simmer for another 10 minutes. Spoon the rice into serving bowls, then top with meat and gravy. *Serves 4.*

Sandhill Fingers

Here is a delightful way to eat crane breasts, and they can be served as a main course or as an appetizer, depending on how many cranes you've got and on how many folks you've got to feed.

    crane breast
    salt
    pepper
    lemon
    butter
    flour

Skin the breast and cut it into fingers about ½ inch thick. Put the fingers into a bowl and sprinkle them with fresh lemon juice and pepper. Let set for an hour or so. Drain, salt to taste, and shake in flour. Let set a few minutes. Heat the butter in a frying pan. Sauté crane breasts on medium-high heat until they are browned. Do not over cook. Allow at least ⅓ pound of crane breast fingers per person.

Note: This recipe calls only for the breast,

but be sure to save the rest of the crane. Try the marsh bird fricassee recipe.

Dr. Frye's Favorite Fried Coot, with Gravy

Some years ago, I got hold of an interesting news release from the state of Florida. They've got lots of coots down there, and maybe they wanted them thinned out for one reason or another. This recipe no doubt helped! It was said to be Dr. O. E. Frye's favorite hunting camp recipe for coot. Head of the Fresh Water Fish and Game Commission at that time, Frye said, "It is indeed unfortunate that more sportsmen don't add a few coots to their waterfowl bag. The daily bag limit is a generous 15 per day [check current bag limits] and the coot may be found throughout Florida. Bagging a coot is not much of a challenge to the average gunner and this, perhaps, may be one reason sportsmen tend to overlook the bird." The news release made it clear that the secret to the coot recipe is in skinning the bird and removing all the fat.

> **coot breasts and giblets**
> **cooking oil**
> **flour**
> **salt**
> **pepper**
> **vinegar**
> **water**

Skin the birds and remove the meat from either side of the breastbone with a fillet knife. Save the liver and the gizzard. (The gizzard should be split and turned.) Make a solution with water, vinegar, and salt in a glass or crockery container. Put coot breasts in the solution and marinate overnight in a cooler or refrigerator. Refrigerate the giblets.

The next day, boil the liver for a few minutes and set aside. Boil the gizzard for an hour and set aside. Salt and pepper the coot breasts, then roll in flour. Fry in hot cooking oil. Dice the liver and gizzard. Set the breasts aside to drain, then add the diced giblets to the pan drippings. Bring to boil, add a little water, and thicken with flour, stirring all the while. Serve coot and gravy with biscuits and hot coffee.

Variations: Frye's recipe is, in my opinon, made even better if a handful of chopped onion is sautéed and added to the gravy.

Note: The recipe above doesn't say how much vinegar and salt to add to the marinade. I suggest 1 tablespoon of salt and 1 cup of vinegar per quart of water. If you plan to try the recipe in camp but don't want to lug a

---

Coot Liver and Gizzard Pilau

A coot liver and gizzard pilau is made simply by cooking available coot livers and gizzards with enough rice to feed as many people as need feeding!

—Marjorie Kinnan Rawlings, *Cross Creek Cookery*

jug of vinegar along, pack a box of ordinary baking soda and marinate the coot in 1 tablespoon of salt and 1 tablespoon of soda per quart of water. (The next recipe recommends 1 teaspoon soda per quart of water.)

New England Coot Stew

Here's a recipe from Colton H. Bridges, of Grafton, Massachusetts, as published in the Ducks Unlimited *After the Hunt Cookbook*.

    4 or 5 coot breasts
    soda
    seasoned flour
    ½ cup butter
    5 medium onions, chopped
    4 cups chopped tomatoes
    1 tablespoon salt
    ¼ teaspoon pepper
    1 or 2 bay leaves
    pinch of marjoram
    ¼ cup red wine
    ¼ cup cider vinegar
    2 or 3 beef bouillon cubes

Mix 1 teaspoon of soda into a quart of water. Marinate the coot breasts in this solution overnight under refrigeration. Trim the fat (and skin) from the coot breasts and cut the meat into bite-sized pieces. Shake the pieces in seasoned flour. Heat butter in a cast-iron pot and brown the coot pieces. Add a quart of water and bay leaves. Bring to boil. Stir in bouillon cubes. Add onions, tomatoes, salt, pepper, marjoram, wine, and cider

vinegar. Cover and simmer for 2 hours. *Serves 4 or 5.*

Ocala Coot

My sister sent me a little recipe book, full of advertisements, from Ocala, Florida. I've fished the flats of Orange Lake, just north of Ocala, a number of times, as well as Lake Weir, south of Ocala, and in the Big Scrub to the east of town. Thus, I can verify that there is no shortage of coots in that part of Florida! In fact, I even *caught* a coot on Lake Weir with hook and line on a cane pole while fishing for bluegills!

The Meat
    2 coots, dressed
    salt and pepper
The Marinade
    ¾ cup of lemon juice or lime juice, freshly squeezed
    ¾ cup of chicken stock
    1 medium onion, sliced
    1 stalk of celery, tops and all, sliced
    1 bay leaf
    1 tablespoons chopped parsley
The Sauce
    ¼ cup butter or margarine
    1 medium-to-small onion, chopped
    ¼ cup catsup
    ¾ cup tomato juice
    salt and pepper

Combine all marinade ingredients. Dress the coots; salt and pepper them inside and out. Put them into a glass container, then pour marinade over them and cover. Put the coots into the refrigerator for two days. Turn occasionally.

When you're ready to cook, preheat the oven to 350 degrees. Combine all ingredients listed under Sauce. Remove coots from marinade, dry, and dip in sauce. Arrange in a suitable baking pan or casserole dish. Pour the rest of the sauce over the birds. Cover. Bake for 1 hour, basting several times with pan liquid. *Serves 2.*

Crow Hash

I've never quite understood the derogatory implications behind the phrase "eating crow." I'll take all the crow that I can get!

The Meat
  4 or 5 crows
  1 can of chicken broth (10¾-ounce size)
  ¼ cup of butter
  salt
  pepper
  juice ½ lemon
  8 to 12 ounces of mushrooms, sliced
  flour
  1 bay leaf
  rice, or toast
The Marinade
  1 pint water
  1 pint vinegar
  3 cloves garlic, crushed
  1 teaspoon salt
  ½ teaspoon black pepper

Skin the crows, cut away any fat, and draw. Cut birds in half. Mix all ingredients listed under marinade above, then pour it over the crow in a suitable glass container. Marinate for 24 hours or longer under refrigeration. Turn several times a day.

Discard marinade and boil the crow in a pot with water and 1 bay leaf. Remove the meat from the bones, slicing it *against* the grain. In a large frying pan, heat ¼ cup of butter. Sauté mushrooms. Add chicken broth and lemon juice. Salt and pepper to taste. Simmer for 20 minutes. Thicken with a little flour. Serve over rice or crisp toast. *Serves 4.*

Crow Breasts

Here's a crow recipe and considerable opinion from Bradford Angier's *Gourmet Cooking for Free.* "Tasting like chicken with savory overtones of duck, the dark meat of the crow is well worth eating. If you've too many for deep freeze and for friends, even when proffered under the more alluring name of rook, why not feast on the breasts?

"Sprinkle each with salt and freshly ground black pepper. Melt a liberal amount of butter in a preferably heavy iron frypan and heat it as much as possible without scorching. Put in the breasts and cover. Lower the heat to moderate and cook about 7 minutes until brown on one side. Then turn and bronze the other.

"Add a cup of sherry, re-cover, and simmer until the meat is tender, adding more wine if necessary. Then move the breasts to a warm

Hunting Crow

Hunters should read their state game laws carefully, looking for off-beat and off-season action. In Missouri, for example, the crow season is open until the first week in March, providing some late-season shooting and, hopefully, some bonus fare for the table.

Anyone who has every tried to stalk a crow knows that these wary creatures are difficult to bag. The successful hunter will usually depend on the skilful use of crow calls and decoys. Often, owl decoys will work better than crow decoys simply because they are natural enemies. But check your game laws before resorting to electronic crow calls or live owl decoys.

place. Spoon off all possible fat. Bring the wine and juice to a bubble, stirring and scraping, and add a tablespoon of heavy cream to bind and thicken. Pour over the meat and serve. By this time the air will be permeated with the fragrant promise of wonderfully good things to eat."

Fried Crow

    4 crow or 6 crow breasts
    2 small bay leaves
    1 medium onion
    cooking oil
    flour
    salt and pepper

Pluck the crow, dress, and halve the breast, or quarter the whole birds. Put into a pot of water with bay leaves. Bring to boil, then reduce heat and simmer for an hour. Let drain. Discard water and bay leaves.

Heat the cooking oil in a frying pan. Salt and pepper the crow to taste, then shake it in flour. Brown the onions, then set aside. Cook the crow, turning once, until it is brown. Set aside. Put a tablespoon of flour into the frying pan and stir until browned. Add a cup of water and the sautéed onions. Simmer until the gravy is of the desired thickness. Salt and pepper gravy to taste. Serve the gravy over the crow, along with hot biscuits. *Serves 2 or 3.*

Ricebird Fricassee

Ricebirds, or small blackbirds, are easy to dress if you pull the skin off the breast and pull or cut out the meat. It's possible to dress out the whole bird—but the breasts on some species aren't much bigger than your thumb, and the thighs and wings simply aren't worth the trouble. Even if you dress them out, most people aren't going to pick the meat off them after they have been cooked. Anyhow, in the recipe below I have figured 5 or 6 birds per person. Very large blackbirds or starlings may go further:

    20 to 25 ricebird breasts
    2 tablespoons butter
    salt
    pepper
    1 cup diced onion
    1 cup sliced mushrooms

½ cup chicken broth
water
½ cup red wine
rice (cooked separately)

Heat butter in a frying pan and sauté the onion and mushrooms. Add ricebird breasts and brown. Salt and pepper to taste. Add chicken broth and enough water to almost cover the birds. Bring to a quick boil, then reduce heat, cover, and simmer for 45 minutes. Add red wine and simmer for another 15 minutes. Serve over rice. *Serves 4.* (If you've got more than 4 people for dinner, make more rice, add a little boiling water to fricassee, add two chopped hard-boiled eggs, and thicken gravy with flour.)

Crockpot Birds

This is a sort of catch-all recipe for cooking blackbirds, crows, and so on. Clean out the freezer. Assorted doves, snipe, quail, coot. You name it.

birds or bird breasts to fill crockpot
    about half full
1 quart spring water
1 teaspoon baking soda
1 teaspoon salt
½ cup margarine
1 cup red wine
½ cup maple syrup
1 bay leaf
black pepper
rice (cooked separately)

Blackbird Stew

Letha learned to cook by watching her mother, grandmothers, and occasionally her father. She tells this story, "I remember when I was a small child, and my mother was sick during a snow so my father cooked. He was a good cook. He killed some birds, cleaned them, and put them in a big iron frying pan with water. He put some sides of hog meat in with the birds. The meat had only been salted one or two days. We called it corned. Anyway, he made some dumplings and cooked the stew down to a slow gravy. We children thought it was the best stew we had ever eaten. My father called it blackbird stew."
                    —*Coastal Carolina Cooking*

If you've got very small birds, use only the breasts. The whole bird, of course, can be used, but you'll have lots of small bones to fish out of the cooked dish. Put cleaned birds in a glass container, then cover with water into which has been dissolved 1 teaspoon soda and 1 teaspoon salt. Refrigerate overnight.

Drain the birds and put them into the crockpot. Turn to low heat. Add margarine, wine, syrup, bay leaf, and black pepper. Cook on low heat for at least 8 hours. Stir once or twice if you're around the house. When you're ready to eat, fish out bay leaf and serve the birds and gravy over rice. *Serves 8 to 10.*

28

DRESSING BIRDS

Birds, like other game, should be field dressed, or drawn, as soon as possible after killing them, and they certainly should not be carried around all day in a game bag. This is especially true in warm weather—and I have hunted early season birds many times in a short-sleeved shirt. In weather like this, the birds really should be put on ice, and taking a light Styrofoam ice chest to a dove field or an early season teal blind is not always out of the question.

Some people "hang" birds in cool air for several days, and longer, until the meat becomes "high." I agree that aging the meat in a cold, dry environment for a few days, after the guts have been removed, certainly won't hurt the flavor. But too many people have gotten sick from eating tainted meat that has been hung too long, and I can't recommend the practice from a safety viewpoint. If you do "hang" birds for culinary reasons, I recommend that you take the guts out and leave the feathers on. Some people argue for hanging the birds by the head, others say that they should be hung by the feet. It really doesn't matter, if you are going to hang them at all. I feel that most modern hunters, especially those who live in the city or suburbs, don't hold with the hanging theory. Their wives don't either, and only the neighborhood cats will be enthusastic about the project.

In my opinion, game birds can be improved by refrigerating the meat for a few days before eating it. The larger the bird, the more important this becomes. But curing is not necesssary for mild birds such as pheasant or quail. Stronger meat, such as coot, is usually marinated before cooking.

255

The Easiest Way to Dress Whole Birds

It may be difficult to take time away from your hunting, but, usually, it's best to dress birds in the field. Pluck the birds first, pulling the feathers in the direction in which they grow. Usually, leaving the feathers in the field or woods won't hurt a thing, and it's better to leave them there than in your kitchen after dark. Also note that most birds are easier to pluck when they are fresh and still warm. (Plucking will be covered in more detail later.)

Plucking the bird first will make the drawing process easier, and certainly less messy.

To draw the bird, most people make a cut near the anus to enable them to remove the innards. Then they remove the crop, or otherwise get the undigested grain or food from under the skin of the crop.

With small birds, the field dressing can be accomplished without the aid of a knife. Pluck the bird (or skin it). Then hold the bird by the head and wring it off by twirling the bird's body around; anyone who has ever wrung a chicken's neck won't have any trouble with this. Then hold the bird in your right hand and insert your left fingers into the tender spot about midway between the end of the breastbone and the tail, pushing up slightly on the end of the breastbone. After opening the bird, remove the innards

BREASTING A BIRD

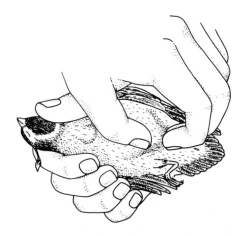

1. Insert fingers into tender spot below breastbone and pull breast upward. Remove innards.

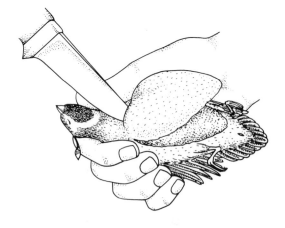

2. Cut breast free; then cut into crop and clean it throughly.

as carefully as possible. (I usually save the liver and the gizzard, and the liver must be removed without breaking the gall bladder. In any case, put all the innards into a plastic bag and dress out the livers and the gizzards later.) Next, break the skin into the crop area and clean it out. I leave the feet and wingtips on the birds, or I might cut them off if I've got a knife handy.

Note that most hunters cut birds in one way or another before drawing them, and many people cut them up the back from the vent to the neck. Usually, a bird cut in this manner will eventually be halved, or flattened. Remember that you, or the cook, may want to stuff the birds later on, and this should be considered when you make an

Location of oil sac. If desired, remove with a knife after bird has been plucked and skinned.

opening to draw the bird. The smaller the opening, the easier it is to close.

Some birds have an oil sac on the rump, just atop the tail. Usually, I ignore this, but some people want it out. Remove it with a knife after the bird has been plucked and skinned. Some people cut off the entire tail bone, and get the oil sac at the same time. Sometimes called the preen gland, the oil sac contains a substance with which birds waterproof their feathers.

If you want to save only the breast of your birds, your field dressing can be even easier. Either skin or pluck the breast clean, then cut it off, starting just behind the breastbone and working toward the crop. Put the breast into a plastic bag and throw the rest away. I much prefer to pluck my birds because I believe that the skin helps keep the meat moist during storage as well as during cooking. But skinning can be much easier on some species, such as quail, and I'll have to admit that I have eaten some skinned birds there were mighty fine indeed. Note that some recipes, such as a fricassee, are better than others for using skinned birds. Usually, fried birds should be plucked, not skinned. But some birds of strong flavor, such as the coot, are probably better when they are skinned, regardless of the cooking method.

Plucking Birds

As stated above, I recommend that the birds be dry plucked in the field. If you've got them at home or in camp, you may want to try wet plucking. This is accomplished by heating

Wet plucking a bird.

growth. Pulling the opposite way may damage the skin, which is quite tender on some birds.

No matter how carefully you pluck your birds, or regardless of your method, you will find that some pin feathers will remain embedded in the skin. There is no easy method of getting these out, and I recommend tweezers. If you use a knife blade and thumb, use a rather dull blade.

The Paraffin or Wax Method

Some birds, such as ducks, are harder to pluck than others, simply because they have more and thicker feathers. Many people prefer to pluck them by the paraffin method. Using low heat, melt some paraffin in a large pan. Fill a bucket with cold water and have it at hand. Pull out the bird's large wing feathers, or cut off the wings if you don't want to keep them. Dunk the bird into the melted paraffin, then quickly dip it into the cold water. The cold water, of course, will harden the melted paraffin. Then you can pull the paraffin off in chunks, and the feathers will come with it. This method takes quite a bit of paraffin, but you can use it over again if you reheat the chunks, melting the paraffin, and then straining it through cheesecloth or meshed wire to remove the feathers.

In a similar method, you add paraffin to a pot of hot water (about 180 degrees), then dip the birds into the water. The paraffin, of course, will float on top of the water, so that

some water to between 150 and 190 degrees. While the water is heating, however, it is usually best to wet the birds down in cold water. Then carefully lower the wet bird into the hot water, but don't leave it in too long, so that you won't start the cooking process. As soon as you remove the bird, start pulling out the feathers, pulling in the direction of dipping the bird into the water will usually get a thin coat of paraffin on the feathers. You may have to dip it more than once, however. Try 1 cake of paraffin per 2 quarts of water.

Singeing

I singe some birds, but not all. Some doves, for example, seem to need it and others don't. This may be a function of temperature or climate. In other words, a late-season bird may have more down on it than an early bird. In any case, the down and "hair" on ducks and other birds can be singed off with a flame. But it is best to avoid very hot flames, although some of the hand held torches are very convenient. I recommend that you use newspaper sheets that have been rolled up loosely. Holding the paper downward at a slight angle will produce more flame, holding it up will reduce the flame. But be careful and be sure you have a good place to drop the burning paper in case the fire is too much.

Singeing should be held to a minimum, and I seldom singe such birds as doves these days. Burning the feathers and feather roots (which stay in the skin) can give an unpleasant taste to the meat. Singe, yes, if necessary—but don't overdo it.

Freezing Birds

By far the best way to keep birds for any length of time is freezing. In fact, home canning is almost obsolete these days. With larger birds, about all you can do is wrap them up as tightly as possible. I prefer to work with cling-type wrap first, then finish the job with heavy duty freezer paper. Small birds can be handled the same way, usually putting more than one bird per package. Be careful that bird legs don't punch a hole in your package.

Smaller birds can be frozen in water like fish. A milk carton works nicely. I even heard of a hunting club in Georgia that froze a 55-gallon drum full of doves and water. While getting ready to cook, they turned the drum over and elevated it. But they had trouble getting it thawed, and doves dropped out for two days. In any case, water works very well for freezing birds because it fills up the body cavity instead of having it open and full of air.

If you aren't going to use water, you might consider freezing the birds two at a time, inserting the legs of the one into the body cavity of the other, snugging them together, and rolling both of them up like a section of log. I also like to cook birds in tandem.

Pheasants, ducks, and other birds can also be put into zip bags of the appropriate size, along with a little water. Most of the air can be removed by first zipping the bag closed all except one end. Then hold the bag under water, leaving the unsealed corner sticking out. Work the bag with your free hand, squeezing out all the air you can. Then seal the corner and remove. This bag can of course be folded and placed into another bag or wrapped for added protection.

Birds that become frozen in the field should be put into your home freezer without thawing them out. When you get ready to eat the birds, thaw them, pluck, dress, and cook as usual. This really isn't a bad way to freeze birds anyhow, especially if you come home late at night with a batch that haven't been field dressed. Just wrap each bird, label, and put it into the freezer. Or, wrap each bird with cling-type film, then bunch several into a larger bundle. The feathers and skin keep the birds from drying out, and the insides insure that the body cavity won't fill up with air.

Save the Giblets

As a few of the recipes in this book indicate, some of the best eating from the bird comes from the giblets. If I am going to freeze giblets, I normally put them under water in a small container. The first step, however, is to dress them out.

The *liver* should be handled carefully, trying to avoid the gall bladder. Cut the gall bladder away without puncturing it. If you do puncture it, consider throwing out that particular piece of liver.

The *heart* should be trimmed, and I usually split it.

The *gizzard* should be cut across the top but not all the way through. Peel the skin from the inside of the gizzard and wash.

The *neck* of larger birds contains some good meat, and it is usually saved along with the liver, heart, and gizzard for making giblet gravy. It should be either skinned or plucked along with the rest of the bird.

The *head* of the bird isn't usually saved in North America, but anyone who has had the

---

Need a Duck Picker?

Consider purchasing a mechanical duck picker when many ducks are to be picked during the season. These pickers employ an electric motor-driven cylinder with rubber fingers attached. The rapidly turning drum with fingers frail feathers from the bird trough a 4-inch flexible hose and into a nearby trash can. Mechanical pickers work fine, but sometimes the rubber projections are too stiff and care should be taken not to tear flesh; yours or the duck's.

—Chandler S. Cheek,
Answering the Call to Duck Cookery

---

pleasure of eating a chicken head will consider trying a pheasant head. The head can be fried or boiled. Gnaw around it, then crack it so that you can get the brains out. If you are making giblet gravy, just put the head in with the rest, then fish it out for yourself, or offer it to your guest of honor.

Removing Shot from Birds

It is best, but not always possible, to remove the shot from birds. This should of course be done after you have drawn the bird and plucked or skinned it. Simply look for holes in the flesh at the point of entry, which will often be darker than the surrounding flesh and will often have parts of feathers in it. Remove the shot with tweezers or with a pointed knife. In some cases, the shot will go on through the bird, or will be removed when the bird is drawn. Anyone who has eaten a lot of game birds will know that getting all the shot out is sometimes not practical, and one should not be offended by running into a shot at the table. But try to minimize this problem and you'll have a more pleasant bird supper.

Once you cut the legs off, as when field dressing, it will be almost impossible to remove the tendons. If you want the tendons out, your best bet is to freeze the birds with the legs and feet still on. When you remove the bird from the freezer for thawing, cut around each leg, just above the knee joint, and break the bone by applying pressure the opposite way from the natural bend in the knee. Then pull on the scaled part of the leg or on the feet. Hopefully the tendons will pull out— but not always.

Removing the Tendons

Some birds, especially the cock pheasant and the wild turkey, have tendons in the legs that make them difficult to carve at the table.

Dressing the Wild Turkey

Some people believe that the turkey should be bled before it is dressed. I don't think that bleeding will do much good, but it is usually

PULLING OUT THE TENDONS

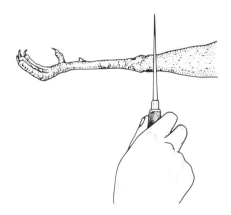

1. Cut around each leg above the knee joint and break the bone.

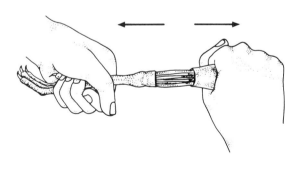

2. Pull on leg to remove tendons.

accomplished by slitting the underside of the neck, then holding the turkey up by the legs. Field dressing should proceed by laying the bird on its back, then plucking a row of feathers from the vent up to the end of the breastbone. With your knife, make a slit from the vent up to the breastbone, being careful not to puncture the insides. (To make the cut, insert the point of the knife, then cut forward with the blade pointed up.) Reach into the cavity with your hand and remove the insides. Get out the intestines, heart and liver, and lungs. This may require two or three steps. Then reach high into the chest area and sever the windpipe. Next, make a small slit at the neck, just above the breastbone, and remove the contents of the crop.

Your turkey contains quite a bit of meat, and it should be cooled down as quickly as possible. It helps to hang the bird by the feet from a tree limb, then prop open the body cavity with a stick to help in ventilation.

Plucking your turkey can be quite a job, and this is made easier by using the scalding method. But you will need lots of hot water. A washtub will hold enough water—if you've got a way to heat it.

Dressing Ducks and Geese

Dry-plucking large ducks and wild geese can be quite a job, and I recommend that you use either the wet method or the paraffin method, both of which are difficult to do in a normal duck blind.

The birds should be drawn as soon as possible after they are brought down. The larger the bird, the more important this becomes. The reason, of course, is that the feathers and down on the birds tend to hold the heat in. So, open the body cavity and empty out the insides. Then keep the birds in a ventilated area, if possible. One trick, which you might remember to try in warm weather, is to dry-pluck the feathers from the breast area, thereby allowing the heat to escape from the thickenst part of the bird's body.

Carving Game Birds

Pheasant and turkey can be carved like domestic chickens and turkey and should present no problems at the table. Carve the breast as usual, and you can cut off the legs and wings simply by working them a bit to determine where the joints are. Duck and geese are different, however, because the leg joints are harder to find. The duck leg is attached more underneath the body than on the side like a chicken or turkey. Some people use poultry shears to cut through the hip joint at the body, and again to separate the leg and the thigh. The wings may also be separated from the body with the shears. If you've never carved a duck or goose, perhaps you should practice on one in the kitchen before you do it at the table.

PART THREE

GAME ANIMALS

29

SQUIRREL

My father left me a 12-gauge double. It had belonged to my grandfather. It was—or is—a Lefever, and, if I remember correctly, my father said it was the first double in our county without rabbit ears. It has a 32-inch barrel, full on the left and modified on the right. The left barrel has worn somewhat, but in better days its pattern of 6's was well nigh perfect; it's range quite long. It was in fact considered to be the best turkey and squirrel gun in Henry County. I retired it years ago when I switched to a rifle and scope for squirrels, but I still like to shoulder the long gun from time to time and think back on different times.

Back then, following the bad Depression years, we ate the whole squirrel, from head to tail. I mean we actually skinned out the head, fried it, and ate it at the table. A fried squirrel head contains some good gnawing all around, and there is a tasty chunk on each cheek. The brain, however, is the real prize. To get at it, hold the head firmly in the left hand, then grasp a tablespoon in your right hand and whop the head hard enough to crack the skull open so that you can get to the brains. It may sound unappetizing to some modern people, but the plain truth is that the head of a squirrel is far better than a chicken head.

Anyhow, before trying the following recipes please note that there is a very big difference between tender young squirrels and tough old squirrels. In short, a young squirrel, properly handled and cooked, is one of the very best kind of game; an old squirrel, improperly handled and cooked, is sorry fare. For this reason, it is important to read the recipes carefully and choose one to suit the squirrels that are available. As a rule, it is not a good idea to cook both young squirrels and old squirrels by the same recipe for the same meal, but there are exceptions, as when a young hunter brings home a mixed bag and wants to feed the whole family. The young hunter, in his enthusiasm, can probably eat most anything that he brings home, but note that old squirrels fried by ordinary methods are just too tough for most people, and old squirrels cooked for a long time atop charcoal are virtually impossible to be bitten into, or gnawed off, by anyone with false teeth.

Brunswick Stew

The following recipe can be made with young squirrels or old, or a mix of the two. If you have more than enough squirrels to make the dish, use the old ones and save the young ones for frying. This recipe is also good when made with squirrels mixed with rabbits and other game.

In my opinion Brunswick stew is best when made with fresh or fresh-frozen vegetables, but of course canned vegetables can also be used, especially in camp.

> **5 to 7 gray squirrels (or 3 fox squirrels)**
> **1 pound bacon**
> **2 cups baby lima beans (or butter beans)**
> **2 cups corn (whole kernel)**
> **8 medium potatoes, diced**
> **4 cups tomatoes, chopped**
> **2 medium onions, chopped**
> **2 tablespoons sugar**
> **1 teaspoon black pepper**
> **½ cup butter or margarine**

> **4 tablespoons of flour**
> **bay leaf**
> **salt and pepper to taste**
> **water**

Dress the squirrels and put into a large pot containing 1½ gallons of boiling water and a bay leaf. An old iron pot seems to work best. Simmer an hour or so, or until tender, skimming off any scum that might accumulate. If you have a mix of old and young squirrels, boil the old ones for an hour, then add the young ones. The squirrels can be removed from the pot one at the time, starting with the more tender ones, letting the older ones cook longer. Remove bay leaf and discard. Remove squirrels and pull the meat from the bones. Reserve liquid in pot. Chop the meat and put it back into the pot.

When all the squirrel meat has been boned, cut the bacon into 1-inch strips and add to pot. You can cut a whole package of bacon instead of dealing with individual slices, especially when the bacon is well chilled or partly frozen. Add the onion. Let simmer for about 2 hours, removing scum if any accumulates.

Add lima beans, corn, potatoes, and tomatoes. Simmer for an hour or two, stirring from time to time. Mix butter (or margarine) and flour into paste balls. Bring stew to a quick boil, add paste balls, reduce heat, and stir for 10 minutes. Test for seasoning and add salt or pepper if desired.

Brunswick stew should be served hot. But it is even better when heated up the next day! *Serves 8 to 12.*

Notes and Variations: Although most cookbook recipes and commercial versions of Brunswick stew use poultry and pork, the

Lots of Squirrels

The Illinois Department of Conservation, in a publication called *Outdoor Highlights*, says that 150,000 hunting Illini will bag an average of at least10 squirrels each per year. They set the annual estimate at from 1.5 to 2 million in the state. If the other states average the same numbers, we bag some 85,000,000 squirrels per year in the United States. Most of'em are fried—and that takes lots of cooking oil. A lot of Americans these days are trying to cut back on fried foods, and hunters should know that squirrels can be cooked, quite successfully, by methods other than frying.

original might well have been made with squirrel. But no one can say for sure how or when Brunswick stew took hold, although serveral places claim it. Brunswick, Georgia, and Brunswick, Virginia, are strong contenders. In any case, the above recipe can be cooked with rabbit as well as with squirrel, and in a pinch, you can throw in a Bantam hen or even a tough grouse.

Belgian Squirrel

With slight variations, I've seen this recipe in several places, and, frankly, I don't know the origin of it. In his *Bull Cook and Authentic Historical Recipes and Practices*, George Leonard Herter said that it was originally used by the Ardennes to cook rabbit, but that the Belgian Immigrants in the United States used it to cook squirrel as well as rabbit. But to be honest about it I'm not sure that this Herter book is as strong on the "historical" end as it is on the "bull." Anyhow, I've never been too fond of prunes, and I was therefore skeptical about the dish—until I cooked it!

> **3 gray squirrels (or 2 fox squirrels)**
> **1 stick butter or margarine**
> **2 medium onions, sliced thinly**
> **3 tablespoons of wine vinegar**
> **salt to taste**
> **pepper to taste**
> **⅛ teaspoon thyme**
> **18 prunes**
> **1½ tablespoons flour**
> **water**

Cut the squirrels into serving size pieces. Preheat oven to 350 degrees. Melt the butter in a frying pan and brown the squirrels. Place squirrels into a well-greased baking dish that has a cover and is suitable for cooking on the stove eye as well as in the oven. (A flat-bottomed Dutch oven that has an oven-proof lid can also be used.) Brown the onions in a frying pan, then reduce the heat and stir in salt, pepper, ⅛ teaspoon of thyme, and 3 tablespoons of wine vinegar. Pour this mixture over the squirrel pieces and put the casserole dish into the oven. Add enough water to barely cover the squirrel. Bake for one hour. Then add the 18 prunes, placing them one at the time between the pieces of squirrels and poking them under the liquid. Reduce the oven heat to 250 degrees and cook for another hour.

Mix 1½ tablespoons of flour into a cup of cold water. Stir until no lumps are present.

Remove casserole dish from oven. Pour flour and water over squirrels and simmer over low heat atop a stove eye for about 15 minutes, or until the gravy thickens to the consistency that you prefer.

All of the recipes that I have seen for this dish recommend that the gravy be served on potatoes or on toast. I also serve mine over rice. *Serves 4 to 6.*

Variation: Also try this dish with a young, tender rabbit. Cook it until the meat falls from the bones when stirred with a fork. Remove the bones, break up the meat into the gravy, and then serve over rice.

Fox Squirrel and Dumplings

  3 fox squirrels (or 5 gray squirrels)
  salt and pepper
  water
  flour
  1 egg, hard boiled and sliced

Clean squirrels and cut into serving size pieces. Put into a pot and cover with water. Simmer until the meat is tender. Remove squirrels and drain, retaining the broth. Pull meat from bones and return to broth. Salt and pepper to taste. Keep hot.

To make the dumplings, put one cup of water into a bowl and mix in flour until you have a stiff dough. Knead. Dust a suitable surface with flour and roll out the dough. Make it very thin—about ⅛ inch. Cut the dough into strips. Bring the squirrel broth to

boil and drop strips into it. Add hard boiled egg slices. Taste for salt and pepper, and adjust if necessary. Simmer for 5 minutes before eating. *Serves 5 or 6.*

Variation: To make cornmeal dumplings, or corn dodgers, mix a little meal, salt, and water until you get the consistency of uncooked hushpupies. Form into small balls, or patties, and put them around the edge of the pot. Simmer for 10 minutes or so.

Fried Squirrel

Once I shot a big gray squirrel off an ear of corn in a field that bordered a wooded creek. I don't know how old this thing was, but he certainly had some credentials of maturity. I gave it to the fellow who owned the corn, and he later told me that it was so tough that he couldn't stick a fork into its gravy. He had fried it, then made gravy from the pan drippings. Of course he spoke in jest, but there was more than a grain of truth in what he was saying. An old squirrel should not be fried as usual. But if you've got tender squirrels, try the following:

  young squirrels
  cooking oil
  flour
  salt and pepper

Dress the squirrels and cut into serving pieces. Salt and pepper to taste. Bring at least 1 inch of oil to heat in a frying pan, then cook the squirrel pieces on medium-high heat until they are brown and done. Do not overcook. If you want gravy, pour off most of the oil, then scrape up the pan dredges. Bring to heat, pour in a little water, and stir in flour. Cook the gravy down to the desired consistency.

Note: If you insist on frying tough squirrels, boil them in water (or in a pressure cooker) until they are tender. Drain them, then fry by the above recipe. Or, you can fry the squirrels first, then add water, bring to boil, cover, and simmer until you can stick a fork into the meat.

Frying Pan to Crockpot Squirrel

I've eaten my share of squirrel, cooked a number of ways. Perhaps my all-time favorite, at least for cooking a mixed bag of young and old squirrels, came from a fellow named Floyd "Jake" Kringer. I don't know him, but he was more or less featured in an article on squirrel cookery in *Outdoor Highlights*, published by the Illinois Department of Conservation. The article was somewhat vague about exactly how much of what to add, and my guess is that Kringer wasn't too eager to talk. But here's what I use, and my boys don't argue with the results:

7 or 8 gray squirrels (or 5 fox
   squirrels)
flour
cooking oil
salt and pepper
1 medium onion, chopped

8 ounces mushrooms, sliced
2 cans creamy chicken mushroom
   soup
2 cups sour cream
2 cups water

Dress the squirrels and cut them into serving size pieces. Salt and pepper each piece, then roll in flour. Heat some cooking oil in a large frying pan and brown the squirrels. Put the squirrel pieces into a crockpot. Add soup, water, onions, and mushrooms. Turn the crockpot to high for half an hour. Then turn the heat to low, add sour cream, and cook for at least 6 hours. *Serves 8 to 10.*

The gravy can be thinned with water, or thickened with flour, as needed. Kringer said, "And the gravy from this recipe over baked potatoes is superb." Indeed it is. Also try it over rice or hot biscuits. As I write this recipe down, there is the first hint of fall crispness in the air, and the squirrels around my place are feeling good and frisky. They had better watch out!

Squirrel Cacciatore

Cacciatore is an old chicken dish of Italian origin. But it has a tomato base—and the tomato is an American vegetable. Who can say that the original "cacciatore" recipe wasn't in fact made with squirrels? In any case, the following recipe works best with young, tender squirrels, but a mixed bag can be used, as discussed below.

5 gray squirrels (or 3 fox squirrels)
⅓ cup cooking oil

flour
2 pounds fresh tomatoes, peeled and
   cut up
1 can tomato sauce (8-ounce size)
2 cloves garlic, minced
1 large onion, sliced
½ bell pepper, diced
6 ounces sliced mushrooms
2 bay leaves
1 teaspoon salt
¼ teaspoon pepper
¼ teaspoon thyme
¾ teaspoon oregano
½ cup wine

If any of the squirrels are old and tough, simmer them in water for 30 minutes. Do not boil tender squirrels. Cut the squirrels into serving pieces.

In a frying pan, heat a little of the cooking oil and sauté the onion, bell pepper, mushrooms, and garlic for a few minutes. Remove, drain, and put into a Dutch oven or other suitable pot. Put the flour into a bag and shake the squirrel pieces. Pour the rest of

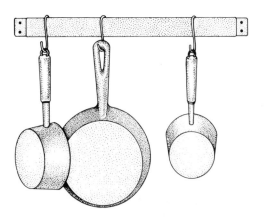

the cooking oil into a large frying pan and heat. Fry the squirrel pieces, turning, until they are golden brown. Add the squirrel pieces to the sautéed onion, pepper, mushrooms, and garlic. Mix in the tomatoes, tomato sauce, salt, pepper, thyme, bay leaves, and oregano. Bring to heat, reduce, cover, and simmer for 40 minutes, turning squirrel several times. Add the wine and fish out the bay leaves. Simmer for another 15 minutes. Eat while hot. *Serves 6 or 7.*

Squirrel Salad

3 gray squirrels (or 2 fox squirrels)
2 bay leaves
3 stalks celery, diced
1 teaspoon onion juice
1 cup mayonnaise (more required
   later)
juice of 1 large lemon
2 tablespoons capers
salt and pepper
Tabasco sauce (optional)
mayonnaise
paprika

Boil the squirrels in water with two bay leaves until the meat is tender. Remove the squirrels from the pot, let cool, and bone. Discard liquid and bay leaves. Chop the meat and put it into a glass container. Squeeze the lemon juice over the meat, then refrigerate it overnight.

Mix meat, celery, 1 cup of mayonnaise and capers. Add onion juice, then salt and pepper to taste. Add a little Tabasco sauce if desired. Serve on leaves of lettuce. Top with mayonnaise, then sprinkle lightly with paprika.

This salad can be eaten on crackers. Also, try thinning it with mayonnaise and then using it as a sandwich spread.

Squirrel Fricassee

I've paid attention to hundreds of recipes called "fricassee." My conclusion is that the word is used loosely, to say the least. Nonetheless, I take the following recipe, whatever it should be called, quite seriously:

2 squirrels
1 bay leaf
4 slices of bacon
1 cup of apple juice
salt and pepper
crab apple slices

Boil squirrels in a little water containing a bay leaf. When tender, drain the squirrels and pull the meat off the bones. Fry the bacon in a frying pan. Remove bacon, crumble it, and set it aside. Pour off most of the bacon grease. Sauté the squirrel meat for a couple of minutes, then pour in the apple juice. Add the bacon pieces. Salt and pepper to taste. Cover and simmer for an hour. Serve over rice. Garnish with red crab apple slices. *Serves 4.*

30

RABBIT

My guess is that the rabbit (including cottontails, snowshoes, hares, jack-rabbits, and the others) are by far America's favorite small game. If they aren't, they ought to be. They can be found in deep woods, hedge-rowed farmlands, surburban yards, unkempt pastures, piney woods, hardwood forests, prairies, and even in swamps. From coast to coast, from Mexico to the Arctic, rabbits are plentiful. They are easy to find. Easy to bag. Easy to dress. Easy to cook. And easy to eat. It's good meat, too, very low in calories and very high in protein.

Moreover, most states have long seasons and very liberal bag limits. No special equipment is needed to hunt rabbits successfully. Many have been taken with bow and arrow, and even with a slingshot. Either a .22 rifle or a shotgun will do fine. But the ultimate rabbit gun, in my opinion, is an over-and-under combo with a .22 rifle on top and a 20-gauge shotgun on bottom.

Tasty Onion Rabbit

1 or 2 rabbits
buttermilk
salt
pepper
1 package onion soup mix (2.6-ounce)
1 cup dry bread crumbs, fine
paprika
butter

If your rabbit is young, cut it up and soak it in buttermilk for 20 minutes or longer. (If the rabbit is old, marinate it under refrigeration for 12 hours or longer in buttermilk. Use a glass or crockery container.) After soaking the rabbit, cut it up and reserve buttermilk.

Preheat oven to 375 degrees. Put onion soup mix in a food processor and zap it a few times, until it is the consistency of the dry bread crumbs. Mix onion soup mix, bread crumbs, 1 teaspoon paprika, 1 teaspoon salt, and ½ teaspoon black pepper. Remove rabbit pieces from buttermilk, then roll or shake them in the crumb mix. Arrange the pieces of rabbit in a well-greased shallow baking pan. Place a small pat of butter atop each piece. Bake for 1 hour. Melt a little butter in a saucepan and baste rabbit pieces several times during cooking. After an hour, baste the rabbit with pan drippings, sprinkle with paprika, and bake for another 10 minutes.

Wiregrass Fried Rabbit

This simple recipe works best for young, tender rabbits. Older rabbits can also be used, but of course they may be a little tough. (The tougher rabbits can be parboiled before frying, but this takes away some of the taste.)

1 or more young rabbits, pan dressed
cooking oil
flour
salt
pepper

Heat about 1-inch of cooking oil in frying pan. Salt and pepper the rabbit pieces to taste, then shake or roll in flour. Fry in oil on medium heat until browned and done. Or listen carefully. My wife says it's done when it gets quiet. She can, in fact, watch TV in the den and tell you when the rabbit (or chicken) is done in the kitchen! Apparently the meat doesn't pop and crackle as much when it gets done, but I always have to look at mine. And sometimes at hers. Anyhow, drain rabbit on absorbent paper before serving so that it won't sound soggy when you bite into it.

Hasenpfeffer

This German dish has been around for centuries simply because it is so good! I've seen dozens of variations of hasenpfeffer, but of course I haven't tested them all. The recipe that I use came, for the most part, from an early edition of *The Good Housekeeping Cookbook*.

The Meat and Marinade
 3 to 4 pounds of rabbit or hare, cut up
 1 cup water
 2 cups red wine
 2 cups sliced onions
 1 tablespoon pickling spice
 2½ teaspoons salt
 ½ teaspoon thyme leaves
 ½ teaspoon coarsely ground pepper
 2 bay leaves
Other Ingredients
 10 slices of bacon
 ¾ cup all-purpose flour
 1 teaspoon sugar

Put rabbit pieces into a large bowl. Pour over it 1 cup of water and 2 cups wine. Add onions, pickling spice, salt, thyme, pepper, and bay leaves. Cover bowl and refrigerate overnight.

Fry bacon in a skillet until it is quite crisp. Drain bacon, crumble, and set aside. Retain bacon drippings.

Remove the rabbit from marinade and pat it dry with paper towels. (Retain marinade.)

Shake the meat in flour, then brown the pieces a few at a time in bacon drippings. Set aside. When all the rabbit has been browned, put it into a Dutch oven or large frying pan. Crumble bacon and sprinkle it over rabbit. Strain the marinade mixture, discard seasonings, and stir 1 teaspoon of sugar into the liquid. Pour over rabbit and bring to a quick boil. Reduce heat, cover, and simmer for 2 hours.

Rabbit Fever

Not long ago, I read that rabbits should not be hunted until two or three weeks after a heavy frost, and that rabbit hunters should carry with them a pair of gloves and a can of Lysol. The gloves, the author said, were for wearing when you handle or clean the rabbit, and the Lysol was for spraying your hands when you finished the job.

The author, of course, was setting forth precautions against the disease tularemia, or "rabbit fever," which can be transmitted to humans. The disease causes a lymphatic inflammation, along with chills, headaches, and fever. Tularemia can be fatal to humans, and of course it should be properly treated.

But the odds against a particular rabbit having tularemia are quite long. Even if a rabbit has the disease, it can be dressed, cooked, and eaten without a problem. The disease is caused by a microorganism, which can be transmitted from rabbit flesh (or other infected rodents) to an open wound or sore on human skin. Thus, it is not a good idea to dress rabbits when you have a cut, scratch, or sore on your hands.

The disease can also be present in beaver and muskrats, both water rodents, and waterborne epidemics of tularemia have been documented in Russia and Turkey. But probably most of the cases of tularemia in this country are caused by bites from the deer fly and ticks. So . . . if you have "rabbit fever" phobia, take mosquito netting and tick repellant along with rubber gloves and Lysol when you go hunting. And stay out of the water! Avoid Russia and Turkey.

Should you wait two or three weeks after first frost to go rabbit hunting? I don't have extensive data, but my feeling is that most of the cases of tularemia are caught, in warm weather, from flies, ticks, and mosquitoes, *not* from dressing rabbits. The best time to hunt (and eat) rabbits is whenever the season is open in your state. True, you can catch tularemia while rabbit hunting on warm days. But you can also catch legionnaire's disease while sitting at home under your air conditioner.

Remove rabbit to a serving platter and cook gravy a while longer, stirring. Serve gravy over rabbit. *Serves 5 or 6.*

Yellowknife Hare Stew

This simple, good, and versatile recipe came from *A Way of Life*, a book published by the Northwest Territories Department of Renewable Resources. It was submitted to that publication by Mary Ann Rabesca of Yellowknife. It's as good with Florida marsh rabbits as it is with arctic hares!

"After the hare has been skinned and cleaned, cut it up into pieces and brown in a frying pan. Place the pieces in a large pot with three cups cold water. Add salt, pepper, and vegetables (celery, carrots, potatoes) and cook until tender. Thicken the stew by mixing flour and water into a paste and adding it to the stew."

Rabbit Salad

Here's an excellent dish for a hot summer's day. Take a rabbit from the freezer, boil it until the meat is done and tender. Bone the meat and put it into the refrigerator for a while before dicing it.

The Salad
  2 cups cooked rabbit meat, diced
  juice from 1 lemon

  1 cup diced celery
  1 cup mayonnaise
  2 eggs, hard boiled and sliced
  ¼ cup almond slivers (sautéed)
  salt and pepper to taste
The Garnish
  lettuce
  1 tablespoon capers
  1 hard boiled egg, sliced
  1 tablespoon mayonnaise
  paprika

Sauté almond slivers in a little butter. Mix rabbit, celery, and lemon juice. Chill. Before serving, mix in 1 cup mayonnaise, slices from 2 hard-boiled eggs, almond slivers, salt, and pepper. Line a bowl with lettuce, then fill with rabbit salad. Arrange slices of hard-boiled eggs on top, then put capers onto eggs. Top with mayonnaise, then sprinkle top of mayonnaise with a little paprika. *Serves 6 as a salad or 4 for a light lunch.*

Note: Rabbit salad makes an excellent sandwich. If you aren't on a diet, use lots of mayonnaise and trim the brown crust from the slices of white sandwich bread.

Oven Barbecued Rabbit

The Meat
  2 cottontails, cut up
  juice from 1 lemon
  salt
  pepper
The Sauce
  ½ cup water
  ½ cup vinegar

1 can V-8 juice (12-ounce size)
½ cup catsup
½ cup Worcestershire sauce
2 medium onions, diced
2 cloves garlic, minced
2 medium green peppers, diced
2 tablespoons butter
1 teaspoon salt
½ teaspoon pepper

Salt and pepper rabbit pieces. Preheat oven to 350 degrees. Place rabbit pieces in a single layer into a well-greased baking pan and squeeze lemon juice on top. Bake for 30 minutes.

Combine all sauce ingredients in a pan and bring to a quick boil. Reduce heat and simmer for 30 minutes while rabbit is cooking.

Pour the sauce over the rabbit, reduce heat to 250 degrees, and bake for 3 hours. Turn pieces a time or two during cooking period. *Serves 4 or 5.*

Germantown Rabbit Stew

For this one you can thank Art Boebinger, who wrote it, and the Commonwealth of Kentucky's *Happy Hunting Ground*, who published it:

"Many German and French immigrants settled in the Ohio River Valley between Louisville and Cincinnati, Ohio, about the time of the Civil War. These people had a tradition of hunting in their native countries and they soon adapted older recipes to the native game animals. Here is a rabbit stew with just a little continental flavor."

1 rabbit
¼ pound bacon, diced
1 tablespoon butter
½ pound sliced mushrooms
8 small white onions
2 tablespoons flour
1 cup beef stock
1 cup red wine
1 tablespoon minced parsley
2 carrots, sliced
bay leaf
salt
black pepper

In a stove-top Dutch oven or similar heavy pot of suitable size, fry the bacon in butter until brown. Brown all the rabbit pieces and remove them to drain. Sauté the onions and mushrooms. Add the flour and blend it into the mixture. Add beef stock, wine, parsley, carrots, bay leaf, salt, pepper, and rabbit pieces. Bring to light boil, then reduce heat and simmer for 2 hours, or until the rabbit is tender. Art Boebinger says they like to serve this stew with corn bread and a salad. *Serves 2 or 3.*

Pea Ridge Buttermilk Rabbit

Once I knew a somewhat chubby poker player who kept a pack of beagle hounds. If there was anything that he liked better than country fried rabbit, it was the rabbit gravy

North Country Rabbits

Trappers commonly eat muskrat and beaver meat and some gourmets eat blackbirds.

Perhaps the best of all the small game animals in Manitoba is the snowshoe hare or bush rabbit. They make excellent sport and eating. Cottontails are good to eat but are much less common in Manitoba. Jack rabbits, more common than cottontails, are also delicious in stews and sausage.
—*Field Handling of Game and Fish,*
Manitoba Natural Resources

served over biscuits! At the time, I lived on Pea Ridge, near Fayetteville, Tennessee, where I played a little poker and cooked this dish often. It can be made with older rabbits as well as young ones.

rabbits, dressed and cut up
buttermilk
cooking oil
flour
salt
pepper

Put the pieces of rabbit into a glass or crockery container. Cover meat with buttermilk and refrigerate for 12 hours or longer (depending, somewhat, on the age of the rabbits).

Heat oil in a frying pan. Season flour with salt and pepper. Remove rabbit from buttermilk and drain. Roll pieces in flour and fry in oil at medium-high heat until brown. Pour off most of the grease. Add 2 cups of water to rabbit, stir, and cover tightly. Simmer for an hour.

Eat the rabbit, then serve the gravy over biscuit halves. I prefer to pepper my gravy rather heavily after I have poured it over the biscuits.

Rabbit Sauce Piquante

2 wild rabbits (cottontail size)
salt
cayenne pepper
½ to 1 teaspoon red pepper flakes
1 cup cooking oil
1 cup celery, diced
1 cup onions, diced
1 cup green pepper, diced
8 ounces mushrooms, sliced
½ cup green onion tops
3 cloves garlic, minced
1 tablespoon parsley
1 can tomato juice (12-ounce size)
1 can tomatoes (16-ounce size)
rice (cooked separately)

Cut the rabbit up and season with salt and cayenne pepper. Heat a cup of cooking oil in a Dutch oven. Brown rabbit pieces on medium-high heat. Pour off about half the oil, then reduce heat, cover, and simmer for 30 minutes.

In a pan, sauté onions, celery, garlic, and green pepper. Add 1 cup water, tomatoes, and tomato juice. Cook for 30 minutes. Add to rabbit in a Dutch oven. Add mushrooms, red pepper, onion tops, and parsley. Cover and simmer for 30 minutes. Eat with rice. *Serves 5 or 6.*

Rabbit Stuffed Peppers

  2 cups diced rabbit, cooked (leftovers
    will do)
  4 bell peppers, medium to large
  ¼ cup onion, finely chopped
  2 tablespoons mushrooms, finely
    chopped
  1 can Rotel(10-ounce) or Mexican-
    style stewed tomatoes
  1 tablespoon butter
  salt
  pepper
  1 tablespoon Worcestershire sauce
  1 cup cooked rice
  ½ cup Parmesan cheese, grated

Cut tops off green peppers, remove seeds, and simmer in slightly salted water for 10 minutes. Drain peppers while you prepare the stuffing. Preheat oven to 350 degrees.

Heat butter in a large frying pan. Cook onion and mushrooms until they are tender. Add rabbit, rice, salt, pepper, Rotel, and Worcestershire sauce. Mix well.

Spoon stuffing into peppers. Stand stuffed peppers upright in a baking dish. Bake for 30 minutes. *Serves 4.*

Note: The meat for this dish can be from a leftover rabbit, or you can boil a rabbit, or parts of rabbit, until it is tender. I normally let mine simmer for about about an hour on low heat. Bone and chop. Chilled meat is easier to chop, making a neater dice, if that matters.

Mock Hassenpfeffer

Here's a quick recipe from Mel Marshall's *Complete Book of Outdoor Cookery*, which explains: "You can always cook a rabbit by the standard hassenpfeffer recipe you'll find in any cookbook, but this one's quicker and easier."

  2 rabbits, cut up
  ½ cup flour
  1 teaspoon basil
  1 teaspoon salt
  ½ teaspoon freshly ground pepper
  ½ cup cooking oil
  ½ cup water
  2 tablespoons red wine vinegar
  1 tablespoon sugar
  1 teaspoon honey
  1 tablespoon chopped parsley
  1 cup sour cream or yoghurt

Swamper Tricks

Swamp rabbits are worthy of a few special comments, simply because they're much more difficult to bag than cottontails. The same techniques are used to hunt them, but keep in mind they're twice as big as cotton-tails, leading dogs on much longer chases. They're much less numerous, too. It takes a lot more work to bag them. When pursued, they'll often take to the water, float a safe distance downsteam, then exit the water and head for thick cover. In slow-moving water, they'll dive and hide nose-up under shoreline vegetation. Such strategies evade even the best dogs, and a disappearing swamper is by no means a strain on a beagle pack's reputation. Instead, it speaks for this rabbit's amazing adaptability.

—Keith Sutton, *Arkansas Game & Fish*

Rabbit à la King

If I had to choose a recipe for introducing wild game dishes to people of squeamish nature, this one might be it.

2 cups rabbit meat, cooked and diced
1½ cups cream
3 tablespoons butter
1½ tablespoons flour
1 small-to-medium onion, finely
   chopped
½ bell pepper, finely chopped
8 ounces mushrooms, finely chopped
juice of ½ large lemon
⅓ cup pimentos, chopped
2 egg yolks
⅓ teaspoon salt
1 bay leaf
salt and pepper to taste

Dress the rabbit, put it into a suitable pan, cover with water, add ⅓ teaspoon of salt and

"Combine flour, basil, salt, and pepper and rub well into the pieces of rabbit. Heat the oil and sauté the rabbit pieces until they brown lightly; don't overcook, or they'll toughen up. Over low heat, in a separate pan, combine water, vinegar, sugar, and honey and simmer—not boil—for 2 or 3 minutes. Pour this over the rabbit and cover the skillet; cook in a 325-degree oven 45 minutes or until the rabbit is tender. Stir in the sour cream and cook covered an additional 5 to 6 minutes to blend the flavors.

Sprinkle with chopped parsley. Serve good cold beer with hassenpfeffer in preference to even the finest wine. *Serves 6*."

a bay leaf, bring to boil then reduce heat and simmer for 1½ to 2 hours, or until the meat comes off bones easily. Bone rabbit and dice the meat.

Heat 1½ cups of cream in a double boiler. In a small container, blend the flour and 2 tablespoons of butter, then stir it into the heated cream. Melt the other 1 tablespoon of butter in a frying pan. Add peppers, mushrooms, and onion; simmer for a few minutes. Beat the egg yolks in a small container and stir in a little of the heated cream. Add the egg yolks to the heated cream, then stir it into the mixture in the frying pan. Stir in lemon juice, salt, and pepper. Then add the diced meat and pimento. Bring to heat but do not boil. Serve on crisp toast. Makes a teriffic lunch. *Serves 4 to 6.*

31

CLASSIC RECIPES for BIG GAME

One of the worst ways to introduce people to the joys of venison and other big game is to bake a whole roast too long. Venison is already much more lean than feed-lot beef, and baking it in an oven is likely to make it too dry. Moreover, this problem is complicated because far too many people tend to cook wild meat *longer* than they cook supermarket meat. (Still another problem, in my opinion, is that too many people follow the old practice of soaking venison in salt solutions—and salt will make the meat even less moist.)

One of the best ways to introduce people to wild game, or to convert skeptics, is to prepare a stew-type, or moist-heat, dish with which they are already familiar. Thus, they will be starting off with a familiar classic flavor, and, if you prepare the dish with tender-loving care, they will be more likely to come back for seconds. Here are some old favorites:

Big-Game Stroganoff

Traditionally, stroganoff is made with beef, but it's classic flavor goes well with the better cuts of deer, elk, moose, caribou, and similar wild game. The recipe given below can easily be cut in half or otherwise modified. If the full measures are used, the volume will be too much for a single frying pan of ordinary size. I use a medium frying pan together with a Dutch oven.

The following ingredients make enough stroganoff to feed 6 or 8 hungry adults.

2 pounds tenderloin or choice venison steak
1 cup chopped onion
2 cloves garlic, minced
8 ounces fresh mushrooms (or 6-ounce can), sliced
2 cans condensed beef broth (10½-ounce size)
⅛ cup tomato paste
¼ cup red wine
16 ounces sour cream
15 ounces medium egg noodles
salt
pepper
flour (all-purpose)
butter or margarine

The success of this stroganoff recipe depends, in part, on having thin strips of tender meat. The first step, therefore, is to get the meat ready to cook. Use tenderlion or other choice steak. Cut against the grain into slices about ¼ inch thick; then cut the slices into strips about ½ inch wide. (If the meat is difficult to slice, try freezing it slightly before cutting it. Or, cut the steaks thicker and then pound them flat with a wooden mallet.)

Melt about ⅛ cup of butter or margarine in a frying pan. Add onions, garlic, and mushrooms. Sauté for five minutes. Remove from frying pan and put into a Dutch oven or similar larger container, together with about half a can of the beef broth. Put on low heat.

Salt and pepper meat, then shake it in a bag with ⅛ cup of all-purpose flour. Add ⅛ cup margarine to the frying pan. Brown about half the meat, then transfer it to the Dutch oven. Put a little more margarine into the frying pan if needed, brown the rest of the meat, and add to Dutch oven.

In the frying pan, make a gravy by stirring ⅓ cup of flour into the pan drippings and beef broth. Go slowly and mix thoroughly, adding a little beef broth and flour as needed. Add tomato paste. Cook over medium heat until gravy bubbles and thickens. Add gravy to Dutch oven with meat and vegetables. Then stir in wine and sour cream. Reduce heat so that the sour cream will not curdle into an unappetizing mess. Do *not* allow to boil.

While the stroganoff sits on very low heat, bring a gallon of water to a rapid boil in a suitable pan. Add noodles slowly. Salt to taste and cook uncovered for 12 minutes, stirring occasionally. Drain in a collander. Top the noodles with a teaspoon of margarine or butter and stir.

Serve hot stroganoff over noodles. Have ready plenty of sourdough French bread and vegetables of your choice. I highly recommend frozen San Francisco style mixed vegetables with this dish.

Leftovers: Stroganoff freezes well and uneaten portions can, therefore, be kept for quite some time. Also, try any leftover gravy on French-cut green beans.

Variations: Stroganoff can also be served over rice or mashed potatoes instead of noodles.

There are hundreds of recipes for "stroganoff," many calling for such spices as nutmeg, basil, mustard, etc. I suppose that a pinch of this or a dash of that won't hurt anything, but remember that the main ingredients in this dish are: tender meat, mushrooms, gravy, and sour cream. I do, however, highly recommend using the tomato paste as set forth in the above recipe, not so much for the flavor, but for the hint of creamy pink color that it lends to the dish!

Note on meat used in stroganoff: The above recipe is based on tenderloin or other choice cuts of tender steak. Lesser cuts can also be used, but the meat should first be tenderized either by a marinade, by sprinkling with commercial tenderizer, by beating, or by cooking for a longer time. I recommend the following: Cut the meat as above—with emphasis on thin cuts—and brown it in the frying pan. Add a cup of water, cover the frying pan, and simmer the meat for an hour or so, or until it is tender. Then proceed with the recipe as indicated above.

Also, leftover meat from such dishes as venison roasts can be sliced up, or even cubed, for use in stroganoff recipes. It is, in fact, usually a good recipe for using up any leftover meat that tended to be on the dry side after the original cooking. Even ground meat, made into balls or patties, can be used. All in all, stroganoff is a good, versatile dish that every cook should know. In fact, any

hunter needing a new .30-06 for birthday or holiday should drop the hint while serving up venison stroganoff at a family dinner!

Game Hungarian Goulash

This is a very old dish, and of course there are many variations. It is also a good recipe to use on venision and other game. Here's my favorite:

2 pounds game meat, cut into 1-inch cubes
1 onion, chopped
3 ripe tomatoes, chopped
2 cloves garlic, minced
1 tablespoon parsley, chopped
1 can beef broth (10½-ounce size)
cooking oil
flour
salt
pepper
2 bay leaves
2 teaspoons caraway seeds
½ teaspoon paprika

Salt and pepper meat, then sprinkle with flour. Add 2 tablespoons oil to a frying pan, then sauté the onion and garlic. Transfer to a Dutch oven. Add more oil to frying pan and brown about half the meat. Add more oil if needed and brown the rest of the meat. Transfer all meat to the Dutch oven. Add beef broth and put on low heat. Add bay leaves. Stir in caraway seeds, paprika, parsley, and tomatoes. Cover and simmer for about 3 hours. About 30 minutes before serving, season to taste with salt and pepper.

Serve Hungarian goulash with egg noodles. *Serves 4 or 5.*

Sauerbraten

This old German dish is an ideal way to serve up a good-sized chunk of elk, deer, moose, and other red meat to guests who might be a bit squeamish about even a hint of gamey flavor.

The Marinade
   3 cups water
   2 cups red wine vinegar
   1 lemon, sliced
   2 medium or 1 large onion, sliced
   10 peppercorns, whole
   8 bay leaves
   12 cloves, whole
   1 tablespoon sugar
   1 tablespoon salt
   ¼ teaspoon ground ginger
The Meat
   4- or 5-pound roast from deer, elk, or
     other venison
   strained marinade from above
The Sauce
   1 cup of crumbled gingersnaps
   pan juices from meat
   ½ cup water

In a large crock or suitable glass container, mix water, wine vinegar, and all other ingredients listed above under marinade. Cover

and refrigerate for 24 to 48 hours. Turn meat every 8 hours or so.

When you're ready to cook the main dish, remove meat from the marinade and dry with a towel. (Strain marinade and save.) In a Dutch oven, heat oil and brown the meat. Add the strained marinade. Cover and simmer for 2 hours. Put the meat on a serving dish and save 2 cups of pan liquid.

To make gravy, put 2 cups of pan liquid into a saucepan, then add half a cup of water and 1 cup of crumbled gingersnaps. Simmer and stir until the gravy bubbles and thickens.

Slice sauerbraten and spoon the gravy over individual servings. *This dish will feed 8 or 10 people.*

Variations: Try an apple cider marinade. Substitute 3 cups of cider for the red wine vinegar in the above list. Also, use 2 tablespoons of brown sugar instead of 1 tablespoon regular sugar.

Leftovers: Sauerbraten doesn't freeze well, so plan to eat the roast within a few days. Refrigerated sauerbraten slices very well, and I highly recommend it with white-bread

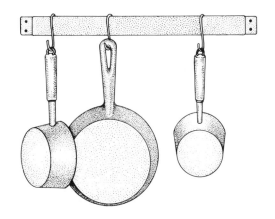

sandwiches. The trick is to slice it thinly, then use several slices per sandwich. My oldest son, Jarrod, likes three or four sauerbraten and lettuce sandwiches together with a couple of packs of potato chips and a jar or two of Kosher dill pickles. For lunch. Then he asks, "What's for supper?"

Venison New England Boiled Dinner

I've always been quite fond of corned beef, and I was excited to find the following recipe in *Game Cookery*, written by E.N. and Edith Sturdivant. As the book said, "There is no better meal than a good New England boiled dinner using corned venison, which in my opinion is far superior to corned beef. For the latter, most packing houses use the cheaper and tougher cuts, such as the brisket, thereby getting a much higher price for the otherwise undersirable parts. For corned venison we use only choice cuts, usually the ham or shoulder blade of the deer. From each ham, as you bone it, you will be able to get three good pieces of meat by separating the muscular segments. Cut these three segments from the bone, being sure to remove all the fat and also the glands between them. When we corn the blade we also cut the meat off the bone, using the same caution as for the hams.

"Use a glass or crockery jar with a capacity of at least two gallons; a three-gallon one is preferable. Use a box of Morton's Tender Quick, following the directions on the box.

Though we have tried other recipes, we find this one is the simplest and easiest. The meat must be kept completely submerged for at least two weeks, and the temperature should not exceed 38 degrees. Upon removing meat from the pickling jar, rinse it thoroughly in clear, cool water. Cook it according to the recipe that follows.

"You should be able to corn enough venison at a time for three or four meals. What you don't cook immediately can be placed in a plastic bag and frozen for future use. In cooking, it will take on a deep red color, and properly prepared it makes the best of eating."

Here is the Sturdivant recipe for Venison New England Boiled Dinner. Be sure to try it:

> 2 pounds corned venison
> 2 strips beef suet
> 2 bay leaves
> 1 teaspoon dried basil leaves
> 4 medium-sized or small onions, left
>   whole
> ½ teaspoon pepper
> 4 potatoes
> 4 carrots
> 1 medium-sized head cabbage

"Rinse the venison thoroughly to remove the salt left by the corning process. Slit the meat with a sharp knife, place the strips of beaf suet in the slits, and tie securely with butcher's twine. Cover with cold water, bring to a boil, and simmer for four or five minutes. Pour off the liquid and cover again with cold water. Add bay leaves, onions, pepper, and basil leaves. Cook over a low fire for six hours at a slow simmer, not a vigorous boil. *This is very important. Corned venison cooked too fast will be tough.*

"Now add the potatoes and carrots, and cook until they are almost done. During the last ten or twelve minutes of cooking, cut the cabbage into wedges and add to the pot. It shouldn't take more than ten or twelve minutes to cook the cabbage.

"Serve with hot corn bread muffins or corn bread sticks, or if you prefer, light bread or rolls. For dessert we suggest a good pan pudding."

Variations: A number of recipes for New England boiled dinner call for different vegetables. If you want to try a recipe a little different from the above, try substituting diced turnips for the carrots. Then add a few separately cooked and sliced beets for flavor as well as color.

Moussaka

This classic favorite of the Greeks and Turks is a wonderful dish to serve whenever you have lots of folks to feed on a minimum amount of meat. Use ground venison or other ground game.

The Meat
  1 pound ground meat
  3 medium eggplants
  1 cup chopped onion
  2 tablespoons parsley, chopped
  1 medium tomato, peeled and chopped
  1 can of tomato sauce (8-ounce size)
  2 eggs
  1 cup of bread crumbs
  ½ cup of sharp American cheese, grated

½ cup of Parmesan cheese, grated
pepper
cinnamon
cooking oil and margarine
¼ cup red wine
salt
Topping Sauce
  butter
  flour
  milk
  salt and pepper
  nutmeg
  1 egg

To start, peel eggplants and cut into ½-inch slices. Sprinkle slices generously with salt and set aside, well spaced, on absorbent paper. (This will require lots of space, so clean off a counter or table. Paper towel can be used, but several layers will be required to fully absorb all the moisture.) Let stand for an hour or so. While the salt is drawing the bitter juices from the eggplant, sauté chopped onions in a little margarine in a frying pan. Add ground beef and cook for a few minutes, until browned. (If you are using ordinary hamburger meat instead of real ground game, be sure to pour off the fat before proceeding.) Stir in tomato paste, chopped tomato, parsley, and wine. Salt and pepper to taste. Simmer on low heat until most of the liquid has been absorbed. Then remove from heat and let cool.

While meat is cooling, rinse eggplant slices

Venison

The term 'venison' comes from the Latin term *venatus* which means 'to hunt.' The latter probably is akin to the Sanskrit term *venati*, which means 'he desires, attacks, gains.' Originally, the word venison applied to the flesh of any beast or bird of the chase, but has now come to apply only to flesh of deer and deer kind.

—Frank G. Ashbrook, *Butchering, Processing and Preservation of Meat*

under cold water and pat dry. Pour a little oil in a frying pan or skillet. Brown eggplant, a few slices at a time, and drain. Again, draining will require space and lots of paper. Ordinary brown grocery bags are hard to beat for soaking up oil.

Preheat oven to 350 degrees.

Prepare the topping in a saucepan. Start by melting 3 tablespoons margarine or butter. Slowly stir in 3 tablespoons flour. Add salt, pepper, and a dash of nutmeg. Pour in milk and stir until the sauce thickens and bubbles. In a small bowl, whip one egg and stir in a ladleful of the sauce. Then add egg to the main sauce mixture and simmer over low heat for a couple of minutes. Remove from heat.

Back to the meat mixture, which should have cooled down by now. First, whip two eggs and stir into mixture. Also stir in half the bread crumbs, a dash of cinnamon, and American cheese.

Now we're ready to put everything together. Into a shallow baking dish (12-by-8-by-2-inches), sprinkle the remaining bread crumbs. Add a layer of eggplant, then crisscross another layer, using up about half the slices. Spoon on the meat mixture, spreading evenly. Add the rest of the eggplant in even layers. Pour milk sauce on top and spread. Sprinkle Parmesan cheese onto sauce. Place in preheated 350-degree oven for about 45 minutes, until a crust has formed atop the dish.

This recipe for moussaka, cooked in the measures given above, feeds from 6 to 8 adults. Serve it with lots of fresh green salad and a good bread.

Variations: Try moussaka cooked and served in small individual dishes. Also, try the dish topped with a layer of mashed potatoes or sautéed sliced potatoes. With sliced potatoes, retain the sauce detailed above. With either sliced or mashed potatoes, sprinkle with Parmesan before baking. And by all means try Kephalotyri cheese instead of Parmesan, if you happen to have some at hand.

Don't tell my son Bill, who is always on guard for "ucky" things, but if you've got some zucchini that needs to be used up, if can be sliced and used along with the eggplant. Also, try using thin eggplant slices with the peeling still on. The peeling adds an unusual flavor, and also provides color contrast for moussaka.

Venison Lasagne

There are a number of excellent lasagne recipes that work with ground venison. I would like to say that my favorite heretofore secret lasagne recipe came from Aunt Anna or somebody from the Old Country—but the truth is that I modified it from one that came in the instruction booklet for a small auxillary oven that I recently purchased. Good stuff. Try it:

1½ pounds ground venison
2 tablespoon margarine
1 medium onion, diced
1 clove garlic, pressed or minced
1 can whole tomatoes (16-ounce)
1 can tomato sauce (15-ounce)
2 tablespoons parsley flakes
1 teaspoon sugar
1 teaspoon dried basil leaves
½ teaspoon salt
9 uncooked lasagne noodles (½ pound)
2 cups cottage cheese
¼ cup grated Parmesan cheese
1 tablespoon parsley flakes
1 teaspoon salt
1½ teaspoons oregano
2 cups shredded mozzarella cheese
¼ cup grated Parmesan cheese

Add margarine to a skillet and sauté the onions and garlic. Then brown the meat. Add tomatoes and liquid from can, tomato sauce, 2 tablespoons parsley flakes, sugar, basil, and ½ teaspoon salt. Bring to boil, stirring constantly. Reduce heat and simmer for an hour.

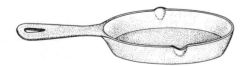

Preheat oven to 350 degrees.

In a suitable boiler, cook noodles according to the directions on package. Take ½ cup of meat sauce from frying pan and set aside. Mix cottage cheese, ¼ cup Parmesan cheese, 1 tablespoon parsley flakes, 1 teaspoon salt, and oregano.

In a 9-by-13-inch baking pan, make three layers in the following order: ⅓ of noodles, ⅓ of meat sauce, ⅓ of mozzarella cheese, and ⅓ of cottage cheese mixture. Repeat layers. Repeat again. Spoon on the ½ cup of meat sauce, then sprinkle with ¼ cup of Parmesan. Bake in preheated 350-degree oven for 45 minutes. Let cool for 15 minutes before serving.

Serve with hot Italian, French, or Greek bread and lots of good tossed salad. *Serves 4 or 5.*

Variations: Most any good red game meat can be used in this dish. Also, try it with ground turtle.

Venison Swiss

Here's a good recipe that can be used on most cuts of steak from deer, elk, or moose. Really tough meat, however, should be tenderized before cooking.

The Meat
2 pounds good venison steak
½ cup of flour
2 tablespoons cooking oil
1 teaspoon salt
½ teaspoon pepper
1 tablespoon mustard powder

The Trimmings
 1 cup diced carrots
 1 cup sliced onions
 1 can stewed tomatoes (14-ounce size)
 1 tablespoon brown sugar

Preheat oven to 325 degrees. Mix flour, mustard, salt, and pepper. Pound flour mixture into steak with a meat mallet, edge of plate, mouth of coke bottle, or whatever you use. Brown on both sides in hot cooking oil. Then place the steaks into a greased roasting pan or casserole dish of suitable size. (I prefer to have a container large enough to hold the steaks in a single layer.) Mix carrots, onions, tomatoes, and brown sugar. Pour over steak. Cover. Bake for 2 hours. *Serves 5 or 6.*

Venison Pepper Steak, Chinese Style

There are at least two types of "pepper steak." One is cooked by pounding freshly ground black pepper into the meat, then broiling it for a short time under high heat. The other kind is cooked with green peppers and other vegetables and Chinese stuff. The recipe below is a little different from most Chinese versions in that it contains no concentrate of monosodium glutamate. It should be served over rice.

 1½ pounds good venison steak, 1-inch
 thick

 meat tenderizer, if needed
 ⅓ cup peanut oil
 1 cup beef broth
 1 medium bell pepper, green
 1 medium bell pepper, red
 1 medium onion
 1 garlic clove, minced
 2 medium tomatoes
 ¼ teaspoon ground ginger
 1 tablespoon cornstarch
 2 tablespoons soy sauce
 ½ teaspoon salt
 ⅛ teaspoon pepper
 2 teaspoons sugar
 rice (to be cooked separately)

Sprinkle the steaks with meat tenderizer, if needed. Pound the steaks with a meat mallet or the edge of a plate, then refrigerate them for an hour. Cut the 1-inch steaks into strips about 2 inches long and ¼ inch wide. Prepare vegetables. Onions and peppers should be cut into strips, long ways. Each tomato should be cut into eight pieces, long ways.

Heat the peanut oil very hot in a large skillet. Add the venison. Stir constantly while it cooks for 5 or 6 minutes. Stir in the beef broth, onion, garlic, and ginger. Bring to boil, then reduce, cover, and simmer for 15 minutes. Add green and red pepper and simmer for another 5 minutes.

In a saucepan, blend cornstarch, sugar, salt, pepper, and soy sauce, then stir it into the meat mixture. Bring to boil. Cook and stir for a few minutes while mixture boils. Put tomatoes on top of meat mixture. Cover and cook on low for 4 minutes. *Serves 3 or 4.*

32

VENISON

One day I was talking to a hefty local farmer who operated a small pork sausage packing operation, and I knew that he was also a deer hunter of some local repute. Carefully, I worked into the culinary aspects of the hunt, and he told me that they hung their deer for 10 days in their sausage cooler. When I asked him how he cooked the deer, a puzzled look crossed his face. "We fry 'em," he said, almost as if it had never occurred to him that there might be another way. He cuts the better parts into ½-inch steaks, then he grinds the rest of the deer into "hamburger" or sausage meat. He wouldn't give me his family sausage secrets, but here's his fried venison recipe:

Fried Venison

venison steaks, ½ inch thick
meat tenderizer
peanut oil
flour
garlic salt
pepper
water
milk

Treat the steaks with meat tenderizer, then sprinkle with garlic salt and pepper. Pound with a meat mallet. Sprinkle flour over steaks, then pound again. Heat 1 inch of peanut oil in a frying pan, then fry steaks until browned. Remove the meat from the pan and pour off most of the grease. Put 2 tablespoons of flour into the pan drippings and stir. Slowly add 1 cup of water, stirring. Next, add 1 cup of milk, still stirring. Put the steaks into the gravy and simmer for 10 minutes. Have hot biscuits for the gravy.

5 til 9 Roast

Here's a good venison roast dish that can be put on at five o'clock in the morning (before you go hunting) and taken out at night (when you get back from hunting). You'll need a crockpot.

> 1 venison roast, 5 or 6 pounds
> 3 strips bacon
> salt
> pepper
> 1 package onion soup mix
> ¼ cup water
> vegetables (optional)

Before you leave the house in the morning, put the whole roast (it can be frozen) into your crockpot. Add ¼ cup of water. Sprinkle onion soup mix on top of roast. Drape bacon over roast. Put crockpot on low heat and leave all day. About dark, add onions, potatoes, carrots, or other vegetables of your choice. Turn up heat and cook until vegetables are done. You can also put the vegetables into the crockpot along with the roast and cook for 9 or 10 hours. *Serves 10 or more.*

Note: The vegetables used in this recipe can be frozen, canned, or fresh. Fresh or frozen vegetables will take a little time to cook, but canned vegetables will only have to be heated up.

Back Country Venison

I designed this recipe for remote camps, where a wide variety of ingredients would not be available. But my boys liked it so much that I decided to switch it to a crockpot dish for home use. Try it!

> 3 pounds venison stew meat
> 4 ounces dried apples
> salt
> pepper
> 1 tablespoon brown sugar
> 1 cup water

Dump everything into a crockpot and cook it on low heat for 8 or 9 hours. The dried apples will cook away, almost, leaving a thick gravy of very nice flavor that goes with venison. *Serves 6 or 7.*

Crockpot Flavors

Meat cooked on low heat for a long period of time, under cover, tends to absorb more flavor from herbs, vegetables, and spices. You might therefore consider cutting back on measures when cooking recipes that were not designed especially for crockpots.

Pan-Fried Venison Parmesan

This tasty dish should be cooked only with fairly tender steaks or chops. Loins or tenderloins work fine.

    2 pounds tender steak or chops
    1 cup cooking oil
    1 teaspoon garlic juice
    salt
    pepper
    1 egg
    ½ cup Parmesan cheese, grated
    ½ cup fine cracker crumbs

Mix cooking oil and garlic juice in a suitable container. Marinate steaks for several hours. Pour marinade liquid into a frying pan and heat. Salt and pepper steaks to taste. Whip an egg lightly. Mix cracker crumbs and cheese. Dip steaks in egg, roll in crumbs, and fry on medium-high heat until batter is golden brown. Eat while hot. *Serves 4 or 5.*

Barbecued Tough-Buck Ribs

Here's a recipe that makes tough ribs tender, moist, and tasty. If you are in doubt about

---

Beef Suet

Beef suet is often added to ground game meat to make it more like ordinary hamburger, and it is put into venison roasts (and other cuts of meat) by "larding and barding." Essentially, the suet adds fat to lean meat. Special larding needles are sometimes used for this purpose, or, more often, the meat is slit with a knife and the suet is poked in. Also, the suet is sometimes placed atop the meat, and the fat can be pumped into the meat with a special syringe.

In any case, beef suet is no longer used in everyday cookery, and is therefore not widely available in supermarkets these days. In fact, a clerk at my local supermarket didn't even know what the term meant. A good butcher, or specialized meat market, can, of course,

provide beef suet. Loosely, it is merely beef fat. More specifically, it is the firm, white fat found in the kidney and loin sections of beef. In a pinch, a "strip of beef suet" can be obtained by trimming such cuts of beef as round steak. Purists may not agree, but in my opinion it is permissible to substitute a strip of bacon. Calorie counters and modern fat-conscious cooks may want to omit the suet entirely.

My wife says that a Greek family living in California taught her that garlic cloves stuck into slits in lean meat will keep it from being so dry after cooking. I don't know what the garlic does—but I no longer argue with the results, for she serves up a succulent roast every time.

the quality of the ribs you are about to cook, then try this recipe. The measures can be changed. I figure about a pound of ribs for each person. If you've got lots of ribs, however, you might consider boning them after boiling. Your guests will eat more and keep cleaner hands. But if you're running short of meat, reduce the boiling time recommended below, leave the meat on the bones, and make 'em gnaw. This sauce is very thick and somewhat sticky so . . . put a bowl of water and a roll of paper towel within easy reach.

The Meat
   4 pounds ribs
   water
   salt
   2 bay leaves
The Sauce
   2 tablespoons butter or margarine
   1 medium onion, chopped fine
   1 stalk celery, chopped fine
   2 cups water (but see instructions below)
   2 cups catsup
   juice of 1 lemon
   ½ cup vinegar
   ¼ cup Worcestershire sauce
   2 tablespoons brown sugar
   2 tablespoons blackstrap molasses
   1 teaspoon chili powder
   1 teaspoon pepper

Put the ribs into a pot and cover with water. Bring to boil, add 2 bay leaves, and reduce heat. Simmer for about 2 hours.

While simmering the ribs, prepare the sauce. Put butter into a large frying pan and sauté the onions and celery. Add water, catsup, lemon juice, vinegar, Worcestershire sauce, brown sugar, molasses, chili powder, and pepper. Stir. Simmer the sauce while the ribs are parboiling.

Preheat oven to 250 degrees. Remove ribs from water and drain. Salt each rib to taste, then arrange in a well-greased baking pan. Pour the sauce over the ribs and place the pan into oven. Bake for 2 hours. Either baste or turn two or three times. *Serves 4 to 6.*

Note: The sauce on this dish is dark and thick, and I like to broil it for a few minutes before serving, thereby making it darker and thicker. If you want a thick sauce, then be sure to simmer the sauce for a long time, as specified above, or, if you're in a hurry, reduce the water from 2 cups to 1 cup. If you want a thinner sauce, add more water or reduce the cooking time.

Venison Shank á la Montana

Here's a helpful recipe from E. N. and Edith Sturdivant's *Game Cookery:* "Most hunters cut the meat off the shank and either grind it or use it as stew meat. But contrary to what many of them suppose, the meat is tender and has a rich, nutty flavor. Here is a different method of cooking the shank, which we like very much. We use the shank of the deer or antelope for this dish, serving one shank per person.

   4 deer or antelope shanks
   2 tablespoons bacon fat or cooking oil
   1 large onion

1 small can tomato sauce
½ cup cooking sherry
¼ teaspoon crushed rosemary leaves
¼ teaspoon thyme
¼ cup brown sugar
salt
pepper
flour

"Flour, salt, and pepper the shanks, and place with bacon fat or cooking oil in deep skillet or Dutch oven and brown lightly over medium heat. Meanwhile, place in another utensil the chopped onion, tomato sauce, water, cooking sherry, rosemary, thyme, and brown sugar. After the meat has cooked for about 10 minutes, pour the sauce over it, cover and simmer for 1½ or 2 hours, depending upon the size of the shank.

"If necessary, add a little water so that the sauce completely covers the meat at the beginning of the cooking process; but do not add any water while it is cooking.

"Serve with fluffy rice or mashed potatoes, spinach, and spiced figs. Follow with a light dessert.

"This recipe should serve four hungry people."

Easy Swiss Venison Steak

2 pounds venison steak
4 tablespoons cooking oil
flour
salt
pepper
garlic powder

3 medium onions, sliced
1 can tomato soup (10¾-ounce)
1 soup can of water

Cut the steaks into serving-size pieces. Season with salt and pepper, then sprinkle lightly with garlic powder. Dredge in flour. Pound with edge of plate or meat mallet.

In a large frying pan or stove-top Dutch oven, sauté the sliced onions in 2 tablespoons of cooking oil. Remove onions and set aside. Brown part of the steak and set aside. Add another 2 tablespoons cooking oil and brown the rest of the steak. Arrange the steak and onions in a Dutch oven, then add soup and water. (Mix soup and water in a bowl before adding to meat.) Bring to boil, then reduce heat, cover, and simmer for 3 hours. Turn once or twice so that bottom steak will be rotated to prevent scorching. *Serves 4 or 5.*

This dish makes lots of good gravy and my

boys like it poured over homemade biscuits. For breakfast.

Alaskan Barbecued Venison

Here is a very good dish—one of my personal favorites—that apparently originated in Alaska.

>   2 pounds venison, boneless
>   ½ pound bacon
>   1 cup chopped onions
>   2 cloves of garlic, minced
>   1 cup catsup
>   ½ cup of red wine vinegar
>   ¼ cup of Worcestershire sauce
>   ¼ cup of brown sugar
>   salt
>   pepper
>   milk (for marinade, if needed)
>   rice (cooked separately)

The better, or more tender, cuts of venison can be used without any sort of tenderization. But tougher cuts should be marinated. I prefer ordinary milk. Simply cover venison with milk and refrigerate for 8 hours or longer.

Cut venison into 1-inch cubes. In the bottom of a dutch oven (or large frying pan) cook bacon until it is crisp. Remove bacon, crumble, and set aside. In a bowl or other container, mix all ingredients except venison. (Salt and pepper to taste, or try 1 tablespoon of salt and ⅛ teaspoon of pepper.) Drain

venison and brown it in bacon drippings. Pour off drippings and liquid. Add the other ingredients. Stir well. Cover tightly and simmer for about an hour, or until the meat is tender. Stir occasionally. Eat the barbecued venison on rice. *Serves 7 or 8.*

Venison Steak Rolls

Here's one that was sent to me by Tammy Ryan of the Montana Fish, Wildlife, and Parks Department.

>   2 pounds venison steak, pounded, cut
>   into serving sizes
>   4 slices bacon
>   ½ cup finely chopped onion
>   ¼ cup finely chopped celery
>   2 cups bread crumbs
>   1 egg, well-beaten
>   1 teaspoon sage
>   salt and pepper
>   slices Swiss cheese (or your choice)
>   ½ cup butter
>   ½ cup cracker crumbs

"Fry bacon until crisp, remove from skillet and crumble. Add onion and celery and sauté. Add the bacon, bread crumbs, egg, sage, salt, and pepper. Spoon about 2 tablespoons of the mixture on each piece of venison (this amount will depend on the size of the venison pieces). Top with cheese and roll up. Secure with toothpicks. Roll each roll in cracker crumbs and fry in butter. Turn often. For tough venison, use a lid and very low heat, then remove lid for crustiness."

Venison Steak, Ranch Style

I've always enjoyed recipes written by people of firm opinion. Here's one from Mrs. Wm. C. Lindmier, Sr., as published in *Cooking in Wyoming*. She said, "We have used the venison steak recipe for years, feeding hunters from Louisiana, Wisconsin, Minnesota, Iowa, and Michigan, and they really go for it cooked this way.

"When you have your venison processed, insist that the butcher cut your steaks and chops at least 1-inch thick, and 1½-inch is even better, since venison is a naturally dry meat, and this will allow the natural juices to remain in the meat, rather than be cooked out.

"If your animal is young, marinate the steaks or chops ½ hour to 1 hour in plain cold water. If the animal is older, or of an indeterminate age, then it is best to marinate for at least 1½ hours. Be sure all hairs are removed.

"For 4 servings, you will need 2 venison rounds, enough seasoned flour (flour with salt and pepper added) to dredge the steaks, and about ½ cup bacon drippings or shortening.

"Remove the steaks from the water, remove all fat, fell the thin, bluish outer layer of tissue around the edges of the rounds, and the bones, and the fat around the bones. Pound each serving, and dredge in the prepared flour.

"Meanwhile, heat fat in a heavy skillet. I use cast aluminum, but cast iron or an electric skillet will do as well. Have the fat smoking hot. Place pieces in hot fat. Allow to brown well on one side, turn, and brown on the other. Do not crowd the meat in the skillet. It may be necessary to reduce the heat once the meat has browned on one side, to prevent burning. It must be watched carefully during the cooking time. It may also be necessary to turn it once more if the animal is very old, or thin, but for an animal in good condition, once is enough. It will be very slightly rare. This preserves the juices and the flavor. Remember, overcooking can ruin otherwise excellent venison."

Hot Crockpot Stew

Because of the rotel, which is a canned mixture of tomatoes and hot chili peppers, this delicious dish has a hint of old Mexico in its flavor. If you don't like hot stuff, reduce the rotel or use regular canned tomatoes.

> 2½ pounds venison, cubed
> ½ cup flour
> 2 cans rotel (10-ounce) or Mexican-
> 　　style stewed tomatoes
> 1 large onion, sliced
> 2 bell peppers, sliced
> 1 tablespoon Worcestershire sauce
> 1 teaspoon Tabasco sauce
> 1 teaspoon salt
> ¼ teaspoon black pepper

Mix flour, salt, and pepper in a paper bag. Shake meat in flour and dump into a crock pot. Also dump all flour from the bag. Add rotel, onion, peppers, Tabasco sauce, and Worcestershire sauce. Cover crockpot and cook on low for 8 or 9 hours. *Serves 5 or 6.*

This dish makes a gravy that is just right for eating with lots of white-meal corn bread. Don't sop it. The procedure is break up the corn bread on a plate and spoon gravy on it. Then mash it all up with a fork.

Crockpot Pepper Steak

2 pounds steak from deer or elk
1 can tomatoes (16-ounce size)
1 large onion, sliced
2 medium green peppers, sliced
6 ounces mushrooms, sliced
3 tablespoons soy sauce
2 tablespoons blackstrap molasses
½ cup flour
1 teaspoon salt
¼ teaspoon black pepper

Cut steaks into strips. Mix flour, salt, and pepper in a bag and shake the steak fingers. Put steaks into the crockpot and dump the remaining flour mixture on top. Add all other ingredients. Cover and turn crockpot to high for one hour. Reduce heat to low and cook for 9 or 10 hours. *Serves 4 to 6.*

Butterflied Tenderloin Barbecue

venison or big game tenderloin
salt
pepper
butter
barbecue sauce

Slice tenderloin across the grain into 2-inch pieces. Then slice each piece almost through. Fold out into a butterfly. Salt and pepper to taste. Melt butter and make a basting sauce with ½ butter and ½ barbecue sauce. Arrange rack in pre-heated broiler so that meat is 3 inches from heat source. Put meat on rack and baste heavily with sauce. Broil for 5 minutes on each side, basting twice.

Whitetail Deer Success

In 1900, there were only about 350,000 whitetail deer in the entire United States. Thanks to modern game management programs, today we have over 14,000,000 whitetails!

Tough Buck Roast

1 roast, 4 or 5 pounds
1 can mushroom soup (10¾-ounce size)
1 package onion soup mix
1 can mushrooms (6- or 8-ounce size)
salt
pepper

Salt and pepper roast, then put it into a crockpot. Mix mushroom soup, onion soup mix, and mushrooms. Pour mixture over roast. Set the crockpot on low heat and cook for 8 or 9 hours. *Serves 8 to 10*.

If you don't have a crockpot, wrap the roast and other ingredients tightly in wide, heavy duty aluminum foil. Put into a slow oven (250 degrees) for 4 or 5 hours.

Easy Venison Steak

steak
salt
pepper
onion
Worcestershire sauce

Advice on Venison from South Dakota

Tender cuts (loins and ribs) can be broiled or roasted. Round steaks, the meat from the leg, and less tender cuts should be cooked with moist heat (stewed, pot roast, or braised). To tenderize the meat, let it stand in an acid marinade—vinegar, tomato paste, French dressing—for 24 hours. Also remember that venison is sweeter than beef, so cut down on the sugar used in beef recipes.

—*Cooking the Sportsman's Harvest*

Preheat oven to 300 degrees. If meat is not quite tender, pound it with meat mallet or the edge of a heavy plate. Treating each piece separately, center the steak on a piece of aluminum foil of suitable size. Salt and pepper to taste. Add 2 or 3 thin slices of onion and a dash or two of Worcestershire sauce. Wrap tightly and bake for 4 hours.

Venison Crust Pie

The idea for this recipe came from the South Dakota Department of Game, Fish, and Park's book *Cooking the Sportsman's Harvest*.

The Crust
  1 pound ground venison
  ¼ cup onion, finely chopped
  ¼ cup green pepper, finely chopped
  ½ cup dry bread crumbs
  ½ cup tomato sauce
  1½ teaspoon salt
  ⅛ teaspoon pepper
  ⅛ teaspoon oregano
The Filling
  ½ cup uncooked rice
  ½ cup water
  ½ cup tomato sauce
  ½ teaspoon salt
  ¼ cup grated sharp cheddar cheese
Late Addition
  ¾ cup grated sharp cheddar cheese

Turn oven to 350 degrees. Grease a deep 9-inch pie pan. (A deep pan is required.) Thoroughly mix all ingredients listed above under "crust." Pat the mixture into the bottom of pie pan, then pinch 1-inch flutings around the edge. Put in a 350-degree oven for 15 minutes.

While the crust is cooking, mix water, tomato sauce, salt, rice, and ¼ cup cheddar. Remove crust from oven and spoon in rice mixture. Cover with aluminum foil. Bake at 350 degrees for 25 minutes. At the end of 25-minute period, the filling should have the texture of soupy pudding. Top filling with ¾ cup of grated cheddar, then bake, uncovered, for another 15 minutes at 350 degrees. *Makes 6 servings.*

Note: This dish may be a little tricky. I had to cook it twice, adjusting measures and temperatures, to make it work with my equipment. So, you may want to cook it once for practice, then make adjustments, if necessary, before depending on it to feed guests.

Venison Fondue

A good friend of mine once said hell no he didn't jog. He ran. He also said that when he ate, he ate instead of messing round with fondue. I tend to agree with him on both counts, but, of course, fondue can be fun. And venison fondue can be different. Something to talk about. So, try it if you've got a fondue pot, a tenderlion of venison, and good company.

   strips or chunks of tenderloin of
     venison
   hot oil
   salt
   pepper

Worcestershire sauce
lemon

Cut the venison into thin strips or small chunks. (I prefer strips.) Prepare a sauce in the proportions of 1 tablespoon Worcestershire sauce to the juice of ½ lemon. Warm the sauce. Heat oil. Salt and pepper venison to taste. Each guest sticks a strip or chunk of venison with a fork, cooks it in the hot oil, dips it into the sauce, and eats it directly.

Note: Any good meat sauce can be used instead of the Worcestershire and lemon juice.

Alaskan Jerky

Here's a good jerky recipe that I got from an article by Karen Cantillion in *Alaska Fish & Game*:

   stripped venison (cut with the grain
     for chewy texture, across the grain
     for crisp texture)
   ½ cup Worcestershire sauce
   1 tablespoon liquid smoke
   1 tablespoon onion powder
   red pepper flakes to taste (at least 1
     tablespoon)
   ½ cup soy sauce
   1 tablespoon black pepper
   1 tablespoon garlic powder
   Tabasco sauce to taste

Put the meat in a glass or crockery container. Mix all other ingredients and pour it over the meat. Marinate for 8 to 12 hours. Drain the meat and put it on a rack in a shallow baking dish. Turn oven to 150 degrees and bake meat for 12 hours, or until dried. Store the jerky in a tightly covered container.

Big-Game Soup

I have always appreciated the word 'soup-bone'—especially in relation to venison and other big-game. First, the idea of making a soup with the bone and some trimmings permits me to be a little careless when boning out a shoulder or other piece of meat. Second, big-game bone, with a little meat on it, can be the makings of a truly wonderful soup. Here's what I recommend, provided that some meat is left on the bones:

venison bones from a hindquarter or
   two shoulders
2 cans of stewed tomatoes (14½-ounce
   size)
16 ounces of fresh frozen mixed
   vegetables
salt and pepper to taste

Boil the bones in pot of suitable size for 2 hours. Add tomatoes, vegetables, salt, and pepper. Cover and simmer for another hour. *Note:* If you use a very large pot to hold the bones, don't put too much water in it. Leave part of the bones sticking out, but cover the pot tightly and steam the bones. Reverse them from time to time. If you put too much water into the pot, the soup will be too thin. It might be best to saw the bones in half and use a smaller pot.

Venison Pot Roast

3- to 5-pound venison roast
oil
flour
salt
pepper
water
6 carrots, cut into chunks
8 onions (golf ball size)
4 medium potatoes cut in quarters
1 bell pepper, cut into ½-inch strips
½ teaspoon garlic powder
¼ teaspoon thyme

If roast is fairly tender and well aged, proceed with the recipe. But if the meat is tough, or in doubt, it may best to marinate the roast for 24 hours or so.

Season the roast with salt and pepper, then dredge it in flour. Heat a little oil in a Dutch oven and brown roast on all sides. Add a cup of water. Sprinkle roast with garlic powder and thyme. Cover tightly and cook on low heat for 3 hours, or until meat is tender. Turn the roast from time to time.

Add onions, potatoes, bell pepper, and carrots. Season to taste with salt and pepper. Cover and cook for 20 minutes. *Serves from 6 to 10.*

33

FANCY OR UNUSUAL VENISON RECIPES

I've always been fond of trying new dishes, new tastes, or new ways of cooking an old dish. Such recipes are not necessarily long, complicated, or difficult. Here are some of my favorites:

Seminole Venison Stew

I seldom marinate meat in salted water, but I confess that the following dish is good. Also, my wife says that she once knew an Armenian woman from southern Russia, a kabob specialist, who quite successfully used pretty much the same marinade on lamb.

In any case, it's not often that you find a recipe calling for green tomatoes, which happen to be one of my favorite vegetables, in season. Moreover, I am including this recipe, in spite of the slightly salty marinade, because it is, I am certain, cooked with unpeeled potatoes.

Permit me to explain. While serving a hitch in the Navy, I peeled no less than 67,000 pounds of potatoes during a 3-month period. I don't peel them anymore.

And I welcome the following recipe on the grounds that no self-respecting Seminole would waste time peeling spuds. Anyhow, here's what you need:

3 to 4 pounds venison
5 cups of water
2 tablespoons salt
6 peppercorns
1 onion, sliced
¼ cup cooking oil
½ cup water
4 ribs of celery, chopped
3 green tomatoes, chopped
3 medium onions, chopped
4 large potatoes, sliced (no doubt unpeeled)
salt
pepper

Mix marinade with 5 cups water, 2 tablespoons salt, 6 peppercorns, and sliced onion. Cut the venison into 2-inch chunks, put it into a glass or crockery container, cover with marinade, and refrigerate overnight (or at least 10 hours).

In a large pot or Dutch oven, heat ¼ cup of

oil and ½ cup of water. Add meat and vegetables. Salt and pepper to taste. Bring to boil, reduce heat, cover, and simmer for 2 or 3 hours, adding more water if needed. Add vegetables, salt and pepper to taste, cover, and cook until vegetables and meat are tender. *Serves 6 to 8.*

Note: The above recipe is based on a book called *Seminole Indian Recipes.*

Rock Salt Venison Roast

I first ran across this recipe in a book called *Dress'em Out* by Captain James A. Smith, and I found it to be very good. Here's my version, which I cooked with a loin roast.

The Meat
small venison roast (2 or 3 pounds)
3 strips of thin-sliced bacon, cut into pieces
black pepper
garlic clove (optional)
rock salt (you'll need from 3 to 6 pounds)
Late Additions
apple slices
parsley
marinated pears
good brandy

Preheat oven to 500 degrees so that it will be very hot. With a fillet knife, make three slits into the roast. Poke the garlic clove into the middle slit, then pack pieces of bacon on either end of the clove. Pack bacon into the other two slits, using up all of the pieces.

Sprinkle the roast with pepper. Spread about an inch of rock salt in the bottom of a roasting pan and put the roast on top. Pile rock salt around the roast, building it up. Use a little hot water here and there to help hold the salt. Completely cover the roast in this manner, then put the roasting pan into the oven.

Reduce the temperature to 450 degrees. Bake for 14 minutes *per pound* of roast. Sample the brandy, just to make sure it is good enough, while you worry about your roast being under a mound of rock salt. Remove the roasting pan at the end of the calculated time. You'll have a hard mound of rock salt, which will have to be cracked with a hammer and chisel. Once cracked, the pieces of crust should lift off the meat easily. Lift the roast out of the pan, brush off excess salt, and put the meat into a serving platter. With toothpicks, stick slices of apple, pears, and parsley onto sides of the roast.

Heat about ¼ cup of brandy in a pan, then, at the table, under dim light, pour it over the roast and ignite it. Slice the meat. *Serves 4 to 6.*

West African Stew

If I were attempting to write a complete history of American game cookery, I suppose I would start with Central Europe, take a quick look at the native Indians from the Aztecs to the Eskimos, and finally bog down somewhere in the continent of Africa. Indeed, I have dipped into some African cookbooks, but they were, for the most part, written for American kitchens. After all, how many kitchens in Duluth, Minnesota, or even Pascagoula, Mississippi, have fresh tenderloin of wildebeest?

Since my name is Livingston, I suppose I could claim roots to the great explorer, Dr. David Livingstone, who recorded the recipe below somewhere in the big bend of the Niger, between Timbuktu and Gao. In truth, I got the recipe from a booklet about cooking with peanuts, to which it was submitted by one Myron Boutwell, of Slocomb, Alabama. The peanut connection is for real, since many of the recipes from Western Africa do indeed call for "groundnuts." Many of the local people in our peanut belt call them "ground peas." Anyhow, . . . here's my venison version of Myron Boutwell's West African South Alabama beef stew:

> 1 pound of venison, cubed
> ¼ cup peanut oil
> ¼ cup peanut butter
> water
> 1 medium onion, sliced with the grain
> 1 large ripe tomato, diced
> salt to taste
> ½ teaspoon red pepper flakes
> 1 tablespoon cornstarch

In a large frying pan, heat peanut oil and quickly brown cubed venison. Add 1 cup of water, cover, and simmer for an hour or two—until meat is tender. Add another cup of water, bring to heat, and stir in peanut butter. Add tomato, onion, salt, and pepper. Bring to quick boil. Reduce heat and simmer, stirring, for 15 minutes. Mix 1 tablespoon cornstarch and 2 tablespoons of water. Add to stew and stir. Bring to quick boil, stir until creamy, then remove from heat. Serve hot.

Serves 2 or 3—maybe 4 if there is plenty of good bread for the gravy. In fact, all connoisseurs of gravy must try this dish. It's hot but smooth. In taste, texture, and color, it is like no other. My wife likes it, she says, because it doesn't seem as greasy as other gravies.

This recipe is a little on the hot side, and anyone who likes bland food might be tempted to leave out the red pepper flakes and maybe substitute a little fine-ground black pepper. Don't do it. The red pepper flakes add to the dish visually.

Venison Coffee Roast

One of my favorite ways to cook venison roasts grew directly from the "Java Roast Beef" recipe set forth in *Southern Family Recipes* by Geddings de M. Cushman and Ora Lou O'Hara Cushman. If you are fond of coffee, as I am, be sure to try this unusual recipe. Its flavor is an experience that should not be missed; and for hours, during cooking, it gives off a tempting aroma.

> **4- to 5-pound roast**
> **1 onion**
> **2 cloves garlic**
> **1 cup apple cider vinegar**
> **2 cups black coffee**
> **¼ cup cooking oil or bacon drippings**
> **water**
> **salt and pepper**

With a long, thin knife cut slits through roast. Cut onion and garlic in slivers and insert into slits. Put roast into a suitable bowl and pour vinegar over it. Refrigerate for 24 hours. Discard vinegar.

Put oil into a Dutch oven and place on high heat. Sear the roast on all sides, heating almost to the burning point. Pour water and coffee over meat, and cover tightly. Simmer on very low heat for 6 to 8 hours, turning several times. About half an hour before eating time, season the roast with salt and pepper. (The roast can also be seared in a frying pan, then transferred to a crockpot for long cooking.)

Slice roast and serve with rice. Spoon gravy over slices of meat and rice. *Serves 8.*

I use very strong coffee with this dish (actually, my brew is made with part coffee and part chicory). It makes lots of very good, black gravy. The gravy can also be thickened with flour and served over biscuits.

Tip: Freeze leftover coffee and save it for cooking this dish.

Golden Venison Steaks

Seasoning steaks with marigold (yes, the flower) dates back to medieval times and probably further. Like saffron, marigold imparts a golden yellow color to venison and other foods. The following recipe is from *The Forgotten Art of Flower Cookery*.

¼ pound butter
1½ to 2 pounds venison steak
½ cup flour
¾ cup red wine
1 cup tomato paste
1 cup chopped onion
½ cup chopped carrot
½ cup chopped celery
2½ tablespoons Worcestershire sauce
salt and pepper to taste
1 cup chopped marigold petals
 [see instructions below]

As the book directed, "Melt butter in skillet; brown meat and reserve. Stir flour into remaining butter until roux is formed. Stir in wine, tomato paste, onion, carrot, celery, Worcestershire, salt, and pepper. Blend well over heat and return venison to sauce. Cook in oven at 325 degrees F. until fork tender (approximately 90 minutes).

"Then stir in marigolds. Turn off oven and let stand in oven another 5 minutes before serving. . . .

"*To prepare marigolds*: Pull entire petals from the stem, and as you hold them firm in your hand, with scissors cut off the white (or pale greenish) 'heels,' as this could give a bitter taste if not removed. Wash petals thoroughly but gently and drain well."

Boiled Venison with Caper Sauce

The recipe below was sent to me from the University of Florida. I sneaked in some red pepper flakes and worked out the following measures:

The Meat
 3- to 4-pound shoulder of venison
 3 bay leaves
 1 medium onion, diced
 ¼ cup parsley flakes
 ½ cup of celery tops
 juice of ½ lemon
 2 teaspoons salt
 1 teaspoon red pepper flakes
The Sauce
 stock from venison (above)
 flour
 1 teaspoon lemon juice
 1 tablespoon orange juice
 3 tablespoons capers
 1 cup milk

Place the venison shoulder, whole, into a suitable cooking container and cover with water. Add bay leaves, diced onion, parsley, celery, lemon juice, salt, and pepper. Bring to boil, reduce heat, and simmer for 3 hours.

To make a sauce, dip out 2 cups of the venison stock and heat it in a saucepan. Mix 3 tablespoons of flour with 1 cup of cold milk.

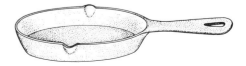

Stir into the hot stock and simmer until it thickens. Add lemon juice, orange juice, and capers. Simmer for a few minutes.

Slice the venison thinly and serve it with the caper sauce. *Serves 6 to 8.*

Kiwi Pepper Tenderloin

Some time ago, the kiwi gained some culinary kudos. I like the fruit very much and I eat one occasionally. I also cook with it from time to time, and here's one of my creations:

tenderloin of venison
kiwi fruit
salt
peppercorns (and a pepper mill)

Peel the kiwi fruit and slice it crossways. Also cut the tenderloin into slices about ¾ inch thick. Pull off a piece of plastic film and lay it flat on a countertop. Make a loaf on the plastic film by alternating slices of kiwi and tenderloin. Wrap the plastic around the loaf and put it into the refrigerator for several hours.

Preheat a broiler and adjust a rack so that it is very close to the heat source. (I prefer that the top of the tenderloin be within 2 inches of the heat, although I admit that this is a little extreme.) Unwrap the loaf and retain the kiwi slices, handling them carefully. Salt the tenderloin, then grind fresh pepper on each slice. Mash the pepper into the meat with your finger or thumb. Turn it over and pepper the other side. Put the meat under the preheated broiler and cook for 5 minutes on

one side. Turn and cook for 5 minutes on the other side. Add the kiwi back atop the tenderloin slices and broil for another 2 minutes. Serve hot.

Galantine of Venison and Pork

This recipe is based on a very old Scottish dish. It takes a little doing, but I can highly recommend it. To do it right, you'll need some venison bones, so save a few the next time you bag a buck. (Freeze some bones for this recipe. Or, if you've already got a venison roast in the freezer, but don't have any bones to go with it, then get a few beef bones from your butcher.)

3 pound venison roast, boned
venison bones
1 pound of pork sausage
½ pound ham
3 hard-boiled eggs, halved the long way
3 cloves of garlic, minced
¼ teaspoon thyme
¼ teaspoon marjoram
6 peppercorns
salt and pepper
8 cups of water

Bone the venison roast. Crack the venison bones (or frozen bones) and boil them in 8 cups of water to which you have added the peppercorns, thyme, and marjoram. Let simmer.

Cube the ham and mix it with the sausage and minced garlic. Place the boned roast on a flat surface and open it up. Season it well with salt and pepper. Spread on about half of the ham and sausage mixture. Cover this with the halves of boiled eggs. Then cover the eggs with the rest of the ham and sausage mixture. Roll up the roast and carefully wrap it in a floured cloth. Tie both ends.

Remove the bones from the pot and put the roast into the liquid. Cover and simmer for 4 hours. Let it remain in the stock while cooling. When cool, remove the roast, take the cloth, and place it into a dish which it fits closely. Cover with foil wrap and put a weight on top of it. Chill overnight. Slice before eating. *Serves 6 to 8.*

Big Horn Venison Birds with Wild Rice

For this recipe, we are indebted to Mrs. Robert E. Helvey, of Big Horn. It was published in the book *Wyoming Cooking*.

> **3 venison round steaks, sliced thin**
> **1 cup uncooked wild rice**
> **water and salt for rice**
> **1 small can mushrooms**
> **1 medium onion**
> **3 tablespoons butter**
> **1 bay leaf**
> **1 carrot**
> **3 tablespoons currant jelly**
> **½ pint commercial sour cream**
> **flour**
> **garlic**
> **salt and pepper**

As the book instructed, "Bring wild rice to a boil in 2¼ cups boiling water and 1 teaspoon salt. Let simmer 1 hour. Meanwhile, trim all fat from venison steaks, rub both sides with garlic and sprinkle with salt, pepper, and flour. Pound until very thin with the edge of a plate and repeat process on the other side. Cut steaks in quarters. Chop onion and drain mushrooms. When rice is done, place a heaping tablespoon on each quarter of steak and fold in half. Secure end with toothpicks or skewers. Brown onions and mushrooms in Dutch oven in 3 tablespoons butter. Remove from pan and brown venison birds well on both sides, adding more butter if necessary. Now add the bay leaf, sliced carrots, the onions, and the mushrooms. Cover and cook slowly over a low heat for 30-40 minutes.

"Remove the birds to a hot platter and make a sauce of the pan drippings by melting the currant jelly, stirring constantly and adding sour cream and salt and pepper to taste, and a little stock if necessary. When the sauce is smooth and bubbling, spoon it over the venison, which has been placed in a nest of the remaining hot wild rice (there will be enough rice left over for 4 servings). Serve immediately while hot."

Backstrap Wellington

Over a period of years, I have eyed a number of Wellington recipes, but they all seemed too complicated for me. Essentially, the Wellington recipe is for a loin or tenderloin, which, together with a liver paté, is encased in a pastry and baked. All this takes some doing, but what really bothered me was the cooking time. The recipes say to cook the dish until the crust is brown, and that the meat should be pink and not overdone. Well, what if you can't get it both ways? It seems to me that it's a matter of proportion and exact timing at the right temperature. Regardless of my fears, I hauled off and cooked the dish. I hit the jackpot on the first try, and I can highly recommend that any hunter take the gamble.

Actually, the recipe that I followed came from an article in *Sports Afield* (October 1967) by Jack Denton Scott, who said, "How should you serve what most of us consider the best piece of venison, the filet, that tender muscle that can almost be cut with a sharp glance? Although the English have the reputation of being unimaginative cooks, I believe they have a method of serving that prized filet that leads all others— even the French. It passes the test of all superior dishes, is dramatically presented, appeals to the eye and is so tasty that once eaten it is never forgotten. I had it in the home of a baronet in Kent who stalked his meal on ancestral acres in Scotland. It was the filet from a royal stag, well hung, and it easily served eight drooling guests. I watched his

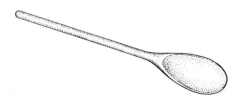

1890

In the not too distant past we have further evidence of the decrease in meat consumption by reading a menu of the 1890s, when game was a food for epicures. Imagine sitting down to an elaborate and sophisticated dinner where the course of soup and fish were followed by 'relieves,' six or more in number, among them turkey *á la Toulouse*, saddle of venison with currant jelly, and stewed terrapin *á la Maryland*. And after that came a number of cold, ornamented dishes; then the entrees and hors d'oeuvres.

The second main course offered canvasback ducks, pheasants, partridges, and grouse, with ten vegetables. And finally came 15 desserts and coffee. Such was the culinary tradition of the inns, taverns, and hotels of our larger cities during the nineteenth century.

—Frank F. Ashbrook, *Butchering, Processing and Preservation of Meat*

---

cook, a gentle and skillful Irishwoman, prepare it. . . ."

Well, when I tried the dish, I wasn't in Kent with an Irish cook and a royal well-hung stag from Scotland, and I don't really know whether the 'filet' in Scott's recipe was a true tenderloin or a loin or backstrap. In any case, the dish fed, Scott said, eight drooling guests. My assumption is that the meat weighed about 4 pounds. This rules out a tenderloin from an ordinary whitetail deer. Therefore, I recommended that the recipe be cooked with a loin or backstrap of a whitetail, or with a tenderloin from an elk or moose. Any very tender, loaf-shaped piece of red meat in the neighborhood of 4 pounds will be satisfactory. I might add that I have changed Scott's recipe somewhat, and, if the results be suspect, blame me, not Scott. If you want to gamble your choicest piece of venison, start with:

The Pastry
  4 cups flour
  1 stick butter
  ½ cup lard
  1 teaspoon salt
  1 large egg, beaten
  water (about ½ cup)

Put the flour, butter, salt, and lard into a bowl and mix it thoroughly. Whisk in the beaten egg. Slowly, blend in just enough water to make a dough. Put the dough in a bowl and place it in the refrigerator. Proceed with:

The Liver Paté
  ¾ pound of chicken livers, minced
  5 tablespoons butter
  4 green onions, finely chopped
  3 tablespoons of Madeira
  salt and pepper

Melt the butter in a frying pan and sauté the onion lightly. Add the minced liver and cook it until it turns pink. Add the wine, salt, and pepper. Mix well and set aside. Proceed with:

The Meat
  1 whole tenderloin or backstrap of 3
    to 4 pounds

¼ cup of butter
1 teaspoon dry mustard
salt and pepper
2 eggs, well beaten (to be used later in
  recipe)

Melt butter in a large frying pan and brown the meat on all sides. Use high heat and do not cook it longer than 10 minutes. Salt and pepper to taste. Remove the meat and sprinkle it on all sides with the mustard. Set the meat aside.

When the meat is cool, spread the paté on top of it. Turn the oven to 425 degrees so that it will be ready.

Take the dough from the refrigerator and put it onto a smooth surface of at least 2 feet by 2 feet. Roll the dough into a rectangle of about 12 by 20 inches. It should be ¼-inch thick. Carefully place the meat on one side of the dough. Then lift the other side of the dough and fold it over the top of the meat. Fold it under the bottom. To seal, brush the bottom well with part of the beaten egg. At both ends of the roll, cut off excess dough, then fold to seal. Brush seams well with beaten egg.

Place the roll, with the seam side down, on a baking sheet. Then brush the entire roll with the rest of the beaten egg. Place in a preheated 425-degree oven and bake for 30 minutes. When done, the pastry will be crisp and golden brown. With luck, your meat will be pink and just right. Overcooking the meat a tad is not disastrous because the jacket of dough helps seal in the moisture.

Serve with good red wine, hearty bread and butter, and vegetables of your choice. *Serves 8 to 10.*

34

GROUND GAME MEAT

Venison and other game can be ground into "hamburger" meat successfully, but remember that most game does not contain as much fat as beef. Thus, the ground meat will be different. (Better, in my opinion, and certainly better for you!) If the ground venison or game is to be used in spaghetti sauce, casseroles, and so on, it can be used as is; but for meat balls and patties, and especially for grilled burgers, the meat may require a couple of beaten eggs, or some such binding, in order to hold it together during the cooking process.

Some books and articles on game cookery recommend that the ground venison or other wild meat be mixed with beef fat (suet) or ground pork. If you grind up a large batch of venisonburger at one time (as many people do), you may want to include up to 25 percent beef suet, which can be obtained from your meat processor. While one could do a good deal worse than making up a large batch of venisonburger, I offer no fixed recommendation for mixing in fat, simply because lean meat is better for you. In my opinion, it is best to grind all lean meat and freeze it in 1-pound packages; then, if necessary, you can always add some beef fat or ground pork. A few of the recipes do call for a mixture of meat.

Creole-style Game Loaf

I've always been a meat loaf fan, and here's one of my favorite recipes for the dish.

The Loaf
  1 pound ground venison
  1 pound lean pork, bear, or armadillo
  ½ medium onion, grated
  ½ green pepper, grated

310

2 eggs, beaten
1 cup milk
1 cup toast crumbs
1 tablespoon Worcestershire sauce
¼ teaspoon Louisiana hot sauce (or Tabasco)
½ teaspoon salt
⅛ teaspoon pepper
The Sauce
½ green pepper, chopped
½ medium onion, chopped
1 clove garlic, minced
2 cups diced fresh tomatoes
2 tablespoons cooking oil
2 tablespoons flour
1 cup milk
1 tablespoon Worcestershire sauce
½ teaspoon salt
⅛ teaspoon pepper

Preheat oven to 350 degrees, then make the Creole sauce. Add oil to pan and stir in flour. Stir while cooking on medium heat until a nice brown color develops. Add onion, garlic, pepper, and tomatoes. Simmer for 4 or 5 minutes. Stir in milk. Add Wor-

cesterhire sauce, salt, and pepper. Bring almost to boil, then reduce heat and simmer for 5 minutes.

While the sauce cooks, mix the two meats thoroughly. Then mix in vegetables, toast crumbs, and seasonings. Shape into a loaf and put into a greased baking pan of suitable shape. Top with Creole sauce. Bake for 1 hour. *Serves 8 to 10.*

Zesty Gameburger Steak

Here's a good, quick one for the frying pan.

2 pounds ground game meat
1 egg, beaten
¼ cup Italian bread crumbs
½ cup tomato puree
salt
pepper
Zesty Italian salad dressing

Mix tomato puree, beaten egg, bread crumbs, salt, and pepper. Add meat, mix thoroughly, and form into serving size patties. (To cook the whole batch at once will require a large, 18-inch frying pan; or, two smaller pans can be used.) Pour a little Zesty Italian dressing into the frying pan and brown patties, over high or medium-high heat, on both sides. Cover, reduce heat, and cook for 10 minutes.

If you want a little more zest, run a can of Rotel (or Mexican-style stewed tomatoes) through a seive and mix it into the meat instead of the tomato puree. *Serves 4 to 6.*

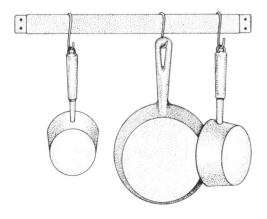

Venison Macaroni

Here's a very good recipe that I adapted from *Cooking the Sportsman's Harvest*, published by the South Dakota Department of Game, Fish, and Parks:

- 1 pound ground venison
- 1 tablespoon oil
- 4 ounces elbow macaroni (uncooked weight)
- 1 can cream of celery soup (10¾-ounce size)
- ½ cup of milk
- ¾ cup catsup
- ½ cup grated cheddar cheese
- 1 cup sliced mushrooms
- ⅓ cup chopped green pepper
- 1 small onion, chopped
- 1 teaspoon salt
- 1 cup crushed potato chips

Cook macaroni according to directions on the package. Drain. Turn oven to 350 degrees. Lightly sauté the onions and green pepper in 1 tablespoon of oil. Add meat and brown. Mix all ingredients, except potato chips. Put mixture into a well-greased 2-quart casserole dish. Bake in oven for 45 minutes at 350 degrees. Sprinkle with potato chips. Bake for another five minutes. *Serves 4 to 6.*

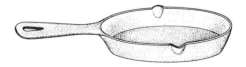

Poyha—Cherokee Indian Meat Loaf

At age eight or nine, one of my sons was the best fish bait digger that I've ever seen. So, I can't say, categorically, that he is lazy. But I do know that he doesn't clean up a tasty quail leg, and, more than once, he has requested "corn off the cob." He likes his food easy to eat, and the following recipe is just right for him. I got it from *Cy Littlebee's Guide to Cooking Fish & Game*, as compiled by Werner O. Nagel and published by the Missouri Department of Conservation. Nagel said that he heard the recipe read over the radio, but, other than that, he doesn't know exactly where it came from. In any case, I tried the Cherokee Meat Loaf and can highly recommend it for those who prefer corn off the cob. In the recipe that follows, I have changed only the format, not the ingredients or proportions.

- 1 pound ground venison
- 1 can whole kernel corn (17-ounce size)
- 1 small chopped onion
- salt to taste
- (absolutely no pepper, Nagel says)
- 2 eggs
- ½ cup water-ground cornmeal

Brown the venison in fat. Drain corn and add to venison. Add onion and cook for 10 minutes. Stir in the eggs, salt, and meal. Cook 15 more minutes, then put into a well greased meatloaf pan. Bake for 30 to 45 minutes at 350 degrees. Slice and serve with gravy. *Serves 4 to 6.*

Game Meat Chili

When first planning this book, I thought I would include several recipes for chili. But things don't always go as planned, and I ended up with a whole chapter on the subject. Chili is just too good when made with game, and there are too many matters of opinion to cover the subject with only a recipe or two. Besides, who says that chili ought to go in a ground meat chapter anyhow? Some people hold that it ought to be made with chunks of meat before it can be called chili. So . . . see chapter 35.

In cooking Cherokee Indian Meat Loaf, I always respect Nagel's command of no pepper along with the salt, because, I suppose, the Cherokee's didn't have any black pepper. I do, however, like a little more seasoning and I have, I admit, chopped up four or five jalapeños along with the onions and called it Apache Indian Meat Loaf.

Tough Meat Stew

Here's a recipe that takes a lot of attention—but it makes good eating from the worst cuts of the oldest, toughest game. It's so good, in fact, that once you cook and eat it you'll be tempted to run a whole bull moose through the meat grinder:

Meat Balls

2 pounds ground game
½ cup of cooking oil
8 small green onions, chopped (save tops)
1 clove garlic, minced
3 cups of soft bread crumbs
2 eggs
1 tablespoon Worcestershire sauce
1 teaspoon salt
½ teaspoon black pepper
½ teaspoon cayenne pepper
¼ cup cold water

Gravy

pan drippings from above
¼ cup cooking oil
3 cups cold water
2 cans beef broth (10 ½-ounce size)
1 ½ cups flour
½ teaspoon salt
¼ teaspoon black pepper

Late additions

onion tops from above
½ cup of minced parsley

Mix the meat, chopped onions, garlic, bread crumbs, eggs, salt, pepper, cayenne, Worcestershire sauce, and water. Form meatballs about 1 inch across, place on a tray, and chill in refrigerator for half an hour.

In a large frying pan, heat ½ cup of cooking oil almost to smoking point and quickly brown a batch of the meatballs. Remove meatballs as soon as they are brown and place in a Dutch oven. Brown the rest of the meatballs and transfer to Dutch oven, which should be on low heat.

To make gravy, add ¼ cup of oil to the drippings in the frying pan, put on medium heat, and slowly mix in the flour. Stir constantly until the flour starts to turn brown; this takes 10 to 15 minutes, so don't quit. Add water a little at the time, stirring constantly. Don't quit. Add beef broth, salt, and pepper, stirring constantly. Gravy should be light brown and thick.

Add meatballs to gravy and simmer. While cooking, stir several times to prevent sticking. After 45 minutes, add chopped onion tops and parsley. Simmer for another 20 minutes.

This dish goes nicely over rice. But, if you don't have fancy company at the table, also try sopping the gravy with bread or biscuits. In any case, this dish has very thick gravy and should be served hot. *Serves 4 to 6.*

Venisonburger Pie

Here's a dish that is very easy to make. It can be made from leftover meat, and it freezes nicely.

    1 pound ground venison
    1 tablespoon bacon fat
    1½ cups mild cheddar or other cheese,
        shredded
    ½ cup chopped onion
    salt
    pepper
    3 eggs
    ¾ cup of milk
    ½ cup mayonnaise
    2 tablespoons cornstarch
    2 store-bought pie crusts, frozen
        (9-inch size)

Preheat oven to 350 degrees. In a skillet, brown venison and onions in bacon fat. Salt and pepper to taste. In a bowl, thoroughly mix milk, eggs, mayonnaise, and cornstarch. Add to ground venison. Add cheese. Stir well, then spoon into pie crusts. Bake for 40 minutes. *Serves 4.*

Southwestern Game Loaf

Here's one to try if you like the flavor of Mexican or Southwestern dishes—but want it mild. If you prefer it hot, add some red hot sauce.

The Meat Loaf
    2 pounds ground venison, elk, or
        other suitable game
    2 strips bacon, minced
    1 medium green bell pepper, chopped
    1 medium onion, chopped
    1 small can tomato sauce (8-ounce)
    1 egg
    2 slices white bread, soaked in milk
    ¼ teaspoon black pepper
    1 teaspoon salt
    1½ teaspoons sugar
The Sauce
    1 cup catsup
    ¼ cup dark brown sugar
    ¼ teaspoon dry musard
    ¼ teaspoon nutmeg

Preheat oven to 350 degrees. Whisk the egg and break up the bread. Then mix both with the meat, bacon, onion, pepper, tomato sauce, sugar, and salt. Shape into a loaf, put into a suitable dish, and bake for about 1 hour.

While the loaf is cooking, make the sauce by mixing brown sugar, dry mustard, and nutmeg. Then mix with catsup. When meat loaf is almost done, cover with sauce and return to oven for a few minutes before eating. *Serves 6 to 8.*

cuts, I cut off all the fat, then cook the deerburger in small amount of bacon grease. After deerburger is cooked break an egg into the skillet then press the deerburger down on the egg hard enough to break the yoke. After egg is cooked, salt and pepper and serve while hot. The egg will moisten the deerburger."

Deerburgers

This unusual dish comes from C.V. Gaugler, of Joplin, Missouri. It was published by the Missouri Department of Conservation in *Cy Littlebee's Guide to Cooking Fish & Game:*

"Many cuts of venison are best ground into a deerburger without adding any other kind of meat. Before grinding the different

Seminole Deerburger

The recipe that I found for this dish called for ground beef. Some Seminoles can afford to eat beef if they want to, and I suppose that any Seminole not in on the tourist or bingo trade can easily make a raid on the large cattle ranches just north of Lake Okeechobee, where, I understand, rustling is more of a problem than it is in Texas. But I feel that honest Seminoles would rather have venison, and I have modified the recipe accordingly.

By the way, the pumpkin was very important in the Seminole diet, possibly because it is so easy to keep without canning or deep freezing. I've never been a real pumpkin eater myself, but the following recipe has gone a long way toward helping me acquire a taste for them.

2 pounds ground venison
½ cup chopped onion
salt and pepper to taste
2 cups of cooked pumpkin, mashed
    like potatoes
2½ cups of self-rising flour
water to make dough
cooking oil or fat

Easy Breakfast Sausage

Everybody has their favorite recipe for sausage, and some people even go to the trouble to obtain natural casings for them. I enjoy any good sausage, but I confess that more often than not I take the easy way out, especially early in the morning when I have a taste for sausage patties.

1 pound ground venison
1 pound of your favorite pork sausage
Mix the above thoroughly, shape it into patties, heat your griddle, and fry on medium heat until done.

Get a Meat Grinder

If you cook a lot of game, you really need a good portable meat grinder. There are some electric models on the market that are fine for most family use, but of course some are better than others. Try to get the old-fashioned kind that you turn with a handle. Probably the best ones are made primarily for grinding meat and have attachments that offer a choice of texture.

Some have a hopper for holding chunks of meat and a worm gear for forcing the meat through a circular "blade" that has holes in it.

I've tried to grind meat with a food processor. Sometimes it works all right, and sometimes it doesn't. Usually, however, you'll have a hard time getting the texture just right, between lumps and mush. But it can be done.

Mix ground meat, onions, salt, and pepper. Set aside. Mix pumpkin, flour, and enough water to make a soft dough. Knead the dough for a few minutes, then separate it into 3-inch balls. Knead and pull the dough some more, until it is rather elastic, and flatten it out like a pancake, about ¼ inch thick. Shape meat into patties, and put each pattie onto a piece of dough. Fold the dough up and seal it into itself. Heat oil on medium high and fry the patties until they are brown on each side. Eat while hot. *Serves 6.*

Note: Cook one pattie at a time, and test for doneness. The first one that I cooked was a little rare because the meat was too thick and the bread browned before the pattie cooked through.

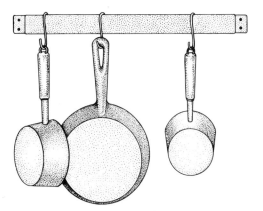

Antelope Sausage

The following recipe was given to me by Michael E. Sievering, who is a wildlife biologist at the Oakmulgee Wildlife Management Area in Brent, Alabama. He is also a wildlife artist. If you like sausage, be sure to try this one.

> **9 pounds antelope meat (boned)**
> **2 pounds pork fat or 3 pounds of hog jowls**
> **3 tablespoons sage**
> **3 tablespoons thyme**

3 tablespoons pepper
3 tablespoons marjoram
salt as needed

Bone the antelope and grind it with pork fat. Mix in the spices, then make the mixture into patties for pan frying, or freezing.

Variations: Use meat from deer, elk, or other game.

Game Stuffed Peppers

This is one of my favorite dishes, and I especially like it with ground game meat. Here's what you need to serve 3 or 4 people, assuming that 1 or 2 will want more than one pepper.

6 large bell peppers
3 cups of ground game meat
1 medium-large onion, finely chopped
2 cloves garlic, minced
salt and pepper
2 cups soft bread crumbs
½ cup melted butter (used in two
    batches)
grated cheese

Melt ¼ cup of butter in a frying pan and sauté the onions and garlic. Set aside. Brown the ground meat and keep warm. Cut the tops off the bell peppers and remove the seeds and pulp. Boil some water with a little salt in it, then add peppers for 8 minutes. Drain.

Preheat oven to 375 degrees. Place the peppers into a baking pan of suitable size and set aside.

Mix the meat, bread crumbs, salt, pepper, and sautéed onions. Toss, adding melted butter. Stuff the peppers loosely with this mixture, then sprinkle with grated cheese. Pour ½ cup of water into the bottom of the baking pan. Bake the peppers for 20 minutes, or until the cheese is ready.

Note. Some stuffed peppers are too bland for my taste, and before cooking the above recipe I sometimes squirt some Tabasco sauce in with the stuffing. Thus, some can be hot, some not.

Venison Sloppy Joe

Here's one that is always a favorite around my house, especially when we have a bunch of children to feed.

1½ pound ground venison
2 tablespoon margarine
1 medium onion, diced
1 clove garlic, minced
1 can whole tomatoes (16-ounce size)
1 can tomato sauce (15-ounce size)
2 tablespoons parsley flakes
½ teaspoon pepper
½ teaspoon chili powder
1 teaspoon salt

Put margarine in a skillet and brown onion and garlic. Add ground meat and brown. Add canned tomatoes (and liquid from can), tomato sauce, parsley flakes, salt, pepper, and chili powder. Bring to quick boil, stirring, then reduce heat and simmer for an hour. Serve over hamburger buns. *Serves 4 to 6.*

Venison Meatballs Hawaiian

The Meat
    2 pounds of ground venison
    1 cup oatmeal
    ½ cup onion, minced
    1 can sliced water chestnuts (8-ounce size)
    1½ teaspoons salt
    ½ teaspoon garlic powder
    ¼ cup milk
    oil for frying

Mix venison, oatmeal, onion, chestnuts, salt, pepper, garlic powder, and milk. Shape the mixture into small balls and fry in hot oil until they are brown on all sides. Keep warm while making:

The Sauce
    1 can crushed pineapple (15¼-ounce size)
    ½ cup chopped green pepper
    ½ cup brown sugar
    ⅓ cup white vinegar
    2 tablespoons cornstarch
    1 tablespoon soy sauce
    1 cup of water

Jackass Stew?

There are some wild, or feral, donkeys, burros, or jackasses around the world, and, believe it or not, they make good eating. Before shooting one, however, check the game laws in the area where you are hunting—or take one for survival food if you need to. According to the big French book, *Larousse Gastronomique*, donkey meat has been eaten for a very long time in some quarters, and in the Orient wild donkey was considered to be choice "venison."

Mix all sauce ingredients except pineapple in a small pan and heat, stirring, until the mixture thickens. Add pineapple and the juice from the can. Pour the sauce over meatballs and bring to heat. Eat while hot. *Serves 4 to 6.*

Spaghetti Sauce

I've always been fond of spaghetti, and I like a sauce that has been cooked for a long time. This is my favorite, made mostly of venison and fresh vegetables instead of canned ingredients.

    2 pounds ground venison
    ½ pound ground fresh pork
    1 can beef broth (10¾-ounce size)
    2 cups of water

10 medium tomatoes
1 green bell pepper, diced
2 medium onions, diced
2 cloves garlic, minced
10 ounces fresh mushrooms, sliced
½ teaspoon red pepper flakes
salt
pepper
¼ cup of Worcestershire sauce
bay leaf

Brown the ground meat in a frying pan. Stir in the red pepper flakes, beef broth, and water; cover tightly and simmer for 6 hours.

Heat water to rapid boil in a large pot. Put tomatoes into the pot and boil for about 15 minutes, until the skin starts to peel. Cool tomatoes, peel, cut out the stem end, and quarter. (Do this over a bowl so that you'll save any juice that comes out.) Pour water out of the pot and put the peeled tomatoes back into it. Simmer the tomatoes for 2 hours, stirring and mashing to break up the pulp. Then dump them into the pot with the meat.

Sauté the onions, garlic, and pepper in a frying pan, then add to the meat sauce. Add the bay leaf and Worcestershire sauce. Bring to boil, then reduce heat, and simmer for 1 hour. (Note: If the sauce needs to be thickened, simmer it without a cover until some of the liquid boils off.) Fish out the bay leaf before serving.

Serve with spaghetti, garlic bread, and lots of tossed salad dressed with oil and vinegar. *Serves 6 to 10.*

35

CHILI

A buddy of mine sports five or six T-shirts from some sort of national chili cookoff competition. I saw his hackles rise a bit when I first asked him what sort of beans he puts into his recipe. Quickly his wife tried to change the subject, and I knew right off that I had to step carefully. And maybe cover my tracks. Also, I remember that some years ago a writer named H. Allen Smith quit Pleasantville, New York, and moved to Alpine, Texas, from which outpost he quickly stirred up the Texans about their chili competition.

Because I don't want these Aggies and other chili freaks after me, I am quick to point out that many of the following recipes are not really mine. I got the first one, for example, from a fellow named Ronny Cooper, of Clayton, Alabama, who in turn got it from somebody in Arizona, whom Cooper met while elk hunting in either Wyoming or Montana or somewhere in the northern part of the Louisiana Purchase, as Justin Wilson would say. (If any of the Texas gang goes after Cooper, they should be warned that he is an accomplished pistoleer. For a hobby, he goes vine pulling for squirrels. This sport works as follows: Find a suitable tree with vines growing down to the ground. Grab the vine and pull as violently as possible, shaking the treetop. This will send the squirrels scampering for the next county, making a target hard to hit even with a shotgun. Cooper uses a pistol. So does his 12-year old son, Chris.)

I could go on with this farce for several more pages, but I see that it won't work. So much for buck passing, track covering, yarn spinning, diversion, and other tactics. I can't get out of it, and I hereby meet this chapter head on and take full responsibility for it.

Venison Chili

1½ pounds of ground venison
2 tablespoons cooking oil
1 pint canned tomatoes
1 can cream of tomato soup
2 tablespoons chili powder
1 can pinto beans
salt
½ cup diced onions
½ cup grated cheddar cheese

In large skillet, brown meat in oil. Add tomatoes, soup, chili powder, and beans. Salt to taste. Bring to quick heat, then reduce and simmer for an hour and a half. Spoon chili into serving bowls and sprinkle the top with onions and cheese. *Serves 4.*

Texas Chili Mel Marshall

I adapted the following recipe from Mel Marshall's *Complete Book of Outdoor Cookery.* Marshall said, "There's nothing better than good camp-cooked chili, and sadly there's no dish which has undergone more wanton tinkering than has chili con carne, if you want to give the dish its true name, which translates as 'pepper and meat.'

"There isn't space enough here for me to list all the reasons why most of the alterations to chili are phony, so please take my word that tomatoes, paprika, sour cream, lime juice, catsup, red wine, Tabasco sauce, soy sauce, butter, or beans of any kind but especially kidney beans, have no place whatever in chili con carne. The following recipe is for genuine chili, and if you want to serve beans with it, fine, as long as they're pinto beans. But don't cook them with the chili itself.

"Now, if you feel like embroidering the recipe that follows, do so by all means. But if you do, don't call it chili—call your version of the dish what it really is, a meat stew seasoned with red peppers."

I don't think I have "embroidered" Marshall's recipe, but I have changed the meat from tough beef to venison. Also, the directions with his recipe were given for cooking outside, apparently over charcoal, and I have changed this to cooking on a gas or electric range.

3 to 4 pounds of tough venison or
    other game meat
¼ to ½ pound of beef suet
1½ teaspoon cumin seeds
2 tablespoons chili powder
1½ teaspoons salt
1½ cups coarsely chopped onion
2 cloves finely minced garlic
water

Crush the cumin seeds and mix them with the chili powder and salt. Cut the venison into chunks, about the size of the first thumb joint. Put the suet into a Dutch oven and sear it on high heat. After the fat has been rendered, remove the browned pieces of suet. To the hot fat, add venison, a handful at a time, sprinkling with the chili powder, cumin, and salt. Brown all the meat. Then pour off most of the fat.

Add onions and garlic. Stir. Add enough water to cover the meat. Bring to boil, reduce heat, cover, and simmer for several hours. Serve with rice and pinto beans, cooked separately.

Embroidered variation: I tried the measures listed above and found that I prefer a little more pepper in my chili. Maybe the chili powder that I used had lost some of its strength. Anyhow, I sprinkled on a little cayenne, which will do the trick, fast.

chopped onions (optional)
oyster crackers (optional)

Dump everything except onions and crackers into a crockpot. Cover tightly and put on low heat for about 8 hours. Serve chili in bowls and top with chopped onions and oyster crackers. Beans can also be added, if you want them. *Serves 10 or more.*

My son Jarrod loves onions, and this chili is one of his favorites. He would like to have a crockpot ready, hot and steaming, day and night.

Crockpot Chili

Here's an excellent, no-bean chili with lots of flavor. If you reduce the measures below, however, you might consider cooking it slowly in a regular pot instead of a crockpot. The crockpot has heating elements in the side and should therefore be almost full for best results.

> **4 pounds ground venison or other red-meat game**
> **½ pound fatty pork, ground (sausage will do)**
> **3 cups water**
> **1 tablespoon salt**
> **1 teaspoon black pepper**
> **2 tablespoons cumin**
> **5 tablespoons chili powder**
> **1 tablespoon garlic juice**
> **1 tablespoon brown sugar**

Hotdog Chili

Ed's Place, a cafe here in my hometown, claims to have the World's Best hotdogs. Ed advertises accordingly. And they are good. I even published an article about them in one of the airline magazines. Everyone wants to know his recipe, but of course that is Ed's commercial secret. All he'll say is that the chili makes the hotdog. Into more detail he won't go. But my notes on the delivery traffic from a local meat market indicate that Ed's chili contains about two parts beef and one part pork. Adjusting a little for venison, I've come up with the following:

1 pound fine-ground venison
1 pound fine-ground pork
1 cup water
1 teaspoon salt
1 teaspoon black pepper
3 tablespoons chili powder
1 tablespoon brown sugar
1 clove garlic, minced
½ cup onion, very finely chopped

Brown garlic, onion, and ground meat in a frying pan. Add all other ingredients, cover, and simmer for 6 to 8 hours. Eat on regular hot dogs, or make chili dogs without the weiner.

The key to good hotdog chili, in my opinion, is to use fine-ground meat and cook it down. Then dip it with a strainer so that there won't be enough liquid to make your hotdog bun too soggy. For maximum results, steam the hotdog buns until they are warm and soft. Any sort of steamer can be used, but I put the buns on a rack in a large boiler over ¼ cup of steaming water. Don't get the buns too soggy.

Pedernales River Chili

Some years ago, the Alabama CowBelles published their *Beef Cookbook*. Their recipe from Mrs. Lyndon Baines Johnson has be-

come one of my favorite chili-type dishes. Lyndon might roll over and bellow from the grave, or otherwise discharge, but I have taken license to change the recipe from beef to venison and beef suet.

The Chili
  4 pounds of venison ground with
    ½ pound beef suet
  1 tablespoon oil
  1 large onion, chopped
  2 cloves garlic, minced
  6 teaspoons chili powder
  1 teaspoon ground oregano
  1 teaspoon comino seed (cumin)
  1 can tomatoes (16-ounce size)
  ½ teaspoon red hot sauce (or more)
  salt
  2 cups hot water
Noche Specials
  tortillas
  cooking oil
  grated cheese
  jalapeño pepper

Heat a little oil in a Dutch oven and sauté the onion and garlic. Brown all the meat a little at a time. Add oregano, comino seed, chili powder, tomatoes, hot sauce, and water. Salt to taste. Bring to quick boil, reduce heat, and simmer for an hour or two. Or longer. Serve with Noche Specials, prepared (from above ingredients) as follows:

Heat at least 1-inch of oil in a large frying pan. Preheat oven to 400 degrees. Cut the tortillas into quarters and fry until brown and crisp. Drain tortillas on absorbent paper. Put 1 teaspoon of grated cheese (I use sharp cheddar) and a slice of jalapeño pepper on each piece of tortilla. Place on a flat baking sheet and put into the oven until the cheese starts to melt. Serve hot with chili. Cool off with ice-cold cola. *Serves 10 or 12.*

Venison Chile Con Carne with Beans

2 pounds of ground venison
4 strips of bacon
1 medium onion, chopped
2 cloves garlic, minced
1 can stewed tomatoes (14½-ounce size)
1 cup catsup
1 can kidney beans (16-ounce size)
3 tablespoons chili powder (with cumin)
½ teaspoon salt
¼ teaspoon black pepper
water

Cook bacon, crumble, and set aside. Brown venison in bacon drippings. Add onion, garlic, bacon bits, and chili powder. Stir and simmer a few minutes. Add tomatoes, catsup, beans, salt, pepper, and a little water. Bring to quick boil, then reduce heat, cover, and simmer for 3 hours. Add more water if needed. *Serves 4 to 6.*

Osmose Zoo Chili

Here's a good large-batch recipe from Greg Rane, who said it was used in the Southeast Regional contest of the International Chili Society's cook-offs.

Group One
5 pounds lean hamburger meat
1 pound deer tenderloin, cubed small
1 pound mild pan sausage
6 ounces rabbit (lean)
6 ounces squirrel (lean)
10 ounces shark (preferably from just behind dorsal fin)
10 ounces chicken (white meat, finely chopped)

Group Two
3 large onions, chopped
2 large green peppers, chopped
1 jar pepperoncini peppers, chopped
2 large jalapeño peppers, chopped
4 chili peppers, punctured several times with fork

Group Three
1 large can chili powder (add to taste)
3 to 5 teaspoons cumin powder (add to taste)
1 teaspoon MSG (monosodium glutamate)
2 teaspoons salt
black pepper to taste (approximately 1 tablespoon)
3 tablespoons sugar

Group Four
2 large cans tomatoes
3 cans tomato puree (10-ounce size)
1 can tomato paste (10-ounce size)
1 lemon
½ stick butter
1 small jar lemon-pepper
2 cans Budweiser beer

Rane says, "Pour tomato products into a

large pot (approximately 3 or 4 gallon). Be sure to squash tomatoes with your hands. Cook on low for one hour, stirring frequently and making sure not to burn. Add ingredients from group three. Stir in and mix. Cover and simmer.

"Lightly sauté onions and green peppers. Add to pot. Brown hamburger and sausage. Drain off, add to pot, and stir in. Sauté cubed deer tenderloin and add to pot. Stir in. Chop rabbit, squirrel, and chicken. Sauté and add to pot. Stir in.

"Melt butter, then add lemon pepper and lemon juice. Sauté shark. When it is cooked, flake it and stir into the pot.

"Add last four items in group two. Stir in. Cook on low slowly for at least two hours, stirring frequently.

"As chili cooks down and consistency

thickens NEVER ADD WATER! Add beer as needed to suit thickness. The longer this chili cooks, the better it gets. Enjoy."

FAT AND PROTEIN IN MEAT
(Based on 100 Gram Edible Portions)

Meat	% water	calories	protein*	fat*
beef	56.7	301	17.4	25.1
beaver	56.2	248	29.2	13.7
opossum	57.3	221	30.2	10.2†
rabbit	73.0	135	21.0	5.0
raccoon	54.8	255	29.2	14.5
venison	74.0	126	21.0	4.0

Note: I made up the above table from data published in *The South Carolina Wildlife Cookbook,* which in turn credited the Georgia Extension Service.

*measured in grams

†this figure seems low to me, but perhaps most of the fat that I associate with the possum is layered between the skin and the meat.

Easy No-Bean Venison Chili

2 pounds ground venison
2 cans stewed tomatoes (14½ ounce cans)
2 packs of chili mix (1¾-ounce packs)
1 teaspoon salt
1 tablespoon cooking oil

In a large frying pan, brown venison in cooking oil. Stir in chili mix, salt, and tomatoes. Simmer for 1 hour, adding a little water if necessary. Serve in individual bowls and top with oyster crackers. *Serves 4 to 6.* For a drink, try chilled V-8 juice.

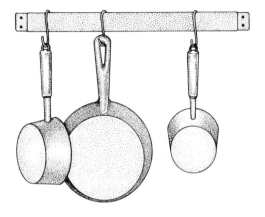

Dr. S. N. Hodges' Buzzard Breath Chili

Here's one that I got from *Ducks Unlimited Cookbook*, which is really not quite as foul as its name might indicate:

- 2 cups ground deerburger
- 2 cups chopped onions
- 1½ cups chopped green pepper
- 2 cans tomatoes
- 2 cans tomato sauce
- 2 cans kidney beans
- 2 to 2 ½ teaspoons salt
- 2 tablespoons chili powder
- 1 or 2 cayenne peppers
- 2 cans mushrooms

In a stove-top Dutch oven or large frying pan, sauté the ground meat, onions, and green peppers until the meat is browned. Mix in the tomatoes, tomato sauce, kidney beans, salt, chili powder, cayenne peppers, and mushrooms. Bring to boil, reduce heat, and simmer for 1 hour. *Serves 8 to 10.*

Opposite-Sex Guest Chili

I don't care what you call this dish. It looks like chili, but it's good clean flavor and consequence, so to speak, are quite different. Carefully note that it has no beans.

- 4 pounds ground moose or other suitable game meat
- 2 cans Rotel (or Mexican-style stewed tomatoes)
- 2 teaspoons salt
- 1 teaspoon parsley
- 1 teaspoon garlic powder
- 1 teaspoon basil
- 1 teaspoon oregano
- chopped onions

Put the ground meat into a crockpot, then add Rotel and all other ingredients except onions. Cook on low heat for 8 hours or more (I have cooked it for 24 hours). Serve in bowls and top with chopped onions. We like to eat this dish with Wheatsworth crackers. *Serves 6 to 8.*

Variation: If you've got vine-ripened tomatoes, chill one or two and dice it. Serve atop the meat dish, with or without the onions. Also try it in taco shells, with shredded lettuce, cheese, taco sauce, plenty of onions, and tomatoes.

Note: This dish can also be cooked in a Dutch oven. Just reduce the cooking time to an hour or two.

Bedfellow Variation: Once the Broad Street boys gathered at our house to discuss a major event. It seems that an out-of-town girl friend would be staying the night at the home of a 14-year old. The several boys who were discussing this possibility were all about 11 or 12 years old at the time, except for my son Jeff, who was only 7 or 8. I overheard part of the conversation, which went pretty much as follows:

"Reckon where she's going to sleep?" one boy asked.

"With him, I reckon," said another.

"I wish I was him!" said a third.

"Man yeah," two or three said.

"Shoot," Jeff said, "*I* sure wouldn't want to sleep with no *girl*. Why, you couldn't even fart. You could lie there all night long and couldn't even fart."

Well . . . under such circumstances, try the above recipe without the onions or the garlic powder. Add beans at your peril.

Black Bean Venison Chili

Here's a connoisseur's recipe from Michael McLaughlin, as published in *The Manhattan Chile Co. Southwest American Cookbook.* He says, "Venison may well have been the original chili meat, and it remains a favorite of serious chili cooks both for its resilient texture, which holds up under long simmering, and for its rich flavor . . .

½ **pound bacon, finely chopped**
2 **tablespoons vegetable oil**
3 **pounds boneless venison, trimmed of all sinew and cut into ½-inch cubes**
2 **large yellow onions, peeled and coarsely chopped (about 4 cups)**

8 **medium garlic cloves, peeled and minced**
⅓ **cup mild, unseasoned chili powder**
3 **tablespoons ground cumin, from toasted seeds**
1½ **tablespoons dried oregano, preferably Mexican**
¾ **teaspoon cayenne pepper, or to taste**
6 **cups beef stock or canned beef broth**
salt
2 **to 3 tablespoons yellow cornmeal, as optional thickener**
2 **cans (16 ounces each) black beans, rinsed and drained**
sour cream, orange peel, and minced clean fresh cilantro leaves, as garnish

1. In a 4½- to 5-quart heavy flameproof casserole or Dutch oven, combine the bacon and oil. Set the casserole over medium heat and cook, stirring once or twice, until the bacon is crisp and has rendered its fat, 15 to 20 minutes. With a slotted spoon remove the bacon and drain it on paper towels. Pour half the rendered fat into a large skillet and set it aside.

2. Return the casserole to medium heat. Add the venison and cook, uncovered, stirring often, until the meat looses all red color, about 20 minutes.

3. Meanwhile, set the skillet over medium heat. Add the onions and garlic, lower the heat slightly, and cook, stirring once or twice, until very tender, about 20 minutes.

4. Scrape the onions and garlic into the casserole with the venison. Stir in the chili powder, cumin, oregano, and cayenne pepper and cook, stirring, for 5 minutes. Stir in the beef stock and the reserved bacon and

Chauvinistic Chefs

One winter night I was talking to Greg Rane, the chili sport, after we had feasted from several venison and bird dishes that I had concocted, and had settled into easy chairs with whiskey and our women, when he made some compliment about my writing style. I told him that poets and nature lovers ought to stay away from making cookbooks, in which genre the language often degenerates into "Me Tarzan; You Jane."

"Well," Rane said, after a while, sipping of his whiskey and smirking ever so slightly, "It's not an entirely bad style. At least one knows who's who!"

bring to a boil. Lower the heat and simmer, uncovered, stirring occasionally, for 1½ hours.

5. Taste and correct the seasoning, adding salt if needed and water if the chili is thickening too rapidly. Continue to simmer, stirring often, for another 30 to 45 minutes, or until the meat is tender and the chili is reduced to your liking.

6. To further thicken the chili, or to bind any surface fats, stir in the optional cornmeal. Stir in the black beans and simmer for another 5 minutes, or until the beans are heated through.

7. To serve, ladle into bowls and garnish each serving with a dollop of sour cream and a sprinkling of orange peel and cilantro."

Note: Mr. McLaughlin sugested that salt not be added until shortly before eating time. I followed this advice when I tested the recipe, and I also plopped a blob of sour cream onto my bowl of chili. I loved it. But I'll have to admit that I failed to add fresh cilantro leaves simply because I didn't have time to drive several hundred miles hunting for them. Also, I passed on the orange peel. In a note to the recipe, McLaughlin said to use a "zester" to remove the orange peel in long, thin ornamental strands. I called the local hardware store up on the town square, which carries cast-iron frying pans and such kitchen items, to see if they stocked zesters. Had to ask twice and push for an answer. After a testy silence, the proprietor said he didn't know what in the hell I was talking about. I informed him that a zester is used for fixing orange peelings with which to garnish black bean venison chili. The guy hung up the telephone. I don't know whether he was a chili freak—or whether he thought he was talking to one.

36

BEAR

It's a good red meat, similar to prime beef or buffalo, with plenty of fat, like pork. A bear of the right age, and in the right season, with proper care and proper cooking, might well be the best of all big game, or maybe the best of all meat. But there is a problem with bear, which keeps it from fulfilling its potential. It must always be cooked well done. Under no circumstances should it be eaten rare because bear, like pork, can carry trichinosis. So, be careful.

When a bear is being field-dressed, it should be gutted and cooled as soon as possible. The thick hide of a bear retains too much heat, and it should be removed quicker than the hide of deer or elk, especially in hot weather. Field-skinning the bear is recommended, if possible. In fact, a large bear killed some distance from ready transporta-tion will probably have to be quartered before it can be packed out.

Aging or hanging bear is not necessary, but leaving it for a day or two in icy water or under refrigeration certainly won't hurt anything. Then freeze it.

Many people hold that bear meat is not fit to eat. But why not? It feeds mainly on berries, grass, nuts, and so on. Mating seasons may have some bearing on the quality of the meat in adult males, but I suspect that most of the trouble with bear is caused by improper field-dressing. Or by chasing the bear all over the country with dogs, and fighting it with dogs, before the kill. Hunting bear, and deer, with dogs is a sport that many people enjoy, and that's fine with me. I'm merely saying that hunting with dogs is not the way to get the best meat.

Bigos

This old Polish dish was originally a hunter's stew and it was served after a bear hunt. It contained, of course, bear and other game meat. The measures below make a rather large dish, which serves about 10 people, and a stove-top Dutch oven will be helpful. I also use an auxiliary frying pan.

½ pound bear meat, cut into cubes
½ pound venison or other game, cubed

½ pound bacon, cut into 1-inch squares
½ pound Polish sausage, sliced
2 medium onions, chopped
8 ounces fresh mushrooms, sliced, or 6-ounce can
2 cups beef broth
½ cup white wine
2 bay leaves
1 teaspoon paprika
½ teaspoon pepper
salt
2 cans sauerkraut (16-ounce size)

Warning

All bears, like all domestic hogs as well as wild hogs (including javelina or peccary), can carry the parasite that causes trichinosis. The only safeguard against trichinosis, if you eat these animals, is to make sure that the meat is done. Avoid rare steaks and roasts, no matter how good they might be. If the meat is cooked properly, there is no danger in eating bear and wild hogs—even if they do carry the trichinosis parasite.

According to my edition of *Encyclopaedia Britannica*, 6 per cent of all the swine in the United States that are fed slop, or raw garbage, are infected with the parasite *Trichinella spiralis*, whereas less than 1 percent of grain-fed swine has the parasite. It follows, I think, that a truly wild bear from deep in the forest would be less likely to have the parasite than those that feed at garbage dumps.

Because of the possibility of trichinosis, I have not included any recipes for broiling, grilling, or frying bear steaks or chops. Typically, these methods of cooking can produce a well done outside and a rare inside. Although I feel that the danger of trichinosis would be slight in most cases, I also feel that many people—including this one—will overreact even to the possibility of getting infected with the trichinosis parasite. Thus, a prime bear steak is likely to be cooked far too much, thereby ruining a good piece of meat. I conclude that it is better to avoid these methods of cooking bear meat altogether.

Also, if you cook a roast that may border on the dangerous, it is best to use a meat thermometer and make sure that the interior of the meat reaches a temperature of at least 150 degrees F.

Freezing bear meat will not prevent trichinosis, but the meat can be cooked safely in a microwave.

Cook bacon in your frying pan, then sauté the onions and mushrooms in the drippings. Remove the onions and mushrooms from frying pan and brown the bear and the venison. Transfer the meat to your Dutch oven. Add onions, bacon, and sausage slices. Pour in beef broth. Add paprika, pepper, salt, and bay leaf. Stir. Cover and simmer for 2 hours.

Just before serving, drain the sauerkraut and stir it into the meat. Serve hot.

Variations. There are, of course, all manner of possible variations to bigos, but I like the two types of meat along with the sausage. (The bacon can be omitted, using cooking oil to sauté the onions and brown the meat.) Ideally, in my opinion, the dish should contain a lean meat such as deer or elk together with a fatty meat such as bear or opossum or armadillo.

Barbecued Bear

Here's a good one from Mike Stephens of the North Carolina Wildlife Resources Commission. It was published by the Commission in a booklet (currently out of print) called *Wild Game Recipes.*

The Meat
    bear roast, 3 or 4 pounds
    salt
    pepper
    water
The Sauce
    ½ cup catsup or chili sauce
    2 tablespoons barbecue sauce
    3 tablespoons Worcestershire sauce

½ cup water
1 clove garlic, minced
1 onion, chopped

Preheat oven to 350 degrees. Salt and pepper the roast, then put it on a rack in a covered baking pan. Bake for 2 hours. After 2 hours, add ½ cup of water to pan, turn off the oven, and let the bear meat steam until the oven cools down. While waiting, heat up the skillet and add ½ cup water, catsup, barbecue sauce, Worcestershire sauce, garlic, and onion. Let simmer. When the bear roast cools down, slice it thinly against the grain and serve with the sauce. *Serves 6 to 10.*

Crockpot Bear

This dish has an intriguing hint of sweet-and-sour in the taste of the gravy.

    bear roast of suitable size and shape,
        4 to 5 pounds
    salt
    pepper
    onion powder
    garlic powder
    2 medium onions, quartered
    2 bell peppers, sliced
    2 medium potatoes, quartered
    8 to 10 mushrooms, if you've got
        room for them in the pot
    2 cups water
    4 beef bouillon cubes
    ¼ cup Worcestershire sauce
    1 cup brown sugar

½ cup prepared mustard
1 tablespoon prepared horseradish
2 bay leaves

Mix salt, pepper, onion powder, and garlic powder. Roll bear roast over seasonings and rub in. Put roast into a crockpot. Heat 4 cups of water and dissolve bouillon cubes. Stir in Worcestershire sauce, brown sugar, mustard, and bay leaves. Pour over roast. Add onions, bell pepper, and potatoes. Turn crockpot to low and cook for 8 or 9 hours. Turn to high

---

Big Scrub Bear

Bear, once so plentiful in Florida that before 1792 William Bartram wrote, 'there are still far too many bears in Florida,' are becoming scarce. I see no reason for destroying the remaining ones, since they live so far from any domestic clearing that they are no longer a menace, as formerly, to stock. But I must admit that bear meat at the proper season, and properly cooked, is a delicious meat. A male bear in the mating season, like a boar hog, is not fit to eat. A female nursing bear not only has tough and stringy meat, but for humanitarian reasons should never be destroyed. A young male bear in the off-season provides meat better than the best beef. I should happily settle for a stupid steer, but on the occasions when I have had bear meat in the Big Scrub of Florida, I have enjoyed it thoroughly.
—Marjorie Kinnan Rawlings,
Cross Crook Cookery

---

and cook for an additional hour. Have plenty of biscuits for the gravy. *Serves 8 to 12.*

Appalachian Bear Roast

Here's one from *Wildlife Chef*, published by the Oklahoma Wildlife Federation. "Trim excess fat from roast. Parboil in water with 4 apples added to each quart of water. When apples start to fall apart remove meat. Salt and pepper meat, and bake it in a roaster in 350 degree F. oven until tender.

"Be sure meat is well done. Even when cooked it may have a pinkish tinge which will darken on contact with air."

Bear Loaf

If you like meat loaf, be sure to try the following the next time you have bear.

1½ pounds ground bear meat
1 can tomato paste (6-ounce)
8 slices American cheese
1 cup cracker crumbs
1 medium onion, diced
½ bell pepper, diced
2 stalks celery, diced
1 egg
1 tablespoon Worcestershire sauce
1 teaspoon salt
¼ teaspoon pepper
½ cup water
1 beef bouillon cube

Preheat oven to 350 degrees. Dice 4 slices of the cheese and mix with bear meat, tomato paste, cracker crumbs, onion, pepper, celery, egg, Worcestershire sauce, salt, and pepper. Form into a loaf and place into a well-greased baking dish of suitable size and shape. Place remaining cheese slices atop loaf. Dissolve bouillon cube in water and add to dish. Bake for 45 minutes, or until cheese is ready. *Serves 4 to 6.*

Dutch Oven Bear Roast

The following recipe has been adapted from *The South Carolina Wildlife Cookbook*. It was submitted by Faye Harris who said that it should be served with saffron rice, stewed tomatoes, and green salad.

The Meat
   1 bear roast to fit your Dutch oven
   salt
   pepper
   cooking oil
   hot water
The Marinade
   1 large onion, chopped
   1 garlic clove, minced
   1 celery stalk, chopped
   1 cup cooking oil
   1 teaspoon dry mustard
   ½ cup catsup
   2 bay leaves
   ¼ teaspoon rosemary
   1 tablespoon Worcestershire sauce
   1 teaspoon celery salt
   1 cup vinegar

Put bear roast in a glass or ceramic container of suitable size. Mix all marinade ingredients and pour over bear roast. Refrigerate for 18 to 24 hours, turning several times. Save marinade.

Remove roast from marinade and rub it with salt and pepper. Put a little oil in a Dutch oven, heat it, and sear roast on all sides. Add enough hot water to cover ¼ of the roast. Then discard the bay leaves and pour the marinade over roast. Bring to boil, reduce heat, cover, and simmer 45 minutes *for each pound* of roast. Turn the meat several times during cooking, and add more water if needed. The gravy can be thickened with a little flour or cornstarch. Allow ⅓ to ½ pound of bear roast per person.

Barbequed Bear Loin

Here's a neat, time-efficient recipe that I got from a booklet called "Black Bear, Nature's Forgotten Delicacy," which was published by the Ontario Federation of Anglers and Hunters:

The Meat
2 to 3 pounds bear tenderloin
The Sauce
¾ cup of vinegar
¾ cup of catsup
1 cup water
1 onion, chopped
1 clove garlic, minced
2 teaspoons salt
¼ teaspoon pepper
1 tablespoon Worcestershire sauce
¼ teaspoon Tabasco sauce
3 tablespoons brown sugar
1 teaspoon dry mustard

Preheat oven to 350 degrees. Slice the meat into ½ inch pieces. Put it into an oblong glass baking dish and cook it for 30 minutes. While the meat is cooking, mix the sauce ingredients in a suitable pan and cook it for 25 minutes. Pour the sauce over the meat and bake at 350 degrees for an hour. *Serves 6 or 7.*

Bear Sobieski with Croissants

If you've got some bear meat and want something special for it, consider the following recipe from *Joe's Book of Mushroom Cookery* by Jack Czarnecki. "This dish bears the name of King Jan III Sobieski (1629-1696), the savior of Vienna and the greatest king in Po-

land's history," Czarnecki says. "There are two reasons for the name. One is that King Jan was, indeed, a bear of a man, being large of girth and fierce of temper. The second reason is that the principal flavor here is cumin, a spice used throughout the former Ottoman Empire, whose expansion King Jan halted at Vienna (1683). Another famous food invented to celebrate that event, the croissant, is used to finish off eating the sauce in this dish. Serve with a good Cabernet Sauvingon."

If this dish sounds a little highfalutin, what with royalty and all, consider exactly what they were doing with those croissants when using them to "finish off the sauce." They were sopping with 'em. Anyhow, I cooked the dish and I can highly recommend it for royalty or common folk.

2 pounds bear meat, cubed
1 quart dry red wine

The Practical Domestic Uses of Bear Grease

Tanya Chasse of the Yukon Renewable Resources was kind enough to send me a copy of a booklet called *Yukon Bear, Bacon, and Boot Grease Recipes*, which, unfortunately, is now out of print. From this booklet I learned that caked bear lard, at room temperature, makes good boot grease and softens leather. I also learned that it makes hair soft and shiny, but my wife insists, still, on paying good money to a cosmetologiest.

1 quart strong meat stock, veal
   preferred
3 cloves garlic, crushed
3 large onions, cut coarsely
1 cup honey
⅓ ounce dried cepes
1 tablespoon crushed cumin
3 tablespoons butter
3 tablespoons sifted flour
2 teaspoons salt
2 tablespoons soy sauce
1½ cups fresh wild or domestic
   mushrooms
4 croissants

Put the bear meat into a stove-top Dutch oven or suitable pot. Add wine, meat stock, garlic, onions, honey, cepes, and cumin. If the liquid does not quite cover the meat, add a little more water. Bring to a boil, then reduce heat, cover, and simmer for 1½ hours, or until the meat is tender.

Dead Bears Are Also Dangerous

There's no doubt that bears can be dangerous. Grizzlies, blacks, browns, and whites all have chewed hell out of numerous citizens. . . . But I have a hunch that more people have been hurt skinning dead bears than were ever injured by bears on the hoof. Reports of knife cuts, ax cuts, assorted hernias, and pratfalls while packing hides to camp are legion.

Even more serious are the home accidents caused by head-mounted rugs lying between the cocktail bar and the gun cabinet. The risk is about one hundred to one, compared to the relative safety of hunting the shaggy brutes across the ice, on the tundra, in the woodlands, and beside the glaciers.

—C.E. Gillham, *Field & Stream*,
November 1968

Colby on Bear

Many hunters prefer the meat of a bear killed just after hibernation in the spring, when most of the animal's fat has been lost and its muscles are soft from inactivity. Others say that the meat of a bear that's been eating berries is best, regardless of the time of year.

This, too, is a matter of opinion and probably depends upon when you are lucky enough to bag a black bear in the first place.

—C.B. Colby, *Outdoor Life*

Remove the meat. Strain the liquid, then cook it down to 3 cups. (If you have a pot with cup gradient markings, strain the liquid into it. You can also pour 3 cups of water into a pot and measure its depth with a ruler. Then discard the water, pour in the strained stock, and cook until the liquid is at the proper 3-cup depth.) After the liquid has been reduced to 3 cups, pour it back into the main pot.

Mix the butter and flour, then cook the mixture in a frying pan until it makes a dark brown roux. Stir constantly so that the mix-

Grizzly Meat

The flavor of grizzly meat is more pronounced [than black bear] and slightly coarser in texture but no less tender or edible. Grizzly meat does not freeze well. Three months is maximum. However, black bear freezes much better, very similar to pork.

—*Yukon Bear, Bacon, and Boot Grease Recipes*

and I therefore worked out the following recipe:

2½ pounds bear stewing meat
2 tablespoons oil
1 medium onion, diced
1 clove garlic, minced
1 teaspoon salt
½ teaspoon pepper
½ teaspoon thyme
1 tablespoon Worcestershire sauce
1 can V-8 juice (10-ounce size)

Heat a little oil in a skillet and sauté onion and garlic. Drain. Add more oil and brown the bear meat. (Brown it in several batches, adding a little oil as needed.) Transfer meat, onion, and garlic to a Dutch oven. Pour in V-8 juice and other ingredients. Bring to quick boil, then reduce heat, cover, and simmer for 3 hours or longer. *Serves 6 or 7.*

ture will not burn. When the roux is ready (after about 15 minutes of cooking and stirring) add it to the liquid in the pot, along with the salt and soy sauce. Heat and stir until the mixture thickens. Add the bear and mushrooms. Cook for 5 minutes. While waiting, warm the croissants. *Serves 4.*

Warning

Do not eat bear liver or feed it to your pets. Bears sometimes secrete Vitamin A in their livers in amounts that can be toxic to humans and dogs or cats. Discard the liver with the intestines.

—Mel Marshall, *Complete Book of Outdoor Cookery*

Bear Fricassee V-8

Once I needed a little water in a fricassee that I was cooking, and I happened to have a can of V-8 juice in my hand. I dumped it in. Both the meat and the gravy turned out just right,

37

ELK and MOOSE

Many people consider the elk to be the best eating of all big game. It resembles beef and has a texture that is a little coarser than deer meat. Moose is also very good; it is of similar texture and is usually not as dry as deer. Moose and elk meat also make good "hamburger" and sausage.

The elk is usually taken in cool weather at high elevations, so that proper cooling of the meat makes for better eating. On the other hand, elk are large and difficult to handle. Also, the elk should be dropped on the first shot. A wounded elk tends to run much farther than a deer, and this of course hurts the quality of the meat. With moose, the big problem is in getting it dressed out quickly, especially if the animal was shot while it was wading in the water.

Most of the recipes in the venison chapters can be used for moose or elk, or you may want to try these:

Moose Mozzarella

This dish works best with a fairly good cut of meat, sliced about ½ inch thick.

> 1½ **pounds moose steak**
> 1 **cup cooking oil**
> 1 **teaspoon garlic juice**
> **salt**
> **pepper**
> 1 **egg**
> ½ **cup cracker crumbs**
> ½ **cup Parmesan cheese, grated**

½ cup onion, chopped
¼ cup bell pepper, chopped
1 can stewed tomatoes (15-ounce)
1 tablespoon chopped parsley
1 teaspoon oregano
½ teaspoon marjoram
6 ounces mozzarella cheese, sliced

Pound the steak with a meat mallet or the edge of a heavy plate. Mix the oil and garlic juice, then pour it over the steak and let it sit for at least 4 hours. Turn the steak several times. Save the marinade.

Preheat oven to 325 degrees. Heat 1 tablespoon of marinade oil in a pan. Sauté the onions and pepper. Stir in tomatoes, parsley, oregano, and marjoram. Let simmer. Put oil from marinade into a frying pan and turn on heat. Whisk an egg. Mix Parmesan cheese and cracker crumbs together. Dip steaks in egg, roll in crumb mixture, and brown in frying pan. Put browned steaks into a well-greased shallow baking dish; ideally, the steaks should cover the bottom but should not overlap. Mix sauce and pan drippings, then pour over steaks. Top with mozzarella cheese slices and bake for 40 to 50 minutes, or until cheese is ready. (Watch cheese carefully toward the end of baking period.) *Serves 5 or 6.*

Moose Steaks Supreme

This delicious recipe is designed for meat that is on the tough side. If you've got tender meat, so much the better.

3 pounds round steak of moose or elk (¾ inch thick)
½ cup olive oil
½ cup red wine vinegar
salt and pepper
½ teaspoon garlic juice
flour
¼ cup cooking oil
1 can cream of chicken soup (10¾-ounce size)
water

Marinate steak for several hours, or overnight, in a mixture of ½ cup olive oil and ½ cup wine vinegar. Turn meat several times.

Drain the steaks. Salt and pepper to taste and sprinkle with garlic juice. Roll steaks in flour, then beat them with a mallet or the edge of a plate. Heat the cooking oil and brown the steaks on both sides. Add a little water, cover, reduce heat, and simmer for an hour, checking from time to time to see whether more water is needed. In a saucepan, heat the soup and stir in a cup of water. Add soup mixture to meat, cover, and simmer for 15 minutes. Serve gravy with mashed potatoes or rice. Or over biscuits. *Serves 6 to 8.*

Big-Game Chow Mein

The following dish is a very good way to feed lots of folks on a little game. I've made it with several kinds of meat, but if you use elk or moose, I recommend round steak or some similar cut. Usually, the "instant" tenderization method recommended below will be sufficient for properly cured or frozen meat—but if the meat is very tough, consider marinating it overnight or longer.

- 1½ **pounds round steak from elk or moose**
- 3 **stalks of celery, sliced crossways**
- 1 **medium-to-large onion, sliced long ways**
- 6 **ounces fresh mushrooms, sliced**
- 1 **red bell pepper, sliced thinly**
- 1 **can bean sprouts, drained (14-ounce size)**
- 1 **can bamboo shoots, drained (8-ounce size)**
- 1 **can sliced water chestnuts, drained (8-ounce size)**
- 1 **cup beef bouillon (made with bouillon cube)**
- ½ **cup soy sauce**
- 2½ **tablespoons cornstarch dissolved in ½ cup water**
- **salt and pepper**
- **peanut oil**
- **chow mein noodles**
- **meat tenderizer (if needed)**

Sprinkle the steak with instant meat tenderizer, then beat it with a meat mallet or the edge of a plate. Let the meat sit for a while under refrigeration, then cut it, against the grain, into thin strips.

In a large frying pan, heat a little peanut oil and stir-fry the meat. Put the meat into a larger pot (I use a Dutch oven) and quickly sauté the onions, mushrooms, celery, and red bell pepper in the frying pan. Mix the cornstarch solution, beef bouillon, and soy sauce, then stir into the sautéed vegetables. Put the sautéed vegetables into the pot with the meat, then add the bamboo shoots and water

chestnuts. Bring to boil, stir, salt and pepper to taste, reduce heat, cover, and simmer for 30 minutes. Add bean sprouts, then simmer for another 15 or 20 minutes. Serve with chow mein noodles. *Serves 4 or 5.*

Moose Pie

- 2 **pounds of moose steak, cubed**
- 2 **tablespoons cooking oil**
- **salt**
- **pepper**
- 2 **cups water**
- 1 **medium onion, diced**
- 2 **teaspoons flour**
- ¼ **teaspoon dried basil**
- ⅛ **teaspoon nutmeg**
- ¼ **teaspoon thyme**
- 1 **tablespoon Worcestershire sauce**
- **paprika**
- **frozen pie crust (or other suitable pastry)**

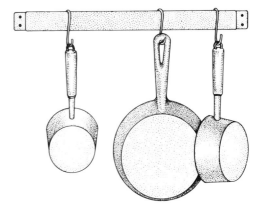

Put 2 cups of water into a small pan and heat to boiling. In a frying pan, brown meat in hot oil. Salt and pepper to taste. Add boiling water, cover tightly, reduce heat, and simmer for 45 minutes. (If the meat is very tender, reduce simmer time; if it's tough, add another 30 minutes or so.) Add onion, basil, nutmeg, and thyme. Mix flour with a little water, stir until smooth, and add to steak. Add Worcestershire sauce and pour it all into a suitable round casserole dish. Cut the pastry into strips and criss-cross it over the meat mixture. Sprinkle with paprika. Place casserole dish in the middle of the oven and bake at 400 degrees for 30 minutes—or until pie crust is done. *Serves 4 to 6.*

Elk with Flaming Bourbon

Most people enjoy a dish if this sort, made with flaming whiskey or brandy. This one is easy, as well as good.

> **2 pounds tender elk steak, cut ½ inch thick**
> **⅓ cup bourbon**
> **⅓ cup butter**
> **½ cup chicken broth**
> **½ cup cream**
> **salt and pepper**

If your meat is not tender, either marinate it overnight or treat it with a commercial meat tenderizer before cooking it.

Warm the bourbon in a small saucepan. Melt the butter in a large frying pan. On high heat, brown the steaks for 3 or 4 minutes on each side. Pour out the butter. Reduce heat. Pour in the warm bourbon and ignite it with a long match. Shake the pan while the bourbon burns off. Put the steaks into a heated platter serving. Add chicken broth, salt, and pepper. Stir. Add the cream, stirring until gravy thickens. Pour the gravy over the steaks. Eat while hot. *Serves 4 to 6.*

Steak Diane (or Jutland Moose)

I got the following recipe, and good information, from an article by Jack Denton Scott, which was published in the October 1967 *Sports Afield*. As Scott explained, "Diane is Goddess of the Hunt, and steaks cooked in her name could make hunting as popular as sex." I first had them in Copenhagen in the home of a Danish friend who

was given a strip of sirloin, well aged, of what they call elk and we know as moose. I had been to Jutland with him to look at the fishing streams and had come to respect his Danish way with food . . . and was eagerly anticipating this 'game' dinner he mentioned. I wasn't disappointed. Here is the recipe as I saw it:

2 boned 1 ½-inch strip sirloins
8 tablespoons butter
½ clove garlic
2 shallots, minced
1 tablespoon parsley, minced
1 tablespoon Worcestershire sauce

"Slice each steak in half horizontally and flatten between sheets of wax paper with wooden mallet or side of cleaver until about a quarter inch thick. In half the butter melted in frypan, quickly sauté the steaks 20 seconds on each side; then remove from heat. Melt remaining butter in chafing dish on sideboard in dining room and stir in all the remaining ingredients, removing the garlic when it is browned. Stir constantly with wooden spoon until sauce is well blended and very hot. Now add the steaks and cook them in the sauce, turning constantly, two or three minutes. They should be pink-rare and served immediately on warm plates. We had

Moose Headcheese

A lot of so-called gourmets have already put in their votes for the 'ultimate' cuisine, but I'd say that if you haven't eaten moose headcheese, you haven't eaten. I discovered this delicacy quite by accident once when, after flying around over the treetops along the Little Gerstle River in Alaska, I got marooned overnight in a cabin that had a small airstrip alongside. We were hunting a murderer who had axed a couple of drinking buddies, and the F.B.I. told us that if we would fly over these woods, the murderer would get nervous and come out. Damned if he didn't, a couple of days later— and I think he got hung. Anyway, in this cabin was a Scandinavian lady named Tecla, making moose headcheese. The head was that of a cow with long ears and a bulbous nose. The hide had been removed and what was left had been

scrubbed as clean as the driven snow. The moose's head was so big that Tecla had put it in a washtub out in the yard, where she boiled it until the meat fell off the bone.

The teeth, jaws, and skull were then fished out and thrown to a disappointed-looking sled dog. More cooking followed, until the chunks of meat were tender, then salt and pepper added. This mixture was put into shallow pans and placed in a cache where the bears couldn't get at it. When cooled, it was a jellied meat that could be sliced and eaten cold, or fried in grease or bear fat. Bull moose heads work just as well but Tecla said that you have to knock off the horns because they won't go into a washtub.

—C. E. Gillham, *Field & Stream*

crusty bread, a hot Danish potato salad and chilled Algerian red wine. Although red wine is not supposed to be served cold, I appreciated it this way. One of our California or New York State dry reds would have been better. But I had no complaints. *Serves 4.*"

Tenderloin of Elk with Mushrooms

This dish calls for elk, but it can be made from any tenderloin or other cuts of very good meat.

Meat and Marinade
 2 pounds of elk tenderlion, cut ½ inch thick
 Worcestershire sauce
 ¼ cup butter or margarine
 salt to taste
Mushrooms and Sauce
 8 ounces fresh mushrooms
 ¼ cup butter or margarine
 juice from ½ lemon
 1 teaspoon onion juice
 ½ teaspoon garlic juice
 ¼ cup chopped parsley
 1 teaspoon Worcestershire sauce
 ½ teaspoon salt
Garnish
 slices from ½ lemon (left over from above)
 fresh parsley sprigs

Cut tenderloin about ½ inch thick. Stick fork into each piece several times. Put in suitable container and sprinkle heavily with Worcestershire sauce. Let marinate for several hours, turning and sprinkling from time to time.

To prepare the mushrooms and sauce, heat the butter in a pan. Stir in the juice from lemon, onion, and garlic. Add mushrooms and sauté for a few minutes. Add salt, Worcestershire sauce, and parsley. Keep warm while tenderloin is cooking.

Heat your skillet. Salt the meat to taste. Melt ¼ cup of butter in the skillet and cook the tenderloin steaks quickly on high heat. Three minutes on each side will be plenty, if skillet is hot. Arrange tenderloin slices on serving platter, pour on mushrooms with sauce, and garnish with parsley and lemon slices. Eat while hot with baked potato and tossed salad. *Serves 4 to 6.*

Moose Ribs

If you've got 3 or 4 pounds of moose ribs and a pressure cooker, try this one from Alaska Department of Fish and Game's *Wildlife Cookbook,* which is now out of print:

"Place the ribs, bone down, in pressure cooker. Lay strips of fat salt pork over top of meat. Add ½ cup water and 2 or 3 sliced onions. Cook at medium pressure for ½ hour. Remove ribs and place in an iron skillet. Mix 1 tablespoon brown sugar and a pinch of dry mustard with fat stock from the pressure cooker, and pour it over the meat. Place in moderate oven, uncovered for ½ hour, or until crisply browned, basting frequently with pan juices."

Slow Oven Barbecued Elk

Here's a good recipe that takes about 12 hours to cook, but it's worth it and is a fun project for a cold, rainy day.

The Meat
  elk roast (5 to 7 pounds)
  ¼ cup cooking oil
The Sauce
  2 medium onions, chopped
  2 cloves garlic, minced
  juice from 2 lemons
  1 can tomato sauce (12-ounce size)
  ¼ cup catsup
  ¼ cup vinegar
  1 tablespoon Worcestershire sauce
  ⅛ teaspoon Tabasco sauce
  2 tablespoons brown sugar
  2 tablespoons salt
  ½ teaspoon dry mustard
  ½ teaspoon pepper
  ½ teaspoon paprika
  ½ cup water

Preheat oven to 200 degrees. Heat cooking oil in a skillet and brown roast on all sides. Put the roast in a suitable baking dish, with a cover. Sauté the onion in the frying pan, then add all other ingredients. Simmer for a few minutes, stirring. Pour the sauce over the roast. Bake for 12 hours. Check from time to time to see if the roast needs water added, and turn in the sauce or baste well. *Serves 10 to 12.*

The Biggest Game?

Hippopotamus meat is highly sought in some parts of Africa. Rhinoceros meat is edible, and better then elephant (which is said to be tough and leathery). Elephant feet and trunk, on the other hand, are delicacies.

Another large animal, the whale, has been hunted around the world and is still eaten by the Japanese and the Eskimos. According to *Larousse Gastronomique*, a French work, "Whale meat was not greatly esteemed by our grandfathers, but they did set some store by the tongue of the animal, usually salted, and Ambroise Pare says that 'it is tender and delicious.' They also much appreciated whale fat which they ate 'during Lent, with peas.' "

Elk Cutlets

  2 pounds elk cutlets
  salt
  pepper
  2 eggs, whisked
  flour
  dry bread crumbs, fine
  cooking oil
  water
  juice from 1 large lemon
  1 tablespoon Worcestershire sauce

Salt and pepper the cutlets. Roll them in flour, dip in beaten egg, then roll in bread crumbs. Heat oil in a large frying pan and brown some of the cutlets. Carefully set the cutlets to drain on absorbent paper and brown the rest. Pour off excess oil. To 1 cup water add the juice of 1 lemon and 1 tablespoon Worcestershire sauce. Stir. Pour this liquid over the cutlets. Add enough water to almost cover the meat. Put the lid on the frying pan. Simmer for 2 hours, or until meat is tender. Serve to plates directly from frying pan, and handle with care. Top individual servings with gravy from frying pan. *Serves 4 or 5.*

Cubed Elk Tenderloin over Rice

Here's a great little dish that is very easy to prepare. I normally make it with a very tender cut of meat, but it can also be made with other cuts that have been tenderized or marinated.

> 2 pounds elk tenderloin or other tender game meat
> 1 medium onion, diced
> 2 tablespoons cooking oil
> ½ cup chili sauce
> 2 tablespoons flour
> ½ teaspoon salt
> ⅛ teaspoon pepper
> water
> rice or noodles (cooked separately)

Cut the meat into 1-inch cubes and dice the onion. Add oil to skillet, heat, and sauté the onions. Brown the meat. Then add 1 cup hot water to the meat and onions. Cook for about 30 minutes. In a bowl, mix ½ cup of cold water, chili sauce, salt, and pepper. Stir in flour thoroughly. Add to meat mixture, increase heat, and stir while bringing to a boil. Reduce heat and simmer for about 30 minutes. Serve over rice or noodles. *Serves 4 to 6.*

Easy Dutch Oven Elk Bourguignon

> 2 pounds good elk steak
> 1 can cream of mushroom soup (10 ¾ ounces)
> 1 small can mushrooms, chopped
> 1 package of onion soup mix (1¼ ounces)
> ¼ cup bacon drippings or cooking oil
> ¾ cup red wine
> ⅛ teaspoon black pepper
> water
> rice

In a Dutch oven or large frying pan, brown the meat in bacon fat or oil. Add ¾ cup of water. Stir in mushroom soup. Add mushrooms, onion soup mix, pepper, and red wine. Cover and cook on low heat for 3 hours, or until the meat is tender. If necessary, thicken the gravy with flour stirred into mixture; go slowly, adding only a pinch or two of flour at the time. Serve over rice. *Serves 4 to 6.*

Variations: This dish can also be cooked in the oven at 350 degrees. First, brown the meat and mix the ingredients in a large frying pan, as above. Then dump it into a casserole dish, cover, and put it into a preheated oven.

Creamy Elk

- 2 pounds elk meat, sliced into thin strips
- 1 can cream of onion soup (10¾-ounce size)
- 1 can cream of cheese (Nacho) soup (10¾-ounce size)
- 1 can cream of mushroom soup (10¾ ounce-size)
- 1 teaspoon salt
- ½ teaspoon pepper
- 4 ounces elbow macaroni (uncooked weight)
- 2 cups mashed Nacho chips

Cook the macaroni according to directions on the package. Drain. Preheat oven to 350 degrees. Brown meat in large frying pan. Add all soups, salt, pepper, and cooked macaroni. Stir until mixed. Pour into a casserole dish and bake for 45 minutes. Sprinkle Nacho chips on top of casserole and bake for another 5 minutes. *Serves 4 to 6.*

Stuffed Elk Steak

Here's a good one that was sent to me by the Alaska Department of Fish & Game in Juneau:

- 2 elk club steaks, cut 1-inch thick
- 1½ slices of day-old bread
- ½ teaspoon salt
- 2 teaspoons green pepper, chopped finely
- 2 teaspoons minced onion
- 2 teaspoons celery, chopped finely
- salt and pepper to taste
- flour to dredge
- 2 tablespoons butter
- ½ cup water

To make a dressing, break the bread into small pieces. Mix in the salt, green pepper, onion, and celery. Set aside. Salt and pepper the steaks to taste and coat with flour. With a very sharp, thin knife, cut slits at least halfway through the steaks, forming a pocket. Stuff the steaks with the dressing.

Melt the butter in the bottom of a pressure cooker and brown the steaks. Add water and cook for 20 minutes at 10 pounds pressure. *Serves 4 or 5.*

Elkburger Quiche

The measures given below fill two standard-size (9-inch) pie crusts. This dish freezes nicely, so you can make up several, cook, cover with aluminum foil, and store in your freezer.

- 1 pound ground elk meat
- 4 slices bacon
- 1 medium onion, diced
- 2 cups milk
- 2 eggs

2 cups cheddar cheese, shredded
1 teaspoon Worcestershire sauce
¼ teaspoon pepper
salt to taste
3 tablespoons flour
2 frozen, uncooked pie crusts (9-inch)

Preheat oven to 400 degrees. Fry bacon in skillet until crisp, remove it, and crumble. Brown onions and set aside with bacon. Brown elk meat. Mix in onions, bacon, flour, salt, and pepper. In a bowl, mix eggs, milk, and Worcestershire sauce. Add about half of the shredded cheese. Combine with elk meat mixture and spoon or pour it all into the pie crusts, dividing equally and spreading evenly. Top with remaining cheese. Bake for 25 to 30 minutes. *Makes 8 to 12 servings.*

2 medium onions, diced
8 ounces mushrooms, sliced
½ cup dry red wine
½ cup strong black coffee
salt and pepper to taste
1 cup of sour cream

Cut meat into 1-inch cubes and marinate overnight, or longer, in 1 cup of water mixed with 1 cup of red wine vinegar.

When you're ready to cook, preheat oven to 300 degrees. Melt the butter in a frying pan. Sauté the onions and mushrooms; set aside. Roll the meat in flour and brown it. Put meat, onions, and mushrooms into a large casserole dish that has a cover. Pour in ½ cup red wine and ½ cup of black coffee. Salt and pepper to taste. Bake for 3 hours. Stir in the sour cream. Turn the oven off, then put the casserole back into the still-hot oven for a few minutes before serving. This dish goes well with noodles. *Serves 4 to 6.*

Maxwell House Moose

2 pounds round moose steak, or other
    suitable meat, cubed
1 cup of water
1 cup of red wine vinegar
flour
1 stick margarine or butter

38

CARIBOU and ANTELOPE

As table fare, the pronghorn antelope is one of the very best game animals, and many people rate it above all other. The average antelope is only about half the weight of a full-grown deer, and it doesn't present as many field-dressing and handling problems. This may help account for its popularity as table fare! As pointed out in the chapter on dressing game, however, a scent gland on the rump, which the antelope uses to signal danger, is quite powerful and should be avoided.

The caribou is also considered by some hunters to be the best of all game meat! It is rather fine-grained in texture. The animal looks large because of its huge rack of antlers, but it is a good deal smaller than a moose or elk. Students of old-world cooking should note that the caribou is the same animal as the European reindeer. Anyone interested in making a complete study of caribou cookery should look into the culture of the Lapps, a people who depend on the animal and use every part of it.

Most of the recipes listed in the venison chapters will do nicely for either antelope or caribou. Or try one of the following:

Rock Springs Antelope Roast

The recipe below rates among my favorites, and I based it on one that I found in a book called *Cooking in Wyoming*. It was submitted to that work by Mrs. W. Robert Dubois of

Cheyenne. She said, "Rob got this recipe from another hunter, who obtained it in turn from a Rock Springs chef. The story goes that he had to ply him with liquor before he'd give up this recipe."

The Meat
　　6- to 8-pound roast—antelope or other game meat
　　¼ pound butter
　　1 can tomatoes (1-pound, 13-ounce size)
　　allspice
　　bay leaf
　　salt and pepper
The Sauce
　　fry out ¼ pound fat pork, ground*
　　⅛ pound butter
　　1 cup chopped celery
　　1 8-ounce can mushrooms (or fresh mushrooms)
　　2 cloves garlic, chopped
　　1 cup chopped green pepper
　　1 cup chopped onion
　　1 pint red wine

Make the sauce first. Cook all ingredients for 1½ hours. Add a little water as sauce cooks down. Keep warm.

Preheat oven to 300 degrees. Heat the butter in a stove top Dutch oven and brown the antelope roast. Add the spices and seasoning to taste, along with the tomatoes. Cover and bake for a total of 5 hours, but after 2 hours start basting with the sauce.

Note: I always use ¼ pound of salt bacon. I fry it crisp, then crumble it. The grease left in the frying pan is discarded. If you don't have salt pork handy, try cured bacon.

Baste often, using all the sauce during the first hour of basting. Then continue basting with pan juices. Also, turn the roast after the first 3 hours. *Serves 12 to 16.*

Caribou Steak in Sour Cream

Here's a very good, easy recipe that can be used with caribou or other game meat. The only problem is whether or not the meat is tough. I am recommending meat tenderizer (if needed) for this one, but remember that your favorite tenderizing marinade can also be used. For flavor, I really prefer the dish without either marinade or tenderizer. If a marinade it really needed, I use ordinary milk.

　　2 to 3 pounds round steak of caribou (¾-inch thick)
　　salt and pepper
　　meat tenderizer, if needed
　　flour
　　½ cup peanut oil
　　1 medium onion, diced
　　8 ounces fresh mushrooms, if available
　　½ cup cour cream
　　hot water

If needed, sprinkle meat tenderizer over the meat, following the directions on your tenderizer package. Sprinkle meat with salt and pepper. (If tenderizer is used, you can cut back on the salt.) Sprinkle the meat with flour and pound it with the edge of a heavy plate. Add flour from time to time while pounding the steak. Rotate the steak 90 degrees, add more flour, and pound crossways.

Choose a frying pan that has a cover and heat the oil in it. Sauté the chopped onion and mushrooms for a few minutes, then drain and set aside. Brown the steak on both sides. Pour off most of the oil. Add boiling water, onion, and mushrooms. Stir in sour cream. Bring to heat but do not boil. Reduce heat, cover, and simmer for about 2 ½ to 3 hours, or until very tender. Check the moisture level from time to time, and add more water if needed. Be sure to have rice or biscuits for the gravy. *Serves 4 to 6.*

Easy Jalapeño Antelope

Once I got on a jag of cooking various kinds of meats with red currant jelly, mayhaw jelly, and so on. From all this came one of my favorite of the "easy" dishes, made in a crockpot.

> antelope roast, 4 to 6 pounds
> salt and pepper
> ½ cup water
> ½ cup red hot jalapeño pepper jelly

Salt and pepper the roast and put it into a crockpot. Pour in half a cup of water and dump the jelly directly atop the roast. Turn on low heat and cook for 8 or 9 hours. Slice the roast and serve with crockpot gravy. *Serves 8 to 12.*

Note: Water and flour can be added to the pot juices to make and thicken more gravy, if needed.

Caribou Stew

> 2 pounds stew meat
> ¼ cup butter or cooking oil
> 1 medium onion, diced
> 2 cups stewed tomatoes (or canned tomatoes, 16-ounce can)
> 1 teaspoon salt
> ¼ teaspoon pepper
> 1 cup sour cream
> mashed boiled potatoes or rice

Heat the oil in a large frying pan (one that has a cover) or Dutch oven. Sauté the onions for 5 minutes, then add the meat and brown it. Add the tomatoes, salt, and pepper. Bring to heat, then add the sour cream. Reduce heat, cover, and simmer, very slowly, for 3 hours. (Add a little water if needed, depending partly on whether the lid fits tightly.)

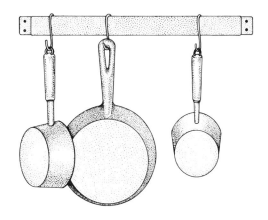

Serve with rice or mashed potatoes. *Serves 4 to 6.*

Variation: For a little more zip, which I really prefer, try two 10-ounce cans of Rotel instead of the tomatoes.

Antelope Ragout

If you have dropped a good antelope and have taken proper care of the meat, the better cuts will need no marinade for this recipe.

> **3 pounds good antelope meat, cut into 1½-inch cubes**
> **½ pound bacon**
> **1½ quarts water**
> **1 can tomato soup (10¾-ounce size)**
> **8 to 10 ounces fresh mushrooms, sliced**
> **3 medium to large onions, chopped**
> **5 cloves garlic, minced**
> **¼ cup beer**
> **2 tablespoons sour mash bourbon**
> **1 tablespoon salt**
> **¼ teaspoon pepper**
> **1 teaspoon curry powder**

Cook the bacon in a large frying pan. Remove bacon and crumble. Brown the meat in bacon drippings and set aside to drain. Pour off about half the bacon drippings. Brown onions and garlic in the bacon drippings left in the pan. Add water, tomato soup, beer, bourbon, salt, pepper, and curry powder. Bring to boil, add browned meat and crumbled bacon, cover, reduce, and simmer for 1 hour. Then add the mushrooms and simmer for another 10 minutes. *Serves 6 to 8.*

Antelope Cutlets in Sherry

> **2 pounds boneless antelope cutlets, ½ inch thick**
> **salt**
> **pepper**

Eskimo Dinner Party

The host's wife is busy boiling meat from the newly caught game over her blubber lamp, and when everybody has had enough of the frozen delicacies, they start in on the steaming walrus or seal meat. The polite guests fart and belch to show how well they are digesting the treats of the house. They continue eating until they are too gorged to get another bite down. If a guest gets tired, he will simply go to sleep where he sits and start in on the meal again when he wakes up. If it becomes apparent that the provisions of the house are about to give out, another hunter will stand up and ask to be allowed to show what his house has to offer. Thus the party goes from house to house, and the feast may last for days.

—Peter Freuchen's *Book of the Eskimo*

2 eggs
flour
dry bread crumbs, fine
cooking oil
juice from 1 lemon
½ cup dry sherry

Whisk an egg. Heat cooking oil in a large frying pan that has a lid. Salt and pepper cutlets to taste. Roll in flour. Dip in egg, then roll in bread crumbs. Brown cutlets in frying pan. Add water to pan until cutlets are almost covered. Stir in the juice of one lemon. Cover tightly and simmer for 2 hours, or until meat is tender. Add sherry and simmer for another 10 minutes. Thicken the gravy with a little flour and serve it over cutlets. *Serves 4 or 5.*

Herb Roast

Here's a very good, rather exacting, recipe that I got from the South Dakota Department of Game, Fish, and Parks. It was published in their book, *Cooking the Sportsman's Harvest*. Frankly, I don't usually get too excited about herb dishes, but I enjoy the flavor of this one and have a yearning for it from time to time. Be sure to try it with antelope, caribou, or other good meat:

3- to 4-pound rump, loin, or rib roast
1 tablespoon cooking oil
½ teaspoon salt
¼ teaspoon pepper
¼ cup flour
2 teaspoons marjoram

1 teaspoon dried thyme
2 teaspoons dried rosemary
1 teaspoon powdered garlic
1 cup apple juice
1 cup water

Preheat oven to 325 degrees. Dry the roast and cut several slits in it, about ½ inch deep. Rub the roast well with oil, then sprinkle it with salt and pepper. Mix the flour, marjoram, thyme, rosemary, and garlic; then pat this mixture onto the roast, and stuff it into the slits. Insert a meat thermometer into the roast. Pour the apple juice and water into a shallow pan of suitable size to hold the roast. Put the roast directly into the liquid, then put, uncovered, into the oven.

Bake about 1 hour, until flour mixture adheres to meat. Baste and bake for another hour, basting several more times. The meat thermometer should read 160 degrees for medium doneness; 170 degrees for well done, according to the book cited above. (I prefer mine at 150 to 155 degrees, if I'm certain that I've got good meat.) *Serves 6 or 7.*

Antelope Stew

This is a good basic recipe that can be used with the tougher cuts of antelope and other game, such as elk or moose. If the meat is very tough and you have a pressure cooker, you might consider stewing the meat and liquids (but not the vegetables) at 15 pounds pressure for 20 minutes. But longer cooking, as described below, will usually make a very good stew. Even longer cooking in a crockpot will also work with this recipe.

>　2 pounds antelope stew meat
>　2 tablespoons cooking oil
>　½ cup beef broth
>　1 medium onion, chopped
>　1 clove garlic, minced
>　4 potatoes, quartered
>　4 carrots, cut into 1-inch segments
>　1 tablespoon vinegar
>　1 teaspoon salt
>　¼ teaspoon pepper
>　⅛ teaspoon nutmeg

Heat 2 tablespoons of cooking oil in a frying pan and brown the stew meat. Put the meat into a Dutch oven or other suitable container. In the frying pan, sauté the onion and garlic. Stir in ½ cup of beef broth, vinegar, salt, pepper, and nutmeg. Pour mixture over meat and bring to boil. Cover, reduce heat, and simmer for an hour. Add the potatoes and carrots, then simmer, covered, for another 2 hours. *Serves 4 to 6.*

Antelope Loin Chops

Here is a delicious recipe that is a switch on the usual "brown and simmer" method.

>　6 chops, about ½ inch thick
>　3 tablespoons cooking oil
>　½ cup flour
>　pepper
>　garlic salt
>　water

Pass the Salt

A mob of Indians and I were floating down the Porcupine River in the Yukon Territory when a herd of woodland caribou started across the river in front of us. We killed fourteen of them, planning to take most of the meat to the hospital in Fort Yukon, Alaska. We camped on the sandbar where we killed the caribou, and I had visions of roast ribs, fillets, and all kinds of delectable items. Instead, my companions set up a tripod of three poles over a whopping fire. In the heart of this blaze they suspended the unskinned head and neck of a caribou. Periodically they turned the thing in the leaping flames, and the burning hair stank to the aurora borealis.

After an hour of this primitive cooking, the caribou's eyes bugged out in the heat, giving the charred head an expression of great surprise. At last it was finished, and we fell to. The burned skin was scraped off. This was hard as a butcher's heart, but the meat beneath was tender and toothsome. Because I had shot eight of the caribou I was paid special honor by my companions; they gave me an eyeball. It might have tasted all right with a touch of salt.

—C. E. Gillham, *Field & Stream*

Season the chops with pepper and garlic salt. Heat cooking oil in a large frying pan that has a cover, then roll or shake chops in flour. Put chops into frying pan, cover, and cook over low heat for an hour or so, turning and adding a little water from time to time. When the meat is tender, remove the cover, increase the heat, and brown the chops.

Note: This is a good recipe to try in camp because you don't have to tote along lots of stuff for it.

Country Baked Antelope

Here's a good recipe for antelope, and for most any other kind of venison or big-game. Really tough cuts, however, should be marinated before cooking it.

2 pounds antelope steak
¼ cup of cooking oil
2 medium onions, chopped
3 tablespoons flour
water (about 3 cups)
½ cup catsup
salt and pepper
2 tablespoons sugar
1 teaspoon prepared mustard
1 ½ teaspoons chili powder
1 tablespoon Worcestershire sauce

Cut the antelope into 1-inch chunks and brown it in a frying pan containing ¼ cup of cooking oil. Remove the meat and set it aside. Sauté the onions. Add the flour and stir well. Add 3 cups of water, a little at the time, and stir until the gravy thickens. Add

the catsup, sugar, mustard, chili powder, and Worcestershire sauce. Salt and pepper to taste. Simmer for ½ hour. Turn oven to 300 degrees so that it will be ready.

Put the meat into a suitable baking dish and pour the sauce over it. Cover and bake at 300 degrees for 2 hours, or until the meat is tender. Add more water, if needed. Serve with rice or hot buscuits. *Serves 4.*

Easy Rotel Caribou

3- or 4-pound roast
1 can Rotel (10-ounce) or Mexican-style stewed tomatoes
salt to taste
1 teaspoon pepper
1 teaspoon chili powder

Put roast into a crockpot and salt to taste. Sprinkle with pepper and chili powder, then pour in Rotel. Cook on low for 9 hours. If your roast is frozen to start with, allow another hour. *Serves 6 to 8.*

39

SHEEP and GOAT, BOAR and JAVELINA

Bunching all these fine game animals into a single chapter certainly does injustice to them. They can all be excellent table fare, and therefore deserve separate chapters. But their range is limited, although some, such as the javelina, might be quite plentiful in some areas. If you are lucky enough to have these animals to hunt, try the following:

Sheep Kabobs

Get a good cut of meat for this dish and don't overcook it. You can, of course, put vegetables on the kabobs in the American patio manner, but also try the dish with meat only. The original kabob was probably cooked with meat only—and was no doubt developed with sheep or goat.

sheep loin or other very good cut
olive oil
garlic
salt

Crush two or three cloves of garlic in olive oil and let it sit for several hours. Cut the meat into bite-size pieces, put into a glass container, and pour the oil over them. Marinate for several hours. Put the meat onto a skewer and broil very close to the heat source for 5 or 6 minutes, then turn and broil the other side for a few minutes, or until the meat is ready. Sprinkle a little salt on the meat and eat.

Variation: Try these kabobs over very hot coals, basting once or twice with oil. Or baste with a mixture of melted butter and lemon juice.

Leg of Bighorn Sheep

Here's a good oven recipe that I cook with the aid of heavy duty aluminum foil.

The Meat
  leg of sheep, 4 to 6 pounds
  salt and pepper
The Marinade
  4 tablespoons vinegar
  1 cup red wine
  ½ cup olive oil
  ½ teaspon thyme
  1 teaspoon garlic salt
  2 cloves garlic, crushed
  ½ teaspoon black pepper
Basting Sauce
  ½ cup melted butter
  juice from ½ lemon

Mix the marinade ingredients. Put the meat into a suitable glass container and cover with the marinade. Refrigerate for at least a day, turning several times.

Just before you are ready to cook, preheat oven to 325 degrees. Remove the meat from the marinade and drain. Salt and pepper to taste. Put the meat into a "boat" made with heavy duty aluminum foil. (Do not close foil and do not let it touch the sides of the leg of bighorn.) Put onto a shallow baking pan, pour all of the basting sauce over the meat, and put the pan into the hot oven. Bake for 3 hours, basting from time to time with sauce and juices from the aluminum foil "boat." *Serves 8 to 12.*

Variations: This recipe can also be cooked under a broiler or over hot charcoal. In either method, be sure to baste the meat frequently. The cooking time will depend on how close you've got the meat to the heat source. Note that the aluminum foil "boat" can also be used under the broiler, but you'll need to turn the meat several times.

Rocky Mountain Bighorn Roast

I've always been fond of roast recipes that called for garlic stuck into the meat, and here's one from E. N. and Edith Sturdivant's book *Game Cookery*. As the Sturdivant's said, "Any sportsman who has eaten properly cared-for sheep will tell you that it tops

Bighorn Shank

The front shank of the bighorn sheep contains some excellent eating. Use the recipe for venison shank á la Montana on page 293.

everything for tastiness among large game animals. This is doubly true of the Rocky Mountain bighorn sheep. A chuck roast from the blade will do in the event that you have cut the loin into chops." Unfortunatley, I've never encountered the Rocky Mountain bighorn, but I did try the recipe with lesser meat. It's good, it's easy, and it doesn't require many ingredients.

> 3 or 4 pounds bighorn roast, from the loin or chuck
> 1 clove garlic
> salt
> pepper
> flour

"Wipe the roast with a damp cloth. Cut two or three gashes in the meat and insert slivers of garlic. Salt and pepper, sprinkle with flour and place uncovered in a 375- to 400-degree oven for 30 minutes to sear or brown lightly. Reduce heat to moderate (325 degrees), and roast for about 2½ hours, longer if necessary to make it tender. Gravy may be made from some of the residue in the roaster. Serve with mint jelly, potatoes, a green vegetable, and a salad of lettuce wedges and your favorite dressing."

Kurdish Goat

Here's a dish that my wife has cooked for me a number of times. It probably originated in the rugged mountain range between Iran and Russia, or in other highlands inhabited by the Kurds. This is mountain goat country.

> 1 pound cubed goat meat
> ½ pound fresh green beans, cut into ¼-inch segments
> ½ onion
> 1 clove garlic
> 1 small can tomato paste
> ⅛ teaspoon cinnamon
> salt and pepper to taste
> 2 cups long grain rice
> water
> oil

Pour a little oil into a frying pan and sauté the onions and garlic. Then sauté the meat and the green beans. Stir in the tomato paste, cinnamon, salt, and pepper. Let simmer.

Put 2 cups of rice into a large pot and cover it with about ½ inch of water. Add 2 teaspoons salt. Bring to a rolling boil, then pour into a colander. Don't rinse the pot. Cover the bottom of the pot with oil. Put on low heat and spoon in a layer of rice. Heat until the oil bubbles through the rice. Spoon a layer of meat and bean mixture over rice. Then add another layer of rice, and alternate until it's all gone. End with a layer of rice. Toward the end, form the mixture into a mound. Take a long spoon and make a hole through the middle of the mound all the way down to the bottom of the pot. Make several similar holes spaced out between the center and the rim. Cover the dish and simmer for 30 minutes.

After 30 minutes, dip the pot for a few seconds into a larger container (or sinkful) of cold water. Eat while hot. If this dish works out properly, the bottom layer will be somewhat crusty, and this is considered to be the best part. *Serves 4 to 6.*

Crockpot Goat with Beer

Meats that are slow-cooked in crockpots are usually tender and full of flavor. It's easy, and the meat doesn't have to be "browned in oil."

America's First Big-Game Hunters

Many thousands of years ago, mammoth ranged the plains of North America, while mastodon browsed along the deciduous forest edges of the Southeast. On the trail of these and other game, hunters from the Old World made their way across the Bering Strait land bridge into Alaska. From there they followed interglacial corridors down into the New World, exploiting the rich environment so successfully that soon their presence was felt as far south as the tip of South America.

We know that these early Indians hunted mammoth because at places like the Blackwater Draw site in New Mexico, prehistoric spear points have been found among the bones of the mammoths they killed.

—Evan Peacock, *Mississippi Outdoors*

---

4 pounds of no-fat goat meat
6 strips of thick-sliced bacon
½ cup flour
1½ tablespoons salt
1 tablespoon paprika
1 tablespoon black pepper
12 small onions, peeled (golf-ball size)
1 pound fresh mushrooms, whole or sliced
1 can beer (12-ounce)
1 teaspoon sugar
1 tablespoon vinegar
½ teaspoon dried thyme leaves
2 small bay leaves

Cut the meat into 1-inch cubes. Cut thick-sliced bacon into 1-inch squares. Put flour, salt, paprika, and pepper into a bag and shake the meat in it.

Place bacon, onions, and half of the mushrooms into the bottom of the crockpot. Add the meat from flour bag. (If there's any flour left in the bag, dump it atop the meat.) Add the rest of the mushrooms. Mix beer, vinegar, sugar, thyme, and bay leaves. Pour over meat. Cover crockpot, turn to low heat, and cook for 10 hours—while you're out hunting or fishing.

This dish goes will over rice or noodles. *Serves 8 or 9.*

Goat Goulash

I'm fond of this dish with most any reasonable meat, and I especially like it with goat. I make it with fresh tomatoes, but of course canned tomatoes can also be used.

3 pounds goat stew meat
cooking oil
7 or 8 fresh tomatoes, peeled and
    quartered (see text below)
2 medium onions, diced
1 bell pepper, diced
4 or 5 tablespoons paprika
1½ teaspoons salt
½ teaspoon black pepper
¾ to 1 cup lemon juice
water for marinade

Put the goat meat into a suitable glass container, cover with good water, and stir in ½ cup of lemon juice. Cover the dish and put into the refrigerator for 2 days, stirring from time to time.

When you're ready to cook, heat a little oil in a frying pan and brown the meat. Set aside. Sauté the onion and peppers.

To peel the fresh tomatoes easily, bring some water to boil in a pan and drop the tomatoes into it for a few minutes. Then cool and peel. Quarter the tomatoes and put them into a pot of suitable size. (I use my Dutch oven.) Add the meat, onions, peppers, salt,

pepper, and paprika. Stir, bring to boil, reduce heat, cover, and simmer for 3 hours. This dish goes well over hot noodles or rice. *Serves 6 or more.*

Wild Boar Chops

If you've got an older hog, it will be best to marinate the chops in cold water with a little baking soda for 24 hours.

2 pounds of boar chops, about ½ inch
    thick
peanut oil
salt and pepper
egg
½ cup milk
fine bread crumbs
5 or 6 green onions with tops
1 tablespoon parsley, chopped
8 ounces fresh mushrooms
2 beef boullion cubes dissolved in 2
    cups of water
juice from ½ lemon
flour (optional)

Salt and pepper the chops to taste. Mix egg and milk, then dip the chops in the mixture. Roll in bread crumbs. Fry the breaded chops in hot peanut oil over medium heat until they are brown on both sides. It may be necessary to brown the chops in two or more batches. After browning, transfer the chops to a stove-top Dutch oven.

While the chops are browning, mince the onions, including about half the green tops, and sauté them in a suitable pan. Add the parsley and sliced mushrooms. Simmer for a few minutes. Add the boullion solution and bring to boil, reduce, and simmer. Add the lemon juice. Salt and pepper to taste. Stir the sauce and and pour it over the chops. Bring to boil, cover, reduce heat, and simmer for an hour. You may need to add a little water, especially if the lid doesn't fit tightly. Remove chops to a heated serving platter. Thicken gravy with a little flour, if necessary. *Serves 4 to 6.*

Seminole Wild Boar Stew

The following dish is from a book called *Seminole Indian Recipes*, by Maria Polvay. It cooks up into a rather thin stew, almost a soup with chunks of meat in it, which, I understand, is characteristic of many Seminole dishes. The recipe below will *serve 6 to 8.*

> 3 or 4 pounds of wild boar
>   hindquarters cut into 2-inch cubes
> 2 teaspoons salt
> ground pepper to taste
> 2½ quarts water
> 2 medium yellow onions, peeled and
>   quartered
> 2 ribs celery, sliced into 1-inch pieces
> 2 carrots, sliced into 1-inch pieces
> 2 tablespoons apple cider vinegar, or
>   more, to taste
> 3 tablespoons flour
> 3 tablespoons lard or shortening

As the book instructed, "Place cut up meat into a large heavy kettle. Add salt, pepper, and water. Simmer uncovered for 25 minutes, skimming the foam off the top. Add onions, celery, and carrots. Bring to boil, reduce heat, cover and cook over low heat for 2-3 hours or until meat is tender. Add the apple cider vinegar; stir well. Remove from heat and set aside for 2-3 hours. Skim off fat.

"In a small saucepan combine flour and lard and cook, stirring often until golden brown. Add 1 cup of the cooking liquid or water if the liquid has cooked down too much. Whisk until smooth. Add to the meat, bring to boil; reduce heat and simmer, stirring occasionally until slightly thickened. Serve in soup plates."

Note: The "wild boar" specified in the above recipe is not the European wild boar. It is most likely a feral hog, many of which roam very wild in Florida. My father called them Piney Wood Rooters. But they are indeed wild—and the Seminoles that I have seen wrestling alligators down in the Everglades, and who have never signed a peace treaty with the United States, can call these rooters anything they want to.

Braised Leg of Wild Boar with Sweet and Sour Sauce

Here's a good one from Jack Ubaldi's *Meat Book*. It's a bit long, but the wild boar isn't everyday fare, and it's worth extra trouble. Ubaldi said, "I always think of wild boar in the mountains of Umbria where I was born, but boar can also be hunted in the United

States in game preserves in Tennessee. Boar is cooked in exactly the same manner as venison, but the marinating time, 7 or 8 days, is considerably longer. The sweet and sour sauce complements the taste of the meat."

The Boar
- 1 leg of wild boar, 8 to 10 pounds
- preserving marinade (below)
- 4 tablespoons butter
- 4 tablespoons oil
- 2 onions, sliced thin
- 2 carrots, peeled and sliced
- 2 celery stalks, sliced
- salt
- freshly ground pepper
- 1 cup dry red wine
- 2 cups veal stock

The Sweet and Sour Sauce
- 6 tablespoons sugar
- 2 garlic cloves, peeled and crushed
- 1 bay leaf
- ¼ cup vinegar
- 4 tablespoons grated unsweetened chocolate
- 1 tablespoon potato starch or a roux of 1 tablespoon flour, 1 tablespoon butter (optional)
- ¼ cup white raisins
- 15 dried prunes soaked in Madeira
- candied citron
- candied orange peel

"Remove the skin from the ham, score it, and place in a large terrine or crock. Cover with the cooked, cooled marinade (see instructions below) and place in the refrigerator for 7 to 8 days, turning the ham at least twice a day.

"Heat the butter and oil in the bottom of a large flameproof casserole and add the sliced vegetables. Cook for 5 minutes, then add the boar and brown it on all sides with the vegetables. Sprinkle with salt and pepper and add the wine. Reduce to half and add the veal stock. Partially cover the casserole and place in a preheated 350-degree oven for about 3 hours, or until the thermometer registers 170 degrees.

"Remove the meat to a serving platter and keep warm; defat the juices from the roast.

"Make the sweet and sour sauce: Dissolve the sugar in a saucepan with the garlic and bay leaf. When it has turned a golden color, add the vinegar. The sugar will congeal, but keep stirring it with a wooden spoon until it dissolves again. Add the chocolate, bring to a boil, lower the heat, and cook until the chocolate is completely melted. Add 1 cup of the juices from the roast and stir well. Strain into a clean saucepan.

"If you feel that the sauce is too thin, thicken with potato starch or a roux of flour and butter. Simmer the sauce until it is the correct density. Add the raisins and prunes, then the candied citron and orange peel. Slice the boar and serve the sauce on the side. *Serves 14 to 16*."

Here are Jack Ubaldi's comments, recipe, and instructions for the marinade: "This cooked marinade is for hunters who have bagged some big game and are without freezer space to preserve it. If kept in a large crock in a cool place, this marinade should preserve your game for months. Double this recipe for large quantities of meat."

Preserving Marinade
- ½ pound of lard or Crisco
- 1 pound onions, chopped coarse
- 1 pound carrots, peeled and chopped coarse
- 1 pound celery, peeled and chopped coarse
- small bunch of parsley, chopped coarse
- 2 bay leaves
- ¼ cup chopped fresh basil leaves or 2 tablespoons dried basil
- 1 whole head garlic, crushed but not peeled
- 3 tablespoons dried thyme
- 1 teaspoon whole cloves
- 1 tablespoon salt
- 2 quarts wine vinegar
- 1 quart red wine

"In a large casserole, heat the lard and add the onions, carrots, and celery. Cook until soft but not brown. Add the remaining ingredients, let come to a boil, lower the heat, and simmer for 45 minutes. Remove from the heat and cool completely. Place the meat in a large crock and cover with marinade, adding water if necessary. Cover the crock tightly. Keep in a cool place. This marinade may be reused by reboiling it and storing it in sterilized jars."

Javelina Chops Parmesan

The top weight of a javelina is about 50 pounds, and the "pork chops" are therefore smaller than those from a mature domestic hog. So, allow 3 or 4 chops per person.

- 12 javelina chops (or slices of javelina "ham")
- peanut oil
- salt and pepper
- juice of 1 lemon
- 1 can cream of celery soup (10¾-ounce size)
- ⅓ cup Italian bread crumbs
- ½ cup Parmesan cheese

Squeeze the lemon juice over the chops and refrigerate for several hours.

When you are ready to cook, preheat oven to 350 degrees. Salt and pepper the chops to taste. Heat a little oil in a frying pan. Brown the chops, then transfer them to an oven-proof pan. Cover with celery soup, spreading it out smoothly. Sprinkle with bread crumbs, then with Parmesan cheese. Bake for 40 minutes. *Serves 3 or 4.*

Sweet and Sour Javelina

- 2 pounds javelina meat, cut into 1-inch cubes
- cooking oil
- salt and pepper
- 1 cup beef broth
- 1 green pepper, sliced
- 1 medium onion, diced
- 1 can pineapple chunks and juice (8-ounce size)
- juice from 1 small lemon
- ½ cup brown sugar
- ¼ cup apple cider vinegar
- 2 tablespoons soy sauce

2 tablespoons cornstarch
1 teaspoon dry mustard
rice (cooked separately)

Add a little oil to a large frying pan and brown the javelina. Add salt and pepper to taste. Pour the beef broth over the meat and simmer until the meat is tender, adding a little water from time to time.

Mix the cornstarch and brown sugar. In a separate bowl, combine the pineapple juice, lemon juice, soy sauce, and mustard, then stir in the cornstarch and brown sugar mixture. Pour over the meat a little at a time, stirring well. Add pineapple chunks, diced onion, and sliced pepper. Let simmer for a few minutes, then serve over rice. *Serves 4 to 6.*

Javelina and Sauerkraut

I got the idea for this recipe from Captain James A. Smith's book *Dress 'Em Out*. I recommend that the javelina be marinated in milk overnight, partly because too many people believe, often incorrectly, that the javelina is strong. Anyhow, if the changes I have made are for the worst, I hearby clear Captain Smith of any responsibility.

2 pounds javelina chops
cooking oil
salt and pepper
1 quart sauerkraut (canned will do)
5 or 6 medium-sized potatoes
milk marinade (optional)

Put the chops into a glass container and cover with milk. Marinate overnight, or longer, in the refrigerator.

When you are ready to cook, preheat oven to 325 degrees. Drain the meat, salt and pepper it to taste, and brown it in a little cooking oil in a stove-top Dutch oven. (You'll have to brown the meat in two or more batches, so you can also use a frying pan if you choose and later transfer the meat to the Dutch oven.) Put all the browned meat into the Dutch oven and dump the sauerkraut on top of it. Cook in the oven for an hour.

Peel the potatoes and cut them in half. Sprinkle the potato halves with salt and pepper, then arrange them atop the sauerkraut. Cover the pot tightly and bake for another hour, or until the potatoes are done. *Serves 4 to 6.*

40

BONUS EATING
from the
TRAPLINE

The animals covered in this chapter are taken primarily by trapping. It's true that coon hunting is still fairly common, but for the most part the hunter is more interested in the performance of the dogs than in the meat that might result from the quest. At one time, opossums were hunted quite often for meat, but that sport has pretty much died out. Just the other day, following the first frost, I ran into a local lawyer at the post office. "It's getting possum hunting weather," I said, rubbing my hands for warmth. The guy laughed a little, but I don't think he even knew exactly what I was talking about. He probably didn't even own a possum dog.

In any case, this chapter covers coons and possums as well as muskrats and beaver. Even skunks get a few words.

OPOSSUM

The opossum has rather light-colored, fine-grained meat that can be quite good. They are sometimes very, very fat—and the fat isn't all on the surface. It is distributed in the lean meat, which makes the opossum more ideally suited for dry cooking as compared to, say, lean squirrel. A young possum can be cooked as soon as it has been dressed, although I prefer to soak mine at least two days in cold water, maybe with a little baking soda mixed in, which adds a touch of freshness to the meat. Many people parboil older possums before cooking them by other methods.

At one time, during the bad depression years of the 1930s, people hunted or trapped more possums than they do today. (Many people called them "Hoover Hens," but this joke was applied to the gopher tortoise, rabbits, and other critters that made a handy meal.) Often, they penned up a possum for a week or so before dressing it for the table, and of course they had special cages for this purpose. The thought was that the opossum is a "scavenger," and keeping it penned up permitted one to "clean it out." No doubt some people still hold to this practice.

Today, the possum is subjected to very liberal game laws in most states, and it is quite plentiful in the wild as well as in the suburbs. And maybe in the inner cities. I've had a few around my house, within the city limits of a small town, since World War II. Several years ago, we had two young possums that ate supper with our dog if we fed after dark. They came right onto the back porch and the three of'em ate out of the same bowl. At first there was only one, and we named him Henry. Then another one got brave enough to climb the steps and waddle onto the porch, and we named him Henry II. The boys wanted to eat Henry II, but everyone agreed that we ought to keep Henry, since he was the first to venture forth.

Possums will fool you. They look bigger than they are. Their hair is thick and coarse, and it tends to stick out every which way. Moreover, they often (but not always) have a very thick layer of fat under the skin. Thus, a big possum, when you hold him up by the tail under the spot of a flashlight, may look and feel as if it will feed eight people—but when you skin it, remove the fat, and cook it down, you've got enough good meat for only two or three hungry boys.

A good many people say that a possum should not be skinned. Instead, they say, it should be scalded in boiling water and scraped or pulled (that is, you pull out the hairs like feathers.) I've tried this, and, in my opinion, it's simply not worth the trouble, and, besides, I had rather skin them in order to get rid of lots of the fat. Still other people

Skunk

When I was just a sprout, I recall a feller who worked for Uncle Ott saying that of all wild meat, he figgered skunk had the sweetest taste. Now I was willing to take his word for it, without trying to prove it. But once you get past the idea of eating skunk, I reckon they ain't no reason why skunk meat shouldn't be as good as any. Ray Parker, from St. Louis, sent us a recipe that looks good enough to try, if any of you folks get the notion:

"Skin, clean and remove the scent glands. Put in strong solution of salt water and parboil for about 15 minutes. Drain off this water, add fresh water, season, and steam slowly for about 1 hour or until tender."

And if you do try it, let me know how it turns out!

—Cy Littlebee's
Guide to Cooking Game & Fish

say to singe the hair off in hot coals, then scrub the hide several times in water. That's not for me, either. In any case, here are a few recipes:

Fricassee of Possum

I have eaten quite a few possums, usually cooked with some sort of stuffing or sweet potatoes, or both, but most of these dishes were far too greasy to suit me. Good, yes. But I really prefer the following:

> 1 possum, skinned
> water for boiling
> 1 cup of vinegar
> 3 bay leaves
> 2 cans of beef broth (10¾-ounce size)
> 1 medium onion, very finely diced
> salt and pepper to taste

Skin the possum, put it into a suitable pot, cover with water, add bay leaves and vinegar, and bring it to a quick boil. Let it boil mildly for 30 minutes, then pour off the water. Add more water and boil for another 30 minutes. Discard the water. (The main purpose of the boiling is to help remove some of the fat from the possum.)

Bone the possum, cutting off as much fat as you can. Cut the larger chunks of meat

across the grain, then put all of the meat into a suitable pot. Add beef broth and onions. Bring to boil, then simmer for an hour. Salt and pepper to taste—and my taste runs toward lots of pepper on this dish. Serve over rice, or over toast. *Serves 3 or 4.*

Note: If this dish is simmered down long enough, the gravy will be just right. But it can be thickened with a little flour or cornstarch, and of course gravy can be increased by adding more liquid before thickening.

Pea Ridge Possum with Chestnuts

Once I lived in a house (on Pea Ridge in Tennessee) that was made of chestnut wood. Years before, the hills had been covered with wild chestnut trees, but a blight killed them. All of them. Only the house stood. A fellow who had been born and raised in the area gave me the following possum recipe, and of course it no doubt goes back to the days when the chestnut was plentiful.

> 1 possum
> 1 gallon water
> 1 teaspoon baking soda
> pieces of sassafrass root (about 1 cup will do)
> salt and pepper
> chestnuts
> applesauce
> bread crumbs
> sweet potatoes (with skin on)

juice of 3 lemons
melted butter

Skin and clean the possum, then scrape off most of the fat. Preheat oven to 300 degrees. Bring a gallon of water to boil, then add baking soda and sassafrass root to it. Insert the possum, bring to boil, and cook for 15 minutes. Drain and cool. Rub inside and out with salt and pepper. Make a stuffing with equal proportions of chestnuts, applesauce, and bread crumbs, then stuff the possum with the mixture. Put the possum in a suitable baking pan and surround it with sweet potatoes. Pour 1 cup of boiling water and lemon juice over the possum. Bake for 2 hours, basting from time to time with pan juices, or until potatoes are soft and ready. Peel potatoes, slice, butter, and serve with the meat. *Serves 3 or 4.*

Variation: Peel the potatoes, slice, and boil until tender. After baking the possum for 1 hour and 45 minutes, arrange the sliced potatoes around and on possum. Sprinkle with brown suger and top with a piece of butter. Bake for another 15 minutes.

Skillet Possum

water
1 tablespoon salt
1 teaspoon red pepper flakes
1 medium onion, sliced
peanut oil
2 cups catsup
¼ cup Worcestershire sauce

Cut the possum into serving size pieces and soak for several hours, or overnight, in cold water. Put the pieces in a pan of suitable size, then cover with water and bring to boil. Add salt, onion, and pepper flakes. Reduce heat and simmer for an hour and a half.

Heat some peanut oil in a large frying pan. Brown the pieces of meat on all sides and remove from the frying pan. Pour off most of the oil. Stir in catsup, Worcestershire sauce, and a little water. Put the meat back into the frying pan and simmer for 30 mintues. Add salt if needed. *Serves 3 or 4.*

RACCOON

I've eaten quite a lot of raccoon, and I enjoyed all of it. The meat is on the dark side, and, at its best, it is sweetish. But many raccoons have lots of fat between the meat and the skin. However, the fat isn't distributed throughout the meat as much as it is on a opossum. I normally like to remove most of the fat before cooking a raccoon. Also, if you've got a big boar raccoon it's best to remove the small scent glands (bean shaped) from under the front legs and thighs.

In my opinion, any raccoon that has been killed by dogs, or that has stayed overnight in a trap, is not as good as one that has been killed cleanly. Older raccoons should probably be marinated before cooking, and any raccoon is better if the meat is refrigerated for two or three days before it is eaten.

Raccoon Casserole

This dish is very good with young racoon, but it can also be used with possum and armadillo that aren't too fat.

The Meat:
  1 small or medium-sized raccoon
  water
  2 bay leaves
  1 tablespoon salt
  juice from ½ lemon
The Filling
  2 cups mashed potatoes (hot)
  4 cups dry bread crumbs
  ½ cup diced celery
  1 medium onion, diced
  1 clove garlic, minced
  1 egg, beaten
  1 tablespoon melted butter
  1 teaspoon salt
  ½ teaspoon pepper
  ½ teaspoon poultry seasoning
The Sauce
  1 cup raccoon stock
  2 tablespoons flour
  salt and pepper

Dress the raccoon, cut it into pieces, and put it into a suitable pot. Cover with water, then add salt and bay leaves. Bring to boil, reduce heat, and simmer for an hour, or until raccoon is tender. Drain (saving stock) and pull the meat from the bones with a fork. Dice the meat. Sprinkle meat with juice of ½ lemon and refrigerate.

Make a gravy sauce by putting 1 cup of raccoon broth into a saucepan, adding 2 tablespoons flour, salt, and pepper, and then cooking until the sauce is thick and smooth. Preheat the oven to 350 degrees. Mix hot mashed potatoes and other ingredients listed under filling, above. Grease a suitable casserole dish. Add a layer of filling to the bottom, then a layer of racoon meat, and a layer of gravy. Repeat layers until all ingredients are in the casserole dish. Bake for 25 or 30 minutes, until browned on top. *Serves 4 or 5.*

Crispy Baked Coon

A lot of peanuts are raised in my part of the country, and many of the fields are dotted with them from harvest time (September or October) until the land is broken again in January or February. Raccoons know this, and from their dens in the river or creek swamp they walk up the ditches and draws and feed in the edge of the fields. Hence, any trap set in a suitable ditch is likely to catch a raccoon—if you can keep the opossums out of it. After feeding on peanuts, these racoons are of course fat and juicy. They are ideal for cooking with the following recipe:

Skin the raccoon, leaving a layer of fat on the meat. Preheat the oven to 300 degrees. Salt and pepper the raccoon inside and out. Wrap it in several layers of cheesecloth, then wet the cloth with a cup or so of water that has been boiled and steeped with two bay leaves. Bake for 3 hours. Remove the cheesecloth. Baste the raccoon with pan drippings and sprinkle lightly with flour. Baste and sprinkle with flour several more times while baking for another 30 minutes or so, or until the raccoon forms a crispy crust.

This one may not be for calorie counters, but it sure is good! *Serves 4 or 5.*

Note: For other recipes suitable for baked raccoon, see those set forth for baked possum earlier in this chapter. If you enjoy wild plants as well as wild meat, be sure to try the Gibbons recipe with Jerusalem artichokes.

Fricasseed Raccoon

3 cups diced raccoon meat (front
    quarters or any other parts)
water
⅓ pound sliced bacon
1 medium onion, diced
1 cup beef broth (or 1 cup water with
    bouillon cube)
juice of one lemon
flour
bay leaf
1 teaspoon salt
⅛ teaspoon pepper
rice (cooked separately)

Boil raccoon in water with a bay leaf for an hour, or until the meat comes from bones easily. Discard liquid and bay leaf. Dice about 3 cups of the meat.

In a frying pan that has a lid, cook the bacon and set aside. Roll the racoon in flour and brown quickly. Pour off the oil or transfer the meat to another pot. Add beef broth, onion, lemon juice, salt, pepper, and crumbled bacon. Bring to boil, then reduce heat, cover, and simmer for 2 hours. Eat on rice. *Serves 6 or 7.*

Barbecued Raccoon

I've eaten several messes of barbecued raccoon, some of which were cooked at a commercial establishment. Some of the best I've ever had, however, were prepared very simply as follows:

raccoon, cut into serving size pieces
2 bay leaves per raccoon
salt and pepper
bacon drippings
barbecue sauce of your choice

Put the raccoon into a pressure cooker and cover with water. Add bay leaves. Cook at 15 pounds pressure for 25 to 30 minutes.

Preheat the oven to 350 degrees. Drain meat, salt and pepper to taste, then arrange the pieces in a baking pan. Pour barbecue sauce over meat. Bake for 1 hour. Baste several times with sauce and pan juices. *Serves 4 or 5.*

BEAVER

For some reason, the beaver's meat never became as popular as its pelt. If it had, the animal might have been wiped out, like the carrier pigeon. Today, the beaver thrives in much of its original range, and is something of a problem in some areas. Some states have open seasons or very liberal game laws for the beaver, and I've even heard of bounties being offered here and there. But check your game laws carefully before shooting or trapping a beaver.

The dark red meat, one of my favorites, is surprisingly moist, as compared to venison. Young beavers are tender, but the old ones do tend to be tough.

Barbara Bara's Beaver Stew

Barbara Bara of Georgetown submitted this recipe to *The South Carolina Wildlife Cookbook*. I tried it, and I'm happy to report that it is very good. And it's a complete meal for 6 or 7 people.

**3 pounds boned beaver, cut into cubes
flour
vegetable oil or bacon fat
salt and pepper
1 or 2 bay leaves
1 dash Worcestershire sauce
water to cover
potatoes, diced**

**carrots, sliced
onions, chopped
turnips, diced
cabbage, cut in wedges**

"Remove all possible fat from beaver meat and cut in cubes. Flour cubes and brown on all sides in small amount of fat in a Dutch oven. Season with salt and pepper, add bay leaf, dash of Worcestershire sauce, and water to cover. Cover and simmer until nearly tender. (Time will vary according to age and condition of animal.) Add diced potatoes, carrots, onions, and turnips, if desired. Cover and simmer until vegetables are tender, but still intact. Add cabbage, cut in wedges, and simmer again until cabbage is tender, about ten minutes. The gravy may be thickened, if necessary, with flour and water paste."

Fried Beaver

Beaver can be fried successfully, but I would recommend only very young beaver for this purpose.

**young beaver
bacon drippings
flour
salt and pepper**

Dress beaver, cut it up, and soak the pieces in cold water, under refrigeration, for 2 days. Boil the beaver in a little water until it is tender. Drain. Salt and pepper to taste. Roll in flour and pan fry in hot bacon drippings until browned all over.

Plum Good Beaver

The idea for this dish came from a recipe in *The Maine Way*, to which publication it was submitted by Kay Tukey of Milo, Maine. I have changed it a little and have adapted it to cooking in a crockpot.

> 7 pounds beaver meat
> 2 pounds onions, sliced thinly
> 1 cup of plum jelly (or other tart jelly, such as scuppernog)
> 1 tablespoon salt
> 1 teaspoon black pepper
> flour (optional)

Dress beaver, remove most of the fat, and cut the meat into pieces. In a glass or crockery container of suitable size, pack beaver pieces with alternate layers of onion slices. Refrigerate overnight.

Remove meat and wash it. Discard onions. In a crockpot, layer beaver meat with plum jelly, salt, and pepper. The original recipe didn't call for flour, but I prefer to thicken my gravy a bit and serve it over rice, mashed potatoes, or biscuit halves. Turn crockpot to low and cook for 9 or 10 hours. *Serves from 10 to 14 people.*

Hard Times

With the stock market crash of 1929 and the depression of the 1930s, many Illinois residents again turned to the state's fur-bearer resource to provide basic necessities for their families, as had Illinois' native Americans for hundreds of years before. Wages of 50 cents per day were then all too common, and trapping and hunting provided an essential source of income and food that helped thousands of families survive the hard times.

—*Outdoor Highlights,*
Illinois Department of Conversation

Suwannee River Beaver Roast

When I was a boy, the beaver was almost gone from Florida. Now, however, they are present in the northern parts of the state in large numbers. In any case, the following recipe is from Suwannee River country.

> 1 young beaver
> 1 pound sliced bacon
> 2 stalks celery, chopped
> 6 carrots, cut into 2-inch segments and split in half
> 4 medium onions, sliced about ¼-inch thick
> 2 clover of garlic, minced
> 1 lemon, thinly sliced
> 4 small chili peppers, chopped
> 2 bay leaves
> 1 teaspoon thyme
> 1 teaspoon marjoram
> 1 teaspoon basil

salt and pepper
beef bouillon

Select a roasting pan with a cover and a rack to keep the meat off the bottom. (If you don't have a pan large enough to take the whole beaver, cut it up.) Preheat oven to 300 degrees. Salt and pepper the beaver, inside and out. Place it on the rack inside the pan. Cover with bacon strips, and place lemons atop the bacon. Add 2 quarts of bouillon. Scatter celery, onions, and garlic over and around the beaver. Add the chili peppers and bay leaves, together with the thyme, marjoram, and basil. Add about 2 quarts of beef bouillon, which can be made easily by adding bouillon cubes to water. Roast for 3 hours or longer, basting several times with pan liquid. Add water if needed.

Fried Beaver Tail

Skin beaver tail and put it into a pot of water. Bring to boil, then simmer for 1 hour or so for young beaver or 2 hours for old beaver. Also, add two bay leaves to old beaver. Let cool. Heat oil in skillet. Cut tail into slices. Salt and pepper to taste. Roll in flour, then fry in hot oil until golden brown.

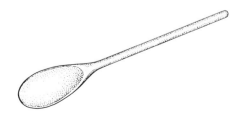

MUSKRAT

The muskrat is one of our better meats, but, unfortunately, most people can't get past the name or the ratlike tail. It is, however, surely one of the cleanest of all animals, since it stays in the water much of the time and eats only vegetation.

Oklahoma Special Muskrat

Here's a recipe that I got from the Oklahoma Wildlife Federation's book *Wildlife Chef*. I have, however, changed it here and there. Normally, I don't soak game meat in salted water, but I did with this recipe and the results were good.

**2 muskrats
1 teaspoon salt
⅛ teaspoon pepper
½ medium sliced onion
½ cup peanut oil
1 cup tomato catsup
½ tablespoon Worcestershire sauce
water**

Soak muskrat overnight in salted water (1 tablespoon salt to 1 quart water). Drain and cut into serving pieces. Place the pieces in a deep pot. Add 1 quart water, 1 teaspoon salt, pepper, and onion. Bring to boil, reduce heat, then simmer for 1 hour. Heat oil in a skillet and fry the meat until it is brown on one side. Turn the pieces and immediately pour the catsup and Worcestershire sauce over the meat. Add a cup of water and simmer for 30 minutes, or until the gravy is thick enough. *Serves 2.*

Back to Basics Muskrat

Anything as good as young muskrat doesn't need spices and all manner of stuff in the recipe. The following basics are all you need:

    muskrats
    peanut oil
    salt and pepper
    flour

Clean the muskrats, cut into serving pieces, and let them sit for several hours, or overnight, in cold water. When you are ready to cook, drain the meat, salt and pepper it to taste, and shake in flour. Let sit for a few minutes. Heat about an inch of peanut oil in a frying pan. Fry the pieces on medium heat until they are golden brown. Serve hot. Allow one muskrat per person.

Variation: If you've got a lot of folks to feed and not too many muskrats, make biscuits and gravy. Pour off most of the oil, then scrape up the dredges left in the frying pan. Add a finely chopped onion and cook until it starts to brown. Mix some flour in a little water, then pour it slowly into the frying pan. Cook until gravy is of the right consistency to suit you, adding more flour or water as needed.

Water Rabbit Pot Pie

Here's a recipe that I adapted to muskrat, with considerable success, I think, from my wife's copy of *The Good Housekeeping Cookbook.*

The Pie
    4 or 5 muskrats, cut into serving size
        pieces (save livers)
    water
    1 pound small white onions, whole
    2 cups carrots, cut into 1-inch sections
    2 cups celery, cut into 1-inch sections
    ½ cup butter
    1 cup half and half
    ⅓ cup of flour
    ¼ teaspoon pepper
    1 teaspoon salt
    1 package fresh-frozen peas (10-ounce
        size)
    piecrust for 2-crust pie
    1 egg yolk
Bouquet Garni
    1 medium onion, sliced
    1 stalk celery, sliced
    3 sprigs parsley
    2 bay leaves
    ½ teaspoon peppercorns
    ¼ teaspoon marjoram leaves

Put the frozen peas out to thaw. To make *bouquet garni,* put onion, celery, parsley, bay leaves, peppercorns, and marjoram leaves on an 8-inch square of double-thickness cheesecloth. An 8-inch square will be about right. Place seasonings on the cheesecloth, pull corners to form a small bag, and tie with an undyed cotton string.

Bring water to boil in a pot; add *bouquet garni* and muskrat pieces. When the water comes to boil again, reduce heat, cover, and simmer for 30 minutes. Add the muskrat livers and simmer for another 20 minutes. Remove meat from pot and drain. Save 1½ cups of the broth. Remove meat from bones, and chop any large pieces.

Preheat oven to 400 degrees. In a saucepan over medium heat, melt ½ cup of butter. Slowly stir the flour into the butter until blended. Stir in the 1½ cups of reserved broth, the half and half, ¼ teaspoon pepper, and 1 teaspoon salt. Stir until blended and bring to heat, *but do not boil*. Let simmer. Prepare the vegetables and put them into a pot. Pour the sauce over the vegetables, add muskrat, and mix. Pour mixture into a 9-by-13-inch baking dish.

Prepare pie crust dough. (If using a ready-mix type, read the directions on the package.) Roll dough into an 11-by-15-inch rectangle. Place dough over the baking dish and trim to about 1 inch of overhang and make a fluted edge. (Fold the overhang under to make a stand-up edge. Place the left index finger on the inside of edge and hold it there. Then with the right thumb and index finger, pinch pastry up around left index finger. Move the index finger a little and repeat the procedure, working your way around the crust.) Make several slits in the crust with the point of a knife.

In bowl, beat an egg yolk with 1 teaspoon of water. Brush the egg yolk onto the pie crust. Put the baking pan into the oven and bake for 40 minutes. Check closely toward the end of cooking period. When done, the crust should be brown and the pie filling should be bubbly. If the crust tends to get

---

Marsh Rabbit

Some people are not fond of the word "rat" and cannot imagine eating one. This is perhaps why muskrats are called "marsh rabbits" when marketed commercially. Muskrat is one of the most tender and flavorful of all wild meats and should never be wasted. It can be cooked without special preparation, though some cooks soak it overnight in a solution of 1 tablespoon salt or 1 cup vinegar in 1 quart water. Cook by most recipes calling for chicken.

—*The Official Louisiana Seafood & Wild Game Cookbook*

---

too brown, cover with foil while baking for the last few minutes.

When serving at the table, watch the pot closely. If the contents diminish too fast, consider whether you should announce the true name of this dish. In mixed company, this revelation will usually slow somebody down. *Serves 4 or 5.*

Muskrat in Cream

Here's a mild dish that may be in order for introducing muskrat to people who might be a bit squeamish.

4 or 5 muskrats
cooking oil

flour
salt and pepper
juice of 1 large or 2 small lemons
½ pint cream (or half and half)

Cut the muskrats into serving size pieces. Arrange the pieces in a glass container and sprinkle with lemon juice. Refrigerate overnight.

Turn the oven to 425 degrees. Rinse the muskrat pieces and let drain. Heat some cooking oil in a frying pan. Salt and pepper the meat pieces to taste, then roll it in flour. Brown in hot oil. Arrange the meat in a casserole and pour the cream over it. Bake for 25 minutes. *Serves 4 to 6.*

Stuffed Muskrat

When looking around recently for ways to cook muskrat, I was inspired by a recipe in Jack Ubaldi's *Meat Book*. He set it up for squirrels, then said it could be used with any small furred animal. I changed it around a little here and there, and added a soak of water and soda. But the basic recipe is Ubaldi's. If you are cooking for people who are not squeamish over mere names, and who would not be put off by a whole stuffed muskrat being on the plate, try the following:

The Meat
  4 muskrats
  1 tablespoon baking soda
  water
  12 juniper berries, crushed

salt and pepper
juice from 3 lemons
1 tablespoon lemon peeling, grated
½ cup peanut oil
½ cup white wine
8 slices of bacon
The Stuffing
  12 ounces mushrooms, chopped
  1 medium onion, chopped
  1 clove garlic, minced
  1½ cups bread soaked in milk
  1 medium egg, whisked
  salt and pepper
The Gravy
  ½ cup beef bouillon
  1 tablespoon butter
  1 tablespoon flour
  2 tablespoons red currant jelly

Skin and dress the muskrats but do not cut them up. Put them into a glass container, then cover with 1 quart of water into which 1 tablespoon of soda has been dissolved. Cover and refrigerate for several hours or overnight. Wash the muskrats and let them drain.

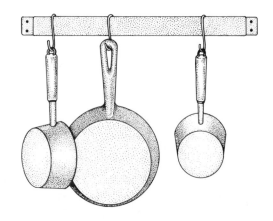

Mix ½ cup of peanut oil, crushed juniper berries, lemon juice, and lemon peeling. Pour this mixture over the muskrats and let sit, under refrigeration, for 2 or 3 hours, turning occasionally.

Make a stuffing with bread, whisked egg, mushrooms, onion, garlic, and 2 table-spoons of peanut oil. Salt and pepper to taste. Preheat oven to 350 degrees. Stuff the muskrats loosely and close openings with skewers. Grease a baking dish of suitable size and place the muskrats into it. Place 2 slices of bacon on each muskrat. Pour the oil left from the marinade over the muskrats, then put into the oven. Bake for 1½ hours. Turn the muskrats from time to time and baste with white wine.

Remove the muskrats from the baking dish and put them onto a warmed platter. Pour most of the bacon grease out of the baking dish. Pour ½ cup of beef bouillon into the baking dish and scrape up the dredg-ings. Pour the contents of the baking dish into a saucepan. Mix flour and butter, then heat with the baking dish liquid. Heat and stir until the consistency looks right. Stir in the red current jelly and serve the gravy over muskrats. *Serves 4.*

41

RATTLESNAKES, ARMADILLOS, and VARMINTS

Once I faced the problem of moving lock, stock, and barrel to another part of the country. Among other tasks, I had to clean out a large freezer. The logical solution, of course, was to eat it out. After two or three weeks, all I had left in the way of meat was a very large rattlesnake and an armadillo. If I had it all to do over again, I would have started on these first!

In any case, if you are lucky enough to have rattlesnakes or other offbeat fare, or have a chance to get any, here are some recipes you may want to try.

Fried Armadillo and Gravy

This critter has been in Texas for many years, and it has now made its way through Louisiana, Mississippi, Alabama, Georgia, and Florida. They are very plentiful in all the Gulf Coast regions, and throughout Florida. I don't know how far north or west they have extended their range, but my guess is that they'll go pretty much where they want.

In any case, they are neither wary nor fleet

of foot, and therefore are not much sport for the hunter. But they do provide some very good eating. I've heard them called possum on the half shell, and there is some similarity. Both meats tend to be rather fatty, and both are tender. In short, an armadillo can be eaten right out of the shell and requires no marinade or aging. Hence, it is an excellent meat for camp cooking. Also, the meat, like pork, can be ground up and used with venison or other game in "gameburger meat," sausage, and so on.

The armadillo is also delicious fried. Cut the critter into serving size pieces, put it into a pot of water with a little baking powder, and refrigerate it for one or two days. Wash, drain, salt and pepper to taste, roll in flour, and fry like chicken in medium hot peanut oil.

If you want some really good gravy with your armadillo, make a batch of biscuits and try the following:

pan drippings from frying armadillo
¼ cup flour
2½ cups milk (used in 2 parts)
salt and pepper

Pour all the oil out of the frying pan, then measure out ¼ cup and put it back into the pan. Heat and scrape loose any tidbits that may have stuck to the bottom of the frying pan. Stir in ¼ cup of flour, adding a little at a time. Stir and heat until flour is slightly

browned. Reduce heat and stir in ½ cup of milk. Then add the rest of the milk, bring to heat, and simmer until gravy has thickened. (If it thickens too much, add a little more milk.) Salt and pepper gravy to taste. I personally like to go a little heavy on the black pepper, fresh from a mill.

Grilled and Barbecued Armadillo

Armadillo meat is very good when cooked over open coals. Salt and pepper is all you need, but butter for basting won't hurt a thing. Generally, the cooking times for armadillo are about the same as for fresh pork. Also, baste generously with your favorite barbecue sauce, or make a sauce with the following recipe:

1 cup butter
½ cup grated onion
½ cup catsup
2 tablespoons prepared mustard

To make the sauce, melt the butter in a sauce pan and sauté the onions. Add the catsup and mustard. Simmer for a few minutes, then let cool.

As a succulent variation, cut the animal into serving size pieces and put them on a sheet of heavy-duty aluminum foil. Salt and pepper to taste, add a little butter, close foil tightly, and cook over medium coals for an hour. Then open the foil and brown the pieces close to hot coals, basting frequently

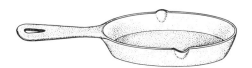

with the barbecue sauce. (This method can also be used in an oven, and the meat browned under the broiler.)

Armadillo Meatballs

> 1 pound armadillo meat, minced or ground
> 1 egg
> 2 tablespoons celery, minced
> 2 tablespoons onions, minced
> 1 tablespoon parsley, minced
> 1 teaspoon salt
> ¼ teaspoon pepper
> flour
> oil

Boil the armadillo for about 30 minutes, bone, and mince the meat or grind it. Mix everything in the recipe except oil and flour. Form mixture into 1-inch balls and refrigerate for 30 minutes or longer. (I have kept them overnight.) When ready to cook, heat oil in frying pan. Roll balls in flour, then fry until golden brown. This recipe will *serve 2 or 3 people*. Increase measures as needed.

Ray Lemelin's Barbecued Porcupine

Here's one from Ray Lemelin of Embden, Maine, as published in *The Maine Way*: "Skin one porcupine. The trick in skinning is to roll the quills under as you loosen the hide. Cut meat in serving pieces. Place in fry pan and brown on all sides. Remove to roasting pan and place in oven, preheated to 325 degrees. Add 2 cups of your favorite barbecue sauce and cover pan. Baste often. Cook until well done, as for pork, about 2 hours. Vegetables may be added to pan during last hour. Porcupine are at their best when taken in the fall when they have been feeding on acorns and beech nuts."

Simmered Woodchuck

This recipe works best for woodchucks that are about one-half to three-quarters grown.

> 1 young woodchuck
> 1 quart water (more needed later)
> ½ cup vinegar
> ½ teaspoon soda
> salt and pepper
> flour
> cooking oil
> garlic
> 1 tablespoon Worcestershire sauce

Cut the chuck into serving size pieces and put them into a suitable glass container. Mix the soda and vinegar into the water and pour it over the meat. Marinate in refrigerator for 12 hours or longer. Drain the pieces. Salt and pepper to taste, then roll or shake in flour. Heat some oil in a frying pan and brown the meat on all sides, a few pieces at a time. Put the meat into a stove-top Dutch oven (or large frying pan), add a little boiling water,

Prairie Dogs

Originally called anything but "dog," prairie dogs would doubtless have regularly appeared on pioneer bills-of-fare. Certainly they are as clean feeders as any of the native rabbits or hares, or the woodchucks that many present-day varmint hunters shoot for meat. Even so, when other meat was in short supply, pioneers didn't gag on prairie dogs. Plainsmen, trappers, and soldiers followed suit, especially when they didn't want to attract the attention of hostile Indians.

Kit Carson, the great plainsman and Indian fighter, himself feasted on prairie dog, cooking the meat by broiling it on a stick after skinning and splitting the carcass.

—Bert Popowski, *The Varmint and Crow Hunter's Bible*

the Commission. Now out of print, the booklet contained the following groundhog or woodchuck recipe from Randy Wilson. *It will serve 4 or 5.*

1 young groundhog
3 apples, halved
1 can sliced pineapple
salt
pepper

"Clean groundhog thoroughly, leaving whole. Parboil until meat is beginning to get tender. Remove and stuff with apples. Garnish with salt and pepper. Toothpick the pineapple rings all over the groundhog and then place in brown'n bag. Cook at 300 degrees until 'whistler' is browned."

and simmer for an hour, or until tender. Add Worcestershire sauce a few minutes before eating. *Serves 4 or 5.*

Randy Wilson's Whistle Pig Delight

The North Carolina Wildlife Resources Commission once published a booklet called *Wild Game Recipes*, which was a collection of "favorite family" recipes from employees of

Clyde's Bobcat in White Wine

Recipes for bobcat are hard to come by, and I was fortunate enough to find this one in *The Maine Way*, published by the Maine Department of Inland Fisheries and Wildlife. It was contributed to that publication by Clyde Noyes of Dennysville, Maine. Here's what he recommends *for 4 or 5 people:*

2 pounds bobcat meat
¼ cup butter
pinch thyme
1 teaspoon chopped parsley
½ cup chicken bouillon
½ cup white cooking wine

salt

pepper

"Remove all fat from two pounds of bob-cat meat. Slice ¼ inch thick and lightly season with salt and pepper. Heat butter in a skillet and brown meat on both sides. Transfer to casserole dish. Combine pinch of

Of Burros and Bobcats

Have you ever thought how closely food prejudices are related to the other kinds? Long ago, during the controversy about the United States joining the League of Nations, I saw a jingoistic orator whip up a frenzy of hatred and disgust against the French because they ate frog's legs and snails. During the late war, when a patriotic speaker wanted to emphasize how alien the Japanese were to our way of life, he would always mention the fact that they ate octopus and raw fish. Only yesterday I saw a newspaper article in which the reporter seemed to think that he had found the final argument against communisn because he had discovered that some of the peoples in Asiatic Russia were eating horse meat. The fact that the horse had been the chief meat animal of these people for a thousand years before communism was ever heard of, was, if it was even known to him, irrelevant. An American governor of the Philippines once told one of the non-Christian tribes there that the American people could not like them as long as they persisted in eating the flesh of dogs. It is a sad commentary on the American mind that what he said was perfectly true.

I was fortunate in being brought up in a family that ate a broad spectrum of meats. Opossum, raccoon, squirrel, frog's legs, turtle, crayfish and even armadillo sausage were not only eaten in our family but were considered great delicacies. Even meat to which I was unaccustomed never seemed to repel me as it did some people. Once, in a wild section of New Mexico, when we had been without meat for some time, my buddy and I shot a fat young burro from a herd of feral animals, wild as any deer, that roamed the dry hills. I thought burro meat delicious at the time, and ate it cooked in several ways with great relish. At another time, on a hunt, finding game scarce, I killed and dressed a porcupine. The meat, cut from the bones and soaked overnight in salt, vinegar and water, then parboiled for 10 minutes and dredged in flour and sautéed, was very good. I cannot claim, however, that I am entirely free of this kind of prejudice. Once a companion and I shot a large bobcat. We had no fresh meat in camp, so we carefully dressed the big feline and fried some of the loin chops for supper. Surprisingly, the meat was clear and white, tender and delicate, as the breast of a quail. The taste was mild and good. As we were eating our unusual fare, my companion remarked, 'The *bob* part of this meat sure is good, but I'm having trouble swallowing the *cat*.' Frankly, I was having the same difficulty.

—Euell Gibbons, *Stalking the Wild Asparagus*

thyme, chopped parsley, chicken bouillon, and cooking wine. Pour this sauce over meat, cover casserole, and bake at 350 degrees approximately 45 minutes."

Baked Rattlesnake

The background information for this recipe isn't quite clear to me, but it apparently came from a great nephew of President Madison. The great nephew is said to be a noted hunter and storyteller. The material was contributed to some publication (I have only an unidentified tearsheet) by Richard Fleetwood Madison of Montgomery, Alabama. I don't know whether Richard Fleetwood is the nephew or more distant kin. In any case, my own nephew, David Livingston, who de-

---

Rattlesnake

Rattlesnake meat is canned commercially in Florida and served as a delicate *hors-d'oeuvre*. I have never tried it and do not intend to. It is said to taste much like canned tuna. . . . Bartram wrote in his famous *Travels* that Governor Grant of Florida had a passion for rattlesnake meat "if the snake had not bit himself," but Bartram, as I should have done, "tasted of the meat but could not swallow it."

—Marjorie Kinnan Rawlings,
Cross Creek Cookery

---

signed the little Stumpknocker creek boat, provided a 5-foot 6-inch diamondback for the recipe below. It fed 4 people, and I can vouch for the results.

> 1 large rattlesnake
> 1 can cream of mushroom soup*
> 6 ounces mushrooms, sliced
> 2 limes, sliced thinly
> salt to taste
> 1 teaspoon white pepper
> 1 teaspoon basil
> 1 teaspoon rosemary

After skinning and washing the snake, cut it into 3-inch sections. Salt each piece to taste and place in a baking dish of suitable size. Top with the soup. Add limes, mushrooms, white pepper, basil, and rosemary. Cover. Bake in preheated 300-degree oven for an hour.

*The original recipe called for "1 recipe" of thin cream sauce. I changed this to 1 can of cream of mushroom soup.

Rattlesnake Patties

I've never eaten a water snake, but I've seen some cottonmouths big enough to tempt me. If hungry, I wouldn't hesitate to eat any sort of American snake except the coral snake. But I don't think I would fry them in pieces. I would use the recipe below, which I have tried with a freezer-burned rattlesnake and found it to be quite good.

snake
water
bay leaf
flour
peanut oil
salt and pepper

Skin the snake and cut off the head. Cut it into 4-inch pieces. Boil the pieces in water with a bay leaf for about 30 minutes. Drain. Pull the meat off the bones. Salt and pepper it to taste. Shake it in flour and pan fry it until brown in a little hot peanut oil.

Note: I've read about putting marjoram, rosemary, savory, and so on in the flour before coating the snake with it. This is entirely unnecessary, of course, unless you don't like the flavor of rattlesnake meat!

Fried Rattlesnake and Ham Gravy

There is a problem with fried rattlesnake. Some of the meat is along a backbone and some of it is along rib structures. If you merely cut the snake into segments, you'll have both types on each piece. If you fry the pieces long enough to cook around the bone, the rib part is going to be cooked too much. This problem is compounded because people tend to cook rattlesnake too much anyhow, and I confess that I certainly want mine well done. But most people who try it are going to fry it anyhow, so here's how:

Soak the snake in cold water and a little baking soda for two days. Drain. Salt and pepper to taste. Shake in flour and cook on medium high heat until snake is done. Pour off most of the grease, then fry some ham in the pan. Remove ham to serve along with the snake.

With a spatula, scrape up the pan drippings. Pour in a little black coffee, bring to heat. Add a little flour. Cook down. Add more coffee or more flour, whichever is needed, until you get the gravy consistancy that you want. Serve gravy over hot biscuits.

Note: This recipe is one that I hit on once when I had two very large snakes to cook, and several high-school boys who wanted to try the the meat. I cooked the ham, just in case any of the boys chickened out on the snake. They ate everything and the snake-and-ham gravy was a big hit!

42

VARIETY
MEATS from GAME

Anyone who likes heart, liver, and such from domestic animals will love similar parts from wild game. They really won't need an introduction to this chapter. They'll dig right in. Anyone who doesn't like, or won't even try, the so-called variety meats from domestic animals won't need an introduction, either. They'll move on to another chapter, no matter what I say here!

The recipes given below should be enough to get anyone hooked on variety meats. Be warned, however, that edible organs should be removed from game as soon as possible. Also be warned that one must proceed with care when dressing out the liver of some animals, lest the gall bladder be cut and ruin the meat. These topics are covered in more detail in the chapters on dressing game.

Skoog's Leverpostej

Here's a recipe from Denmark, which I received from the Alaska Department of Game and Fish. It is from their *Wildlife Cookbook*, which is now out of print, and it was contributed by Ronald O. Skoog, who was a Game and Fish Commissioner when the book was published.

1 pound of deer or caribou liver
½ pound bacon or pork fatback
1 onion, peeled and quartered
3 or 4 anchovies (optional)
¼ cup butter
½ cup flour
1½ cup milk

Getting Liver Ready

Mrs. Wilson Bell of Big Piney, in preparing liver for frying, and especially the liver from game, soaks the thinly sliced liver in a solution of warm water to which 2-3 tablespoons of vinegar have been added. This treatment was told to her by Rives Holcomb, a cowboy from Virginia, who was a cook on a destroyer during WW I. My mother rolled thinly sliced liver in ⅔ cup cornmeal to ⅓ cup flour before cooking in bacon drippings. This makes liver crisp and delightful.

— Mrs. Mae E. Mickelson in
Cooking in Wyoming

2 medium eggs, beaten
1 teaspoon ground allspice
1 teaspoons salt
¼ teaspoon black pepper

As Skoog said, "Wash liver, remove sinews, and cut into strips. Put liver, bacon, onion, and anchovies (if used) through the grinder 3 times (or use food processor until ground fine).

"Make roux with butter and flour and stir in milk to make a smooth, thick white sauce. Let it cook for a few minutes, then add the liver mixture, eggs, allspice (if used) and salt and pepper.

"Pour the mixture into a well-greased oblong baking pan and bake in the lower part of the oven at 350 degrees for 45 to 60 minutes, covered with foil to prevent a skin from forming."

Fried Venison Liver

liver
cooking oil
salt
pepper
flour

Heat oil in frying pan. Slice liver ½ inch thick. Salt and pepper each slice. Roll in flour

Porcupine Liver

Porcupine liver is the sweetest of all the wild-game livers I have tried. This sweetness is due to the animal's diet, which consists almost exclusively of the cambium layer of bark, plus buds, leaves and even blossoms of deciduous trees. The porcupine also has an overpowering yen for anything salty, as witness by the many ax and paddle handles he ruins.

Preparation of porcupine livers is simple. Just trim off any fat or tissue, and slice in desired thickness. Dust the slices with flour, season with a bit of salt and pepper, and fry as you would calf's liver.

Porcupine livers are particularly delicious when fried with bacon for breakfast. Fry until the slices are fully cooked and uniform in color throughout.

Small pieces of porcupine meat and bits of the liver can be used with bacon, tomatoes, and mushrooms to make an unusual and highly delicious shish kebab.

— C.B. Colby, *Outdoor Life*

and fry in hot oil. Do not overcook. On medium high heat, 5 minutes on each side should be plenty. Cooking the liver much longer will cause it to be tough.

Game Liver Casserole

The recipe below is a good one for most any kind of liver, from eelpout to elk. It is highly recommended for liver from deer, antelope, and other big game.

 2 pounds of liver
 ½ pound bacon
 2 cups of chopped onions
 2 cups cracker crumbs
 3 eggs, beaten
 1 cup half and half
 salt and pepper to taste
 ¼ teaspoon thyme

Boil the liver for 10 minutes. Let it cool, then slice it thinly. Set four slices of bacon aside and then cook the rest in a frying pan until it is crisp. Add bacon to onions and set aside.

Preheat oven to 325 degrees and grease a casserole. Place about a third of the onion and bacon mixture in the bottom of the dish, then top with a layer of sliced liver. Add another third of the onion and bacon mixture, then top this with a layer of cracker crumbs. Next, add the rest of the sliced bacon, the last of the onion and bacon, and another layer of cracker crumbs.

Mix the beaten eggs and the half and half. Sprinkle thyme, salt, and pepper over the

> ## Liver & Port
>
> W. G. Howe, from La Grange, Missouri, was quoted in *Cy Littlebee's Guide to Cooking Fish & Game* on the subject of cooking deer liver in camp: "Pour a little port wine over the liver while it's frying," says Mr. Howe. "It not only improves the taste, but the smell is sure to bring in any lost hunters that might be near-by and down-wind."
>
> —Missouri Department of Conservation

casserole, then pour the egg mixture over it. Place four strips of reserved bacon on top. Bake for 1 hour. *Serves 6.*

Sautéed Liver with Onions and Mushrooms

I've cooked this dish a dozen times or more, and it is one of my favorites. I've never figured out the exact ingredients, but any reasonable measures work. But a little liver goes a long way, usually, and I allow ¼ pound per person.

 liver
 butter
 salt and pepper
 flour
 onion, sliced lengthwise and separated
 mushrooms, sliced

Slice the liver into fingers. Salt and pepper them to taste, then coat them lightly with flour. Heat a little butter in a large frying pan—or on a griddle. Sauté the liver for a few mintues, then add in the onion and mushrooms. Cook until onions start to brown. Add more salt and pepper if needed. Add a little water and stir up the pan drippings.

Tasty Tongue

Moose and elk have tongues about the size of beef, or larger, and can feed four or five people. Tongue from smaller animals, such as deer, won't go so far. One of the most popular methods of serving tongue is as an appetizer or snack, in which case size isn't of too much importance. In any event, the recipe below will work with large and small tongues.

1 or more tongues
2 quarts of water
1 medium onion, diced
3 bay leaves
3 cloves
1 tablespoon salt
½ tablespoon red pepper flakes

Place the tongue into a suitable pan, cover with water, and bring to a boil. Add onion, bay leaves, cloves, salt, and pepper. Reduce heat, cover pan, and simmer until tongue is tender. (Allow 2 hours for large tongues, and 1 ½ hours for smaller tongues.) When the tongue is done, remove the skin.

The tongue can be served hot or cold. Slice against the grain and serve on crackers or thin pieces of rye. Either mustard or prepared horseradish goes well with boiled tongue. I am fond eating tongue with the brownish Creole-style mustard.

Bone Marrow

I've always enjoyed bone marrow whenever I happen to come upon it while eating meat, such as the small bit left in a T-bone, a turkey neck, or a backbone cooked in greens for seasoning. I've never cracked any elk or moose bones open to get at the marrow, but I wouldn't hesitate do so in an emergency situation. Some people do take the trouble to get at bone marrow—and eat it raw. In the arctic circle, it is sometimes called Eskimo butter.

Crockpot Elk Tongue

The crockpot is ideal for cooking game tongue, and the results are highly recommened.

1 elk tongue
1½ cups water
6 peppercorns
juice from two lemons
1 bay leaf
2 tablespoons salt

Put water and tongue into a crockpot. Add peppercorns, lemon juice, bay leaf, and salt. Put on low heat for 8 to 9 hours. Peel tongue, slice, and serve, hot or cold, for use as sandwich meat or on crackers. *A large tongue will serve 4 or 5 for lunch.*

Tongue Salad

Some people are squeamish about eating tongue. The shape of the tongue has got a lot to do with it, and sometimes merely slicing it into cross sections isn't enough disguise. If you've got such people to feed, chop up the tongue up and use it in the following recipe:

1 cup boiled tongue, minced
2 tablespoons onion, chopped
2 tablespoons salad pickle relish
½ bell pepper, chopped
2 tablespoons nuts, finely chopped
creamy buttermilk salad dressing

Mix tongue, onions, pickle relish, bell pepper, and nuts. Stir in a creamy buttermilk salad dressing. Eat on crackers.

Stuffed Venison Heart with Brandy Gravy

There is a considerable difference in the size of the heart in deer and larger game. Usually, the heart of an average deer will serve 2.

Big Heart

Pound for pound, wild animals usually have larger hearts than their domestic counterparts. Apparently this is because wild animals run more, thereby pumping more blood and giving the heart (a muscle) more exercise.

heart of deer, antelope, or other
   venison
saltwater marinade
¼ cup bread crumbs
¼ cup chopped celery
¼ cup chopped onion
milk
⅛ teaspoon ground sage
1 teaspoon butter
salt and pepper to taste
½ cup of beef broth (canned will do)
¼ cup brandy
bacon (optional)

Put the heart into a suitable container and pour saltwater marinade over it; this is made by adding 1 tablespoon of salt to a quart of water. Let heart stand overnight, or several hours, under refrigeration.

When you're ready to cook, preheat the oven to 350 degrees. For a stuffing, mix the bread crumbs, celery, onion, sage, and butter. Salt and pepper to taste, and add a little milk to bind and moisten the stuffing. (Note: The measures given are in the correct proportion, but the amount used will vary according to the size of the heart being stuffed.

If you have any left over—and you will—wrap it with bacon and bake it along with the heart.) Stuff the heart, then close the opening with skewers. Put the heart (and leftover stuffing) into a suitable size pan then pour in ½ cup of water and ¼ cup of good brandy. Cover the pan and bake for 2 hours, or until tender.

When the heart is done, remove it from pan and slice it carefully on a small serving platter. Pour the pan juices over the slices.

Marinated Heart

Seldom do I use exact cooking methods on heart that has been marinated as indicated below. Hence, several methods of cooking it are suggested.

The Meat
  heart from deer, elk, or other game
  salt and pepper to taste (after marinating)
Marinade
  ½ cup good cooking oil
  ¼ cup grated onions
  ½ teaspoon garlic juice
  ¼ cup Worchestershire sauce

Trim the fat and tubes from the heart. Cut heart into ½-inch strips. Mix the marinade and steep the heart meat for several hours at room temperature. Or put into refrigerator overnight. Shortly before cooking, remove meat from the marinade; salt and pepper to taste. (Save marinade.) Cook the meat by one of the following methods:

1. *Broil:* Put meat strips very close to heat source. In fact, it helps to have the broiler going for 10 or 15 minutes before cooking. Broil for about 5 minutes on each side. Baste with marinade.

2. *Charcoal:* Put meat strips on rack over hot coals. Cook until done, basting with marinade.

3. *Stir fry or quick fry:* Cook on high heat in a skillet or wok. Eight to 10 minutes will be about right. Pour a little marinade into the wok.

4. *Fry & simmer:* Cook quickly in frying pan, add all of the marinade, reduce heat, and simmer for about 2 hours. Gets better by the minute.

Deer Heart Sandwiches

The heart of deer, antelope, and other game animals can provide an excellent sandwich meat. The antelope, by the way, has a large heart for its size. (The larger hearts from elk and moose can also be used; double the measures given below.) Here's how:

  deer heart
  3 cups of water
  1 teaspoon salt
  ½ teaspoon red pepper flakes
  ½ teaspoon marjoram
  2 bay leaves

In a suitable pot, bring the three cups of water to a boil and add salt, pepper flakes, marjoram, and bay leaves. Cut the heart in half lengthwise. Put both halves into the pot and boil, covered, for an hour. Let the heart steep in the liquid while it cools. Put the heart into a suitable dish, then cover with part of the pan liquid. Refrigerate and slice (across the grain) as needed for sandwich meat. Very thin slices work best. Use it as sandwich meat with lots of good mayonnaise. One deer heart will usually make enough sandwiches to serve from 2 to 4 people for lunch. Also, try thin slices atop thin crackers along with a dab of creole or Dijon mustard.

Stuffed Heart

The measures below for this choice dish will make enough stuffing for a large heart from elk or moose. The recipe can be reduced for hearts from animals the size of deer or antelope:

The Meat
  1 large heart
  4 slices bacon (thick sliced)
  salt
  pepper
The Stuffing
  ½ cup mild sausage
  4 slices bacon, chopped
  ½ cup chopped onions
  1 cup diced mushrooms
  salt
  pepper
  1 large egg
  2 slices bread, soaked in milk
  1 tablespoon parsley, chopped

Trim fat from heart and remove tubes. Cut a hole into heart. Sprinkle with salt and pepper. Preheat oven to 350 degrees.

To make the stuffing, brown chopped bacon and onions in frying pan. Add sausage, mix well. Add mushrooms and simmer a few minutes. Salt and pepper to taste. Put the mixture into a bowl. Soak 2 slices of bread in milk, then mash it. Add bread, egg, and parsley to bowl and mix.

Spoon the stuffing into the heart and close the opening with skewers. Wrap the heart with slices of bacon and secure with skewers or tie with string, or both. (I often use round toothpicks for skewers, but some of the flat toothpicks aren't quite stiff enough.)

Carefully place the stuffed heart into a pan and put it into the oven. Add 1 cup of water to the bottom of the pan. Bake for 1 ½ hours for large hearts (moose and elk) or 1 hour for smaller hearts (deer and antelope). When serving, carefully slice the heart and spoon a

Mattak

We were invited to Uvdluriak's and there for the first time I tasted rotten *mattak*. This dish, which is a great delicacy for the Eskimos, consists of huge flakes of narwhale skin that have been in meat caches for several years. In the low temperature they do not become rancid, they just ferment, so that the skin tastes very much like walnuts while the blubber, turned quite green, tastes sharp—almost like roquefort cheese.
—Peter Freuchen's *Book of the Eskimos*

little of the pan drippings atop the meat and stuffing. *Serves 4 or 5.*

Ginnie Peppard's Venison Kidney

Here's a good one that I found in *The Maine Way:* "Melt butter in an iron fry pan. Slice the kidney into ¼ inch thick slices and add to melted butter. Just a spoonful of water helps to simmer them slowly and keep them from becoming crusty before cooked. Don't cook them so slowly that they stew along. At the same time, don't fry them so quickly that they don't cook from the inside out. Be sure to scrape the pan for the crispy pieces left behind. These with baked beans are favorite fare for all."

Menudo

Anyone who is fond of tripe will already have a favorite recipe or two. Those who think they don't like it should try *menudo.* This is a simple Mexican dish that I ran across in Sam Fadala's book *Game Care & Cookery.* It is, of course, the stomach lining that is found in ruminants, or cud chewing animals such as elk, antelopes, goats, cows, giraffes, and so on. I confess that I have never been too fond of tripe, but I immediately took a liking to *menudo.* Fadala said that some of his Mexican

---

Kidney

Kidney from the deer carcass may be prepared as from any domestic animal. Kidneys from young animals should be cooked very briefly while larger ones may be chunked or sliced, browned, and added to a stew.

—Cooking the Sportsman's Harvest

---

friends from across the border credit the dish with medicinal and even supernatural powers. I wouldn't go that far, but it *is* good.

2 pounds tripe from elk or other ruminant
water
2 cans hominy (15½-ounce size)
2 tablespoons chili powder
2 cloves garlic, crushed
1 medium onion, diced
salt and pepper, as needed

Wash the tripe and cut it into 1-inch squares. Put the tripe into a stove top Dutch oven or suitable pot. Cover with water, and have about 2 inches of water above the tripe. Add chili powder, garlic, and onion. Bring to boil, cover, reduce heat, and simmer for 1 ½ hours. Check from time to time to see whether more water is needed.

Open a large can of hominy and drain off the water. Add the hominy to the pot and mix well. The dish should be eaten like soup, so you may have to add a little water, especially if the lid of the pot or Dutch oven doesn't fit tightly. If you choose, add salt and pepper, or other seasonings, and let the dish simmer for a few more minutes. Fadala recommends that *menudo* be combined with freshly made thick corn tortillas. I like it with baked corn pone, or fried corn bread. Or, even better, crackling bread. *Serves 6 to 8*.

Fried Brains

If you like pork, calf's, or lamb's brains, be sure to try those from deer, antelope, and other wild animals. I've always been quite fond of eggs scrambled with brains, as explained in the next recipe, but I also greatly appreciate them fried.

  brains
  vinegar
  salt
  pepper
  flour
  egg yolk, lightly beaten
  cracker crumbs
  cooking oil
  lemons

Put 2 teaspoons of vinegar and juice of ½ lemon in a quart of water. Soak brains in water for several hours, under refrigeration. Prepare another quart of water with 1 teaspoon of vinegar and heat to boiling. Drop the brains into boiling water and leave for 4 minutes. Remove the brains, drain, and cut into 1-inch cubes. Salt and pepper to taste.

Heat at least 1 inch of cooking oil in a frying pan. Roll brain pieces in flour, then dip in beaten egg, roll in bread crumbs, and fry in hot oil. Drain. Provide a lemon wedge for each plate.

Brains 'n Eggs

My favorite way to cook brains is to scramble them with eggs. Many people bake brains and eggs, but in my experience it is easier, and much better, to cook them in a frying pan. Exact measures aren't too important, but I usually have about half brains and half eggs.

  brains
  eggs
  salt and pepper
  butter
  green onions (optional)

Chop up a green onion or two, top and all. Heat a little butter in a frying pan. Sauté onions. Add brains. Cook and stir. Add eggs. Stir. Salt and pepper. Scramble on low heat, stirring constantly, until the eggs are done. Serve with toast and sliced tomatoes.

Fried Animelles

In France, *animelles* is the culinary word for testicles. So, call this dish whatever you choose. Moose *animelles* has a good reputation in some parts, and I have heard of folks eating the testicles from boar hogs and bulls.

Anyhow, here's a recipe that I adapted from *Larousse Gastronomique*. If you like this sort of thing, try it with deer, elk, or moose. Usually, dishes of this sort are cooked and served along with plenty of more ordinary fare.

testicles
salt and pepper
2 teaspoons tarragon vinegar
2 teaspoons oil (more needed for
    frying)
⅛ teaspoon thyme
small bay leaf
1 medium onion, sliced
juice of ½ lemon
flour
cooking oil

Scald the testicles, skin them, and slice into bite-sized pieces. Soak in cold water with a bay leaf for several hours, then drain and cover with a marinade made of 2 teaspoons tarragon vinegar, 2 teaspoons oil, ⅛ teaspoon thyme, sliced onion, and juice of ½ lemon. Let sit for an hour. When you are ready to cook, drain the testicle slices, salt and pepper to taste, shake in flour, and fry on medium heat until golden brown.

Sautéed Animelles with Mushrooms

Scald *animelles*, skin them , and slice. Marinate in 1 pint of cold water with the juice of ½ lemon for 3 hours or longer. Drain. Sauté in melted butter for a few minutes. Remove. Sauté diced onion and mushrooms until tender. Add the sliced *animelles*, then salt and pepper to taste. Garnish with fresh parsley sprigs.

43

COOKING GAME
ON the PATIO

I have mixed feelings about cooking prime game meat on the patio. On the one hand, I believe that such game as venison is better but more difficult to prepare than domestic meats. This is true primarily because the meat is not as fat, and therefore doesn't lend itself very well to dry cooking methods. In short, wild meat is easier to cook in the kitchen. On the other hand, I'll have to admit that some of the best game meat that I've ever tasted was done on a grill over charcoal—and in camp.

If you want to try game on your grill, then by all means do so. I would, however, recommend that you start with small, tender cuts and save the roasts and larger cuts until you gain experience. Or you might start with the following, which I guarantee:

As You Go Barbecue

This recipe is designed to make a believer of anyone who doubts that game meat is good, and who has little confidence in cooking it.

The Meat
 4- or 5-pound venison roast, leg
  quarter, etc.
 salt and pepper
 bacon drippings
The Sauce
 ½ pound bacon
 1 medium to large onion, minced
 3 cloves garlic, minced
 1 cup catsup
 1 cup red wine vinegar

½ **cup Worcestershire sauce**
½ **cup brown sugar**

On the kitchen stove or over hot coals, fry the bacon in a large frying pan. Remove the bacon and pour off most of the drippings. (Save the drippings for basting.) Sauté the onion and garlic in a little of the bacon grease. Mix in the catsup, wine vinegar, Worcestershire sauce, and brown sugar. Heat and stir. Crumble the bacon and put it back into the sauce.

Start a hot charcoal fire in the grill. Salt and pepper the venison, then baste with bacon drippings. Put the meat on the grill, and put the sauce in a pan beside the meat or keep it on a separate hot plate or other source of heat. (Do not boil or bubble the sauce, however; merely keep it hot.) Grill the meat, basting often, until part of the outside looks ready to eat. Slice the crust off in strips about ¼ inch thick. Add the strips to the pan of sauce. Baste and cook until you are ready to slice again, then repeat the process. After you have sliced up all the meat, stir pan and serve the meat over hamburger bun halves. *Serves 10 to 12.*

Rabbit Over Coals

I've never cared much for squirrels cooked over coals, possibly because old ones are simply too tough to chew with false teeth, but rabbit is another matter. I much prefer it to chicken. Of course, young rabbits are better than old ones.

The Meat
    rabbit halves (allow ½ rabbit per person)
    salt and black pepper
The Marinade and Basting Sauce
    1 medium onion, grated
    2 bell peppers, grated
    2 cloves garlic, grated
    ½ cup red wine vinegar
    ½ cup orange juice
    1 tablespoon orange marmalade
    juice from 1 lemon
    2 tablespoons olive oil

Mix the marinade. Dress the rabbits and cut in half, lengthwise. Put the halves into a suitable glass container and pour the marinade mixture over them. Put the meat into the refrigerator overnight or longer. Drain. Retain the marinade. Salt and pepper the rabbit to taste.

Have hot coals ready in the grill. Put the rabbit halves onto a greased rack. Cook for 30 minutes or so, turning, and basting frequently with leftover marinade mixture. If your experience is with plucked chicken (cooked in the skin), you might keep in mind that the rabbit is skinned and will dry out more than chicken unless you keep it well basted.

Grilled Filet Mignon

Many people consider filet mignon to be the ultimate in meat cookery. Essentially, it is a fillet of meat wrapped in bacon and grilled or broiled. Use tenderloin or loin from deer, elk, or other big game—but I do not recommend that you use bear or pork because these meats, for safety's sake, must be cooked until well done whereas the filet mignon should be eaten rather rare to be at its best.

> **tenderloin from deer, elk, or other big game**
> **bacon**
> **1 cup of cooking oil**
> **juice from 4 cloves of garlic**
> **¼ cup red wine**
> **salt and pepper**

Cut the fillets of tenderloin ¾ inch thick. Wrap tenderloin with part of a strip of bacon, pin, and place in a glass baking dish or some such suitable container. With a garlic press, squeeze the juice from four cloves. Mix garlic juice, oil, and wine. Pour this mixture over the fillets and refrigerate for 2 hours.

Bring coals to high heat and adjust grill so that it is close to the heat source. Broil fillets as quickly as possible, being careful to avoid a fire from the bacon juice. In fact, it's best to have a hinged grid and cook this dish over two beds of coals (or one long bed) switching from one to the other if fires start. In short, cook the fillets as quickly as possible, but don't burn. Baste with the marinade liquid once or twice when the meat begins to look ready. Exact cooking times are difficult to pin down, but the filet mignon is probably ready to eat when the bacon looks done. Do not overcook. Salt and pepper to taste after the meat has been taken from grill. Allow from ⅓ to ½ pound of meat per person.

Big Game Ribs with Beer and Honey

Use this recipe for ribs from deer, elk, caribou, moose, bear, or other big game.

> **1 rack of ribs**
> **1 can of beer**
> **1 cup of honey**
> **juice from 1 large lemon**
> **2 teaspoons salt**
> **½ teaspoon pepper**
> **1 teaspoon dry mustard**
> **2 teaspoons ground ginger**
> **½ teaspoon ground nutmeg**

Boil or steam the ribs for an hour. Meanwhile, make a sauce from the honey, beer, lemon juice, salt, pepper, mustard, ginger, and nutmeg. After the ribs have steamed for an hour, cut them into serving size pieces. Put the ribs into a suitable container and pour the beer sauce over them. Marinate for 4 hours, turning several times.

Heat coals in a "smoker cooker" or a grill with a hinged cover. Lay the ribs on heavy aluminum foil and pour ¼ cup of the sauce over them. Seal the foil. Close the lid and cook for 30 minutes. Then open the lid, remove the foil from the ribs, and cook over hot coals until the ribs are brown. Baste sev-

Cougar

Among many of the Indians who relied on wild meat, cougar was preferred to all other game including venison. Like lynx, it has no game taste whatsoever.

—Bradford Angier,
Gourmet Cooking for Free

eral times. If you've got any sauce left, pour it over the ribs when you take them off the grill.

Note: if you are working with tender ribs that tend to come apart, put them into a hinged wire rack for the final browning over open coals.

Game Kabobs

Kabobs are fun to eat and fun to cook inside or outside. The key, of course, is in having good meat to work with. The following recipe is quite suitable for cooking over coals, but before cooking I use a marinade that I got from John Weiss's book *Venison: From Field to Table*.

The Meat
   **tenderloin, loin, or other choice cut of
      meat
   thinly sliced bacon
   salt and pepper
   onions**

   **tomatoes
   green peppers**
The Marinade
   **Italian salad dressing
   white wine
   garlic powder**

Mix a marinade of about 2 parts wine to 1 part Italian salad dressing, then stir in a little garlic powder. Cube the meat and put it into a glass container. Cover with marinade and refrigerate for at least an hour. (I marinate it overnight, usually.)

An hour or so before you are ready to cook, drain the meat (but retain the marinade). Quarter the onions, green pepper, and tomatoes. Put meat and vegetables on skewers, alternating in usual kabob fashion. Get a suitable container to hold all the skewers, and marinate them in the same mixture of wine, Italian salad dressing, and garlic. Prepare fresh marinade if you need more. Leave the kabobs in this marinade for an hour.

Fire up the grill. Cook the kabobs until they are done, turning every 10 minutes or so.

Smoked Venison and Dove Breasts

Because venison tends to be dry, I don't normally recommend that it be cooked over coals except by accomplished backyard chefs. It can, however, be successfully cooked on a grill or in a hot smoker. Here's one that I recommend trying:

> **deer meat, cut into chunks about the size of dove breasts**
> **dove breasts**
> **bacon**
> **bacon drippings**
> **garlic salt**

If the meat is really tough, sprinkle commercial tenderizer on it, following the instructions on the bottle or box. (Or, if you prefer, the meat can be soaked overnight in a tenderizing marinade.) Fire up the smoker with charcoal and have hickory chips ready (either soaked or green). Put venison chunks and dove breasts in a glass bowl and drizzle bacon drippings over them. Sprinkle liberally with garlic salt and toss about. Wrap each piece of venison and each dove breast with half a strip of bacon and pin with a round toothpick or tie off with cotton twine.

When charcoal is ready, cover with hickory chips and close cover. Adjust temperature to about 200 degrees. Grease the rack and place bacon-wrapped venison and dove on it. Smoke for an hour and test for doneness. Smoke longer if necessary, but do not overcook.

Patio Grilled Rib Chops

For a combination of tender bites and good gnawing, rib chops from deer, antelope, and such game are hard to beat. Allow 3 or more chops per person.

> **rib chops**
> **3 strips of bacon**
> **1 medium onion, finely chopped**
> **1 clove garlic, minced**
> **1 cup water**
> **juice of 1 lemon**
> **1 can tomato paste (6-ounce size)**
> **2 tablespoons brown sugar**
> **¼ cup red wine vinegar**
> **salt and pepper**
> **½ teaspoon powdered mustard**

Cook bacon in a frying pan. Set bacon aside. Sauté onion and garlic in bacon drippings. Stir in 1 cup of water, lemon juice, tomato paste, brown sugar, red wine vinegar, salt, pepper, and mustard. Simmer for 15 minutes.

Bring coals to heat in the grill. Cook chops about 4 inches from coals for 10 minutes, then turn. Baste heavily and cook for about 8 minutes. Turn, baste, and cook for a few more minutes, or until done. If you have sauce left over, serve it with the chops.

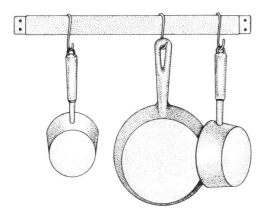

Grilled Gameburgers

If you like to cook hamburgers outside, then by all means try gameburgers cooked over the coals, or in your smoker/cooker. Use your favorite recipe and technique, but be sure to grind up some beef suet or beef fat along with your venison or other game. Otherwise, your burgers may be too dry. To make the gameburger meat from scratch, I recommend that you try 3 pounds of venison (or similar meat) to 1 pound of beef fat.

If you don't have a favorite recipe, try adding a little finely chopped onion, salt, and pepper. Shape into patties and put into a well-greased hinged grill. Cook over hot coals until done, turning from time to time.

Grilled Game Ribs

4 pounds of ribs, more or less
2 bay leaves
¼ cup cooking oil
1 large onion, minced
1 clove garlic, minced
1 green pepper, minced
1 can tomato sauce (8-ounce size)
½ cup catsup
water
1 cup vinegar
¼ cup Worcestershire sauce
salt and pepper

Cut the ribs into serving size pieces. Simmer in water with 2 bay leaves for an hour. Drain ribs; salt and pepper to taste.

While the ribs are boiling, mix a sauce with the oil, onions, garlic, bell pepper, tomato sauce, catsup, vinegar, 1 cup of water, and Worcestershire sauce. Simmer the sauce for 20 minutes.

Outside, bring coals to medium heat. Cook meat on both sides until browned, about 20 minutes, depending on coals. Baste heavily with sauce and cook for another 15 minutes, basting several more times. Serves about 4, but remember that a good deal depends on how much meat is left on the ribs.

Grilled Game Roast

One of the best venison roasts I've ever eaten was cooked on a patio grill with a hinged cover. The fellow who cooked it made deep slits into the meat with a fish fillet knife and poked chunks of salt pork into these slits. Then he sprinkled the roast with lots of pepper and garlic salt. Next, he wrapped the roast very tightly in extra heavy aluminum

---

Lion

Lion meat, though edible, is seldom used in cookery. It is rather tasteless and must be steeped in an aromatic marinade before cooking.

All recipes for beef are suitable for lion.
—*Larousse Gastronomique*

More than One Way

Just in case you haven't noticed, hunters are inclined to be an opinionated lot. A good many of the clan enjoy cooking the game they bring home. Not infrequently a hunter believes his way of handling the job is THE way. So be it, but there is more than one way to skin a cat, or cook a cat squirrel, as any veteran of the wild game dinner circuit will attest.

—Morrie Naggiar, *Florida Wildlife*

are different. The best bet is to read the instruction book that came with your unit, then, before cooking, remember that most game, except bear, is likely to be less moist than beef or pork. I therefore recommend that you consider larding your roast before cooking it by this method. If you don't have a larding needle, consider using a boned roast and rolling strips of bacon or salt pork inside it. Or wrap bacon or salt pork around the roast.

Pit Roast

Some years ago, I was reading a book on outdoor cooking, and it contained a section on pit cooking. It said to dig a hole, as usual, build up a bed of coals, as usual, wrap the meat, put the meat atop the coals, and cover the whole thing up with dirt. Fine. Then it said to check from time to time to see whether more coals were needed! Back to the drawing board, I said, in different terms, rather loudly!

I've always been uncomfortable about the coals burning out, or else about the meat burning up, or both, but if either happens there's really nothing you can do about it. Once you cover up meat on a bed of coals in a pit, *leave it alone*. In fact, I like to prepare my fire during the night, put in the meat, cover it up, and sleep on it! In any case, I've never eaten any pit cooked meat that wasn't good.

If you want to try it, I recommend that you get a fairly large chunk of meat. Try the whole ham from a wild boar, or a 10-pound

foil. He cooked it all morning over low coals, along with some other meat that he was preparing for a Thanksgiving dinner.

The aluminum foil, he said, kept the venison from drying out. He said that the aluminum foil should not be opened at all, simply because after it got hot it was hard to seal it again. Consequently, he didn't sample or even peep at the meat all morning long. He did say that the roast should be turned over on the hour, thereby keeping all sides of the meat moist. I couldn't argue with the final product!

Rotisserie Roasts

There are all manner of neat rotisserie units available for home and patio use. It is difficult to give valid general directions for cooking meat on these units simply because they shoulder roast of venison, made by boning both shoulders then wrapping them up together and tying with cord. Or try a whole venison "ham" or hind quarter.

I recommend using the same method that was described for cooking pit turkey (chapter 22). If you use boar, try the barbecue sauce that was recommened in the turkey text.

Instead of using barbecue sauce with venison, elk, moose, and so on, I would recommend that you try a mixture of prepared mustard, brown sugar, and good black pepper. You'll need lots of mustard if you soak the cheesecloth properly, so buy a large "commercial" jar. And use plenty of cheese-cloth, or a few layers of cheesecloth followed by burlap.

Have plenty of good hardwood at hand, or else have very large bags of charcoal ready. I often use green pecan wood which doesn't burn quickly. Consequently, I may burn wood for several hours before I am ready. I dig the pit shortly before sundown, build the fire, and sit around it with the boys until after midnight. I put the well-wrapped meat onto the coals and cover it up with dirt. Then I sleep on it. At about 11 the next morning, I uncover the meat and get it ready for dinner. It is usually hot, tender, and moist. And good. Try it. Allow ½ pound of meat per person.

Digging a Pit

For some reason, cooking game or meat in a pit seems to strike man's fancy. The method does, or can, produce some very good eating, and it can be fun. My boys enjoy it thoroughly, and they like to invite their guests for such a feast. Building a wood fire, instead of using charcoal, seems to add to the fun.

There are exceptions, of course, but the place to dig a cooking pit is in your backyard, or in the corner of your garden, instead of deep in the woods, assuming that you've got plenty of firewood available. If you're looking for easy digging, elect a spot that will be soft and free of roots or telephone cables. And use the same spot each time you cook, so that the ground will be rather soft, thereby making it easier to dig the hole. A good, sharp scoop helps. And post hole diggers. It also helps to soak the ground thoroughly before digging. Put a garden hose on the spot, crack the valve open just a bit, and let the water ooze out before digging the pit. Don't worry; the fire will dry out the dirt long before you get ready to cook.

44

COOKING
GAME in CAMP

Something romantic fills our souls when we envision the hunter in camp. We see visions of meat frying over wood coals or a venison rump roast cooking in a Dutch oven. It's all true. Some of the most enjoyable meals available to the outdoorsman are in the woods or along a stream. Or at the seashore.

Indeed, one of my fondest memories of boyhood was in setting out afoot on a Saturday, hunting first across our small farm, and then beyond and into the countryside pretty much where my fancy led. More often that not, I shot birds or a rabbit for a noonday meal, stopping to rest while a fire burned. I went lightly, already loaded, I felt, with a gun, and usually did not carry cooking gear. A good knife to help dress the game and to cut a forked spit was about all I needed, along with a little bacon and salt. I wrapped the bacon around the meat and roasted it.

I also remember eating fried quail, cooked on the tailgate of a pickup truck, that were simply wonderful. These meals I enjoyed with my father and some older men, who smoked and told jokes and tales of fox hunting. I suspect that the company and the circumstances made the birds taste better!

Even so, game is not usually the best meat to eat in camp. For one thing, game meat, almost without exception, is better if it is allowed to cure, under refrigeration or at a low temperatrue, for a few days before cooking it. Also, it is more difficult to cook most game meat, and the kitchen might be the best

401

place to do it simply because you have more equipment and better control of your heat.

But I repeat that game *can* be cooked in camp, and should be enjoyed at every opportunity. Some cuts, such as tenderloin and deer liver, are rather traditional, and this chapter concentrates on cuts and cooking methods, as well as a few recipes, that are more suited for the camp. Note that most of the fried dishes and some of the more elaborate recipes set forth in other chapters can also be cooked in camp merely by packing in all the ingredients and bringing along a suitable pan—and paying close attention to your fire.

In any case, be sure to try the following:

Camp Stew

Here's a no-frills stew, hearty and good, that can be cooked in camp with only a few ingredients.

8 grey squirrels or 5 fox squirrels (or similar small game)
8 potatoes, quartered
4 medium onions, quartered
salt and pepper
branch water
cornmeal (optional)

Skin the squirrels and boil them until they are tender. (Old squirrels should be cooked

---

Campfires

The best campfires I've ever made were on the banks of an inside bend in the Chawtawhatchee River. We camped on the spot several times a year, and we took the trouble to cut an oak tree each year for use the following year. The wood was split and stacked between two trees, and it was just right whenever we made camp. Getting good wood is not always easy, and of course dry, seasoned wood burns much better than green or rotten wood. For one thing, good wood makes less smoke than green or rotten wood. It also produces good coals faster. Green hardwood will, of course, make a good fire after you get it started. But you'll have to build a larger fire and wait for it burn down before you'll have good coals for cooking. Owing to the diffi-

culty in finding good wood quickly, more and more people are taking store-bought charcoal into the woods.

There are various schemes for building a good campfire, and I lean toward the keyhole concept. The keyhole is made with rocks. The fire is built in the main part and coals are raked into the small part for cooking. The rocks in the small part should be steady, and should be laid to accommodate your cooking pan or pot, or a suitable grill. Finding suitable rocks is not always easy. Logs of suitable size can also be used, but these are not always available either. So, your best bet for cooking over a campfire may be to bring along a portable grill with folding legs.

longer than young squirrels. Cook in two batches, or keep up with what's what.) Pull the meat from the bones and put it into a suitable pot, preferably one with a lid. Add potatoes, onions, salt, and pepper. Barely cover with fresh water, put over fire or coals, and cook until potatoes and onions are tender.

If you've got fine-ground cornmeal in camp, try some corndodgers in with the stew. Simply mix some of the meal with salt and water until it forms a mush that will hold together when dropped into hot water. Make patties about 2 inches in diameter and ¾ inch thick. Drop these into the simmering stew and let them steep for 20 minutes. *Makes a full meal for 8 people.*

Camp Stew with Canned Vegetables

This recipe was designed for cooking rabbit, squirrel, and similar small game in camp. It provides several vegetables, and is a complete meal for the hunter. Moreover, it calls for canned goods that do not require refrigeration.

**1 rabbit, cut into pieces (or 2 or 3
    young squirrel, etc.)**
¼ cup cooking oil
½ cup flour
salt and pepper
**commercial meat tenderizer (may or
    may not be needed)**
1 can onions (about 12 ounces)

1 can tomatoes (about 12 ounces)
**1 can mixed vegetables (about 12
    ounces)**
1 envelope chicken soup mix
water

If you've got a young rabbit or young squirrel, fine. If it is tough, however, you may want to sprinkle it with meat tenderizer and let stand a while. (Follow directions on the tenderizer package.) Or, you can boil the meat until it is tender, then let it drain.

Heat 1½ cups of water and simmer with chicken soup mix, following direction on package. Salt and pepper the meat to taste. Coat in flour and let sit for a few minutes. Rake out a few coals from the campfire and heat the oil in a large frying pan or Dutch oven. Brown the meat. Add onions and cook 5 mintues. Add chicken soup. Cover and simmer for about 15 minutes. Add potatoes, tomatoes, and mixed vegetables. Cover and simmer on very low heat for 20 minutes, add salt and pepper to taste, and simmer for another 10 minutes. *Makes a full meal for 2 or 3.*

Camp Fried Tenderloin

I don't normally recommend that big-game be fried in camp, but the tenderloin can be very, very good. Also, it can be cut from a deer or elk from the inside of the body cavity, without having to skin the animal. Moreover, it is usually a tender, mild-tasting cut of meat, which needs no aging. I allow from ¼ to ½ pound per person, depending on who I am feeding.

The Pot Tripod

There are dozens of ways of suspending a pot over a fire or coals, but the best one I've ever seen is the camp tripod. A chain drops down from the apex, and the pot handle is attached to the chain by an S hook. The chain and the S hook are the key elements, and can be suspended from three poles, a tree limb, or other overhead structure of suitable strength. The nice thing about this rig, of course, is that the height can be easily adjusted—especially if you install a second S hook higher up the chain just in case the bottom one gets too hot to handle during cooking.

But bear in mind that fried meat can become tough if it is cooked too long. It's best to cook it fast in very hot oil—but not too hot. If the oil starts to smoke, move the frying pan or Dutch oven away from the coals very quickly. Be careful. Hot oil is dangerous. Before you ever start cooking, plan exactly how you will move the frying pan or Dutch oven if you have to. If you use a frying pan, it should be large and its handle should not be short. If you use a Dutch oven, make sure you can move it.

Apart from caution, here's all you need to fry delicious game meat in camp:

**tenderloin, cut across the grain into
   ½-inch thick rounds
cooking oil
salt and pepper
flour**

Salt and pepper each piece of meat to taste. Coat with flour and let sit for a while. Rake some coals from the fire and heat the oil in a Dutch oven or large frying pan. Carefully drop in one piece of tenderloin to see if the oil is hot enough. There ought to be a word to describe the reaction of floured meat to just-right oil, and I can't think of one. My wife says that "sputters" is the word, and I can't think of one any better. Anyhow, when the oil sputters, cook all the tenderloin, a few pieces at the time, and drain.

Note: If you want gravy, first cook all the tenderloin, then pour off most of the grease from the pan. Pour in a little water. Bring to boil and scrape up the bottom dredgings. Sprinkle in a little flour, mix, and let simmer. The thickness can be adjusted by water or flour, whichever is needed.

Camp Liver and Heart

If you are as fond as I am of the so-called variety meats from beef, lamb, and so on, then this dish, or something close to it, will probably be your favorite camp eating. The recipe below calls for venison heart and liver, but those from other game or fowl, large and small, can also be used.

**liver and heart
bacon
salt and pepper
flour
chopped onions
water**

Cut the liver and heart into strips about ½ inch thick. Salt and pepper to taste, then coat in flour. Let stand a few minutes. Rake some coals from the fire and cook the bacon until crisp in a camp frying pan. Set aside to drain. Brown the liver and heart in very hot bacon drippings. Set aside to drain. Add chopped onions and cook for about 5 minutes. Crumble the bacon and add to onions. Add the liver and heart, then slowly add just enough water to cover the meat. Cover the frying pan and simmer for 30 minutes. Stir from time to time. Thicken gravy with flour, and add more salt or pepper, if desired. This gravy goes well over rice or biscuits. The liver and heart from an average deer will feed 4 or 5 people.

Grills or Racks for Camp

A grill is one of the most useful items you can have for cooking over a campfire. The best ones for a camp for a number of people are large and steady, such the racks in a refrigerator, so that they can be put atop rocks around the fire. But smaller racks with legs can also be used.

My favorite for one or two people is a hinged double wire grill with long handles. Meat can be cooked in it on both sides merely be flipping the rack over. Also, the rack can be rested atop rocks, or it can be hand-held, or, more often than not, a combination of the two. Long handles are highly recommended for such double racks for use over a camp fire.

Moose Fries

Some of the French Canadians are fond of fried moose testicles, and of course similar parts from other animals are also eaten.

**testicles
butter, cooking oil, or bacon
salt and pepper**

To prepare these parts for cooking, scald, skin, wash, slice thinly, and soak them in water for several hours. Drain the slices, then salt and pepper them. Heat a little oil or butter, or bacon drippings, in a frying pan. Sauté the slices for a few minutes, browning on both sides. Allow at least ¼ pound per person, unless this recipe is used to prepare a side dish, as is often the case!

For fancier recipes, see Chapter 42.

Easy Neck Roast

If you've got an oven in your deer camp or cabin, this is a good easy recipe to try. Any good roast, not too tough, can be used for this method; but a neck roast is usually juicier than other cuts of venison, and can therefore be cooked without pampering it. I like the recipe for camp because you don't need lots of stuff to cook it. Just pack a few envelopes of soup mix. If you get a deer or elk, use it. If not, eat soup.

**1 neck roast
2 envelopes onion soup mix**

salt
pepper
¼ cup water

Preheat oven to 300 degrees. Tear off a suitable length of wide, heavy aluminum foil. Pour soup mix in center and roll roast in it, coating all sides. Salt and pepper roast to taste. Fold aluminum foil up a bit and add water. Then cover roast with foil and fold edges together to seal. Bake for 3 hours.

Easy Dutch-oven Antelope Roast

Antelope is a fine meat, and, if properly handled before it gets to the cook, it needs very little pampering. It can be cooked by campfire successfully. Here's a basic recipe, which can be modified somewhat if you've got onions, carrots, and such in camp. Also, you can cook other meat by this recipe, especially a roast from a young buck or a tender doe.

The Camp Frying Pan

I prefer a cast iron frying pan for everything, but it is, I admit, a bit heavy for some camp use. Whatever kind of frying pan you choose, get one that is rather deep and has a long handle. Short handled pans are just too hard to handle on a campfire.

Dutch Ovens

Once I knew a tall girl who was going through college on short money. The only thing she had to cook in was a Dutch oven, and she prepared everything in it. There is no doubt that the Dutch oven is one of the best and most versatile cooking tools ever invented. It is, however, a little heavy for many camp cooks to lug around. It all depends on your transportation, how long you will be in camp, and so on.

A camp Dutch oven is different from the ordinary kind made for stove top or kitchen use. The real camp model has three legs on it, and the cover is flanged so that it will hold coals on *top* of the main part. This type of lid makes it easy to keep stews and stuff hot, and it can aid in baking bread in camp. The lid itself can also be used to fry food in camp.

---

antelope roast, 3 to 5 pounds
salt and pepper to taste
1 envelope of onion soup mix

Build two fires or one "long" fire and let it burn to coals. (The idea is to have coals under, around, and on top of a Dutch oven.)

Put the antelope roast onto a piece of heavy-duty aluminum foil, then sprinkle it with salt, pepper, and onion soup mix. Fold and seal the aluminum foil tightly. Put a rack, if available, in the bottom of the Dutch oven and place the foil-wrapped roast on top of it; if you don't have a rack, put several rocks on the bottom so that the aluminum foil won't have direct contact. Put Dutch oven on top of coals, then move coals around the sides, and put some on the lid. (Presumably, you've got a camp-model Dutch oven, with a lid made for holding coals and with 3 legs on the bottom.) Keep a good fire going away from the Dutch oven, and replenish the coals on top of the oven from time to time. Cook for 2½ hours. *Serves 6 to 10.*

Camp Rabbit or Squirrel

Here's a recipe that I designed for use in a camp. Note that only easy to tote and store ingredients are used. It is good, and can also be cooked at home to good advantage. Also try it with armadillo or other small game, as well as with venison tenderloin. *The measures below serve 2.*

> 1 cottontail or a couple of squirrels
> 2 tablespoons cooking oil
> flour
> salt and pepper
> ½ cup Coffee-Mate
> water
> 2 beef bouillon cubes
> rice or egg noodles

Skin and dress the rabbit or squirrels. If the game is young and tender, it can be used without boiling. Old or tough game should be boiled until tender. Cut the game into pieces. Salt and pepper to taste, then roll the pieces in flour. Heat the oil in a frying pan that has a cover, or in a Dutch oven. Brown

the game. Heat 1 cup of water and mix in ½ cup of Coffee-Mate, then pour it over the game. Cover the pan and simmer for 1 hour. (If your pan doesn't have a cover, add a little water from time to time.)

Prepare the rice or egg noodles according to the directions on the package. Remove the game from the frying pan and let it cool a bit. Add a little water to the pan and stir in 2 beef bouillon cubes. Let simmer until the gravy reaches the right consistency to suit you. Put the meat into the pan with the gravy. Simmer for a while. Serve over noodles or rice.

Roast Beaver Tail

The old mountain men, some say, liked beaver tail roasted over a campfire. The trick is to hold the tail over an open flame until the skin blisters and cracks. Let cool off. Peel off skin. Then roast the tail over coals. Try it—but be warned that a beaver tail is, for the most part, a sort of edible gristle. Some people like it, some don't.

Kiwi and Meat

If you want to travel light, but want some fresh fruit along on your trip, consider the kiwi. This little fruit is now widely available in the United States, and it keeps for a long time without special care, provided that it isn't mashed or bruised. Also, it has a thin skin and edible core, so that almost all of it can be eaten. Even the skin can be used to tenderize meat. Just put the skin, fruit side down, onto the meat and let it sit in a cool place for an hour or so. Also, you can mash up the meat of the kiwi and spread it over meat to tenderize it.

Or, slice up the fruit and put it between slices of meat on a skewer, or in a double rack. Let sit for an hour or so, then grill over coal or even over an open flame until the meat is done. Sprinkle on a little salt. Eat the kiwi right along with the meat.

Big-Game Ribs in Camp

Most of the meat on your deer or other big-game should be aged for several days before you eat it. But not all. Liver and tenderloin, for example, are traditional meats for cooking in camp. Also, try ribs from deer, antelope, elk, caribou, and so on. Your best bet is to cook the whole rack atop a wire grill, which in turn is over hot coals. But you can also devise ways to prop a rack of ribs alongside hot coals, then cook them for a long time, turning them upside down as well as around from time to time.

Salt and pepper the ribs. If you've got bacon drippings, baste the ribs from time to time, or use any sort of barbecue sauce if you've got some in camp. Some of the best ribs that I ever ate had nothing but lemon juice squeezed on them. I'll normally eat a pound or so of ribs, but of course much depends on how much meat is on them.

Survival Cooking

I've read several accounts of game being cooked in open fires. For example, the Indians of the Southwest are said to have thrown prairie dogs into a fire, whole, skin and all, and stirred them around until they were done. They were said to be done when they "popped open." Then they were raked out of the coals, cooled a bit, and apparently skinned before eating whatever parts the Indian wanted to tackle or could get at.

Cooking animals with the fur on them doesn't sound appetizing, and certainly wouldn't smell good at first, but it does make a point: you don't have to have tools and equipment in order to cook. If you've got a knife to help clean and skin the game or fish, your fare can be made more appetizing by wrapping it in wet leaves or wet clay before cooking, or by skinning the game and holding it over a fire with a stick. Some small animals, such as crayfish, can be cooked quite successfully in their shell. Also remember that if you have water and a suitable container, you can cook meat by putting hot rocks into the water. And don't forget that a flat rock can be heated and used as a cooking surface. So, if you find yourself in a survival situation, remember that a fire is all you need in order to cook meat, fish, and shellfish.

45

WHAT
to DO with
LEFTOVERS

I've kept this chapter short on purpose. If I have done a good job with the rest of this book, and if you do a good job in selecting your game and caring for it properly, there won't be many leftovers!

In any case, I don't like to throw food out, and at our house we frequently freeze leftover meat and gravy to use in vegetable soup. We also freeze leftover vegetables, or we fill in with mixed frozen vegetables purchased at the grocery store. A recipe for leftover soup, of course, is impossible simply because the ingredients at hand are always different. I might add, however, that some of our very best eating came from mixing leftovers.

In any case, here are a few recipes that you may want to try:

Venison Curry

Here's an excellent way to prepare leftover venison roast if you've got enough for a hot meal. Although curry is not one of my favorite herbs, I found this dish to be quite good. (If you aren't certain of your taste for curry, cut the measure listed below in half the first time you try this dish.) This recipe was

Aluminum Foil

A little aluminum foil can save the day on camping trips. With it you can wrap food for cooking in or under the coals, or you can fashion a reflector oven. The extra-heavy type can even be shaped into a pan or cooking utensil of sorts.

adapted from *Game and Fish Cookbook* by Harriet and James Barnett.

2 cups cooked venison, cubed
3 medium-sized onions, diced
1 cup diced tart apple
1 cup beef stock (or 1 cup water and 1 beef bouillon cube)
½ cup Madeira
¼ cup butter
2 tablespoons flour
1 tablespoon curry powder
1½ tablespoons fresh lemon juice
⅛ teaspoon nutmeg
salt and pepper
rice (prepared separately)

Heat the beef stock in a sauce pan and leave on simmer. Melt the butter in a frying pan. Sauté the onions and apple for a few minutes. Take up the onions and apple; set them aside to drain. Slowly stir the flour into the butter left in the frying pan. (Add a little more butter if needed.) When the flour browns, slowly add the heated beef stock and the Maderia, stirring as you go. Add the lemon juice, nutmet, salt, and pepper.

Leave the mixture over low heat and stir constantly until it starts to thicken. Add the sautéed onions and apple. Bring to simmer, then stir in the venison. Simmer for a few minutes, then serve over rice. *Serves 3 or 4.*

Leftover Venison Salad

1 cup leftover venison or other meat, minced
2 tablespoons salad pickle relish
2 tablespoons onion, finely chopped
¼ red bell pepper, finely chopped
¼ green bell pepper, finely chopped
mayonnaise

Mix venison, pickle relish, onion, and pepper. Add mayonnaise, stirring, until the desired consistency is reached. For lunch, serve on leaves of lettuce or eat with wheat crackers. *Serves 2.*
Variation: Try sour cream or yogurt instead of mayonnaise.

Leftover Roast with Brandy and Mushrooms

This happens to be one of my favorite meals, but I seldom cook it exactly the same way more than once. Have a loaf of good sourdough bread ready, hot and well buttered. Slice the leftover roast into very thin strips, about an inch wide and about ⅛ inch thick. Salt and pepper these strips to taste. Melt a little butter in a frying pan. Sauté some mushrooms until tender. Add the meat strips and bring to heat. In a small saucepan, heat a little brandy. Flame the brandy and pour it, burning, into the frying pan with the meat and mushrooms. When the flame dies down, stir the dish and serve it with the hot sourdough bread. *Allow ⅓ to ½ pound of meat per person.*

Jerky

Drying meat in the sun is the oldest way of preserving it, and the process is known to all cultures. In Africa it is known as *biltong*, a corruption of the words for buttocks and tongue. Apparently this refers to where the meat came from (the hindquarters), and what it looks like after the long strips have been dried.

In the West Indies, the French-African inhabitants of the early 17th century lived on a diet of dried beef made from the wild cattle which roamed the islands. In French these dried-beef eaters were called *boucaniers*, and since many of the islanders were pirates who preyed on Spanish shipping, you now know where the word 'buccaneer' comes from.

The spanish word for dried meat is *charqui*, and it is from this word that we get our word 'jerky.'

—Art Boebinger,
Kentucky Happy Hunting Ground

Leftover Pot Roast Pie

This is an easy dish and makes good use of leftover roast—especially when the vegetables were cooked along with the meat. In the recipe below, other leftover or fresh vegetables, such as onions or celery, can also be put into the pie:

2 cups leftover roast, cubed
2 cups leftover gravy
2 cups leftover potatoes, diced
2 cups leftover carrots, sliced
1 package of refrigerator biscuits

Preheat the oven to 450 degrees. Mix the meat and vegetables. Put the mixture into a greased casserole dish. Place biscuits on top. Bake for 20 minutes, or until biscuits are browned on top and done on bottom.

I recommend using the regular size biscuits for this recipe. The large "Texas" style biscuits may brown on top but become gooey on the bottom. *Serves 4 to 6.*

Leftover Elk Sandwiches

2 cups elk roast or other game meat, finely ground
¼ cup finely chopped onion
¼ cup finely chopped celery
¼ cup salad pickle relish
¾ cup mayonnaise

Mix everything and spread it over thin white sandwich bread.

Leftover Game Meat Barbecue

This recipe is an excellent way to use leftover roasts and other cooked meat.

**3 pounds cooked venison roast or
 other game meat
1 medium onion, chopped
2 cloves garlic, minced
1 can tomato sauce (15-ounce size)
¼ cup Worcestershire sauce
¼ cup red wine vinegar
¼ cup brown sugar
1 teaspoon pepper
1 teaspoon paprika
1 teaspoon dry mustard
1½ teaspoons salt
cooking oil**

Add a little oil to a Dutch oven or large frying pan. Sauté the chopped onions until tender. Add all other ingredients (except meat), stir, and simmer for 30 minutes. Chip cold meat and add to sauce. Cover and simmer for 20 minutes. *Serves 6 to 8.*

Serve this barbecue on hamburger buns or use in sandwiches. It can also be served over rice.

Brunswick Stew in Camp

If you've got the time, ingredients, and facilities, a Brunswick stew is hard to beat in camp. It provides a complete meal, and the vegetables can be brought to camp in easy-to-store cans. The basic recipe for squirrel (see page 266) can be used, or it can be modified to fit the game and ingredients at hand. Use rabbit or pheasant for squirrel, for example. Or use a combination of jackrabbit, armadillo, etc.

46

GAME from FIELD to TABLE

The first step to getting very good game meat is to select a young animal. This often creates a conflict between hunting for the table and hunting for a trophy. Does are often better eating than bucks, yet many states that have a doe season (and want the doe population thinned down) have trouble getting hunters to take advantage of it.

After you have selected the right animal, your job is to kill it cleanly. A wounded animal that runs a long distance, or an animal that has been chased by dogs, simply does not taste as good as one that has not been pumping adrenalin. Any farm boy that has ever butchered hogs or goats or other farm animals knows that they should be calm at the time of slaughter. I remember having breakfast before daylight one chilly morning in a small cafe in Williston, Florida, where a

group of deer hunters were talking to a local farmer who was getting ready to kill hogs. The farmer said that a big boar ought to be scratched down before hitting it in the head with a ball peen hammer! By scratching down, he meant scratching the hog's back until it lay down and went to sleep. It's a good image to remember if you want the best possible wild game meat. Kill your animal the first time you shoot it. Some hunters like a head shot or a neck shot, but most experts these days go for a lung shot. A good deal depends on the situation at hand, on what and on how you are hunting.

In any case, after you have dropped your animal approach it carefully to make sure that it is dead. Once you have determined that fact, proceed with field dressing the animal as soon as possible.

FIELD DRESSING A DEER

There are, of course, different methods of dressing out a deer. I recommend the following method for beginners. Experienced hunters may want to change the sequence, or combine some of the steps.

1. If possible, place the deer on its back with its head pointed slightly uphill. Brace the body with stones or tree limbs to keep it from rolling over.

Straddle the body and make a cut into the deer's skin at a point in the no-bone area just below the rib cage. This initial cut should be made by bunching up some of the skin in your left hand and slicing into it with your knife blade. Try to cut through the skin only, not into the muscle tissue. Of course, your blade should be sharp.

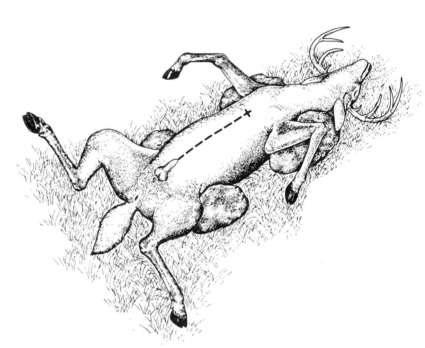

2. Insert the index and middle fingers of your left hand into the cut, spread them into a V, and insert the knife blade with the cutting edge up.

3. Working your way with your finger V and following with the blade, cut the skin all the way down to the pelvic area. Note: Do not cut through the muscle tissue. *Important:* If this procedure is followed correctly, you will be cutting the hide from the underneath. This will help prevent getting hair on the meat, and will not dull the blade as much as cutting the hide from the hair side. Some people start at the pelvic area and cut toward the head. But I prefer to work down, cutting with the lay of the hair instead of against it. Pull back some of the skin from either side of the cut, opening up the area.

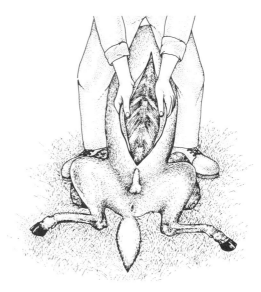

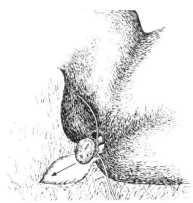

4. Starting at the rib cage, make an insertion into the muscle tissue. Then, using the same finger V technique, cut through the muscle tissue to the pelvic area. Avoid cutting into the organs or intestines. Many people combine steps 2 and 6, thereby making only a single cut. If you have a doe, carefully cut a circle around the anus and the vagina. Work with this circle of flesh until you can see the two tubes (rectum and urethra). Loose these tubes and pull them back enough to tie them off with a piece of string, you should have brought with you.

5. If you have a buck, note that the urethra curves over the pelvic arch to the penis. Hold the penis with one hand, pulling on it, and cut down toward the rectum with your knife. Do not cut it and the scrotum off completely. Instead, cut a circle around the penis and the rectum so that both can be tied off and removed together. Make sure that the tubes will go through through the pelvic bones. It is not necessary to saw or hack through the pelvic bones, if you have cut around the anus deeply enough.

6. Turn the animal on its side and empty the contents onto the ground. This should clear the tubes (urethra and rectum) as well as the bladder and small intestions.

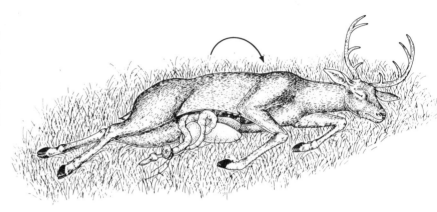

7. Work on the chest cavity. The diaphragm, which separates the chest cavity from the lower part of the body, must be cut. Reach into the chest cavity with your knife and cut along the rib cage, thereby slicing the diaphragm.

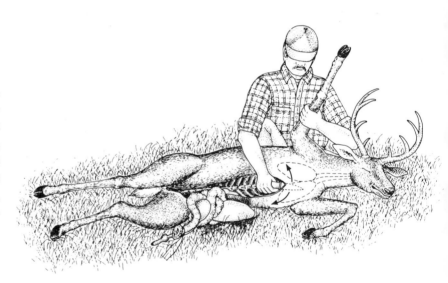

8. Reach up into the throat area with both hands to remove the windpipe and the gullet. Grasp these tubes with one hand, then cut them with the other. Pull down on the windpipe and gullet, which should loosen the heart and lungs. Pull all these organs free and onto the ground.

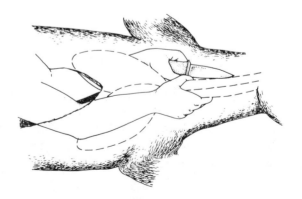

9. Turn the animal over on its stomach, away from the innards, so that it will drain. It should be turned the opposite way from the pile on the ground. Prop the body if necessary so that it will not roll over. While the body is draining, separate the heart, liver, kidneys, and other parts

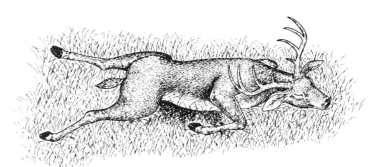

that you want to eat. (Note that the deer liver does not have a gall bladder, so you don't have to worry about it.) Trim off any blood vessels and place the parts in a plastic bag with a little water.

10. Wipe out the inside of the cavity with a dry cloth, then turn the deer on its back. Prop the cavity open with 2 or 3 sticks.

The field dressing is now complete, unless you choose to remove the tenderloin from either side of the inner back and put the pieces into a plastic bag. These choice pieces are not covered by skin, and will tend to dry out if your deer is to be left hanging or will be in transport for some time. (See page 432 for a further discussion of the tenderloin and the loin.)

If there will be any delay in transporting the deer, it should be hung up, if at all possible. If hanging is not feasible, put the deer onto a ventilated bed of limbs or stones.

Dressing Out an Elk

Generally, dressing out an elk is quite similar to dressing a deer. Of course, an elk is much larger and presents bigger problems of handling and transport. Also, the larger volume makes it even more important to field dress the animal quickly. If possible, position the animal so that its head is elevated more than the rump. Proceed as follows:

1. Make the first incision in the middle of the breast, starting at a point half way between the legs and ending at the rear end. Cut through the skin first, as discussed in the section on deer. Next, cut through the muscle layer. Do not cut into the intestines or organs.

2. Cut free and tie off the rectal tubes and the urethal tubes, as was discussed under deer.

3. Turn the animal on its side and empty out the organs and intestines.

4. If you want to save the cape for a mount, you must now skin out the neck and the brisket area. Then proceed with the field dressing by cutting through the rib cage .

5. Grasp the wind pipe and gullet. Cut them as high up as you can. Then cut the diaphragm free of the rib cage and remove the organs.

6. Now get your elk to a meat processor as soon as possible, or take it to your home or camp if you are going to butcher it yourself. If you have transportation problems at this time, it is best to cut the elk into six parts, as shown in the illustration. This is much easier if you have a block and tackle or some other means of hanging the animal. Use the same procedure as for butchering deer, discussed

later in this chapter. Start by cutting the animal in half, preferably with the aid of a saw.

You can either skin the elk before you move the pieces, or you can leave the skin on the pieces. If the weather is hot, it may be best to skin the animal entirely to help cool the meat. Also, the hide is heavy and may become a factor if you are backpacking.

When transporting the meat, use game bags or wrap it in cheesecloth.

Dressing Out a Moose

In general, dressing out a moose is similar to dressing out an elk and the instructions given above will be applicable. A moose, of course, is very large—and can weigh almost a ton. You need heavy-duty equipment to manage a moose, and of course you should have this equipment if you are hunting the animal. A moose shot in water can be almost impossible to handle.

Cold Meat Is Easier

Most butchers and many hunters know that cold meat is easier to slice, dice, or otherwise cut. This information can be especially useful for cooking dishes and recipes that call for thinly sliced meat. Also, proponents of "deerburger" or sausage should also know that game meat, from javalina to moose, is easier to grind when it is cold.

If you have enough help, someone can be skinning the moose while the field dressing is in progress. Getting the skin off as soon as possible helps in cooling the meat. Also, keeping the animal, or parts of it, such as a hindquarter, off the ground helps cool it. Either hang the pieces or put them on a ventilated bed made of limbs or brush.

Caribou

Although a caribou can have a set of antlers as wide as an elk's, and hoofs the size of a moose's, dressing out the animal, which weighs about 600 pounds, doesn't usually present as much of a problem as an elk or a

Watch for Glands?

A number of people who have written about dressing game have warned readers about glands, and they have recommended that they be removed from squirrels, raccoons, deer, and other animals. For the most part, the hunter who dresses out game reasonably well is better off ignoring the glands. This is especially true of the tarsal glands on the hind legs of deer; let them be, since they are on the part of the leg that is normally thrown away anyhow. As John Weiss pointed out in his book *Venison: From Field to Table*: "The tarsal glands—those moist, dark tufts of hair located midway on the hocks of each hind leg—cease functioning when a deer dies. They also are situated a good distance from the prime venison of other body parts. Consequently, there is only one way for the tarsal glands to cause tainted or spoiled meat and that is when unskilled hunters begin slashing away at the glands with their knives, trying to remove them, and in so doing inadvertently cause oil from the gland ducts to come in contact with other parts of the deer."

I feel pretty much the same way about the glands in other animals. The javelina, for example, has a potent gland on the rump, but it will usually come off when the animal is skinned. Therefore, trying to remove it before skinning will usually be unnecessary, and could ruin the meat. Be aware that the gland is there, then check after skinning to see that it is gone. If necessary, cut it out after skinning. Another animal that has a bad gland is the pronghorn antelope. As with the javelina, this gland is on the rump, just under a white patch of hair. The gland will usually come off with the hide, but watch for it. If you use a skinning knife on either the javelina or the pronghorn, watch out when you are in the rump area.

I've never had any trouble with glands from small game, but be aware that the glands in an opossum (just under the forelegs and along the top of the rear back or rump) might need attention if you scald and scrape the animal instead of skinning it. In rabbits, the glands are under the forelegs, and in the beaver, opossum, muskrat, woodchuck, and raccoon the glands are under the forelegs as well as on the rump. The glands are waxy little nodules, usually reddish in color. I never worry about these glands in small game, and I've never had any trouble with them.

How Much?

Steaks from venison and similar game are smaller than comparable cuts of beef. Often these cuts can be made to look larger by cutting at an angle instead of 90-degrees to the grain. Don't overdo this, however, lest your meat become stringy. Also, loin and tenderloin can be made to appear larger by using a butterfly cut.

---

moose because it is smaller. Follow the instructions for elk if you want to save the cape for mounting. In general, follow the field dressing instructions given for deer.

Bighorn Sheep and Rocky Mountain Goat

The bighorn sheep usually lives in rugged country, and that can sometimes present transportation problems. If you are after only the meat, then proceed to field dress the sheep just as you would a deer.

If you want to keep the cape for a trophy, start by cutting through the skin all the way around the upper part of body. The cut should be made entirely around the body, just behind the front legs. Cuts should also be made around the front legs, above the knees. Next, cut along the back of the neck, up to a point about 4 inches behind the horns. Then cut to the base of each horn.

Skin the cape. Then cut through the neck at the base of the skull.

Proceed with the field dressing, following the general instructions set forth under deer.

Follow the same procedure for goats.

Both sheep and goats are easier to field dress if you don't want to keep the horns or cape. Just dress either like a deer. But be warned that the bighorn has a bad gall bladder attached to the liver. If you puncture it, you will likely ruin some good meat.

Pronghorn

The pronghorn antelope is easy to field dress as compared to a moose or an elk. Its maximum weight is about 140 pounds. On the other hand, it is an animal of the plains, where the temperature is usually much warmer than at the higher elevations of the elk. In short, field dress the pronghorn as quickly as possible. The instructions given under deer, above, will be applicable. On your initial cut from the chest to the rear end, you can usually make do with one cut instead of first cutting the hide and then making a second cut through the muscle. Use the finger V cut.

If possible, get your pronghorn into a shady area as soon as possible after field dressing it.

The antelope has a powerful scent gland, used to alert the herd in case of danger, and this thing can cause some problems. The gland is located just under the white patch of skin on the rump. It's best to leave the gland alone and hope that it comes off with the skin, as it often will. Inspect the spot, however, looking for a group of yellowish nodules. If necessary, cut it out, working around it very carefully with your knife. Then wash your knife.

Wild Hog

There are two basic types of wild hogs in North America, in addition to the javelina (which isn't really a pig). The European wild boar can weigh up to 400 pounds, whereas the smaller "feral hog" usually averages about 100 pounds. The boar is therefore harder to dress out simply because it is bigger.

Either type of hog should be scalded and scraped before it is dressed out. This is accomplished by lowering the hog into hot water, and then scraping the hair off it. (A large barrel or some sort of vat is highly desirable for scalding. You really need lots of water at about 145 degrees, or at 150 degrees in cold weather.) Domestic hogs are treated in this manner, and scalding is the first order of business after the animal is killed. Of course, when dressing out domestic animals the hot water can be at hand—and this would be impossible in the woods. It is possible to scald and scrape the hog by pouring hot water on it, but, again, this is not very practical when you are on a hunting trip. It is therefore best to field dress the hog first. Accomplish this by cutting it open from the rib cage to the rear end, then removing the organs and intestines just as you would for a deer or other animal.

After you have gutted the boar, then worry about scalding it. A good meat processor is your best bet to get the rest of the job done. The hog should be taken there as soon as possible.

To Bleed or Not to Bleed

A few years back, most hunters and most authorities on the subject recommended that deer and other big game animals be bled before field dressing. Although the practice is still widespread, it is not recommended by most up-to-date books and magazines. Modern thinking has it that a shot in the lungs with modern ammunition, along with normal field dressing, is all the "bleeding" that is required. It is more important to remove the organs and open the body up as soon as possible. Don't waste time with "bleeding."

Javelina

The javelina, or collard peccary, isn't really a pig and it isn't normally scalded and scraped like a boar. The javelina seldom gets larger than 50 pounds and should be dressed out like a small deer.

One potential problem is a musk gland located on the animal's rump. Usually, this gland will come off with the skin and therefore will not present a problem. If it doesn't come off, remove it carefully with your knife. In my opinion, you should not try to remove the gland before you skin the animal. There are other opinions on this matter, and some people do recommend that the gland be cut out before skinning.

Dressing Out a Black Bear

A large black bear can weigh over 600 pounds, and of course some of the other bears are even larger. The average adult male black, however, will weigh in at 300 to 400 pounds. That's a big chunk of meat—and it is covered with very thick black hair, which holds in the body heat. It is therefore important that the bear be field dressed as soon as possible.

The instructions below are based in large part on a booklet that was published by the Ontario Federation of Anglers and Hunters. Proceed as follows:

1. Turn the bear on its back. Cut into the skin at a point just beneath the lower jaw, being careful not to cut into the meat. Insert two fingers and, holding the blade edge pointed up, start cutting through the skin toward the tail. The cutting edge of the knife should follow along as your work your fingers down the skin. Proceed slowly, being careful not to cut into the abdominal cavity, until you reach the top of the tail. Next, cut the skin on the inside of each leg all the way to the paw pads. Do not skin the animal, however, until you complete the following steps.

2. Working in the cut that you have already made in the skin, carefully insert the knife, cutting edge up, into the abdominal cavity near the pelvic bone. Cutting with the blade between your two fingers, work carefully all the way up to the breastbone.

Do not cut into the intestines if you can avoid them. Do not waste time at this point to cut through the breastbone or the pelvic bone.

3. Reach into the cavity and locate the diaphragm or membrane that separates the heart and lungs from the liver and stomach. Cut this diaphram away from the rib cage.

4. Reach up under the rib cage and cut the windpipe, gullet, and arteries.

5. Cut around the vent with your knife as deeply as you can. Tie off the tube and pull it from the body cavity. If you have a male bear, cut off the penis at its base and pull it from the body cavity.

6. Roll the bear on its side. Pull all the organs and innards out of the body cavity, using your knife to help free any connective tissue.

7. Insert several sticks into the edge of the body cavity to help in ventilation.

8. Separate the heart, liver, kidneys and other innards that you want to keep. Put these in a plastic bag or other container, if you've got it, and leave in a cool place.

9. If possible, skin the bear as a final part of the field dressing. This will help cool the meat much quicker. It will, of course, be much easier to skin the bear if you can hang it up. Hanging will also help cool the carcass. A block and tackle is highly desirable for hanging a bear. Hang from the hind legs, first inserting a strong limb between the tendon and the leg bone.

10. Unless you have plenty of help, you might also have to cut the bear into pieces

FIELD DRESSING A BEAR

Dashed lines show cuts to
be made when dressing
out a black bear. Cuts
along legs are for skinning
the bear after field dressing is completed.

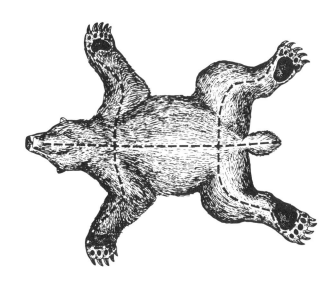

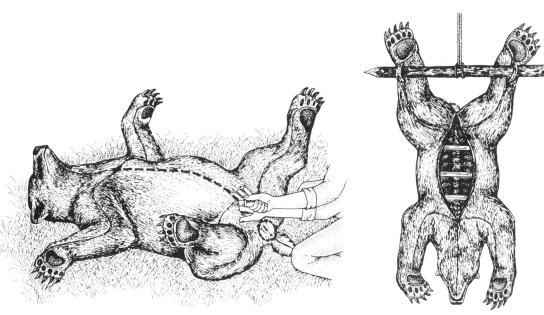

After making first cut from jaw to tail, work
in the same cut from pelvic bone to breastbone, cutting into the abdominal cavity.

Hanging a black bear from the hind legs. A
strong limb should be inserted between the
tendon and leg bone.

before you can transport it. You'll need a saw. First, cut through the neck. Then saw down the middle of the bear, starting at the pelvic bone. Next, cut off the hindquarters. Cut through the back where it joins the front quarters.

In any case, get your bear to a meat processor as soon as possible. If you butcher the bear yourself, cut the meat up into whatever cuts you want, wrap them, and freeze them as soon as possible. I don't recommend that you try to "hang" or otherwise cure bear meat. Cut the fat from the meat before you freeze it, for the fat has a much lower freezing point. It is difficult to freeze this much meat at one time in most home units. It might be best to refrigerate or ice the meat, adding a few packages at a time to your freezer.

Dressing Small Game

Generally, small game is easier to dress out than big game. Such small game as squirrels don't hold the heat as long as bear. Consequently, field dressing is not as critical. But, for maximum quality, *any* game, fish, or fowl should be field dressed as soon as possible. Too many people put small game into rubberized game compartments of hunting jackets and leave them there, unventilated, for as long as the hunt lasts.

When dressing any small game, I normally skin it first, then gut it. Other people may want to gut the game and skin it later, but I don't. I put my dressed game in plastic bags (one squirrel or rabbit per bag) and try to keep it in a cool place. I always like to wash small game in a stream when it is field

dressed, but many hunters object to this practice.

There are many ways to skin small game. I always begin by making a cut across the back with a very sharp knife. Then I loosen the skin a bit with the point of the knife. Next, I work a finger into each side of the hole, crook the finger, and pull in opposite directions. Then I pull the skin all way down to the head and front feet on one end, and to the hind feet and tail on the other. These parts are cut off with my knife, or with shears. Then I gut the animal and fish out the liver if I want to keep it.

I seldom make an exception to the above procedure, but of course some people will want to save the hide of an animal. In this case, it is best to cut the skin on the underside from the chin to the tail. Then make cross cuts along each leg to the feet. This method makes skinning harder, but it gives you a hide that can be tacked to a barn wall. (If you are

---

Dressing a Rattlesnake

Snakes are very easy to dress out. I nail the head to a tree or something, or hold it (carefully) with pliers. Make a cut around the body, near the head, and start the skin down. Grab the skin with pliers and pull. It comes off easily. Then gut the snake down the middle of the belly, and pull out the innards. Cut it into 4-inch segments.

Put the snake into plain water and refrigerate the meat for 2 days or longer before eating. The snake can also be frozen, preferably in water like fish.

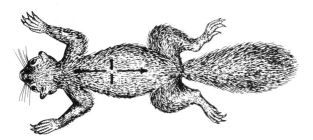

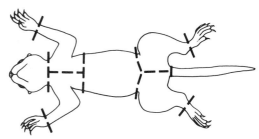

Skinning a squirrel. Cut at dotted line, then pull with fingers in opposite directions.

After pulling skin all the way to feet and head, cut them off, plus the tail. Then cut up squirrel as shown by dashed lines.

selling hides from a trapline, then of course you should follow the procedure recommended by people who traffic in hides. This could be very, very important.) I've read about other methods of skinning squirrels and such, but none of these work any better than the one discussed above, at least not for me.

In any case, the method above serves me well for all small game except the armadillo. Some people scald the opossum like a hog, and then scrape the hairs off before gutting the animal. But this is more trouble than it is worth, and the method leaves far too much fat on the animal.

Transporting Game

Often, the hunter can save himself a lot of work, and end up with better meat, if before the hunt he considers how he will pack an animal out in case he does kill one. Once, for example, a young friend of mine had a map

of a game management area and he pointed out the spot where he wanted to make a deer stand. He had good reason for choosing the spot, but he had to walk some 3 miles to get to it. Wanting him to get closer to the road, I asked him how he was going to get a big buck out. He hadn't thought of that. But he didn't want to get near the road because he

Warning

Transporting a deer or other animal, especially bear, elk, or moose, can be very hard work. Moreover, the hunter may be heavily dressed. This combination is dangerous for people who are not in good shape. Remember also that having a heart attack while shoveling snow in your driveway is indeed dangerous—but it is not as dangerous as having a heart attack while trying to move a moose out of the deep woods, many miles from a hospital.

thought that, late in the season, the deer would be deeper in the woods during the day. He also knew that there would be too many hunters in the area. He was right on both counts.

Finally, he chose a stand even farther into the forest, near a very small stream. He got to the stand by canoe—and he got his buck out by canoe. He floated in, and, after bagging his buck, he field dressed it and floated on down to the next bridge, where he got another hunter to give him a ride back to his own truck. Thus, a little planning paid off.

Of course, it is often necessary to transport game on your back, on a pack horse, or in a backpack. (I do not recommend that good meat be dragged on the ground for any distance.) The best bet is to consider all this before you go hunting. Get topo maps of the area, and plan where you will be and how you will get your game out. Then take the proper equipment, and know how to use it.

A backpack frame is often a big help in getting meat out—but be careful about sticking antlers up over the top, unless you want your head shot off. If you pack out antlers, or whole animals, be sure to make good use of bright orange tape. And lots of it.

If you are alone, you can make a frame of two poles and drag the deer so that it isn't touching the ground. This method works even better with two people. Also, if you've got help you can transport the deer on a makeshift stretcher.

If you have to drag the deer, it's best to tie a

Two methods of transporting a deer out of the woods. If you're alone, you can make a framework of poles and drag the deer out. With a partner, you can make a pole stretcher.

rope or cable to the base of the antlers. Tie the front legs to antlers so that the feet won't drag. Have a comfortable handle, if possible, on short rope. The antlers should be lifted slightly so that they won't stick into the ground while you drag the body.

Sometimes the best bet is to leave the animal and go for help. If at all possible, field dress it before you leave and hang it so that it clears the ground. If you don't have a small block and tackle with you, consider lifting it with a tripod made from poles.

Usually, you will move your animal from the point of kill to some sort of vehicle. Your problems may not be over. Never put a deer or other animal across the hood of a car if you have other options. The heat from the engine will not be good for the meat. The longer you have to travel, the worse this problem will be.

If you have a choice, it is best to travel after sunset in relatively warm weather. If you are driving in very cold weather, it may be better to travel by sunlight to help prevent the meat from freezing. Snow packed into the body cavity may help keep the meat cool by day, and may help keep it from freezing by night.

In any case, get the animal home or, better, to a professional meat processor as soon as you can.

Hanging or Aging Meat

Most meat is better, no doubt, if it is aged properly. This is especially true of deer, elk, and similar animals. For the larger animals, aging is best accomplished at a meat pro-

Hanging a deer from a tripod of poles.

cessor's facility, where the animal is hung up in a controlled, refrigerated environment.

Many hunters will want to hang their deer at home, but this is seldom advisable unless you have the facilities. It is usually a mistake to hang the deer outside at night in freezing temperature, and then have it thaw out as the sun comes up during the day.

If you don't have adequate facilities, your best bet is to cool the deer off as much as possible and butcher it. Then put the pieces on ice for five days. I know some local deer hunters who always butcher their meat as soon as possible, then put it into large ice chests. They ice the meat, drain off the water every day, and add more ice, for five days. I have tried their method, and I like it. Such ice chests can often be carried along on a hunting trip, so that the deer can be butchered and packed down in camp or near the back of a pickup truck.

Still another method is to butcher the animal, wrap the pieces, and freeze it. Freezing the meat for a month or so has an effect quite similar to aging. Often, it is best to proceed with a combination of ice chest and freezer methods, simply because most home units won't quick freeze a lot of meat at the time. In any case, there is no doubt that cured venison is better in texture as well as flavor if it is cured by hanging, icing, or freezing.

Small game is also better if it is aged. A few days in the refrigerator will help the meat of squirrels, rabbits, muskrats, and other small game.

Skinning

It is difficult, in a book like this, to get first things first simply because there is more than one way to skin a deer and other big game. Except possibly for the bear and very large game such as fully grown moose or elk, I recommend that skinning be delayed until the animal has been transported to the place where it will be butchered. My thinking is that the hide will protect the animal during transport and will keep the meat from drying out while the deer is hanging. On the other hand, the animal is much easier to skin while the body is still warm. So, many people will want to skin it as part of field dressing.

Special skinning knives have been designed, but a good general-purpose blade will do the job. The drop-point design is a good choice for field dressing as well as skin-

ning if the blade is kept sharp.

In the field or at home, it is much easier to skin deer and similar animals if you first hang them by the head. Unless you want to mount the head, start by cutting completely around the top of the neck with your knife. First insert the blade, then work around the neck with the finger V technique that was used to field dress the animal. Do not cut into the meat if you can avoid it. Then cut off each leg at the knee joint.

Start working at the neck, pulling down on the hide with one hand while working the skinning blade with the other. The knife helps in slicing the tissue, freeing the skin from the meat. Do not cut into the meat. The knife is an *aid* in skinning and should not be used to cut off the hide. If the hide comes freely, you may not need the skinning knife at all after you get started. Try working with both hands, rolling the hide as you go. You can skin and roll the hide all the way down to the tail, bringing it all off in one piece. (At

Typical drop-point knife design—good for skinning and field dressing.

the shoulders, you'll have work on each front leg as well as the body.) It is easier to cut the tail off, leaving the bone in the hide. But if you want the bucktail to tie jigs or flies, you might carefully split the hide on the underside before skinning the tail.

Skinning to save the hide. If you want to save the hide, the above procedure should be modified as follows: Cut around the neck and remove the legs at the knee, as described above. Next, go to the cut you made in the first step of field dressing. Extend this cut straight up to the cut around the neck. Next, made a cut underneath each leg, going from the knee joint in to the center of the animal. Then skin as usual. This will give you a hide that can be tacked to a wall, or that can be salted and rolled up until it can be delivered to a taxidermist or hide processor.

Skinning to save the cape. If you want to save the cape of the animal for a trophy, you should start by hanging the deer by the hind legs instead of by the head. Also, your cape should be skinned and removed as soon as possible instead of hanging it for several days.

To begin skinning a deer or similar animal for both meat and cape, you must make cuts in the hide around the hind legs at the knee joints, then down the middle of the leg to the cut you made while field dressing. Next, make a cut across the chest or brisket area and down the inside of the legs. On the top side of the cape, make a cut around shoulder (behind the legs, joining with the similar cut that you made from underneath) and down the center to a point behind the base of the antlers. Then skin out the entire neck. Cut off the head at a point where the skull joins the neck bone. Salt the hide thoroughly and pour salt into the neck opening, ears, nose, and mouth. Keep the head in a cool place and get it to your taxidermist as soon as possible. Then skin out the rest of the animal for the

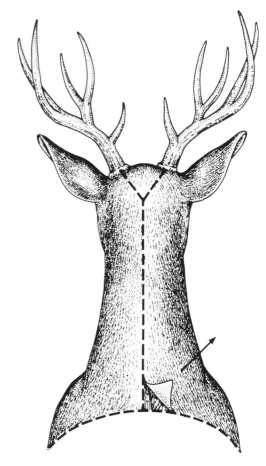

Dashed lines show cuts for caping a deer.

meat, starting at the hind legs and working toward the neck.

Butchering your Meat

I recommend that you take your big-game animals to a professional meat processor for proper aging and butchering. The average kitchen simply isn't the best place to butcher a large animal, and most homes lack meat saws and other tools. But it can be done at home, and of course there is nothing wrong with getting a few choice cuts and cutting the rest up into cubes or pieces to be used in stew or in gameburger. There are several good books on butchering meat, but there are a thousand different cuts and variations, and in the end you'll have to make your own decisions anyhow.

It is best to butcher the animal after it has been chilled considerably, simply because cold meat is easier to cut. If your animal is hanging by the head, start butchering it by removing the hind parts. If it is hanging by the hind legs, start butchering by first removing the neck and the front quarters. (Usually, your best guide to butchering any animal is simply to follow the natural divisions in the meat.) At this point, further reduce the primary parts, wrap the meat, label it, and get it ready for freezing.

You can bone the neck for a boneless neck roast, leave it as is for a bone-in neck roast, or trim off the meat for stew, saving the boney part for soup.

The front shoulders can be cut up into three parts: blade roast, arm roast, and shank. Usually, the shank is used for gameburger. If you want a large roast that is easy to bard with bacon, bone both of the shoulders. Put one down flat and lay strips of bacon on it. Then cover the bacon with the other flattened boned shoulder. Roll both up together with the bacon in the middle.

To remove the hind legs, work with your knife blade, cutting along the dotted lines shown in the drawings. Go slowly, working

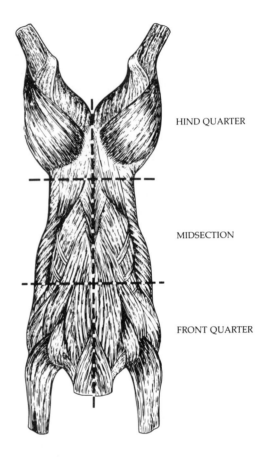

HIND QUARTER

MIDSECTION

FRONT QUARTER

Initial cuts for butchering big-game.

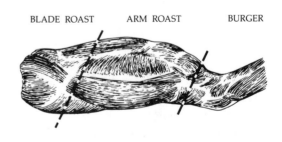

BLADE ROAST   ARM ROAST   BURGER

Shoulder should be cut into three pieces.

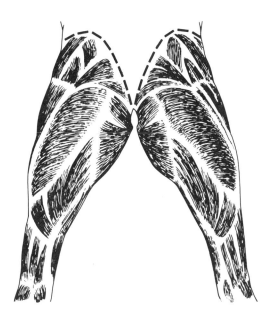

Cuts for removing the hind legs.

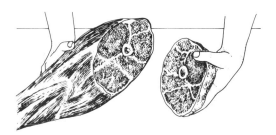

Large end of leg is cut into round steaks.

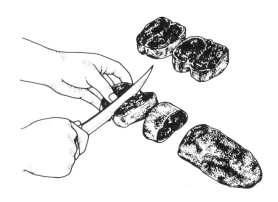

Cutting leg muscle into small steaks.

your way around and down to the ball joint. After you have separated the hindquarters, you can slice the large end into round steaks, complete with a little round piece of bone in the middle, if you've got an electric meat saw. Or you can divide the sections up into smaller roasts. The large end of the leg has separate muscles that go around the bone. (If you want to see a cross section of these, look at a piece of round steak at your supermarket.) If you divide the leg muscles into roast-like pieces, these can be sliced into chops or small steaks.

The lower part of the hind leg, below the knee, is usually sliced up into stew meat or ground into gameburger.

So . . . we've cut off the neck, the front quarters, and the hindquarters. Decide now whether you want to remove the loin (and tenderloin, if you haven't removed this while field dressing) from along the backbone or whether you want to cut it up into chops or steaks. I recommend that you remove the loin, or backstraps, and then cut up the ribs and the rest of the animal the best way you can, using an ax or, better, a saw. If you elect to get the backstrap, you may want to remove it first instead of last.

Generally, the muscle that is not used much is more tender than a muscle that is constantly exercised. Thus, the loin and the tenderloin, both along the backbone, are not used as much as the muscles in the legs, and are therefore more tender. Because these two cuts of meat are really the best that the animal has to offer—no matter whether it be deer, elk, or bear—and because there is a lot of confusion about the cuts, I am treating them separately. Besides, it won't hurt a thing to save the best until last:

Loin and Tenderloin

Almost everyone will agree that the loin and tenderloin cuts from almost any animal make the best eating. But there is a lot of misunderstanding, if not downright disagreement, about what, exactly, these cuts are. Some people assume, without really thinking about it, that the "loin" and "tenderloin" are the same thing. Most books about wild game, and meat in general, are vague on the subject. Moreover, there are a thousand ways to cut up a deer or a cow, and practices vary widely from one country to another and from one region to another. But I, for one, do make a distinction between loin and tenderloin. Both are very good cuts of meat. They come from the body of the animal, between the ribs and the hind legs.

Each animal has two loins *atop* the backbone and running parallel to it, and two tenderloins *under* the backbone and running parallel to it. If you took a cross section of the backbone in the loin sections (or sawed out a 1-inch segment of the backbone and the surrounding muscles) you would have two T-bone steaks joined together. Cut the back segment in half, and you have T-bones like you see packaged in the meat market. As every T-bone fan knows, there are two main parts to this steak. The larger part is actually a slice of the loin, or *top* muscle of the back assembly; the smaller part is a slice of the tenderloin, or *bottom* muscle of the back assembly. Again, every T-bone fan knows that the smaller side is more tender; hence, the name "tenderloin." In addition to the T-bone, the porterhouse and the sirloin steaks also can contain part of the loin and tenderloin.

Obviously, if you cut the meat up into high-quality steaks, you can't have a loin or a tenderloin. In other words, you can't have your tenderloin and eat it too. But you can, by altering the cut of your steaks, cut out both a loin "roast" and a "tenderloin" when you butcher an animal. Both of these cuts of meat are very, very good, with the tenderloin being the very best. To get at these cuts, first cut the animal in half, straight down the backbone, with a saw. Working with either half, locate the loin muscle on top of the backbone. Carefully cut it out with a sharp knife. Then locate the tenderloin muscle on the bottom side of the backbone, and carefully cut it out. *Note*: The tenderloin will be smaller than the loin, but both will be oblong, shaped rather like a long loaf of French bread.

INDEX